BISON
BOOKS

DOFF ABER   *Photograph of Painting by Author*

TO DOFF—IN MEMORIAM

Sleep gently, Cowboy!
In the shadow of a Western hill,
Under the warm, soft sun.
The clamoring crowds you used to thrill,
Only memory now recalls them still,
And all the trophies won.

The wild broncs that used to buck,
When you rode them out and made your luck,
Have other riders now . . .
But to that Land beyond the Sky,
We know you rode with honors high,
To make your final bow.

MAN, BEAST, DUST

The Story of Rodeo

by

Clifford P. Westermeier

Foreword by Bill Crawford
Afterword by Kristine Fredriksson

UNIVERSITY OF NEBRASKA PRESS
LINCOLN AND LONDON

Copyright 1947 by Clifford P. Westermeier
Foreword and Afterword copyright 1987 by the
University of Nebraska Press
All rights reserved
Manufactured in the United States of America

First Nebraska paperback printing: 1987

Library of Congress Cataloging-in-Publication Data
Westermeier, Clifford P. (Clifford Peter), 1910–
Man, beast, dust.
Reprint. Originally published: Denver: World Press,
1947.
"Bison book."
Bibliography: p.
Includes index.
1. Rodeos—United States—History. I. Title.
GV1834.5.W47 1987   791'.8   86-25082
ISBN 0-8032-4743-5
ISBN 0-8032-9715-7 (pbk.)

ISBN 0-8032-9843-9 (pa.: alk. paper)

Reprinted by arrangement with Clifford P. Westermeier

TABLE OF CONTENTS

CONTENTS

ILLUSTRATIONS

FOREWORD

It's unfailingly remarkable how unplanned and often commonplace individual actions result in historical events of great import. The events leading to the publication of *Man, Beast, Dust* could hardly have been more ordinary and explainable.

Clifford P. Westermeier graduated from college during the 1930s world-wide depression. On a trip through the western United States before commencing a career in art, Cliff saw a poster advertising a rodeo in Sidney, Nebraska. Believing the competition might provide interesting material for his sketchbook, he went to the rodeo. He left the rodeo grounds that day with a series of sketches, all right, and one more thing—a devotion to the cowboy sport—and rodeo hasn't been the same since then.

His art degree "almost worthless" for finding a job during the depression, Cliff decided upon an academic career. He built that distinguished career upon the sport of professional rodeo. The sport and its society have benefited as well, for Cliff had in the word's truest meaning discovered a genuine American subculture, and like all true pioneers, he explored the country he discovered.

Cliff began and concluded his exploration of the sport and its culture with the true scholar's unblinking gaze for meticulous investigation, warts and all. He spent months reading and copying out in longhand the skimpy information he found—a search rather than an examination of facts, or even hearsay. The harder he looked, the less he found. In conducting field research, he spent ten years of his life and traveled more than 100,000 miles, sometimes with cowboy contestants who often traveled with their families; but usually he took the road alone, from the Mexican border to the Canadian Provinces, from his native New York to the Pacific shores. If he missed anything, nobody's ever been able to call him on it.

That's the reason for this reprint, forty years after *Man, Beast, Dust*'s first publication in 1947. It was the first scholarly study of the rodeo game and the first book-length study of any kind, and it's still the starting place for any serious study of professional rodeo. A world champion bulldogger, Dave Campbell, wrote, "Cliff has succeeded in giving a true picture of rodeo and the rodeo cowboy. He knows us."

Those forty years have not faded the picture.

Bill Crawford, Editor
Prorodeo Sports News
Official Publication of the
Professional Rodeo Cowboys Association

PREFACE

In my travels through the West I became interested in rodeo, and, fortunately, my trips were so planned that I was able to see many of these contests. They revealed to me an interesting part of the old West and seemed to keep alive the traditions of an era which was past. To keep in memory more vividly the various rodeo feats that had so aroused my curiosity, I made a number of sketches, which I later, in my studio, completed as paintings. In order to enrich my background for this type of painting, I began to investigate the origin of rodeo, its growth, its relation to the cattle industry, its popularity in the country, et cetera.

For this book I used three sources for information, which I gathered by interviews, by the use of statistical questionnaires, and by consulting published material.

The first and most important source was the interview. This manner of gathering information proved to be the most interesting of the three approaches. Interviews were held with cowboys—old-time and modern contestants. This demanded traveling and living with the contestants under all kinds of circumstances—at the "two-bit," one-day-stand rodeos, as well as at the larger, more spectacular contests of four weeks' duration. Thus, over a period of seven years, I had the opportunity to study the cowboy closely. However, these interviews did not take place on first introductions.

Frequently, the interviews were conducted with several cowboys present. This proved more efficacious, for the cowboys were less prone to exaggerate in the presence of their friends, who in most cases, were rivals. I found that the information received under these circumstances was fundamentally accurate and that it stood the test of further investigation. These "bull sessions" were invaluable, for they were spontaneous expressions, and the men were relating their own experiences or ideas.

I also questioned the cowboys individually and found them willing to talk and, at times, willing to spend many leisure hours in giving information, unusual and minute in detail. The cowboys, especially after I had known them for several years, often came to me and related some incident or fact which was of interest in the story of rodeo.

The wives of the cowboys were also interviewed. The majority of these women were not performers, and their ideas concerning the sport were of a different nature from those of the cowboys and the strict outsiders. Often, they successfully clarified very important details when I had failed to "hog-tie my cowboy" for the answers.

The statistical questionnaires were successful and very useful when they were sent to the stock contractors, rodeo committees, and allied organizations—any of the businesses related to rodeo.

From these questionnaires I was able to visualize a pattern of success and failure of rodeo contests, the moves of well-known cowboys, the preference for certain horses and bulls at contests, the types of stock used in the various sections of the country, the prizes offered, and the entrance-fees paid. Often the questionnaires were supplemented with additional information which was offered because of the interest in the idea of a story of rodeo. The questionnaires, however, were complete failures with respect to the cowboys, who did not answer them, for they seldom write letters to anyone.

However, there was one exception. Doff Aber, not only answered the questionnaire, but even invited me to come to the Madison Square Garden Rodeo, to look him up there and ask more questions. Doff introduced me to real rodeo. I was no longer one of the countless, insignificant spectators, I was on the "inside." Here, *The Story of Rodeo* really took shape. During the several summers that followed I traveled with the cowboys—to the Cheyenne Frontier Days, the Boulder Pow Wow, the Greeley Spud Rodeo, the Monte Vista Ski-Hi Stampede, the Pendleton Round-Up, and the Calgary Stampede. When the circuit brought them East in the spring and the fall, I always arranged to spend some time with them—in New York, Boston, Buffalo, Cleveland, and Pittsburg.

More and more information came my way; some in answer to direct questions, but a large part of it, the part that gives the personal element to *The Story of Rodeo,* was quite accidential. Before the shows, while sitting around the chutes; during the shows, while waiting for their turns; after the shows, while relaxing at dinner; at bars, and in night clubs, the cowboys would remember "just one more thing to tell me." They were interested and "they loosened-up." Again and again they came to me with such remarks as, "here's something," "wanna hear about?" and "did cha ever know?" Information from these accounts has been very valuable.

In searching for published material on rodeo, I soon became aware that not a great variety was available. Five periodicals are published which deal strictly with this subject. Various other periodicals, which give space to the sport, are of interest to ranchers, stockmen, horsemen, and devotees of outdoor life. Occasionally, feature articles on some aspect of rodeo appear in popular magazines.

There are really no books on rodeo which treat the subject as such. Numerous books of fiction have been written in which the main character is a rodeo performer, but in them a romance is usually the principal theme, and the story of rodeo is lost. Scattered references to the sport are many, but I have found no specific evidence of a thorough study. The modern cowboy, a combination of ranch and rodeo contestant, seems to have stepped over the border into a new frontier, as yet, rarely explored by writers.

Because of my close association with the men of rodeo, I have tried to write, as much as possible, in a simple, direct manner. This book is not for the reader who expects a popular, glamour-filled account of rodeo. I portray the cowboys as I have found them in relation only to this sport.

After years of research, when I finally began the actual writing, the three divisions which I use, *Man, Beast, Dust,* seemed to fit the pattern of the whole. Part One does not treat solely of man, nor does Part Two deal entirely with beast—these two woven together—result naturally in Part Three—rodeo as a whole.

I realize that this work may not be exhaustive in the early, historical background. That part of cowboy life and activity has been thoroughly treated by other writers. My purpose is to portray rodeo and the rodeo cowboy of the present day and to show how stupendous the growth of the sport has been. Every year more towns and cities in all parts of the United States are scheduling performances to capacity crowds—certainly its popularity is not waning!

I should like to acknowledge the many sources of information and, also, the sincere encouragement which I, through my good fortune, have had in the preparation of this work.

If this story, in any way, reflects a sincerity of purpose, it is because of the guidance, the innumerable kindnesses, and the ever-present encouragement of Dr. Henry D. Abbott of Buffalo, New York, who first opened for me the many vistas of our West.

Through the acquaintance and warm friendship of Mr. and Mrs. W. W. Thurber and Mr. and Mrs. Max Berueffy of Boulder, Colorado, I became aware of the fine character and the understanding spirit of our Western citizens. Doff Aber, S. P. Aber, Jerry Ambler, Wag Blessing, Clyde Burk, Mr. and Mrs. David Campbell, Bart Clennon, Jackie Cooper, Mr. and Mrs. Carl Dossey, Colonel and Mrs. James Eskew, Mr. and Mrs. James Eskew, Jr., Bob Estes, Turk Greenough, Mr. and Mrs. Dick Griffith, Mr. and Mrs. Dick Herren, John Jordan, Harry Knight, Tom Knight, Bill and Bud Linderman, Tad Lucas, Toots Mansfield, Chet McCarty, Bill McMacken, Marie Messinger, George and Hank Mills, Homer Pettigrew, Gene Pruett, Mr. and Mrs. Floyd Randolph, Harriet Ranney, Gerald Roberts, Carl Shepard, Smokey Snyder, Buck Sorrells, Bud Spilsbury, Leonard Stroud, and Fritz Truan not only opened to me their vast fund of knowledge and experiences of rodeo, but many of them became my friends. Also, I am indebted to the many other cowboys, past and present, who by their participation in the sport have unknowingly contributed much to this story of rodeo.

In addition, I am indebted to Oren Allison, secretary of the Chamber of Commerce, Pendleton, Oregon; Ben the Rodeo Tailor, John T. Caine III, manager of the National Western Stock Show, Denver, Colorado; Fog Horn Clancy, William J. Clemens, Bruce Clinton, Leo Cremer, Mr. and Mrs. Verne Elliott, David Hamley, vice-president, Hamley and Company, Pendleton, Oregon; Robert D. Hanesworth, secretary of the Chamber of Commerce, Cheyenne, Wyoming; Mrs. Ethel A. Hopkins, editor of *Hoofs and Horns;* Clifford Kaynor, Fred J. Koller, R. J. Leonard, the late Herbert S. Maddy, Fred S. MacCargar, Thomas B. MacFarlane, Councillor of the Royal Agricultural Society, Sidney, Australia; Chuck Martin, Ed McCarty, Harry Rowell, Carl A. Studer, and J. Charles Yule, general manager of the Calgary Stampede, Calgary, Canada.

Most of all, however, I am indebted to my wife, Thérèse, (known to the cowboys as Tracy) to whom I express my sincere appreciation in the following cowboy lingo:

> Here's to my wife, a sweet gal,
> In this work she's been a real pal,
> With punctuation she wrangled,
> Participles she undangled,
> Praying the damn thing will sell!

Part I

MAN

In the beginning was man . . . .

dP

CHAPTER I

DEATH RIDES AT THE RODEO

He jumped into the saddle,
The crowd shouting, "Ride him or bust!"
Then a hushed silence . . . and
Another knight lay in eternal dust.

"Out of chute No. 3, Pete Knight riding Duster!"

It was the event of rodeo that the spectators liked best. They sat silent in the grandstand; they watched the small group of cowboys gathered around the chutes, the men on horseback, and the brilliant waving flag for one brief moment, before a horse and rider, with a sudden leap, appeared on the horizon to blot out all distractions. It was a fascinating spectacle for which the crowd never lost its thrill—as if at this moment, once more primitive man were making a final struggle to overcome the beast. For the spectators there was always an element of unknown terror in the bronc-riding contest.

And in Hayward there were other things besides fear of an unexpected turn of events. It was the hour when the sun was hottest and the air grew still. In this hour too, heavy with dust and the odors of sweating bodies, the hawkers and vendors with their persistent clamor were wearing on the nerves of a crowd, eager for action. Restless, crying children brought sharp rebukes from fond, but weary parents, who at this critical moment wished that their offspring might cease the endless prattle and demands for attention. And always at this hour, too, came the husky voice of the announcer, calling the names of the riders and horses and the past accomplishments of both; interspersed with this statistical parade were those worn witticisms, used to carry the drama along through the appalling gaps of time that appear in the small contest.

As if relenting and attempting to ease the tension, the tempo of the contest changed. Suddenly appeared a man on horseback. The very design of things brought muted whispers to the full pitch of shrill screams. Before they had died down to the harsh rumble of excited inquiries, a man lay trodden in the arena dust. Pete Knight had been bucked off Duster!

It was just an ordinary Sunday in May, 1937, the twenty-third day of that month to be exact. For some eighteen years a rodeo had been an annual event at Hayward, California, and it was rodeo time again. The contest was sponsored by Harry Rowell, one of the cowboys' favorite rodeo producers; it was a small contest but it drew a number of prominent contestants.

Doff Aber had just been bucked off his horse and was on his way back to the chutes, when Pete came out. Pete rode Duster until almost the last second before the signal. As he came off, he fell in such a position that the horse could not avoid trampling him. A bucking horse usually avoids any obstacle in its way by jumping over it. What unfortunate reason prevented Duster from avoiding Pete is not known, but the animal came down with his full weight on the fallen cowboy. Among the first to reach Pete's side was his closest friend, Harry Knight. Slowly

Pete got to his feet and Harry asked, "Are you hurt?"
"You're goddamned right I'm hurt!"

Aided by his friends, he was taken to the waiting ambulance that stands ready in the background of every rodeo. Babe, his wife, was among the spectators and was unable to reach his side immediately but followed in a private car, only to find, when she reached the hospital, that Pete had died on the way.

Had Pete grown careless? Had he ridden so many broncs that he had complete assurance and faith in his own ability? Had he reached his peak at the age of thirty-five? Was Pete Knight the legendary rider of rodeo that so many people thought he was? Could his ability have been overrated?[1] Was this the ordained fate of bronc riders? Are the conjectures just so many questions that can never be answered?

---

[1] See Chapter XXVI., p. 325.

CHAPTER II

THE GREAT ARENA

Over wide wasteland, parched prairies,
Onward they drew . . .
Driven by dreams of horizons,
Far distant and new.

It was early spring of the year 1866, less than one year after the quenching of the flame of war that had seared the nation. Both victor and vanquished, unable to return to the tranquillity of an age that had passed from the pageant of civilization, turned toward new frontiers.

Youths who had become men during the nightmare of four years of war, sought, with a taste of thrill, adventure and outlawry, further excitement.

Thus, during that spring and the many that followed, men on horseback appeared on the plains of Texas. Weary men, but strong men, hopeful of furthering their fortunes, pushed into the heart of the great cattle country. Dressed in the remnants of their blue and grey uniforms, they wore with pride this last insignia of erring brothers. They sought a life of freedom, adventure, and fortune, and in the cattle industry their quest came to an end.

The Civil War had drawn on the man power of Texas, and while the herds of cattle had been rapidly increasing up to the time of the war, they continued to multiply un-attended. By the close of the great struggle, their numbers had increased until one-half million was considered a conservative estimate. The greater number of these were unbranded cattle or mavericks, and anyone who took the trouble to drive them to market became their owner. Thus, by the spring of 1866, the cattle industry stood on the threshold of becoming one of major importance if adequate markets could only be reached.

The thousands of fat, sleek steers were worth only a few dollars each in Texas, but in the Northern markets they brought extraordinary, even unbelievable prices. Now began the round-up of a trail herd and the driving to a Northern market. Weeks and months were spent in the assemblage and movement of these herds. Once underway, the numerous perils and problems that confronted the drivers were of no minor nature. Harassed by marauding and treacherous Indians; living in fear of some whim of nature or of the beasts in wild stampede; crossing streams swollen with the spring rains—horses, cattle, and men lost their lives in this moving adventure.

Because of the success of the cattle drives, ranching became a thriving industry in Texas and eventually in the High Plains. The drives had grown to such an extent that five years later a law was passed which required all persons purchasing cattle that were to be driven to markets beyond the northern limits of the state to brand their beasts with "a large and plain mark composed of any mark or device he may choose, which mark shall be branded on the left side of the back behind the shoulder."[1]

At the close of the sixties, herds of considerable size still existed in the northern section of the High Plains and

---

[1] *Laws of Texas*, 1871, Session 12, 119.

the surrounding mountain valleys. These herds had been
recruited from the stock of travelers using the Oregon
Trail, from the mineral seekers, from the Mormons, from
the ranchers of California and Oregon. Because of the
converging of the herds from the North and those from
the South in the beginning of the seventies, the great flow
of cattle eastward became an important Western industry.
The basic motive which started the Texas herds northward
was the fact that the cattle taken from the breeding
grounds of the South made wonderful gains in weight in
the feeding grounds of the North. A Texas longhorn
would gain two or three hundred pounds in the transition.
As a stock growing area the Northern ranges had demonstrated their usefulness, and in the early seventies the
plains south of the North Platte in Wyoming were rapidly
being stocked every year by this Texas invasion.

An important barrier had to be removed before the
cattle industry had complete control of this area. This
barrier was the fierce Indians who inhabited the greater
portion of northern Wyoming and much of Montana.
During the seventies the cattle range industry was moving
up to the edge of this territory and attempting to break
down the barrier.

There were also difficulties of the time; for example,
the constant moving westward of the farming frontier
and the strict quarantine legislation in Kansas against
Texas tick fever. As a result, Northern trails formed a
great crescent which swept west from the Panhandle of
Texas and cut into eastern Colorado. Colorado became the
path of invasion toward the ranges of the North. Both
Colorado and southern Wyoming formed a corridor, perhaps the most attractive approach to the North. The long

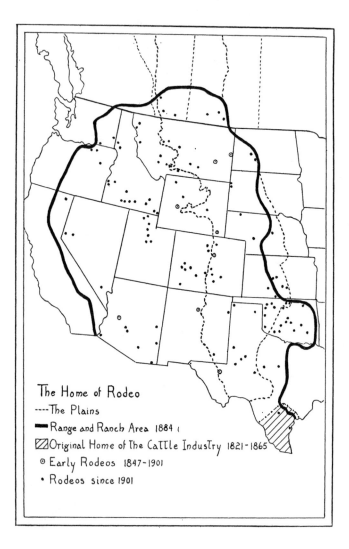

The Home of Rodeo
----The Plains
━━━ Range and Ranch Area 1884 (
▨ Original Home of The Cattle Industry 1821-1865
⊙ Early Rodeos 1847-1901
• Rodeos since 1901

stretches of sweeping plains were conducive to an easy moving of the herds.

The opening of these Northern trails offered greater opportunities to the drivers. If the prices offered along the Kansas Pacific Railroad line were not satisfactory, about one hundred and fifty miles to the north was the Union Pacific. This railroad made attractive descriptions of the advantages of the Northern ranges.

The drives to the Northern ranges have been immortalized in story and song, and in no period of our rapidly moving frontier has an activity been so singled out by its contemporaries and future generations for glorification as were the Texas cattle drives. Each drive was a new experience to those who took part. For the men it was daily work. Each spring meant the rounding-up of the cattle, the branding of calves, and finally, taking to the trail, at the end of which was the cowtown.

The tales told of these early termini of the drives lead one almost into the zone of folklore and fantasy. These towns were wide-open, rugged and earthy. In them the suppressed Adonis of the Plains was given every opportunity for self-expression. It was no novelty to see the ever-flowing bars of Cheyenne lined with Texas cowboys, but, when the thrill of 'having been to town' had worn off, the boasts and exaggerations of these men brought out exhibitions of their particular skills. The problem of keeping the peace was always a difficult one, and it did not improve with the converging of several different outfits in the same place.[1]

---

[1] *Cheyenne Daily Leader,* July 6, 1872; August 31, 1882.

CHAPTER III

EARLY RODEOS, STAMPEDES, AND ROUND-UPS

. . . at last appeared the town,
They gave a rousing yell,
They longed for beer and whiskey
And a chance to raise some Hell!

An exact date of the first exhibition of the daily work
and later, of the sport of the cowboy cannot be given. If
such an attempt were made, it would bring forth vehement
and justified protests from the various parts of the West,
steeped so long in the traditions of the growth of the cattle
industry. Each section jealously protects its contribution
to the development of the cowboy sport. One may assume,
however, that the first exhibitions of cowboys' skill of
range activity took place about the same time throughout
the West. The cowboys and the cattle owners in these
early days were often months, and sometimes even years,
in getting to towns of any size, and their pleasure was
curtailed to such an extent that, in order to indulge in relaxation, play, and sport, they made their daily duties fill
the need.

When their work became a sport, it is natural to assume
that within the various divisions of duty there developed
men of superior skill, especially among the riders and
ropers. They became the champions of the outfit of which
they were members. The approach toward the terminus

of a long drive signaled the opportunity to make new friends and to meet old ones in the numerous saloons of the cowtowns. The gay moods of the men mounted because of companionship, food and drink, and their conversation was brilliantly studded with bragging and boasting about the feats of individual members of each outfit.

The tales grew until, eventually, the veracity of the statements was challenged. The challenge was immediately followed by a division of the gathered group. Usually two camps were formed—one whose members bolstered the story and the narrator with accounts of their own experiences or embellished the original tale; the adherents of the other camp stood by the challenger with stubborn denials and doubt. The arguments usually led to an exhibition of the skills in question at the first opportune time.

Contests took place not only between members of one outfit but also among rival or competitive outfits. It was quite natural that the roping of steers was accomplished with greater ease and dexterity by some men than others, and a difference in skill applied likewise to those men best suited to break horses for the remuda. Yet, it is difficult to say when and where these rivalries first started, and whether they first existed within one outfit or between rival outfits. Information comes from tradition rather than from recorded statements.

Therefore, in the work of the range riders appears the beginning of a genuine, lusty, American sport with its full share of hard competition.

That there is a relationship between the fiestas of the Southwest and the beginning of rodeo, is a logical sequence of thought. This is justifiable in part, for the celebrations of California, New Mexico, and other sections of the

Southwest adjacent to the Rio Grande, did offer, as a form of entertainment, riding and roping by the skilled Mexican horsemen. The common ground of both fiesta and rodeo was the cattle industry. However, it is erroneous to assume that rodeo is a direct outgrowth of these celebrations. The greater portion of the fiesta was devoted to dancing, music, religious observances, and feasting.

The cattle industry, as it flourished in the seventies and eighties, was borrowed from Mexico where it had been planted by the Spaniards. Cattle and horses were Spanish in origin, as were the saddle and gear. The lariat—from the Spanish *la reata*—or as it is known today, the rope, is Mexican in origin, and for many years in the cattle industry the best ropers were Mexican vaqueros who had moved northward from the Rio Grande and had joined the large cattle outfits. The early Mexican dons owned the first herds in the Southwest and also held the first rodeos with the aid of their picturesque vaqueros, a group of the finest horsemen ever to ride the ranges.

The word rodeo is a Spanish word and is pronounced ro-day-o. This word was borrowed by the Anglo-Americans when they began to herd cattle on the plains. The Spanish pronunciation is found more often in the Southwest, while the anglicized form is used in the Northwest. Today the word *rodeo* is used as the name given to the form of entertainment which depicts the range activities of the cowboys and is pronounced both *ro-day-o* and *ro-dee-o*. Among the people connected with, and especially the contestants participating in this work, the latter form is preferred. There has been some confusion in the use of the term. Originally it meant to round up the cattle for branding, or to take them to the cattle market, which was often held during a fiesta. Hence the association with the early Spanish and Mexican celebrations. Today the rodeo is a round-up of cattle and horses, it is true; it is a celebration, however, in which there is a commercial element and also one of entertainment, both of which are very important. In the field of entertainment the words, *Rodeo, Stampede, Round-up,* and *Frontier* or *Pioneer Days* are all, more or less, synonymous and are applied to contests depicting these cowboy activities.

The Spanish-American influence was of great importance in the beginning of the cattle industry and set many of the standards of the work. When it was taken up by the influx of Anglo-Americans into the West, before and especially after the Civil War, it lost much of the significance of its earlier identity and followed the American tradition.

Therefore, one may say that the early beginning of rodeo is found in the inter-camp competitions on the range and, more often, in the cowtowns at the end of the trails. The men of the range talked, thought, and dreamed cattle and horses, and to back a preference by a wager was as natural as to have a preference. The two things went together as do rider and horse.

One of the earliest references to rodeo is found in a letter dated June 10, 1874. In this letter Captain Mayne Reid[1] wrote concerning a rodeo held in Santa Fe, New

---

[1] Captain Mayne Reid was born at Ballroney, County Down, Ireland, April 4, 1818. He came to this country in 1839. At the outbreak of the Mexican War, after an unsuccessful career as a writer, he joined the army and was given a commission as a second lieutenant in the 1st New York Volunteers. He was the author of such "hair-raising" books as *The Rifle Rangers* and *The Scalp Hunters*. He died in London, October 22, 1883. Information offered by Mr. Colin Johnston Robb, Drumharriff Lodge, Loughgall, County Armagh, Ireland.

Mexico. Of this event held nearly a hundred years ago, he says:

> The town from which I write is quaint; of the Spanish style of building and reposes in a great land kissed by the southern sun. You have cows in old Ireland, but you never saw cows. Yes, millions of them here, I am sure, browsing on the sweet long grass of the ranges that roll from horizon to horizon. At this time of year the cowmen have what is called the round-up, when the calves are branded and the fat beasts selected to be driven to a fair hundreds of miles away.
>
> This round-up is a great time for the cowhands, a Donneybrook fair it is, indeed. They contest with each other for the best roping and throwing, and there are horse races and whiskey and wines. At night in the clear moonlight there is much dancing on the streets.[1]

Some twenty-five years later, farther north, on the Fourth of July, 1872, the citizens of Cheyenne were given a minature preview of things to come. The populace was regaled with an exhibition of Texas steer riding. Some months later an exhibition of bronc riding took place. It is of great interest to note that one of the local editors looked upon this spectacle with dismay and considered it unnecessarily cruel.[2]

In the early eighties, the boys representing such brands as the Hashknife, the 101, the Mill-Iron, the W, and others

---

[1] A letter written by Chaptain Mayne Reid to Samuel Arnold of Drumna-kelly, Seaforde, County Down, Ireland, inscribed "Santa Fe, 10th June, 1847." (Now in the manuscript collection of Colin Johnston Robb, Drumharriff Lodge, Loughgall, County Armagh, Ireland. Permission to use.)

[2] *Chevenne Daily Leader*, July 6, 1872. "There was quite a crowd and some quiet swearing. But would not such exhibitions be in better taste out on the prairie?" *Cheyenne Daily Leader*, (September 11, 1873).

run by the Aztec Land and Cattle Company, settled their differences by having a steer-roping contest in Pecos City, Texas. The courthouse yard was used as a corral, and one by one the beasts were set free with the ropers in pursuit. The path of the run was directly down the main street of Pecos. There were no awards or public recognition; the winning outfit of the event stood treat to the losers. A. T. (Trav.) Windham, a Texas cowman of renown, was the winner of the contest.

Exhibitions and competitions, similar to the one witnessed by the citizens of Pecos City, were going on throughout the West. The oldest continuous annual rodeo performance on record in the country is said to be the event held at Prescott, Arizona, in 1888. This event—known as Frontier Days Celebration—took place on July 4, of that year. Juan Leivas was the winner of the award, a mounted silver medal. This award, known as the Citizens Prize, is the earliest known rodeo trophy and perhaps the first of its kind (plaque) to be given at a Frontier Days Celebration. In the years that followed, this award disappeared but was recovered from the silver scrap donated to the Aviators' Fund during World War I. It was purchased by C. W. Davis and H. D. Aitkins and presented on July 4, 1919, to the Prescott Frontier Days Association.[1]

About 1891 a cowboy contest was held for trophies and money at Miles City, Montana, as an entertainment for the members of the Montana Stock Growers Association. Then came the first known commercial rodeo at Lander, Wyoming, in 1893. This event was staged by E. Farlow, and with the regular rodeo events were a ten-

---

[1] A letter and facsimile of the First Cowboy Medal sent to the author by the Prescott Frontier Days Association, Prescott, Arizona, 1941.

mile three-horse-team relay and a stage coach hold-up. This show was known as Frontier Days, a name since made internationally famous by Cheyenne, Wyoming, as the name of its annual contest. The promoter of this early Lander rodeo, Mr. Farlow, is still active, and the portrayal of this celebration as an event in the present Pioneer Days is under his supervision.

On July 4, 1896, a rodeo was held in a little old cow-town of Mingersville, now known as Wibaux, in eastern Montana. A year later, in 1897, came the Frontier Days celebration at Cheyenne, Wyoming, which has been staged annually since that time.

Thus, in the late nineties the possibilities of rodeo as a public entertainment were beginning to be realized. Great rivalry existed among the many Western towns in trying to outdo one another in their annual celebration.[1] This

---

[1] Evidence of this rivalry between Pendleton and Walla Walla is found in the following paragraphs from the *East Oregonian*:

"Walla Walla's effort at a frontier show is a plain infringement on the Round-up and in view of the proximity of Walla Walla to Pendleton and the previous friendly relations between the towns is inexcusable. Walla Walla has shown a poor spirit in this case and it is a fair inference that those in charge of affairs over there are men of small calibre or they would have acted differently.

"From a Round-up standpoint the worst features about the Walla Walla show and other imitation performances is that they discredit the game. None of the numerous shows held from Winnipeg to Los Angeles have been up to the standard. They have all been money making affairs and usually have sought to take much and give little though a conspicuous exception seems to be shown at Ontario, Oregon.

"If these secondary shows are continued long enough the inevitable effect will be to 'queer' the whole thing. People will see them and being misled into believing each and every one is 'like the Pendleton Round-up' they will fail to come to the Round-up. The fact the Thursday Round-up crowd this year was small may be charged chiefly to the fact almost every other town in the country had been having a frontier show of its own." *East Oregonian*, Pendleton, Oregon, (September 22, 1913).

was the case in the Cheyenne and Denver feud.[1] Eventually, Denver dropped out as competitor of the southern Wyoming show. About this time the Wild West Shows began to get under way. Buffalo Bill, his imitators, and rivals saw the opportunity of turning this Wild West horsemanship and cowboy skill into commercial advantage. The riders of those early shows were, or had been, working cowboys, and to that extent these shows were a genuine portrayal of the life of the range.

As the old cattle days faded into the background of our rapidly changing age, Western communities awakened to the opportunity and the need of keeping alive the memory of those bygone days. The stage was set for all the pageantry, thrills, adventure, and competition that are a part of rodeo. Rodeo is made up of competition and that touch of the spectacular which is necessary for all sport and for intensely living drama. It is a national institution, it has its great and near-great personalities, and across its stage have moved men and women internationally famous for depicting a vital phase of American life.

---

[1] Reference to this existent feeling is made in the following newspaper account:

"It is no longer disputed among those acquainted with the wild west exhibitions given here and elsewhere that the championship for bucking and pitching, steer roping, wild horse riding and ladies cow pony race, are determined at any other place than at the Frontier Celebration in Cheyenne. Merit determines the best contestants and it is almost universally admitted, aside from those promoting the Denver bucking and pitching contest, that the best riders and best ropers in the world are to be seen exclusively at Cheyenne." (*Cheyenne Daily Leader*, (August 19, 1902).

"Now comes the annual suggestion from residents of the larger city that, inasmuch as Frontier days is so successful, the celebration should be appropriated by Cheyenne's big neighbor, Denver, and there made a fete of greater magnitude.

"The suggestion that Denver appropriate Frontier Days is old. It has been made every year for a decade, and, as previously herein stated, on two occasions two disastrous attempts to consummate the appropriation have been perpetrated." *Wyoming Tribune*, (August 20, 1912), 4. See Chapter XXX, pp. 438-450, 454-464.

CHAPTER IV

EIGHTY YEARS ON THE TRAIL

The cowboy lives a life of his own,
Riding his horse, and above him the sky;
Under the stars at night his royal throne,
The hard earth where he may lie.

The exact time when the term "cowboy" was applied to the men who made a life work of tending cattle is not known. However, during the American Revolution the name *cowboy* was tagged to a group of American Tories who played havoc with the stock of the Whigs and Loyalists by swooping into their districts of occupation to steal cattle. Today, as formerly, the word *cowboy* is used to designate those men who care for the cattle on the Western ranges of the United States. The probable source of the word is found in the Spanish word *vaquero*, the word *vaca* meaning cow; the word *vaquero*, *cowman* or *cow tender*. Whatever the source may be, the cowboy was a part of the West, and it is impossible to understand one without the other.

The cowboy is considered the last of the various types of individuals who have been products of the West. He shows characteristics that are distinct. Although his appearance on the stage of this epic-making drama was but a short half-century in length of time, his stride was

taken with measured steps that have left an indelible
pattern.

Before the days of the cattle drive, the cowboy did
exist, but as an individual he had not been characterized.
It was the trail drives that made him a type—gave him his
personality and exalted his specialized form of work. The
trail drives produced a man unlike any other that had as
yet appeared in the West.[1]

The early range riders, as a group, were made up of
peculiar stock, for among them were the crude and illiterate, as well as the cultured and educated. The lure of
the cattle industry not only drew upon the manhood of
the surrounding areas; there also was a noticeable influx of
young men from the deep South and the industrial North,
from good families and of education. The War between
the States widened their horizon. They were fascinated
and intrigued by the life of the Plainsmen and entered into
it with a deadly sincerity.[2]

---

[1] The following contemporary reference is of interest:

"I have met among these stockmen highly educated men, as herders,
whose essays on literature would throw into the deepening shade some
of the sentimental so-called aesthetic sickly nonsense which society calls
poetry.

"If you wish to do so, you can find as highly educated and refined
gentlemen among the 'old settlers' and 'cow punchers' of the many
years ago, of these arid plains, as they were formerly called, as you can
in those who come now in their Pullman cars, with Oscar Wilde, aesthetic manner, accompanied with Patchoulli, [sic] Essence de miilefleures
[sic] or seal skin sacques." Stanton, Fred J., *Cheyenne Daily Leader,*
(May 25, 1882).

[2] Further evidence is found in the following:

"For a time, cowpunching was almost a mania among eastern college men. Cultivated youths were fascinated by the free, open life. In
some parts of the west, notably in Colorado, there arose a curious and
delightful society. The ranchman was only a cowboy in chief. He was
emancipated from many prejudices and localisms. In particular, it was
noticed in Cheyenne and Denver in the most high and palmy state of
the cattle business, that cowpunching was a sure receipt for reducing the

Therefore, the assumption that every cowboy was un-
couth, wild, and a desperate character, prone to carousing,
shooting up towns, and possessing no virtue, is as false a
conception as to encircle his head with a halo and make
him a patron saint of Law and Order. To bestow upon
him virtues possessed by no man or saint, both of whom
are children and heirs of the weaknesses of human flesh, is
to mark him without consideration of the age in which he
lived. The early cowboy was, first of all, a human being.
He had all the vices and many of the virtues which are
characteristic of the human family, but because he was
reared in an atmosphere of absolute freedom and unusual
hardship, his life was perhaps more individualistic. The
pleasure of his existence was crammed into a shorter space
of time. In truth, what pleasures the cowboy had, were
usually found in the ragged little Western communities
known as cow towns. These oases of pleasure, found at the
end of the long trails, supplied outlets for the crowded
emotions of these bold, fearless, and daring men.

Their opportunity to "turn loose" and celebrate followed the long drives and round-ups, after weeks and, in

---

Bostonian morgue." *Calgary Daily Herald.* (September 4, 1912), 7.

"As you mingle with these cowboys, you find in them a strange
mixture of good nature and recklessness. You are as safe with them on
the plains as with any class of men, so long as you do not impose upon
them. They will even deny themselves for your comfort, and imperil
their lives for your safety. But impose upon them, or arouse their ire,
and your life is of no more value in their esteem than that of a coyote.
Morally, as a class, they are toulmouthed, [sic] blasphemous, drunken,
lecherous, utterly corrupt. Usually harmless on the plains when sober,
they are dreaded in towns, for then liquor has the ascendency over them.
They are also so improvident as the veriest 'Jack' of the sea. Employed
as cowboys on six months in the year—from May till November—their
earnings are soon squandered in dissoluteness, [sic] and then they hunt,
or get odd jobs, to support themselves until another season begins."
"The Cowboys of the Western Plains and Their Horses," reprint from
the *Providence Journal* in the *Cheyenne Daily Leader,* (October 3, 1882).

Cowboys' Attire (1910).
—*Courtesy Chamber of Commerce, Cheyenne, Wyoming.*

most cases, months of self-denial and restraint. It was their opportunity to indulge, in the brief span of their visit, in whatever vices they knew, and to add to their repertoire as many more as possible. The most important necessities of every cow town, the dance hall and saloon, were taken for granted. A town could not exist without them, although it did manage beautifully without a church. But these men, while on the range, were perhaps closer to their God than they ever could be within the four walls of an unpainted, weather-beaten, uninspiring church. It would be ridiculous to make an attempt to soften the relationship which existed between the cowboy and the people in the early communities. It is unfortunate that the characterization of the man of the Plains is, in most part, built on this contact. Because of the actions of this brief visitor in the cow towns, a picture has been drawn, inaccurate and without justification, one that people insist upon keeping and enlarging as the measure of the cowboy. It is unfortunate that the early cowboy is best-kown through these records of vice and excess. The stories of the cowboy had as a basis the same elements of weakness as are found in any city of yesterday and certainly in any of today.[1]

---

[1] Further corroboration of the statements is found in the following:
  "The accessories, the 'properties' as the stage managers say, of the cowboy, his sombrero and chaperajos, and jingling heavy spurs, have struck the imagination and blinded it to his qualities and services. There rises up the distorted image of him in his most reckless moment, in his hours of gross merrymaking, when he tones down his constitution with frontier whiskey and rides through the town shooting and whooping. Yet all observers of his class paint him as far from quarrelsome, sudden and quick in quarrel, indeed, but not seeking it; courteous as self-contained, as men who live out-of-doors and carry dangerous weapons, and know that their associates carry them, are apt to be; truthful, honest, brave, of course, and not merely in action, but endurance, laborious, full of reserve. He belonged to a highly-skilled profession." *Calgary Daily Herald,* (September 4, 1912), 7.

The crudest and rowdiest men of that age earned the ever-clinging reputation of vulgarity and lack of restraint, and although this had a certain foundation, environment was the important contributing force of this reputation.

Not until the rough edges of this last frontier had been smoothed by the velvet-clad hand of civilization, bringing in its entourage law, order, local and national improvements, and eventually, the flame of civic pride, which is, so obviously, a part of every community of the West, did a change take place. As proof of his underlying and dormant virtues—steadfastness, respect, intelligence, and hard work—the cowboy met the challenge and proved to be what he has always been, the aristocrat of the West, the man in the saddle. Now a citizen, he went about his daily work in the manner of its heritage, but under the new tempo of changed conditions.

At the end of the eighties, the long drives were gradually coming to a close. The advent of the home seekers and the railroads is the outstanding contributing factor. The endless, rolling plains, which stretched out in one continuous sweep northward, were at this time crossed and recrossed by wire fences. The large ranches from the south to the north of the High Plains were fenced in, in order to hold rich grazing areas and choice positions on river fronts. The extension of the railroads into the various sections of the cattle country obviated the necessity of the long trails. The appearance of the law-abiding farmers, of steady, sober citizens and villagers was another factor; these people brought credit to themselves and their settlements with progressive and prosperous farming methods or small ranches of improved stock. The growth of hundreds of towns and cities was the outward expression of their hopes and labor. The dawn of this new era was not so spectacular and colorful as the previous period, but its foundation was rooted more securely in the soil that had been wrested from the mythical Great American Desert.

The spirit and ideal of democracy that had permeated the citizen of the period of the transitory frontier, as exemplified by the cattle industry, continued after the "cooling-off" stage had made itself apparent. He was neither ashamed of nor dismayed by the humble beginning of this lusty, noisy infant, the cattle industry, that had eventually grown into an almost uncontrollable colossus, which had, by its mighty grasp, molded the character of the cowboy and stamped upon it the personality of the frontier.

The citizens of the many towns wished to retain in vivid memory the era that had taken upon itself the brunt of the vicious blows of the forces of nature. From the scene had passed the thousands of range cattle, the great round-ups, stampedes, the long drives, and much of the tinsel of the early cowtowns. Yet, there remained one of the most important features of that era, one which cannot be isolated from the cattle industry, that unique character of the plains, the cowboy. During the "gentling" process of the frontier, the cowboy had slowly fitted into the change which was gradually taking place. He worked as an all-around hand on small ranches, he was slowly becoming the forgotten man of a waning age. It would have been a great mistake, had the people of the Plains permitted the drifting of such an era, as expressed by the cattle industry and with it the cowboy, into a deepening haze of tradition and folklore.

Therefore, with pride of heritage and in recognition of the age which had given it birth, the Plains country, in memory of the cattle industry and the unique figure allied with it, the cowboy, annually holds a celebration with gusto in almost every community. Early in this century, from the border towns of southern Texas, northward, and beyond the border into Canada, the cattle industry and the cowboy were being immortalized in rodeo.

The old time cowboy was in a class by himself, ready for any adventure or romance that might come his way. He was not one to fuss about wages, hardships or food; his work not only involved the cattle, but also patrolling the frontier and fighting the Indian, and later the cattle thieves and border outlaws. In most cases, he came from pioneer stock and was, like his ancestors, ready to step forward and prepare the way for others. It was such men as he, who, around their camp fires, in their homes, or at the early rodeos, showed themselves to be the finest and most congenial of companions.

Among the many courageous men who have been a part of this vital industry, some were destined to ride through this stirring time and pass on, leaving no particular mark or distinction. There were others, however, who were to leave a more definite imprint. Not all were to carry on the traditions of the West in the form as expressed by rodeo, and while many did follow rodeo and made it a very definite part of their lives, on occasion, others were associated with it in an indirect fashion because of their love for horses, cattle, and the men of the range.

The roster of the early rodeo contestants—both women and men—who were prominent during the last of the nineteenth century and the first two decades of the present century, contains names of many who have passed on and of others who have retired. This list includes Prairie Lilly Allen, Nan Gable, Dorothy Morrell, Lucille Mulhall, Prairie Rose Henderson, Fannie Sperry Steele, Paul Hastings, Curley Griffith, Eddie McCarty, Eddie Burgess,[1] Joe Gardner, and Johnny Murray; these last two, the companions and friends of the fabulous and now almost legendary Clay McGonigal.

More stories have been told perhaps about the roping ability of Clay McGonigal than any other individual in rodeo. The term, "to do a McGonigal," was the sweetest kind of praise to reach the ears of roping men of that day. McGonigal was one of the outstanding cowhands of the age; he had great ability as a bronc rider and became famous through his reputation as an artist of the rope. His specialty was the roping and tying of wild steers, and after roping had been outlawed in most of the Western states, he turned to calf roping, as did many ropers of that time. In this event he was no less skilled; in November, 1919, he won first prize of one thousand dollars at the Arizona State Fair at Phoenix, when he made the best time for three calves.

His artistry took him throughout the Western hemisphere; he appeared in roping contests in both North and South America, and for the first two decades of this century all acclaimed him the premier roping man of rodeo.

---

[1] "Eddie Burgess, Oklahoma rider, breaks world record — ropes and ties a steer in 23 4/5 seconds." *Calgary Daily Herald*, (August 30, 1919), 7.

His skill as a roping expert cannot be questioned, especially if the conditions of the calf roping event, as they now prevail, are taken into consideration. Consider the difference between the roping and tying of a steer and that of a calf; consider the earlier start of thirty to one hundred feet with that now, which is practically none! The amazing time of twenty-three seconds flat on a one hundred-foot start, when he roped and tied a steer at Tucson, Arizona, in 1901, is an excellent example of his skill and finesse. Fifteen years later his time was 18-4/5 seconds on a thirty-foot start at an exhibition at Chicago, Illinois. The time of these events is breath-taking, if one considers the changes that have taken place in this roping event.

The New York Stampede, at Sheepshead Bay Speedway, was held during the month of August, 1916, under the leadership of Guy Weadick, one of the first producers of rodeo in the East and West. This was one of the first occasions when name contestants of the West were introduced to the East. The names of three, among the many to appear there, were long to be remembered by those who witnessed this spectacle and by all associated with rodeo in its infancy. The names of Prairie Lilly Allen, Dorothy Morrell, and Leonard Stroud conjure up in the minds of old-timers the dash, flare, and glory of those early days. All three were high class performers and received considerable publicity. Of them, only one, Leonard Stroud, is still active in the work.

Stroud was born at the end of that era—the dying age of the range cattle industry. Originally from Texas, he was related, more or less, to the passing industry through his father's business, which was that of supplying feed. About 1909 he attracted considerable attention as a bronc rider, but that was only one of his many talents, for a few years later he was to qualify, without question, as the All-Around Cowboy Champion of that time. Between 1916 and 1921, he entered into practically every arena event of rodeo. His capacity as a performer was so varied that it necessitated the rearrangement of programs to permit him to partake in the various contests.

Leonard Stroud was one of the most popular performers at the early Fat Stock Shows and Rodeos of Fort Worth, Texas; he also appeared with the Howe Circus, and still later with Ringling Brothers as their star performer. Following his brilliant performance at the Sheepshead Bay Show, Stroud joined Pawnee Bill and made an extended tour of this country.

In the annals of bronc riding, it is said that he was the first to ride the famous "Tipperary," a bronc of great bucking ability some years ago, at the Belle Fourche Round-up. His well-known ride on "Indian Tom" was preserved by R. R. Doubleday's camera, and wherever rodeo is known, this picture is recognized as the personification of its spirit.

Leonard Stroud was one of the first cowboys to make a business and, certainly, a career of contesting. His list of activities reads like that of several men rather than that of one. Stroud was not only a bronc rider, but also a calf and steer roper, a steer rider, a bulldogger, and a contestant in several types of relay races. In addition to these accomplishments, he was a serious contender for the fancy roping championship, and for nearly ten years was the undisputed champion trick rider.

At the present time Leonard Stroud no longer participates in contests as bronc rider or bulldogger, but he is still an important figure in the business of promoting, producing, and directing rodeos. This latter interest was not developed as a result of age, when the strenuous activities of the arena caused him to slow up, because he was already promoting rodeos at the height of his career in 1919. Today, he is in the business of directing contests, and contacting and contracting units for fairs. He still appears on many Western programs and is active as a trick roper and rider.

Leonard Stroud is one of the few genuine men of the West who have a remarkable gift for showmanship with qualifications to back it up. He was able to retain that Western freshness of action that so often loses its punch because of repetition. He truly might be called a career cowboy. He now lives at Canon City, Colorado, where he is engaged in the feed business, when he is not "rodeoing."

The famous Prairie Lilly also reached the height of her long career at the New York Show of 1916. She had come a long way from the town of her birth, Columbia, Tennessee, to win first place in bronc riding for cowgirls. Her dangerous career led her into the various paths associated with this type of work. She supplied stock for Western motion pictures, operated a riding school, and joined several circuses as a feature performer; all this was in addition to her active part in rodeo.

From the time of her remarkable performance at the New York Stampede, which crowned her as first lady of the bronc riding event for cowgirls, until about 1927, she was an active performer and also promoted contests and shows. At this time, however, she gradually began to slow

Cowgirls' Attire (1910).
—*Courtesy Chamber of Commerce, Cheyenne, Wyoming.*

up in her bronc riding activities. Upon retirement, Prairie Lilly settled in New York City, and her home today is the center of activity for visiting rodeo, Wild West, and circus performers.

CHAPTER V

HIGH, WIDE, AND HANDSOME

You can always tell a cowboy,
He's been that way fore'er,
Sombrero, spurs, and chaps,
A shy, independent air.

During the first twenty years of this century, rodeo as a business was not the smooth running organization that is found today. It was the day of fitting what rules there were to the needs of whatever might be the occasion. The variation in the rules and regulations for contests and contestants makes one wonder how it was possible to honor, with any degree of justice, the prowess of the superior man or woman in the work. This problem was more obvious, for every community and every exhibition of cowboy sports had its champion, and the end of the season brought forth several World Champions in the many events, as well as the several All-Around Champions that cropped up. It was the day of no chutes, no dead lines, and of questionable timing facilities. The adjustment of these difficulties and the establishment of several organizations relating to rodeo have eliminated much of this earlier confusion.

The difficulties presented by rodeo in its infancy make it impossible to compare the present-day cowboy-contestant with the working cowboy of earlier periods. This is a question that very often is asked by those looking for a discussion. This is a question that offers possibilities for endless discussion and argument, but is not necessarily one that has sound reasoning as a basis. In other words, at best, it only offers something to quarrel about.

Nearly a quarter of a century separates the present-day spectacular performances of Nick Knight, Hub Whiteman, Everett Bowman, Burel Mulkey, Gene Ross, Smokey Snyder, Toots Mansfield, Homer Pettigrew, Dick Griffith, Chet McCarty, Jackie Cooper, Dave Campbell, Junior Eskew, Bud and Bill Linderman, and the late Pete Knight, Doff Aber, and Fritz Truan, and those of Thad Sowder, Yakima Canutt, Floyd Carroll, John Murray, Tom Minor, Paul Hastings, Ed Lindsey, and John Rock. Another quarter century separates the endeavors of this latter group and those of the boys who came off the ranges or the drives and gave exhibitions of their skill by entering competitions between rival outfits.

Rodeo today is as different from the early cowboy contests as bulldogging is from the early bull leaping contests, as practiced by the ancient Cretans. There is a relationship, but the element of time, be it fifty years or three thousand, brings change.

In the last twenty-five years the physical change in the presentation of rodeo makes a comparison between the forenamed groups of men impossible. The economic and social aspects of our country that have made possible the development of rodeo, as we know it today, must be considered with reference to the change in attitude of the contestants and the growth of rodeo as a big-time business. The latter is especially important, for rodeo is eagerly looking forward to recognition as one of the major sports of this country. With this in mind, that is the sport angle, one may assume that the modern cowboy-contestants of today are better developed athletes than those of former days. It must be remembered that the rodeo contestants have considerably more at stake than the earlier individuals who made rodeo a part of their relaxation and fun, an avocation from their more strenuous work on the range and ranches.

The modern cowboy must attain a certain degree of professional skill, or he is at a great disadvantage in competitions of considerable size. He is a specialist in his work and must constantly work for improvement, just as does any big league football or basketball star. He is as different from the cowboy of the range as the league man is from the sand lot player.

This is no attempt to belittle the skill of the working cowboy, nor is it an attempt to heap glory on the modern rodeo contestant, but rather to make a point of the fact that there has been a transition period during this last half century. Out of this early group of men in their daily work there has developed another type of man for whom this work has become specialized and made into a business, sport, and entertainment. Both groups have been contributing forces in the development of rodeo as a major American spectator sport.

The cowboy of earlier days did not have the incentive to make a highly specialized study of his work from the standpoints of speed, time and showmanship, nor did he reap great financial returns. With regard to finances, he was hired for a monthly wage, to ride herd, to work at the round-ups, to rope and brand cattle, and to break broncs. Efficiency was an important item, but the time element was not as essential as it is in rodeo. The competition or pride in ability, with which the range cowboy was faced while doing his work, did not interfere with his eating or sleeping, unless he was almost hopeless. Elimination of the less competent cowboy took place long before his pride could be injured because of failure in his work. The ability of the man to survive during this time was based on the fact that he was geared to a life of endurance, one of physical strain, hard-riding, and rough living—all spread over a period of time until he became hardened.

Today, with many of the hardships of this life removed, the man who comes off the range does not have the finesse when he enters a contest as is displayed by the regular contestant. This cannot be expected of him, but, in turn, he should not regard the smoothness and skill of the rodeo contestant as easy. These qualities are the result of hours of practice, hard work, and not of fun or play.

The rodeo contestant of today works as sincerely as does the man of the range, but with added objectives and certainly more inhibitions which entail a greater amount of efficiency. Speed, time, showmanship, and the fact that he must earn money on the basis of the first two objectives, create a mental hazard. He is not hired for a wage, and therefore he must be sufficiently skilled to get some financial return, in order to exist and continue his work.

The element of competition is omnipresent for the veteran performer because he is faced with the necessity of making time and speed, and because his superiority is constantly being challenged by the influx of younger blood. This is intensified because his endeavour is not in the form of group activity but that of one individual against all others.

The modern cowboy-contestant is keyed to an existence of marked mental and physical strain in shorter periods of time, but of greater intensity; although he can be trained to his work, the mental strain of competition cannot be measured in concrete terms. Any form of work which involves nervous strain brings in its wake the attendant evils of shorter span of active participation, lack of efficiency, and "slowing-up." This strain is found in all sports and is the result of competition.

The belief that every working cowboy is as good as, or better than, the rodeo contestant is as erroneous as the belief that every contestant would hold up as a work hand. However, the majority of the rodeo contestants are very excellent ranch cowboys. They own and operate ranches for themselves or for others. Certainly, from a physical standpoint, both ranch cowboy and rodeo contestant are blessed with healthy bodies that are, in most cases, typical of hard working people, but the abilities and skills of their respective activities would differ if their positions were switched.

A spectator at any of the performances in modern rodeo is more conscious of the faster action and snap decisions of these men than are necessary for those on the open range. But this very swiftness of action and speed on the range would bring the average working cowboy to his knees before a half day's work is over. The pace demanded of the cowboy's horse in rodeo work could not be maintained throughout the day on the range, while the range horse would, in many cases, be left dust-smothered in rodeo. Both man and beast are conditioned for their particular work. Thus, the discussion of the supremacy of cowboys old and new, is one that can go on forever and gives occasion for interesting, if not logical, argument.

In a discussion of the modern cowboy-contestant, a composite picture reveals those characteristics that might be grouped together and classed as typical of the man in this work. What is the general portrait of the man in rodeo?

Perhaps the first characteristic of him is the fact that he, in most cases, is western-born and wishes to impress this upon the people. The factor of birth place does not seem important, since several years of investigation about the man in rodeo reveal the unexpected fact that some people in rodeo are of eastern birth. The hold that rodeo has taken upon the country has not left any section of the nation untouched, and all areas have offered individuals who aspire to the fame and fortune of the rodeo arena.

It should not be considered unusual, but rather as not probable, that a good bronc rider might come from Massachusetts, as well as from Montana. There is no reason to believe that a snappy quarterback could not come from the latter state and that he must come from the former. Although there are not many contestants from the East, the Easterner is, nevertheless, an important force in the development of rodeo as a sport. If environment had been conducive to the development of contestants, many an Easterner would have been able to hold his own with the best. The factors of background and environment become more questionable when one considers the source of the early cowboy during the range cattle industry. The Easterner and Southerner were in no small measure a force in the development of the typical man of the West, and why there should be any feeling today, especially among the rodeo contestants, of uniqueness of species is not understood. Nevertheless, three or four generations removed from an Eastern background, there has developed a personality distinct in its character, known as the Westerner. This same distinction exists among the followers of rodeo, although less obvious among them and especially so, when an individual of a different environment has proved himself worthy of a position in this work.

Doubtlessly, there exists a degree of social distinction between the Westerner of two and three generations and the man whose ancestry is more recent, and there is even greater distinction between these two groups and the outsider who might try to become a participant in this sport. There is a distinction between those who participate in various rodeo events such as bronc riding, calf roping, steer wrestling and others, and those who are classed as Wild West performers. This latter group includes trained animal acts, novelty roping and riding acts. The genuine rodeo contestant has little time for this type of thing but realizes that it is a drawing feature and essential for its entertainment value. In the first group mentioned, it is obvious that strained but friendly relations exist between the bronc riders and the calf ropers. This is a rather serious aspect which has led to professional jealousy and, in the long run, has brought about many changes in these two events.[1]

---

[1] Rodeo cowboys are quite conscious of the distinction between riders and ropers and the contract performers. This idea goes back to the days when the bronc buster was looked upon as a distinct type of cowboy. The breaking of wild horses demanded a certain talent and men so gifted become professional horse breakers and went around the country doing this hazardous work. They were looked upon as a class set apart from the ordinary cow-puncher.

A second characteristic of the man in rodeo is his youth. It is something that should not evoke surprise on the part of the observer, for only youth has the essential spark, power, dash, and the freshness which are essential in sports of any type. Therefore, it is not unusual that the men in this work are young, but certainly their type of work has put its mark upon them, for they do look more mature than men in other sports. This work demands of them a life in the open, subjecting them to extremes in weather and to rapidly changing working conditions; furthermore, a nervous, high-tension existence, change in food and eating habits, late hours, and the hardship of constant travel. All this shows that their work stamps a mark of maturity, both physical and worldly, on these young men. The general ruggedness of their work removes that look of naive youthfulness which their age, and sometimes their action belie, for during their moments of relaxation their exuberance is astounding. In fun and humor the cowboy of the rodeo is one of the best companions, and there is much of the "boy" about him, for that is what he really is.

These boys begin their careers at the age of fifteen or sixteen, and already in their early twenties they rank as top performers in rodeo. Among the rodeo contestants, it is commonly conceded that a man should taper off from full participation in the work when he is in his middle thirties, for the danger element increases steadily; forty is generally thought of as the retiring age. The span of twenty years of active participation is considered the length of time for successful work.

A third characteristic of the man in rodeo is his enthusiasm for his work. Many of the men have a sincere love for it, not only men who have been making a living and also reaping some of the fame and fortune connected with the work, but many who barely make a living wage to keep themselves, not to speak of their horses, equipment, or the entrance fees needed to participate as contestants. It would be a severe blow to these men to give up this life with all its dangers and precarious financial difficulties, and also the lure of competition, travel, and general laxity of formal living.

Many men in rodeo have been successful in winning money, prizes, and honors, and the motive that keeps them in the game is the likelihood of winning more. They are not especially enthusiastic, they love the sport, and they will continue in this occupation as long as it is a paying business. Others say that they are ready for a change and wish to make it as soon as possible. However, they do nothing about it, make no effort to break away, and thus continue to follow along. The truth of the matter is, that rodeo, when it gets into the blood, is difficult to remove, whether it be a cold-blooded business proposition, a successful work, or a series of disappointments.

One revealing characteristic about the people in rodeo is this: they are not conscious of the fact that they are keeping alive "the traditions of the Old West," as is stated so naively by many publicity directors, nor do they care about this fact in one way or another. Rodeo is a business and livelihood for them; they make the best of it.

Another characteristic of the typical cowboy-contestant is the preference he shows for the various divisions of work. Just as there were specialists in the earlier days on the ranges and ranches, there is a similar division today.

There are really only two types of cowboys, the ropers and the riders. This situation existed during the early days of the cattle industry and still exsists today. This is not an attempt to say that calf ropers cannot ride broncs, nor that bronc riders cannot rope, but rather that there is this obvious division of labor. The contestants in modern rodeo are calf ropers and bronc riders. Then, the question arises: What about those who participate in the events of steer riding, bulldogging, and steer wrestling? In reality these latter events have nothing to do with the actual cowboy activities of the range and were, for the most part, the fun and sport of the men, and have now been included for some years in rodeo for additional thrills. This has certainly been achieved, for without a question, they are really dangerous sports; at least the event of steer riding offers all that can be taken by the most rugged of men. The men of the two main divisions, namely riders and ropers, have, in most cases, added one or two of these other activities.

It is interesting to note that Smokey Snyder, five times World's champion steer rider, is also a bareback rider. Carl Dossey is a rider of bareback broncs, steers, and has the added accomplishment of steer wrestling. Wonder Boy, Fritz Truan, All-Around Cowboy for 1940, was not only a saddle bronc but a bareback bronc rider and a steer wrestler. Bob Walden and Chet McCarty are bareback and saddle bronc riders, Bill McMacken, a saddle bronc rider; all three do steer wrestling with considerable success. Alvin Gordon, Burel Mulkey, Jackie Cooper, Nick Knight, Bart Clennon, and Gene Pruett are, for the most part, straight saddle bronc riders; however, the last mentioned does some steer wrestling.

This confirms the statement that there is a division of work, for in a survey of the activities of the men who are specialists in roping a similar point can be made. Toots Mansfield, Buck Echols, Roy Lewis, Everett Shaw, Juan Salinas, the Burkes—Jiggs, Dee, and the late Clyde—all are straight calf ropers. Homer Pettigrew, All-Around Cowboy for 1941, is a calf roper and a steer wrestler, as are Dave Campbell, Buckshot Sorrells, Hugh Bennett, and Everett Bowman. The former president of the Cowboys' Turtle Association, Everett Bowman, has always been a hard man to beat in either calf roping or steer wrestling, and he is still a serious threat to the contenders in either event.

A survey of this list of activities shows that there are not many instances in which a bronc rider or steer rider participates as a roper, or in which a roper uses bronc or steer riding as an additional accomplishment. This statement should not be taken too seriously, for obviously in a survey of this type, it was impossible to make a complete check of the activities of the many contestants; however, in most cases it can be regarded as fact.

A further development of the idea of a division of work is the fact that most bronc riders are from the north and northwest sections of this country, while the ropers by birth are Southwesterners. In the latter case this is quite logical, since the art of roping was inherited from the Mexican vaqueros and, of course, is directly related to the Spanish-American era of occupation, which was closely followed by the development of the range cattle industry. The need of expert ropers for work with the cattle and the eventual rounding up of the beasts for the move to the North was first felt in the Southwest.

There seems to be no explanation, however, of the fact that the bronc riders come from the North and Northwest. Burel Mulkey, Bill McMacken, Jenny Ambler, Alvin Gordon, Chet McCarty, Jack Wade, the Linderman brothers, all are top men in the bronc riding event and are from the North.

Another characteristic that appears to distinguish the bronc rider from the roper is the differences in the physical appearance of these two groups of men. The riders in appearance are generally tall, slim, broad-shouldered, with an easy posture, while the men from the Southwest are, in many cases, heavy set, husky, and compact. There are exceptions to this general rule, but the infrequency of them tends to prove the contention more often than not.

It is impossible to make a statement as to which particular section of the country produces the steer wrestler and rider, for they are the product of all sections west of the Mississippi River. Both of these events have been added to rodeo as attractions of daring and skill to create more entertainment in the sport of cowboys.

In concluding the portrait of the typical cowboy-contestant, there are various sides of this individual that cannot be ignored. However, it is impossible to say in a general way that the characteristics discussed above are typical of all contestants. These seem to be the obvious characteristics made evident through information gathered by close association with the men of rodeo in their work and play, and by visiting numerous contests of the big-time type, as well as those of a smaller, community nature.

The cowboy-contestant has a certain gracious independence about him that is related to his rather suspicious nature. With regard to his gracious independence—and there are no better words that adequately describe some of his actions—it is praiseworthy, for his type of work and existence are of such a nature that no one can possibly help him other than he himself. He is young, and, in many cases, he reaches success during his youth, if he is ever to be successful, and this gives him the idea that the world is his corral. The tremendous appeal that the cowboy and his work have for the public makes him, at times, the "dashing darling of a daring drama." In all fields of entertainment or sport his work is most unusual and offers an opportunity for the truly spectacular.

These facts and the exploitation of his work by unscrupulous promoters, people of undesirable character, and the curious, hero-worshipping fan, make the cowboy assume an attitude of casualness toward proffered courtesy. The rodeo contestant is not discourteous in any way, but with an almost studied nonchalance, or, if it is possible, sophistication, he is usually a "cool customer." He is never lacking in generosity or kindness toward his own people or toward friends in his own circle, but he is genuinely suspicious of the outsider. It is almost impossible to break into his circle by any other means than by the sheer ability to ignore his attitude, and this is most ungratifying, when at some later date, on meeting the acquaintance, there is a complete lack of recognition.

One meets the people in rodeo by introduction, usually by a fellow performer, and never by persistence. Any attempt to become acquainted by chance at a rodeo, a bar, or in the particular haunts of the cowboy, very frequently results in a boring one-sided conversation studded with brilliant verbal gems of, "Yes!" "No!" and "Uh-Huh!" A conversation of this kind does not show any marked progress, even after several minutes. One may be greeted by a pair of depthless, crystal-blue, cool eyes and encounter a pair of broad shoulders, which might at any moment turn away, as the cowboy courteously remarks, "See you later!" This paints too gloomy a picture, but the cowboy, and wisely too, is not to be misled into wasting his time. Unlike the many people who are a part of the field of entertainment, the cowboy is not inclined to "talk shop," and especially not with some one who spends a great deal of time asking witless questions. There is not a cowboy in rodeo who would not talk about the work, but he expects some other reaction besides being plied with questions.[1]

The man of rodeo wishes to be, in most cases, amused, wishes to talk generalities, wishes to sit by and watch; he does not care to "talk shop" with the uneducated stranger. It takes time to draw the cowboy out and get him to talk about his experiences. Above all, he likes to be remembered not by the experiences of the afternoon, evening, or the past week, but rather by his work of several years ago, or at the different shows of the season throughout the country. If an individual can say he saw a contestant in action on a certain date at a certain show, or better still, at a two-day stand in Montana and then several months later in New York or Boston, he is practically a "blood-brother" of the contestant and accepted in the rodeo world. The cowboy is not particularly interested in talking about himself or his work at any time, but he becomes more expansive if he has the feeling that the outsider is truly in-

---

[1] Observed by the author while contacting contestants at rodeos, bars, and in their homes. One needs a "friend" to aid in *knowing* the cowboys.

terested. In other words he is poor copy, poor theatre, but genuinely sincere.[1]

Related with surprising affinity to the characteristic of suspicion is his indomitable curiosity. Never one to make a point of questioning, like his earlier prototype, he believes everyone has a right to his own way of thinking and living, with no questions asked; nevertheless he is curious. He is attracted by curious objects, actions, clothing, jewelry, and interests of others. One may consider it almost an honor to be quizzed by the cowboy, for his sincerity and interest are genuine, if he takes the trouble to disclose his curiosity.

Perhaps one of the more amusing traits of the rodeo contestant is his attitude toward the various superstitions that have grown up about him, his work, and his relation to life. These superstitions are not in any way based on supernatural or religious grounds, but simply upon cause and effect. The mystery as to why one is able to ride a horse on one occasion and is thrown at some later date, is explained by some peculiar situation at the time. The situation might involve any number of the taboos, or better, some lucky talisman which is a part of the cowboy's existence.

Taboos of the cowboy are numerous and include the common ones, such as Friday, the thirteenth, and the black cat. Many contestants will not work in a building in which there are cats, and black cats at all times and anywhere are bad luck. In the same category with the cat taboo is that of walking under a ladder. Eating peanuts before or

---

[1] The rodeo cowboys love to reminisce about their activities, especially after the evening performance, when they gather at the bars or in their rooms for a game of poker.

during a contest is practically fatal, and placing a hat on a bed is bad. This latter taboo is very vivid in the mind of the author, who, in the spirit of friendship and also in the quest for information, laid his hat on the bed of a contestant who had suffered a broken leg in a calf roping event. At that time—the fact may be mentioned now—a record was broken, that is, a calf roper sat still longer than five minutes—a record established only because the contestant was helpless! This unfortunate roper had been away from his work and from the influence of his companions for some three weeks, and had had just about all the misfortune a contestant could have under the circumstances. He was not too quick to grasp the situation, but a few seconds later, upon seeing the hat, in a bated breath he suggested that it be removed to a nearby window sill—"just in case . . . " Banishment was too good for the perpetrator of such a *faux pas,* but ignorance takes the blight off such an incident. Some contestants deny a belief in superstition, but it is interesting to note that they so very often prefer certain numbers for their automobile license plates and similar combinations of numbers which they wear while participating in the arena.

Perhaps the most interesting superstition of all, and one which has a double connotation of good or evil, concerns the clothing they wear. The cowboy is clothes-conscious and he certainly wears one of the most extreme styles of garb that has ever been devised for man. Except for the boots, his outfit follows the usual trouser-shirt-hat-jacket-belt variety of clothing worn by men, yet it has a cut, a line, a texture, and a color that might be called a conservative-extremeness, and it is certainly of good quality. If he wears a new hat, shirt, or some other article of clothing and ends a show with a streak of bad luck, financial set-back, several nasty spills, or serious injury, the unfortunate man, in many cases, disposes of the entire outfit, and will have absolutely nothing more to do with the clothing that he wore during that show. If good fortune smiles upon him, he jealously guards that article of clothing which has brought him luck. The garment, even after repeated launderings, is worn at subsequent performances.

It is no secret that Burel Mulkey, All-Around Cowboy for 1938, presented, with great ceremony, the shirt in which he won his honors to Paul Carney, who became the All-Around Cowboy the following year, 1939. The lending or giving of lucky garments to a close friend is not an unusual occurrence, and although this may or may not have any significance, the psychological effect on a good man is certainly stimulating. Fritz Truan, the All-Around Cowboy of 1940, was a passionate advocate of lucky clothing.

The wearing of lucky clothing exists not only with the contestant but extends to members of his family. Mrs. "Contestant" wears a new hat, blouse, pin, or shoes on the opening evening; if her husband wins, she wears the talisman whenever he is "up for" later performances. If he continues to win, the lady practically wears out the talisman.

Many contestants are not willing to admit that they have nerves, but they do suffer from the effects of their highly-keyed existence. They draw their mounts for every performance by lottery, and having followed the actions of the beast, or having heard of these actions from other riders, they anticipate what is to take place. It is not fear of bodily injury that causes anxiety on the part of these men, but rather the fear of failure to ride a difficult animal well, or the fear of not qualifying and thus winning no money. This worry causes the nervous upset. If the animal is not difficult to ride, it means that the man himself must put on a still better performance, in order to "get into" the money. The winning of any riding event is based on points allotted to the man and beast and on adherence to the rules, and not on the fact that the man stays on the beast for a specified length of time.

While the contestant thinks about making a good ride and winning money, he builds up within himself a condition, of which nervous indigestion is only one of the obvious results. Throughout the day this nervous strain builds up gradually until the time of participation. In a few seconds the action is over, and there is no gradual "cooling-off" period, slowing down, tapering, and gradual relaxation of tired muscles and taut nerves. The end is sudden and complete. It is this sudden shock that causes the greatest harm, and it cannot be overcome. Many are the ragged nerves at the end of a rodeo season.

This nervous condition is not allayed by the amount of leisure time the cowboy of rodeo has—and he has a great deal more leisure than other people of sport. In proportion to the amount of time spent at his actual work, his free time is too great. While much rest and leisure are necessary for the man in this work, leisure especially works against him, in that it gives him more time to anticipate his next appearance in an event. It is difficult to say, and especially in the case of the cowboys, what rest, pastime, or leisure really are. These men are famous for their poker games; in the East, when the cowboys are not appearing

at every show as contestants, the games are of long duration. Many men are avid readers and spend much of their
time with books. Some men are fond of Western "pulps,"
and although they have no objection to this type of reading, they have a distinct aversion to the life of the Westerner as depicted by the "quickie" motion picture. Cowboys enjoy drinking, but are not strong addicts to this
habit. The great amount of free time, however, gives them
an opportunity for great indulgence, and planned and
more hardy imbibing usually takes place in the late evening after a show, when almost everyone has, at least, a
"night cap," and some really have a celebration. However,
the cowboy in rodeo realizes his capacity and also knows
what over-indulgence will do to his work. A hard-drink-
ing man in this sport will not make the grade; if he does,
it will be of short duration.

Among the contestants a picturesque type of pro-
fanity prevails. They have not added any new oaths to
the long list that is used so easily and unconsciously by men
among men. Their greatest contribution in this line is
the unusual and almost weird combination of words that
can flow from the lips of a disappointed rider or roper. The
cowboy is careful to the point of speechlessness around
women and children; he has a respect for them both in his
speech and actions that would put many a so-called gentleman to shame.

CHAPTER VI

CENTAURS, ROPES, AND AMAZONS

With ropes twisting and turning,
They fly through the air,
As hippodromes, vaults,
And cartwheels they dare.

A part of every rodeo is the performance of those men and women who have made a specialty of certain phases of the cowboy's work. They are known as the contract performers—men and women who are hired to exhibit their skills as expert, fancy, and trick ropers, or as trick and fancy riders. There is a division of work but it is not as evident as in the case of the regular contestants.

The contribution made by the men and women who have taken up riding and roping, and who demonstrate the many possibilities of the work, is merely one of entertainment, and it must be remembered that their exhibitions of today have never been a part of the work of the range cowboy. Among the early cowboys there were, no doubt, outstanding trick riders and ropers, but this skill was used only as a hobby or pastime in leisure hours. The trick riding and roping of today is the development of a natural ability and skill by experts in these activities for the purpose of exhibition and entertainment.

In this group of contract performers are the rodeo clown, the trained horse and animal acts, and other novelty acts related to rodeo. Often the trick and fancy ropers and animal trainers also participate as contestants in the regular rodeo events, and many of these performers are among the best in the work. Such a specialty assures them an income, even though they may not win in the regular contests.

While these people make a specialty of a certain type of work, they are no less skilled, nor are they doing less of a fine job of promoting rodeo than the regular cowboy-contestants. An appreciation of their performances is not lacking, but there is a noticeable lack of knowledge in regard to the months and years of the hard work involved in "whipping into shape" a good riding or roping act. The grace and ease with which the performer acts is deceiving to the untrained eye and to those not acquainted with the difficulties of the work. The trick rider may not be able to give the grunts and groans to his work, as does a steer wrestler or rider, but he takes chances that are as dangerous as those of the bronc and steer rider and the steer wrestler.

When a performer is doing a shoulder or tail stand, his horse can easily trip and fall. Likewise, the performer is exposed to great danger when he rides under, over, and around a horse and, "to add zest to the act," throws in crupper somersaults and Russian drags. These are only a few of the difficulties in trick riding. There is also the problem of finding a suitable mount that will "take to" the training required and remain constant at all times. The laborious hours of practice involve coordination of the human and the animal actions, knocks, bruises and bumps —all this before the rider can even hope to have the act in shape to present to the public. The grace and ease of the performance with which the trick rider pleases the public and which appears so easy is actually the result of much hard work. Any rider can get on a steer or bronc and "be with it" for a few seconds; trick riding demands not only skill in riding, but smoothness and showmanship which eliminate the possibility of just any horseman producing a good riding act without the necessary practice.

The trick riding horse must have a combination of characteristics such as natural ease, gentleness, and a blissful state of indifference to his immediate surroundings. These are not to be found in the ordinary horse. The lack of the last mentioned characteristic is apparent as soon as the performer tries the many stunts which involve action about the hind quarters and the belly of the beast. It is possible to develop the ability to run straight with a steady, easy gait, but not the other qualities.

The trick rider always faces the disadvantage of his act "blowing up"; if this should happen, the rider and not the horse is to blame in the eyes of the public. But this is not true with the bronc or steer rider, the steer wrestler or calf roper; he just had a tough animal to handle.

Famous in the work of trick riding are Bernice Taylor, Myrtle Goodrich,[1] Pauline Nesbitt, Georgia Sweet Gilliam, Norma Holmes, Alice Sisty, Polly Burson, Nancy Bragg, Don Wilcox, Monte Montana, Buff Brady Junior, and Dick Griffith.

---

[1] Myrtle Goodrich, the daughter of Colonel Cy Compton, followed in her father's footsteps in Wild West Shows and Rodeos. Colonel Compton, in his boyhood days, joined Buffalo Bill's Wild West Show, toured the United States and Europe with that troupe. Later he had charge of the Wild West concert of the Ringling Brothers and Barnum and Bailey Circus. He died June 19, 1944.

A lovelier lady than Bernice Taylor will certainly not be seen in the rodeo arena in many a day. It is perhaps the exquisite, fragile beauty of this magnificent horsewoman that dazzles one at first, for if one should never witness her skill of riding, this characteristic is the only thing that impresses one, upon seeing her for the first time. With the added qualities of freshness and femininity, which are ever present, even under adverse conditions, she offers to the follower of rodeo a new thrill which is more exciting, because this genuine beauty and charm are combined with a rare and unusual ability. No matter how many riders, both male and female, may enter the arena, if the lovely Mrs. Carl Dossey (Bernice Taylor) is present, one is conscious of a riding sensation—an optical thrill.[1]

Wherever the fascinating and dangerous profession of trick riding is known, the name Dick Griffith is to this occupation what Whizzer White was to football. The Griffith boy is a true son of rodeo; his father, Curley Griffith, was one of the best rodeo contestants for many years. In 1920 Curley took his young son with his Shetland pony and an act, which they had worked up during the winter months between show seasons, and introduced them to the rodeo world. In the following years Dick "took to" riding calves and trick roping. The fans of the early twenties of this century fondly remember Dick as a youngster of remarkable personality and ability and,

[1] Personal interview with Bernice Taylor (Mrs. Carl Dossey) New York City, 1942, 1943; Buffalo, New York, 1942; Denver, Colorado, 1945, 1946. (Bernice Taylor is considered one of the most beautiful, talented and gracious women in rodeo. She is known in the East as the Gardenia Lady, because of her appearance and charm, and because so often she wears a gardenia in her hair while performing. She is famous for her "Hippodrome stand" and for going under the neck of the horse while riding at full gallop.)

perhaps, more vividly as the boy riding Roman on a team of Shetland ponies. The tragic death of his father in 1926 ended the rodeo career of Dick, and for the next five years he lived with his grandparents and went to school. In 1931 he returned to rodeo and since that time has been one of the vital personalities in the work. By the early thirties Dick was not only a brilliant horseman, but a rider of steers and bareback broncs. In the year 1934, Dick Griffith added the most lustrous laurels to his already bedecked crown which made him world famous as a trick rider. In this year he was one of the cowboys selected for the Tex Austin Show which went to London, England, to give an exhibition of American Cowboy Sports. He learned that trick riding was to be a featured contest and worked earnestly and with his characteristic sincerity to build up his repertoire. He returned later that spring from the London Show as the International Champion Trick Rider and since then has won every major trick riding championship of this country.

Dick began to learn trick riding when he was six years old. He spent three years on a preliminary trick known as the vault and worked to perfection on this basic move, which is so very important to everyone who attempts this type of riding. It was possible to learn to get off the horse, hit the ground with the feet, and get back on the horse in a very short time; however, to learn to vault in correct form and in perfect timing required years of hard work and a certain amount of natural ability. Dick had the natural ability, as well as the courage and willingness to put all his mental and physical strength into the perfection of this trick, which is the basis of his success in th work.

Dick mastered the vault and worked continually on perfecting his timing; he then added to his initial tricks the split, which is done on the neck of the horse. This was a vault to a backward position on the neck. A third trick, and a more spectacular one, is the cartwheel. The performer stands in the saddle in a crouch, then, holding the saddle horn, he drops forward head first to form a cartwheel by keeping the body in a circular movement and swinging up into the saddle upon completion of the run. By using the saddle horn as an anchor or center of action, one can perform some fifty tricks or more from this position on the saddle.

The most difficult tricks are those that are performed from the hips of the horse. These are known as crupper tricks. The first of these crupper tricks to be learned is the straight crupper. The rider, by moving back over the rump of the horse and grasping the hand-holds, hits the ground with his feet and goes a full arm's length above the running animal before returning to its back. The roll-up, one of the most difficult tricks of this type of riding, is done by hitting the ground behind the horse, turning a forward flip, and landing in a sitting position in the saddle. The most spectacular of all crupper tricks is the one invented by Dick Griffith, and he features it at the many shows that "he works." This stunt is the crupper somersault, and the intricate movements of the rider's body in the execution of it, almost defy description. He moves back on the rump of the horse, grasps the hand-holds, and drops to hit the ground behind the animal; the impact and his agility throw him at full arm's length above the horse; then he dives first on the left side of the animal, pivots in the air, and lands in a sitting position on the horses's hips.

Dick's work leaves the spectator breathless. The flashing movement of his well-trained body; the skill and technique that he displays are not unlike a symphonic poem, rich and full in interpretation of the theme, but not half enough to satisfy the greedy desire for more and more of his horsemanship and wizardry. Unless one has seen Dick perform, one has not seen trick riding. He has, undoubtedly, won considerable fame in contesting in the bull riding event, and this is perhaps his pet interest in rodeo, but rodeo fans hope that, as long as trick riding is a part of modern rodeo, Dick Griffith will always be seen.[1]

He was not content with the honors that his skill in trick riding brought him and that he was the premier trick rider of the age; for four consecutive years, 1939-1942, he also had the honor of being the World Champion Steer Rider. From June, 1941, to June, 1942, Dick made an unprecedented record by not "bucking off" a single bull. He attended the largest contests of the country and rode the outstanding beasts of rodeo. Bull riding for Dick is a particular enjoyment, and his accomplishments in this event are a matter of great pride to him. Trick riding he considers work.

Dick is an attractive-looking fellow with great charm and personality, and had he not been the outstanding trick rider of this century, he still would not have missed his mark in some other field of endeavor. Rodeo people have

---

[1] Dick presented his new act at the Denver Show in January, 1947. It is a very spectacular display with two Buick Roadmasters, two trailers, and two beautiful horses, which he rides Roman style. His wife, Velma, assists him in the act.

a deep affection for him; they respect his abilities and point them out with great pride.

There are many people in the work of trick riding, but few have the foundation on which to build a repertoire which will carry them to the position of champion. There are numerous women trick riders who never use the vault as a basic move; their type of work does not require this trick, for they do strap tricks. The Hippodrome Stand,[1] the Russian Drag,[2] the Shoulder Stand, and the Tail Stand are strap tricks; there are some twenty others of this type. The two best of these are the one in which the rider goes under the horse's neck, and the one in which he goes under the belly while the animal is running at full speed. These tricks are not to be looked upon as being simple, but are best suited for women performers. There are some women in this work who are superior to many of the men, even in the ground work, which is so essential for trick riding.

Any good trick rider can do almost any stunt humanly possible if his horse runs slowly. The test of the skill of the rider is in the speed of the horse he rides. In a championship trick riding contest, 50 per cent "goes for" the speed of the horse, 30 per cent goes for grace and ease, and 20 per cent for variety of tricks.

Junior Eskew, the oldest son of Colonel Jim Eskew, occupies today the position of first trick roper in the rodeo world. He and Dick Griffith are two of the finest young men representative of rodeo. Both were born and raised in this environment and have become notable figures

---

[1] Hippodrome stand—standing upright with feet in straps and leaning forward while the horse runs at full gallop.

[2] Russian drag—one foot in a strap with the head hanging off the side of the horse.

in the work. They are excellent examples of the character and the type of individual found in rodeo work. Both are answers to the question so aften asked about the children reared in the vigorous life surrounding rodeo; both are splendid examples of American manhood.

Junior Eskew was "raised" in rodeo; at the age of four he was working with the rope; at eight years he was going under the belly of a running horse. Regardless of his diversified talents, Junior's chief interest and outstanding accomplishment is the rope and what he can do with it. Junior is a husky lad, six feet tall, weighs about 190 pounds —a good looking blond and blue-eyed young man with a remarkable shoulder and arm development. Because of this unusual arm length, he is able to do things with rope with a certain grace and ease that most trick ropers are unable to achieve.

His actions have a certain rhythmic style that does not tire or confuse the eye or mind of the spectator, but rather leads him gently through a soft, undulating, poetic pattern. His approach to the work of roping is restful and soothing; he never lacks in dramatic appeal, and it is a vital experience to witness his talent. Every performance by Junior Eskew is a challenge to his competitors and his onlookers. His artistry creates a tremendous urge in the spectator—the desire to take a length of rope and try to do something with it. Junior can spin anything from chewing gum to a hawser!

At the J E Ranch, Waverly, New York, Junior told his story of ropes and roping, which is the substance for this discussion. The work of fancy roping is a fascinating study, and in the rodeo arena one sees two exhibitions involving the use of the rope different from its use in

the events of calf, steer and wild cow roping. These are
rope spining and trick roping. Rope spinning is done with
a cotton rope about ten to twenty-five feet in length and
about one-fourth to three-eighths of an inch in diameter.
One end of the rope is "whipped" to prevent unraveling.
The other end forms an eye, known as the *honda*, through
which the rope is placed to form the loop. That portion
of the rope from the hand to the *honda* is known as the
spoke. In rope spinning the rope moves only in two directions, clockwise or counter-clockwise, and forms a flat or
vertical loop. Tricks in rope spinning are accomplished by
placing the loop in various positions and angles with combinations of flat and vertical loops. By bringing the rope
up over the head and down around the body, by skipping
in and out of the whirling loop, by somersaulting and leaping through the loop, it is possible to embellish the art.
Some of the variations of the two original positions of the
rope are: the Butterfly, the Zigzag, the forward and backward Ocean Wave, and the Roll-Overs. All these tricks
are practiced so that they may be done with either hand
or in a reverse motion.

Trick roping not only involves handling a rope in
various positions, but also catching a horse and rider by
the performer on foot or on horseback. The rope in this
exhibition is of a different type from that of rope spinning.
It is known as Maguey rope; the fibers are from one of the
species of the aloe plant and come from Mexico.[1] The
Maguey rope is made by hand under water and it is not
seasoned, as are the ropes used for steer and calf roping. It
is made and finished as one complete rope and is not cut

---

[1] The American aloe is the century plant.

off in lengths from a coil. The oustanding characteristic
is its stiffness. Any ordinary rope in the semi-tropical heat
of Mexico would lose its life and go limp; the Maguey,
however, retains its shape and working qualities. The trick
in handling this type of rope is the ability to control the
many characteristics of the lariat which include the peculiar quality of stiffness. Some performers prefer a very
stiff lariat, while others prefer one that is limber.

The Maguey rope weighs about four and one-half
pounds. It is brown in color, hard and slick. This type of
lariat costs from three to eight dollars, but a roper will pay
as much as twenty dollars for a good one. Good Maguey
ropes are hard to find, and Eskew relates that during the
spring of 1942 he purchased eighteen ropes before he
found a useable one among the lot. The ropes for use in
the arena are tinted white so they will show up against
the sawdust and earth background. This tinting has a
tendency to add stiffness and slickness to the rope. Naturally, ropes that are so difficult to find are given the best
of care in order to preserve them as long as possible. They
are carefully cleaned and coiled and are kept in canvas
bags. The atmosphere changes the working quality of a
rope; sometimes it is necessary, after using a rope, to put
a moist sponge in the bag to restore its vitality. This
tends to keep the rope hard and stiff. To plunge the rope
in a bucket of water would "kill it"; a fine spray or mist,
however, will restore a rope.

Junior Eskew modestly admits that he has learned a
great deal about trick roping from watching and prac-
ticing with such experts as Chester Byers, Vern Goodrich, and Weaver Gray. He also admits that he has spent
years in practice and experimentation. He has used stiff

and limber, heavy and light ropes; weighted *hondas* of all types; he has also changed the bit of his horses, in order to see which type would be best suited for a performance.

Junior has taken great pride in his horses. His first one, "Little Eagle," has now been replaced by "Old Blue," who performs so beautifully with his master in the arena today. "Old Blue" was bought for thirty-eight dollars at the stockyards in Chicago in 1933; a three-year-old at that time, he was, because of his training, worth one thousand dollars the following year. "Old Blue" is so well trained that he knows how to take care of himself in the arena; he walks out of the way of the whirling loop when Junior steps off him, and he approaches his master when he is needed for the next trick.

About three years ago Junior started to use "Old Blue" for calf roping, and since then he has been used for steer roping, bulldogging, trick riding, and for the wild cow milking contest. Although this horse is about fifteen year old, he has no visible effects of injuries—no wind puffs. In the fall of 1941, just one month before the opening of the Madison Square Garden Show, "Old Blue" was hit on the eye by the *honda*. Due to careful nursing by his master, he was ready to appear at the Show of Shows. One of Junior's duties is to wash the head and mane of his horse; he entrusts this task to no one, for he maintains that, if anyone else does this before a show, it affects the quality of "Old Blue's" performance.

Trick roping involves the use of the flat and vertical loop in forms, such as the Butterfly, forward and backward Ocean Waves, forward and backward Spanish Flats, with Lift-Overs, Pop-Overs and Push-Offs. "Making a catch" of a running horse and rider is based on one of the above mentioned moves. One of the tests of a skilled trick roper is to "call his catches" and then "make the catch." Roping a horse may look difficult to the spectator—it is difficult! To say that one will "catch a horse over the top" by the neck, or by four legs, is one thing; to say he will "make the catch" by the rear legs or the front leg from underneath, is an accomplishment; however, to say this and then do it is a still greater art. Almost every trick roper will catch the animal, but "calling the catch" and accomplishing it, shows skill of the highest order.

Another test of skill is actually throwing the loop at the running animal and "making a catch" rather than "setting" it, such as by rolling it in front of the animal and allowing the beast to run into it, then drawing up on the loop to "make the catch." Tricks, such as standing on one's head, somersaulting, or tumbling, and, at the same time, roping a running animal necessitate setting of the loop so as to "make the catch" when the animal runs into the loop. If the horse should swerve left or right from the planned path, the trick fails. The trick roper, after he has put his lariat through the various moves, may stay on horseback or step to the ground, and as the running horse approaches, he is able to gauge his throw and place the rope as he wishes, no matter what deviation may take place in the run of the horse, as long as the animal comes toward him.

The Roll Back is one of the outstanding accomplishments of Junior Eskew. It has been achieved by only a few, for it is not considered a "sure thing." Junior is the only roper who does it as a part of his regular routine; he can catch one, two, or all four legs of the horse. Trick roping is a career for Junior, but he also considers it as fine an exercise as swimming. It demands the use of all muscles, without a severe over-development of any particular group. Roping can be dangerous because fingers, hands, and arms are often twisted, wrenched, and cut by the rope. This is especially true if the hand is entangled in the coil and the loop is fast around the neck of a running horse. Such injuries are rare; however, they are possible. Some years ago Junior disjointed the first joint of his ring finger of the right hand when it was caught in a twisting rope. The injury was so severe that he nearly lost the tip of his finger.[1]

The technique of trick roping is constantly making progress. Young men with new ideas are entering this field of work, and new men are appearing every year. Junior Eskew has not only made a brilliant career of the work, he has also contributed much to the work through his knowledge of roping, which he acquired through years of practice and a natural talent for the art. Other men, in addition to him, who have brought roping to the level of an art, are Chester Byers,[2] Weaver Gray, Vern Goodrich, Gene and Don McLaughlin, and Buff Brady, Jr.— all of whom are found in important arenas of this country.

---

[1] Many days were spent by the author at the "Jim Eskew" Ranch with the Eskew family. He painted portraits of Colonel Jim and Junior Eskew, and enjoyed their friendship, talents, and hospitality and, on occasions, rode "Sport."

[2] Chester Byers, internationally known trick roper, died Nov. 1, 1945. He started his roping career at the age of 13 and during his life he performed with the early Wild West Shows, such as "Pawnee Bill's Roundup," Lucille Mulhall's Congress of Rough Riders, and the Miller Brothers 101 Ranch. In 1915 he started out as an independent contestant in rodeos. He was the author of *Roping, Trick and Fancy Rope Spinning.*

FAMOUS RIDERS

Upper: Prairie Rose Henderson on "Brandy," Round-Up 1922.
—*Courtesy Chamber of Commerce, Pendleton, Oregon.*

Lower: Bertha Blanchett, Champion Lady Bronco Buster of the World.
—*W. S. Bowman, Photographer.*

More than 90 per cent of the contestants in rodeo are men. However, the feminine contribution to the development of the sport has been of such importance that to ignore "women in rodeo" would be unfortunate, and, certainly, unjustifiable in this study.

Women in rodeo have presented an interesting study. Though never particularly welcome as participants in the work, they have carved a niche for themselves by sheer audacity, courage, and female persistence, and have won the respect of all who have witnessed their daring and skill. When it is a question of sheer courage and grit among the athletes in various branches of sports, great tribute must be paid to the cowgirl who competes in rodeo.

In 1901 the first woman appeared in a bronc riding contest. This took place at the Frontier Days Celebration, Cheyenne, Wyoming. The contestant was "Prairie Rose" Henderson, the daughter of one of the ranchers. She entered the contest against the protests of the judges, who had no rules or legal right to exclude her from competing in the cowboys' bronc riding event. Her ride was magnificent; she achieved such notoriety and created such a sensation that many of the rodeos soon included, as a feature event, a cowgirls' bronc riding contest.

Since that day the position of the cowgirl in rodeo has not been challenged, and the list of famous names, headed by "Prairie Rose," includes Lucille Mulhall, "Prairie Lilly" Allen, Mildred Douglas, Mrs. Ed Wright, Eloise Fox Hastings, Dorothy Morrell, Ruth Schook, Mrs. Ed Lindsey, Rose Davis, Grayce Runyon, Paris Williams, Alice Adams, Alice and Margie Greenough, Gene Creed, Vaughn Kreig, Dorothy Gaskill, Tad Lucas, Mary Keen Wilson, Claire Thompson, Lucyle Richards, Peggy Long, Cherry

Osborne, Mildred Mix Horner, Iva Del Draksler, Vivian White, Mary Parks, Hazel Burns, Fox Wilson, Fanny Sperry Steele, Maud Tarr, Bertha Blancett, Reine Shelton, Florence Randolph, Jessie Roberts, Marie Gibson, Bea Kirnan, Louis Hartwig, Opal Woods, Ruth Benson Wood, Bonnie McCarroll, and Brida Gafford.

The cowgirls are not only addicted to riding broncs, trick riding and relay races, but several have been adept with the rope and have given exhibitions of steer and calf roping. Some have taken up the hazardous occupation of bulldogging steers and steer riding. The women of rodeo have entered into all the phases of the work and have put on as great exhibitions of skill, nerve, and daring as the men.

The late Lucille Mulhall was one of the most outstanding horsewomen in the country and was, undisputedly, the foremost lady steer roper of the world. Her skill with the lariat made her famous on two continents. She was the daughter of Colonel Zack Mulhall; early in the century she worked with such famous stars as Tom Mix and Will Rogers, and participated in every important exhibition of cowboy activity in this country. On a Grand Tour of Europe she was acclaimed by the crowds as the outstanding woman of her profession. Her feats with the rope marked her as the leading woman roper; she could catch six and eight horses with one throw. In 1920 at Ardmore, Oklahoma, in a steer roping contest she made the fastest time and won over a large group of men ropers. As a promoter of rodeos, Lucille put the Fort Worth Show in the lead as the center of one of the largest exhibitions of rodeo events in the Southwest.

In her later years she retired from active participation and resided on the few remaining acres of the Mulhall Ranch at Mulhall, Oklahoma, which had gradually shrunk in size during the declining years of the great ranches of the cattle industry. Her death, in 1940, removed from the scene of rodeo one of the few remaining figures of the early days of the sport.

Several women in rodeo have made the bulldogging event a part of their exhibition work. This dangerous sport demands not only daring and nerve, but it also requires great strength. It does not seem possible that women could handle the beasts. Several of the best-known women who have made this event a part of their activities are Grayce Runyon, Lucyle Richards, and Fox Hastings Wilson.

The last mentioned, Fox Wilson, began her career as a trick rider and bronc rider in 1917. In 1924 she entered the bulldogging event and first appeared at Houston, Texas. Her opinion of this rough activity is found in the following statement: "I like bulldogging better than bronc riding. Bronc riding is a question of strength and endurance, but in bulldogging you don't tackle two steers exactly alike, you have to learn the difference in the animal's size, strength, formation of the horns, build of neck and shoulders and a lot of things. And every move has to be perfectly timed to a split second."[1]

This work is very difficult and has many hazards. Fox Wilson has repeatedly sustained many injuries, such as broken ribs and legs. Evidence of her courage and her showmanship was expressed at *La Fiesta de los Vaqueros*

[1] "Fox Wilson, World's Only Woman Bull Dogger," *Hoofs and Horns* 4 (December 1934), 13.

in 1935 . . . "notable among the special attractions was Fox Wilson, who, though she had suffered a broken rib the day before the show opened, bulldogged her steer each of the three days of the rodeo proper. She had a contract to fulfill and she couldn't let the management down, even though it took a shot of cocaine to put her through the performance."[1]

Among the many cowgirl bronc riders of today, Alice and Margie Greenough, the female members of the Riding Greenoughs of Red Lodge, Montana, and Tad Lucas of Fort Worth, Texas, are best known and admired by thousands of rodeo fans. The two sisters have competed and exhibited in various parts of the world and have added considerable glory to the name of Greenough, which has attained an almost legendary rank in the business of rodeo. Both are magnificent riders. They are found at every important contest of the East and West and give consistently their usual thrilling and brilliant performances.

Among the lady bronc riders Tad Lucas holds the affection and admiration of more followers of rodeo than any other performer of her sex. Since her childhood, her life has always included horses and riding. Shortly after World War I she began as a contestant and appeared at the County Fair and Rodeo at Gordon, Nebraska. Because of her skill in handling horses, she entered contests of steer riding and horse racing. In 1923 she participated in the cowgirls' bronc riding contests, and her first appearance was at Madison Square Garden in New York City. A year later she began trick riding. The combination of trick and bronc riding and relay racing has carried Tad

---

[1] "Rodeo News" *Hoofs and Horns* 4 (March, 1935), 13.

Top left: Rose Wenger, Noted Cowgirl Rider, at Baldwin Ranch
Rodeo, 1912.
—*E. A. Brininstool, Photographer.*

Top right: Mrs. Dick Stanley.
—*E. A. Brininstool, Photographer.*

Lower: Early Cowgirls.
—*W. S. Bowman, Photographer.*

Lucas to the top of the ranks in rodeo and has brought her the championship in trick riding at Cheyenne, Wyoming, from 1925 to 1933, with the exception of one year when she did not participate.

The year 1933 brought disaster to this lady of rodeo. Suffering from a badly injured arm, she continued to perform, although the recovery from the injury took several years. Her collection of trophies and honors is the envy and delight of rodeo contestants. She won the Ten Thousand Dollar Metro Goldwyn Mayer Trophy for the best All-Around Cowgirl; she is the proud possessor of two of the Denver Post Trophies for the best relay riding, and is the winner of the Gordon Selfridge Trophy of London, England, for being the best All-Around Cowgirl at the Chicago Show in 1929.

A champion among champions, Tad Lucas has attained honors and recognition that few achieve in this life and she has brought dignity and honor to her sex. The people of rodeo deeply admire and respect her. Among the friends and admirers, who are, in many cases, unknown to her, she is considered one of the greatest horsewomen and she has their heartfelt wishes for continued success and good fortune.

CHAPTER VII

VOICES ON THE WIND

In jargon, jokes, and words they warble with ease,
'Ladies and gentlemen, your attention, please!'

In any discussion about the men and women who have helped rodeo gain national prominence and have made it a success from the standpoint of the audience, one cannot neglect the announcer. The present-day system of loud speakers and microphones is a far cry from that of the earlier days when the man with the loudest and heaviest voice in a community made, with the aid of a megaphone, the announcements of the events in the show. Anyone acquainted with this latter system knows how unsuccessful such a method can be during the excitement and confusion that reign at a rodeo.

The accoustical properties of a large, open field are nil. When combined with shifting air currents, a restless excited crowd of spectators, and milling animals, anything but a much amplified voice is a failure. The names of riders, horses, the time achieved, announcements of results, reach only about one-quarter of the crowd and, in the crescendo of noise, are lost to the other three-quarters of the spectators.

The spectator, no matter how well versed he might be in rodeo, loses much of the thrill of the contest if he does not know which contestant is "coming up" or, in the case of bronc riding, which horse is to be ridden. To the average individual who sees only one or, at most, two contests a year, it is of interest to have a brief biographical sketch of the personages, as they appear in the events. If, under the old system of announcing, it was possible for the announcer to reach the entire audience for only the first hour of the contest, it was a miracle; for no human larnyx could meet for several hours the severe demands of shouting. Thus, a great deal of information, which was of interest to the spectator, was lost. During those lulls that precede and follow the events, the old-time announcer could not keep up the pace nor fill the gaps because of the exhausting quality of the work. Among the old-time announcers, before the advent of the public address system, the most prominent ones were: Angelo Hughes, D. D. Johnson, Fog Horn Clancy, and John A. Striker. Abe Lefton and John Jordan, two of the best-known men in the work today, began announcing before the use of the microphone.

Upon the introduction of the public address system of amplifiers with a microphone under the control of an announcer, the entire method of keeping the audience informed was changed. This system permits the announcer to reach every individual in the crowd, it allows him to give out intimate and personal sketches of contestants and horses, and amusing sidelines that were formerly missed, in part, by the on-lookers. The announcer is now a very definite part of the action in the arena. By keeping a sharp eye on the action taking place; with a controlled voice that either builds up or calms the emotions of the spectators, he increases or eases the suspense of the moment.

Therefore, a large share of the responsibility of the success or failure of any rodeo rests upon the announcer. His position is the prevailing voice of the entire contest and makes him an absolute dictator of the tempo of the contest. This is a great responsibility.

From the beginning to the end of the show, the rodeo announcer, as any other announcer working in the field of sports, must be wide awake, see and hear everything, in an instant place some evaluation on the action, and constantly keep in mind that there is a crowd to be informed, thrilled and amused.

The rodeo announcer of today needs more than just a reading knowledge of rodeo. He must have first-hand and intimate knowledge of the men and women who are performing, in order to give each one a short but worthy build-up, as he appears for his part in the contest. He must know those amusing and serious details of their lives, work, and abilities and reveal these in such a way as to arouse a feeling of well-being; in other words, he must create a bond of friendship and interest between the audience and contestant. Unless the rodeo announcer is acquainted with every phase of the various events, the rules, and requirements; unless he has all this at the tip of his tongue, the fast moving action of a contest soon overtakes his ability of expression, and the necessary explanation of the events, needed so often for complete understanding, is lost to the spectators, many of whom are seeing a rodeo for the first time.

The rodeo announcer is required to have information not only about the contestants and the events of the regular rodeo work, but he must "build up" many tricks and actions of the fancy ropers, trick riders, and clowns. To do

Announcer using megaphone, Pendleton, Oregon (1912).
—*Photograph by Marcel, Portland.*

a worthy job, he needs more than just a typed script of information concerning these performers. The various mishaps and changes of movement happen so rapidly that he must have complete command of the situation; he needs a quick but tempered wit and a smooth flow of language to fill in those unsuspected but ever-appearing gaps. Such an announcer is able to cover up, without the knowledge of his audience, the rough spots that are found even in the best-regulated and planned programs. It takes a man who knows rodeo from all its angles to be able to see the many things that happen during a performance and to give this information in short, concise, forceful statements. Such a man knows when to expand this information in order to keep the action of the show running smoothly; when to inject wit and barbed humor; when to relieve the tension of suspense following a serious mishap to contestant or beast—all in all, he is a man who has "lived" the intensely moving pageant of rodeo.

It is fortunate that most of the men in the field of rodeo announcing have been a part of rodeo for many years. Several have been, and still are, active contestants, and others have been so closely associated with the work that they know it from every angle. Jimmy Hazen, Cy Taillon, Glake Merrill, Abe Lefton, and John Jordan are prominent in this work. In the hands of this group rests the success of some of the largest and most spectacular shows of the country. They have all added, with their vast fund of knowledge gained by years of experience in this work, to the enjoyment and education of hundreds of thousands of fans and followers of rodeo.

The men behind the microphone, the rodeo announcers, have different personalities and are distinct and unusual in their method of expression. Several have been mentioned by name, but any comment on rodeo announcing would not be complete without a consideration of the personality and qualifications of John Jordan.

There is perhaps no one better qualified for the position of announcing at rodeos than John Jordan. He has been a part of the business for more than twenty-five years; he knows all about it, for he himself, in the past, has been a successful rodeo contestant—a bronc rider of no mean ability. John took part in this event everywhere on this continent, was selected for special exhibition work at the Chicago World's Fair of 1933, and the following year was an important rider with the Tex Austin Show in London. John has ridden such broncs as "Five Minutes to Midnight," "Golden Rule," "Tumbleweed," and "Jack Dempsey."

Early in his life he owned a string of broncs which he took to various rodeos in the West. He has worked in Western motion pictures and eventually owned and managed a Wild West Show. About two-thirds of his life has been devoted to rodeo and, at one time or another, he has experienced all of its various phases. He was holder of the title of North American Bronc Riding Champion, acquired in 1937 at the Calgary Stampede, the winner of many day monies as well as finals; however, because of a serious injury suffered in his work, he gradually turned to the business of announcing. Since then John has given more and more time to it and now places as one of the best men in the work. His ability has brought to him such fine contracts as the Madison Square Garden Rodeo, the Boston Garden Show, the Calgary Stampede, the contests at Phoenix, Arizona; Ellensburg, Washington; Houston, Texas; and Lewiston, Idaho, and for several consecutive years the San Angelo Fat Stock Show and Rodeo.

John Jordan has ability which is based on years of personal experience. He is one of the few people in this work whom one can meet again and again, and each time, upon leaving, feel better for the experience. Quiet and unassuming, John has a way of speaking that makes one feel he is being singled out and addressed personally. With this quality of thought and expression John makes everyone in the vast audience his friend and confidant. He makes the action of the rodeo a personal experience. There is nothing spectacular or sensational about John Jordan; the gentleness and deliberateness of his speech, the rich timbre of his voice, the traces of excitement which grow with the action let the people know that he is with the boys as they "ride 'em." John is more than an announcer of rodeo events, he is one of the boys in action; his voice carries every grunt and groan, every snort and squeal of both man and beast in their struggle for supremacy.

CHAPTER VIII
ORGANIZIN'

In time they learned the "if's" and "why's"
And decided 'twas best "to organize."

The Story of Rodeo would fail completely in its purpose, that is, in the analysis of forces contributing to the development of the work, if it were to devote the greater portion of the narrative to the personal aspects of the work and neglect those greater, and more abstract social and economic conditions that have brought about significant changes in the business.

The social and economic forces that have made themselves felt in the work have come about through the founding and development of two organizations that are now the dominating influences in rodeo. A business and sport of such magnitude as the rodeo could not have reached such proportions and continued to grow without some guiding influences. These are found in those two organizations related directly to the work. The first organization to be founded and developed for the purpose of creating some standard of conduct and the pursuit of such conduct within the rodeo was the Rodeo Association of America. The other organization of importance, the Cowboys' Turtle Association, (now known as Rodeo Cowboys' Association; see footnote p. 126) was established with the purpose of promoting the standards of the organized rodeos—that is, the member-shows of the Rodeo Association of America. This new organization had the added purpose of increasing the opportunities of the contestants.

Because of the continued and phenominal growth of rodeo during the last decade as one of the most important forms of American entertainment, several organizations similar to the above have made their appearance and are related directly to them, in that their purpose is to aid and to continue to promote the ideals set up by the parent organization, the Rodeo Association of America.

These several organizations: the Southwest Rodeo Association,[1] the Cowboys' Amateur Association of America, (now known as the Cowboys' Association of America)[2] the Rodeo Fans of America[3] have been founded, primarily, for the purpose of further promotion of rodeo as a major sport in this country, and with the added purposes of the respective individual groups. The Associations are discussed, regardless of chronological order, in proper relationship to the divisions in this work.

The Cowboys' Turtle Association was not the first attempt to organize the cowboy-contestants into a group for the purpose of mutual protection and benefits. Several attempts had been made previous to the inception of the Association, but all were doomed to fail. This failure was not due to the lack of realization that an organization was needed to further the welfare of the contestants, but rather to the difficulty of reaching agreement of ideas among the prospective members. The cowboy has always

---

[1] See Chapter XXVII., pp. 339-342.

[2] See this chapter, footnote, p. 130.

[3] See Chapter XXVIII., pp. 352-355.

been an individualist, if nothing else. Formerly he made it a part of his existence to ask for nothing and to give only what he desired. Differences of opinion and unwillingness to part from those differences have been two of the main factors in the many disagreements that have arisen in regard to the relationship existing between contestents and management of rodeos. There is a certain healthy opportunity for progress because of various opinions on a subject; however, there must also be a willingness of some acquiescence of ideal, if the long range point of view, that is, the general good for the greater number is to be considered.

These earlier attempts to organize the contestants for the express purpose of improving their working and living conditions, and of giving opportunities for increased benefits, was looked upon with suspicion, and this with justification. The cowboy has had some of his most unfortunate experiences through organizations of promoters of rodeos. The unscrupulous promoter had done more to instill suspicion of group activity than any other single force. To be inveigled into traveling great distances; into spending what small funds he had been able to save from former contests; into working several days only to be cheated out of his just earnings by a dishonest promoter—all this was not conducive to a feeling of well-being and encouragement of the cowboy's faith in organizations. Whether they consisted of one or two individuals or of a membership of several hundred, the cowboy was wary of them. The cowboy had reached the point, when his only satisfaction, upon not receiving his just dues for his labors, was to go out after it; the violence and destruction that followed caused nothing more than brute satisfaction to the cheated, but in the eyes of the honest promoter or the community holding a contest, such actions did not increase the desirability of conducting rodeos.

The laxity in formal living—or, at least, in what is considered the standard of conduct among other people—which has been a part of the cowboy's existence, also brought up problems that could not be solved unless handled by some organization with rules that could be enforced. The problem of the conduct of the contestant during a contest in a community had always been a difficult one. The type of man that one sees in rodeo today has undergone considerable change in the last ten or fifteen years. Having received fair treatment, he has lost much of his belligerent attitude, which was at no time a part of his nature, but had been assumed in protection of self and of interests.

However, in a heterogenous group of people, there are many intellectual, social, as well as moral levels, and the group of rodeo contestants was no different from any other group. The cowboy-contestant shifted for himself since no one was particularly interested in his welfare. His actions, upon arrival and during his stay in a town, were not always commendable; his personal habits and appearance were not always elevating; there was evidence of neglect in the care of his body and general appearance that was deplorable.

The newcomer in the work did not, in many cases, stand a chance of making a name for himself, even after several years of good work. Not too many years ago recognition of one's skill depended upon having a friend among the judges, or, at least, having one's name brought to their attention. It is doubtlessly true that the judging of rodeo events before this time of organization was a part of a rotten system, and it was the contestant who suffered. The judges were not above accepting a cut from the winner's money, when such an arrangement could be made, and it was not an uncommon procedure. One must not assume that this was a general condition, but it happened often enough to lower the morale among the contestants and to cause among them a great distrust of officials.[1]

Another force that caused much disagreement and dissatisfaction among the cowboys was the lack of ability on the part of the judges to evaluate the contestants' skill. While there may have been no question as to the integrity of the judges, they were incapable of judging the events because of lack of experience. In many cases, they were ranchmen, old-timers, pioneers, and often, old-time contestants. Because modern rodeo had undergone so many radical changes—rules change year by year as in other sports—these men were incapable of judging unless they spent a great deal of their time in the work.

Dissatisfaction among the contestants also resulted from the announcement of prize lists of considerable sums of money and, upon arrival at the contest, the entrants often found a much smaller sum making up the purse. Many times the entry fees paid by the contestants were much larger in the total amount than the purse offered. Not only did the cowboys pay in more money than it was possible to take out, but they had traveled a long distance and had paid their own expenses, only to find that the monies listed were misrepresented. This type of dishonest

[1] A complaint registered by many of the contestants before the founding of the cowboys' organization.

advertising did not promote a feeling of friendship and cooperation between the contestants and rodeo officials. Because of these many faults, the cowboy looked with suspicion on all rodeos, whether they had been established many years or were just in the beginning stage.

Upon consideration of the disadvantages faced by the cowboy, one finds that many of his difficulties were brought about by his own actions. He was not a dependable creature, in that he often, when called to enter an event he had signed up for, neglected to appear for obvious reasons. Among these was free use of liquor which resulted in inability to work, participation in a crap game on the side lines resulting in absence from the rodeo grounds, as well as the many other reasons and excuses a cowboy can give.

Quarrels with the judges over decisions, both unjust and fair, did not add to the already established and unfortunate reputation of the contestant. Braced with liquor, he was a "tough customer" and could cause considerable trouble for himself and his less billigerent fellow workers.

His attitude toward people was not a healthy one; it was suspicious and distrustful, for he lived in constant fear of being cheated of his earnings; and, receiving little recognition for his efforts, he took the path of least resistance. As a result, the cowboy of a few years ago was a surprisingly happy-go-lucky lad, ready for hard work, ready to whip the man who chiseled him, ready for what fun and pleasure life had to offer him. He took many knocks and often came back ready for whatever was offered to him as an opportunity. Thus, the existing situation was unfortunate, and because of it, the contestant lost considerable opportunity for improving his position in the work; in addition, the rodeo was also losing ground as a popular sport and entertainment.

The founding of the Rodeo Association of America[1] in 1929 solved many of these problems. It, however, brought forth and amplified many of the old grievances because of the united front. Earlier, this Association made a fairly successful attempt to standardize the conduct of its member-organizations, and was, more or less, able to guarantee the appearance and performance of contestants, if the prize money was sufficient to make it worth while. The Rodeo Association of America did splendid work in standardizing events, rules, regulations, judging, refereeing, timing, and arena conditions; and also, in as far as it was able, in working for better purses. But its hands were tied and it was powerless to control the appearance and behavior of the participants. It was unable to raise the standards that it had already created for the improvement of the contest and the contestants.

The Association had no legal right to speak for the cowboy, and could only strive for better working conditions, in the hope that it could bring about a happier relationship between the cowboy and the rodeo committees.

In November, 1936, during the Boston Garden Show, the Cowboys' Turtle Association came into existence. The cowboys organized to raise the standards of rodeo as a whole. They hoped to achieve this by classing as unfair those contests which used rules detrimental to the contestants and which offered purses so small as to make it impossible for the cowboy to make expenses. The chief

---

[1] See Chapter XV., pp. 183-188.

purpose of the Association was to secure a fair deal for the cowboy, as well as to secure better results for rodeo organizations, with the hope that both units working together in harmony would achieve more.

The guiding principles of the Cowboys' Turtle Association, which had no restriction as to membership, are found in four rules. These rules, with some modifications and further elaboration, make up the present articles of the Association, its rules, and its by-laws.

The rules are revised here to give a better idea of what the organization planned, and of the character and tone of approach to the problem. The following rules are those found in *Hoofs and Horns Magazine,* December, 1936. Six months later, at the semi-annual meeting at Cheyenne, Wyoming, this magazine was made the official publication for the Cowboys' Turtle Association.

The rules are as follows:

Rule No. 1—Any cowboy or cowgirl will be assessed and required to pay $500.00 to the Association to re [-] enter the Union if he or she performs or competes in that particular rodeo where a strike is called. The re [-] entry of said strike-breaker must be voted upon by silent vote by all members of the Turtle Association.

Rule No. 2—The $500.00 paid to the United Turtle Association by the strike-breaker or violators of the association will go to a trust fund, to be used for lawyer fees, telephone calls, telegrams, or for a representative to be sent to any rodeo committee, which the Cowboys' Association agrees is offering insufficient and unfair purses. It is further understood and agreed that a fine of $100.00 must be paid to the Association by any cowgirl or cowboy for disgraceful conduct, which must be proven before the Board of Directors.

It is to be the ruling of this organization that each member shall be assessed a yearly fee of $5.00, which will go into the trust fund, to put into a bank that is agreeable to all members of the Association. It is further understood that no one member of this organization may check on this fund. All checks must be signed by at least four members of the Board of Directors or officials. No representative, speaker or member of the Board of Directors is to be paid a salary for his services. [sic] This is to be given free of charge to the organization.

It is also understood that a representative must be present at that certain rodeo on which a strike is called, and be able to prove that any member of this Association has competed at that certain rodeo.

Rule No. 3—Strikes are not to be called by any one member of this Association, because he or she may be dissatisfied by the decision of the judges, rules and regulations, or by finding fault with the committee or prize list, but [the matter] must be passed upon by all members of the Association, and if it is passed upon, a representative is to go to the committee with a list signed by all of the members. After a member has once signed his or her name to this list, the Association has the right to use . . . [that] name on any list, that is to be sent to a rodeo committee . . . [whose] purses are considered unsatisfactory and unfair. No one person has the right to send in a list that is not approved by all members of this organization, and should anyone do this, he or she will be expelled from this Association, and will be assessed the $500.00 as stipulated in Rule No. 1. to re [-] enter the Union.

Rule No. 4—It is not the rule of this organization to interfere with personal disagreements among members, nor with personal demands of a cowboy for his rights. For instance: Should a show have a judge who is thought unfair in his decisions, a cowboy has the right to demand a fair deal, without the interference of the Association. The Union has a right to demand capable judges, and should there be judges who do not come up to this standard, the Union reserves the right to send a representative to the rodeo committee to ask for a change of judges.[1]

In considering the rules of the Association, the general opinion was that harmony, among the contestants and between contestants and rodeo organizations, was the reason for existence. This, however, was not the case, and the following three years brought forth many differences of opinion fraught with controversy. These were: the annual conventions and subsequent controversies and argu. ments at Reno, Ogden, and Fort Worth; the retalitory measures of contestants against long established rodeos of Pendleton and Ellensburg; the strike at Tucson; and the Prescott "Amateur" Contest controversy. Basically, all the disagreements had just foundations and could have been settled by concurrment on both sides, but the personal ele-

---

[1] "Cowboys' Turtle Association," *Hoofs and Horns* 6 (December, 1936), 24.

ment of the leaders of the two organizations, or of the contestants and rodeo organization, reduced, in many cases, the disagreement to a garbled squabble of irate personalities, and the significant and important issues of the question were lost.

Perhaps the underlying causes of the many disagreements that followed the organization of the Cowboys' Turtle Association were found in the complete and utter surprise on the part of the cowboys, that, united, they could have a voice in their welfare, could foster development of better conditions in the contests, and could make demands that, in many cases, were heeded. As in similar instances, this power, unrealized at first, was a dangerous weapon, not only for those wielding it but also for those who were rightly in need of checking. Power, fame, fortune—all have great possibilities for creating good, but they have also the possibilities for bringing about evil and eventual destruction to the possessor.

In its new found and unexplored power, the united organization of cowboys was not in complete agreement concerning the changes desired, nor were the men convinced that these changes could be made without causing severe hardship in the organizations that for many years had been the source of their income. This was unfortunate, especially for the older local rodeo committees of many years standing, who had shown fair treatment toward the contestants. They were subjected to the feeling of "we are strong and will get what we want," which, in many instances, influenced the new Cowboy Association in making its demands. The Association members were not conscious of the fact, that their demands, just before the opening of a contest, required much more than compliance or disagreement with them. In the case of the large rodeo, these demands could not be met without considerable discussion among its committee members and the disruption of plans that had taken months for formation; consequently any disturbing force which brought pressure at the last moment resulted in a breakdown of commitments, preferential obligations and contracts, and the many financial and business arrangements that make up the background of a rodeo contest.

It must be remembered that in making demands of the various rodeo committees, many members of the Cowboys' Turtle Association, with a sense of justice and honesty, did not favor the severe and sudden requests, especially when brought forth just before a contest opened. However, as in all associations, some members of this group banded together and made unreasonable, last minute demands, which the committee of the contest often met lest it face disaster by trying to promote a contest without cowboys. Into this breach then, would step local talent from the various outlying districts to carry on the show. The severe action of calling a strike by the Cowboys' Turtle Association, if its demands were not met before the opening of a contest, did not endear the Association to the rodeo committee of that instant, and it instilled fear of failure into the committees of other rodeos.

A contestant member of the Cowboys' Turtle Association who took it upon himself to "work a show" which did not grant the demands of the Association was blackballed and subjected to heavy fine; then possible reinstatement rested with the members of the Association upon payment of the fine. Thus, cowboys, not members of the Cowboys' Turtle Association, just off the ranges and appearing for the fun of it, or non-members of the Association, who made a career of competing at rodeos, were blacklisted, and, if at some future date, they wished to join the Association, they were reminded of their indiscretion. If they appeared and were allowed to compete at a rodeo which had no differences with the Cowboys' Turtle Association, the Association could and did demand that they be refused the right to compete and threatened to strike if the blacklisted contestants were not rejected. These retaliatory measures were enforced, and during the crisis of a strike they only emphasized the unfortunate situation and often led to quarreling and brawling between the Association members and Non-Association members.

The disagreement and points on which the arguments were based referred directly back to the original and almost perpetual grievances of the cowboy. False advertising of the purses offered at a contest; the payment of entry fees that equalled more than the purses offered; the question of adding entry fees to the purse; the division of final monies; the division of the purse among the various events—all these grievances were emphasized, and especially the difference in the monies offered for the bronc riding and calf roping events. There also existed the controversial question of capable judges and referees, and the innumerable questions relative to timing events and arena conditions.

It was impossible to come to an agreement on all the questions. At the first Rodeo Association of America Convention held at Reno, Nevada, in January, 1937, about two months after the inception of the Cowboys' Turtle Association, several members of the new cowboy organization appeared. An attempt was made to work in the di-

rection of harmony. At this convention it was agreed
that the member-shows of the Rodeo Association of
America, must have their prize lists in circulation at least
thirty days before their shows took place, and at this time
there must be on file in the office of the Rodeo Association of America a guarantee that the prize money would
be paid. This would enable the contestants to determine
whether or not they were interested in competing in the
show. This procedure was to eliminate the possibility of
strikes by the contestants, upon arrival at the contest. At
this convention, too, the contestants asked for the assistance of the Rodeo Association of America to request their
member-shows to guarantee the average one hundred dollars a day in each contest. To this amount they also
wanted to add the entrance fees, and if this should not be
done, an equivalent sum was to be added to the purse. The
officials of the Rodeo Association of America agreed to do
everything in their power to grant the requests as soon
as possible.

By April of that year (1937), the Rodeo Association
of America was having difficulties in securing guarantees
of the purses from its member-shows, and a statement
was sent out by the Secretary that they had voted unani-
mously in making this requirement; that the cowboys, in
consideration of this promise, had withdrawn all their
other demands at the January Convention. Previous to
this plea and following it, there was evidence that several
disagreements had come about among the contestants because of misunderstanding of the agreement at Reno. Also,
several of the shows represented at the Convention had
not complied with the plan of that time. Failure to comply, due to neglect and carelessness of listing the purses

offered and the amount of the money guaranteed, was, perhaps, the chief fault of the member-shows.

Perhaps the most severe blow in the undercurrent of harmony that existed during the obvious discontent and prevailing misunderstanding of the time was the ultimatum delivered in the form of a letter (April 20, 1937) to the Rodeo Association of America by the Cowboys' Association. The demands at this time were not only directly adverse to the working plan as laid down at the Convention earlier that year, but were dictatorial and threatening and far from being conducive to bringing about better relationships. This ultimatum practically destroyed what had been achieved in favor of harmonious activities. Just who, or what group of individuals, was responsible for the serving of these demands is unknown; unfortunately it was signed by the President, Everett Bowman, and over his head broke a storm of controversy that was to unleash not only the bitterness that grows from disagreement, but all the petty, personal, and unrelated intrigue and hatred, that result from misunderstanding and confused issues.

The demands made by the Cowboys' Turtle Association at this time were in the main: the right to have cowboy judges and flagmen; the day monies as well as final monies to be divided 40-30-20-10; the shows must belong to the Rodeo Association of America or there would not be any guarantee of cowboys' entrance after their arrival at the contest; to have the shows "put up" what they could afford for purses and add all entrance fees without exception. These demands were further emphasized by requesting the Rodeo Association of America to send a letter to each member-show explaining what the Cowboys' Turtle

Association expected of each show, and that, in any trouble resulting from failure to comply with these demands, the member-show would be considered at fault.

This arbitrary decision on the part of the Cowboys' Turtle Association met stiff resistance and resulted in bringing the disagreement to a head. Unfortunately, the ensuing arguments only intensified the emotion of bitterness and little was achieved in the way of settlement. The cowboys had agreed at the Reno Convention to make no further demands, but following this meeting a strike ensued in the month of February, 1937, at Tucson, at *La Fiesta de los Vaqueros*. This strike was threatened the night before the show opened. The Association demanded that the officials of this contest accept its (the Association's) blacklist. One of its members had violated a rule and was entering the Tucson Show. The threatened strike was so ominous that it was evident that the black-listed individual had to be rejected as a contestant or the show would not take place. By arrangement among the directors of the contest, the cowboy was paid his expenses and his entry fees were returned. This action on the part of the directors placated the Cowboys' Association; it brought forth a promise to cause no further trouble. However, immediately following the settlement of this trouble, further demands were made. A new request, to be granted if the cowboys were to appear as participants, was the right to select the three bronc riding judges. The air was not cleared on these latest conditions until the solution was presented which allowed the Cowboys' Association to name one judge, the directors of the show, another, and the two selected men, a third. This ended the controversy and the threatened strike at Tucson, which was to take place one month after the agreement at Reno, was called off.

By June of 1937, the difficulties between the Cowboys' Turtle Association and the member-shows of the Rodeo Association of America had reached such a point that rodeo as a sport and entertainment was in danger of being destroyed. The Prescott Frontier Days Association, the oldest rodeo organization in the country, then a member-show of the Rodeo Association of America, had evidently received demands from the Cowboys' Association that only members of this latter organization could appear at the show, or the contest would be threatened with a strike. Telegrams flew back and forth between the Prescott Rodeo Committee and the Rodeo Association of America, which resulted in the following decision: The Rodeo Association of America placed stress on the point that the agreement at Reno, made with the Cowboys' Turtle Association, had only consisted of a guarantee of a published prize list and a guarantee of money to be paid. They had made no agreement with reference to limiting their member-shows to Turtle Association members, nor to the selection of judges, nor to the consideration of entrance fees.[1]

The Cowboys' Turtle Association, in its anxiety to secure its place in the sun, was now striking out blindly left and right, without consideration of the significance of its demands. In their desire to make themselves secure, its members were rapidly sacrificing benefits already achieved, as well as the right to secure for themselves those benefits which they felt were theirs. In their mad scramble for security, they were undermining whatever opportuni-

---

[1] The C. T. A. evidently withdrew its threat of strike for nothing more is heard of the matter and prominent "Turtles" contested at the show.

ties they had for future success. The feeling grew that the Turtle Association was unreliable, and that one of its leaders was even more so. The established rodeo committees felt this power could be checked only by refusing to become members of the Rodeo Association of America. This refusal, on the part of the member-shows, to remain in the Rodeo Association of America, was only proof that the Turtle Association, in its desire for security for itself and its members, was destroying the ground work already laid in that direction. In this attempt to separate the parent organization, the Rodeo Association of America, from its member-shows, the opportunities secured by the Rodeo Association for the contestants were rapidly being lost.

Following the difficulties at Tucson, several incidents of a minor nature, relative to the demands made by the Cowboys' Association of the member-shows, intensified the already charged atmosphere. The stage was gradually being set for the eventual spark that was to set off the explosion that follows pent-up energy. Among the minor but incendiary incidents that completed the movement were: the troubles at Salinas, California; Hinton, Oklahoma; and Monte Vista, California.

In the summer of 1937, the rodeo committee at Salinas, California, in an attempt to avoid misunderstanding with the Cowboys' Association, used cowboy judges for the first time. Disagreement resulting over the time made by one of the contestants in the calf roping event and then the reversal of that decision by one of the judges brought forth a flood of controversial letter-writing, even though the issue had been settled agreeably at that time.

The demands at Hinton, Oklahoma, resulted in the most unfortunate, long drawn-out disagreement to come out of the mounting troubles that were surrounding the sport of rodeo. The difficulties early in the fall of 1937, at Pendleton, Oregon, and Ellensburg, Washington, had continued until the late summer of 1938. It was, perhaps, this major altercation that brought the Cowboys' Turtle Association to its senses, and did more to make its members realize the dangerous ground they were treading upon and the unfortunate path they were following.[1]

The story behind the Ellensburg and Pendleton controversies is of great interest, for it reveals, only too clearly, how far the Cowboys' Turtle Association had stepped from its path of purpose and its promises made at the Reno Convention, and how, consequently, it had been reduced to an organization of monopolists, strikers, and unrealible racketeers. Yet, this story reveals the remarkable change of this same group, drunk with power and with the desire of self-protection, into a normal organization. The settlement of these controversial questions shows the remarkable character of the many individuals who were a part of the organization and fought for its just rights, but in a fair, sincere, and honest way.

The Ellensburg and Pendleton controversy grew out of the demands made by the Cowboys' Turtle Association for cowboy judges. The boycott would have prevented the shows from going on, and in order to prevent this, the committee invited local cowboys and non-member contestants of the surrounding countryside to participate in

---

[1] The rodeo committee at Hinton refused to accede to the C. T. A.'s demands. They immediately put their show on a non-professional basis. The strike hurt the business of the show on the first day, but after that the "amateur" cowboys came in and performed.

Monte Vista agreed to the demands of the Cowboys' Turtle Association and the threatened strike was called off. The demands made at both shows centered around the naming of cowboy judges.

the rodeo. The officials promised these men that, if they helped make the 1937 shows a success, these organizations would help protect them in every way.

Immediately the Cowboys' Association "slapped" a five-hundred-dollar fine on any of its members participating and wishing reinstatement and also black-listed the boys of a non-member status. Among those fined were some of the outstanding contestants of the Northwest, bronc riders of ability.

The hectic year of 1937 in the rodeo world drew to a close with a feeling of discontent and unhappiness. The year from the time of the Reno Convention up to the Northwestern controversy had a series of unfortunate happenings. Hardly a month passed without the flames of dissatisfaction being fanned into more brilliant intensity by the demands and broken promises of the Cowboys' Turtle Association. Rodeo as a business, sport, and entertainment had gone through its most severe trial to date, and there was a feeling of disintegration, and a return to the older and more haphazard aspects of the work. Several shows of importance signified that they planned to go non-professional during the next year rather than cope again with the difficulties of 1937. If a great many had agreed to follow suit, the very worthy and untried advantages of the Cowboys' Association would have been lost, and the contestant would have found himself in his former position.

Many of the members of the Cowboys' Turtle Association were not in sympathy with the actions taken by that organization; on the other hand, they favored the accomplishments of these demands through less drastic means. The temper which would prevail at the coming convention at Ogden, Utah, in January, 1938, was bound to be tense.

At this gathering a new element of contention arose with the appearance of the North American Cowboys' Association, the members of which were cowboys black-listed by the Cowboys' Turtle Association. Whether this new group produced a threat in the form of a split among the organized contestants, or whether the Cowboys' Turtle Association membership had taken a change of heart and mind is not known, but the result was that the tenor of the convention was, at least, level-headed and logical, and much of the aggravation of the past was mitigated.

Prior to the convention at Ogden the Rodeo Association of America had requested that the Cowboys' Turtle Association submit the demands of its members for presentation at the January gathering. This plan was to prevent any misunderstanding from cropping up as a result of discussions, such as had been the case at the Reno Convention and the so-called compromise at Redwood City, which had been held that spring (April, 1937) between the leaders of the two Associations. In preparation for the Ogden Convention, the Cowboys' Association submitted its proposed rules for the coming year, subject to change at this meeting. The following rules give a clue to the changes that took place during the difficult year of 1937. The changes are found in:

Rule I—At all shows or rodeos for the year 1938 all entrance fees must be added in each event to the prize money.

Rule II—Each rodeo must have as . . . [its] judges . . . two active cowboy contestants.

Rule III—All members of the Cowboys ['] Turtle Association are not allowed to compete at any amateur rodeo or work in any way connected with [such a] . . . rodeo.

Rule IV—Any cowboy who makes as many as four rodeos in one year shall be classed as a professional, and must have a Cowboys ['] Turtle Association card before entering at any rodeo contest in 1938.

Rule V—[If] any member of the Cowboys ['] Turtle Association . . . leaves a room or board bill, the Cowboys ['] Turtle Association will pay . . . [it], or any other bill [it] see[s] fit to pay. Cowboys that owe bills of this kind will not be permitted to contest or work at any rodeo until the Cowboys ['] Turtle Association has been paid in full. They will be subject to fine also.

Rule VI—Instead of the Cowboys ['] Turtle Association giving a thirty day notice to a rodeo that the members of the Cowboys ['] Turtle Association will work after they get to a rodeo, [the Association asks] each rodeo [to] write to the C. T. A., if . . . it want[s] a guarantee that the members will work after they get there and have it printed on . . . [its] prize list OK. by the C. T. A. officials. . . . If the contestants are not satisfied with what the officials have done, they should stay away. The officials of the C. T. A. should have plenty of time to see all representatives of the C. T. A. and [have] each representative and [the] president sign his name to the OK.

Rule VII—Any contestant that has contested at any place where the C. T. A. has refused to work, . . . shall be fined before he can work again with the members of the C. T. A. Any time any member of the C. T. A. finds a . . . [cowboy] contesting or working on the chutes or with the stock, who . . . [has] not lived up to the rules of the C. T. A. should report this . . . [cowboy] to the management of the rodeo. His entrance fees should be refunded and [he should] not [be] allowed to contest or work until he has squared himself with the C. T. A.

Rule VIII—Any cowboy who is paying on a fine should pay not less than $50 down and one-quarter of what he wins until his fine has been paid. The first time he refuses or neglects to send in one quarter of what he wins, then he is laying himself liable to be put out again and forfeits all he paid on his fine.[1]

The rules contained the desires of the Cowboys' Turtle Association and what they wished to accomplish during that year. For the greater part, they were acceptable to the representatives of the member-shows of the Rodeo Association of America. It was agreed to allow the contestants to select from their membership two judges, if the judges already chosen by the rodeo were not acceptable to them. However, they must first protest this choice and then come to some agreement over the selection of the new ones. It was also agreed to allow variations in the rules set down by the Rodeo Association of America for the operation of a rodeo, if these variations were printed

---

[1] "Cowboys' Turtle Association," *Hoofs and Horns* 7 (January 1938), 19.

in the prize lists of the rodeos desiring the changes. This was important in regard to the new ruling that all entrance fees must be added.

The printing of a variation of rules in the prize list sixty days before the contest and in the *Rodeo Association Bulletin* thirty days before the event would allow the contestants to decide whether or not they wished to compete at the rodeo. The hazard of working under various interpretations of the standard rules of the Rodeo Association of America was not desirable but had been in existence for some time. Much trouble and dissension could be avoided and eliminated if all rodeos were to operate under one set of rules. The Convention, however, was one in which the spirit of harmony, cooperation, and satisfaction was manifested. Still, this spirit was not destined to last long, for dissension was to result in protesting the selection of judges and flagmen. The most serious flare-up came from the 1937 trouble at Ellensburg and Pendleton. By mid-summer of 1938, the trouble was fully blown. A definite split in the membership of the Cowboys' Turtle Association was quite evident. It had been agreed at Ogden that there would be no retaliations against these two rodeos, nor the contestants participating in them. Likewise, the Ellensburg and Pendleton officials would not retaliate against the Turtles, who would be welcome to appear at the two contests that year. One group of Turtles, under the leadership of the spokesman of the Board of Directors of the Cowboys' Association, held to this ruling made in Ogden. Another group, with President Bowman of the Association, maintained that the agreement held only in that they agreed to work with the Northwest contestants at Ellensburg and Pendleton, but not at other

contests. Much discussion resulted over the proper interpretation of the word *retaliation*. The breach widened,
and if these differences had remained impersonal, it seemed
probable that a solution would have appeared shortly. The
petty, personal, and unjust accusations on both sides only
served to keep the "pot boiling."

The question of the district rodeo appeared at this time.
The district rodeo problem was a new source of friction
and was based on the idea of a rodeo in a restricted area
at which only contestants of that area could compete. This
was found particularly in California and in some parts of
Arizona. Coming just at this time, it did not serve to
ease the tense situation.

Some of the members of the Turtle Association, though
not all, took the position that this was a lockout, and that
any one who would contest or work at these rodeos could
not compete or work at a so-called open rodeo. It must
be understood that at such rodeos the Rodeo Association
of America point-awards[1] were not given.

Considerable discussion over the district rodeo took
place. The matter was settled after the majority of members of the Cowboys' Turtle Association agreed that members of that Association who were from the district holding
such a rodeo could compete if points were not awarded,
and if there were separate events open to all with Rodeo
Association points to take care of the non-district contestants. The settlement took place after some discussion
on the part of the leaders of the Cowboys' Association
and the officials of the Reno Nevada Rodeo of 1938. When

---

[1] For every dollar won at recognized contests the R. A. A. gives a point,
the sum total of points at the end of the year gives the cowboys their positions in the championships.

the Nevada State Championship offered an event in bronc rilding and calf roping, with points for one group and no points for the other groups, the trouble of the district rodeo was ended. A similar situation was faced by the Prescott Frontier Days Rodeo but it was settled without further difficulty.

About this time the Cowboys' Turtle Association received national publicity of a nature that could hardly be classed as helpful to its cause. On July 9, 1938, in the *Saturday Evening Post,* an article appeared entitled, "No Turtles Need Apply." In this article the difficulties of the organization at the Pendleton Round-Up were aired and given wide publicity. This type of publicity, although written in no way to be harmful, did carry with it a potent charge of unreliability on the part of contestants' organization. Evidently it put a scare in their camp—for it appears that, although there was a series of disruptions and threatened strikes at contests during the last half of the year of 1938 and into 1939, the general tone of the threats did not equal their former belligerency.[1]

Some objection was raised to the Fort Worth prize list and program, because it did not include a cowgirls' bucking contest for 1939. This objection made by the President of the Cowboys' Association was not sustained by the membership of the organization. The cowgirls had been granted membership in the Cowboys' Turtle Association in 1938 but they had no vote in the organization.

---

[1] The newspapers at this time became curious about the friction between the two organizations and asked questions. The officials of the R. A. A. asked the newspapers not to publish anything and the papers complied. To quote a statement made in the *Bulletin,* 2 (May 1938): ". . . we hope that we will have the cooperation of all who read this bulletin in keeping it out of the papers, inasmuch as possible as the matter is all cleared up."

The cowgirls had made a set of rules agreeing not to accept less than fifteen dollars for riding bronc at smaller shows and not less than twenty-five at larger contests. They worked out a series of fines for the members who failed to follow the rules. However, the cowgirls, like the contract performers who had taken membership in the Turtle Association, had no vote in the organization and therefore had to work out their own rules and regulations. They could expect no help from the Cowboys' Turtle Association in their difficulties: The above-mentioned trouble at Fort Worth received no attention from the members of the contestants' association. They refused to go on strike because of the fair treatment shown them for many years by the Fort Worth Rodeo Committee.[1]

Other controversial questions gradually tapered off, except for the almost amusing flare-up that took place before the opening of the Prescott Frontier Days Rodeo, which decided to go non-professional in 1939. The Rodeo Committee of that city decided to produce a show with men who came directly off the ranges and were not in the business for a living, and special rules were to prevent injury to the beasts and men.

The Cowboys' Turtle Association advised its members not to compete at this contest. The disagreement resulting from this change did not come from any strike or demands or violations of rules, but the Prescott officials resented their contest being called "amateur," and the Cow-

---

[1] The Cowgirl Bronc Riding Contest was being dropped out of rodeos as a competition. The cowgirls hoped to revive interest in the contest by having the "Turtles" back them. On becoming members of the Cowboys' Association, they really gained nothing, for the association did not assume the responsibility of making the cowgirls' contest one of the required R. A. A. event. Today the Cowgirl Bronc Riding Contest, when held, is an exhibition and not a competition.

boys' Association members did not like the odor of the word "professional." The impression that one receives, upon examining the correspondence and printed statements in that discussion, is that the solution of the problem moved farther away and became more heated because of the interpretation of and the play on the two words, *amateur* and *professional*. The Prescott Rodeo still remains a contest for the cowboy of the range; because of this, it has received nation-wide publicity and, also, because it is the oldest rodeo organization in the country.

In July, 1939, the Cowboys' Turtle Association made its last demands of a rodeo that could be classed as a threat of a strike. This took place twenty-four hours before the opening of the Ogden Show. The demands came from the leader of the contestants' organization and insisted that the prize list be raised one thousand dollars. It is evident that the membership of the Association was changing its tone in making threats against rodeos, for, again, a great many of the men refused to support their leader and were willing "to work" the show if they would not be black-listed by the Rodeo Association of America or subjected to a five-hundred-dollar fine. At this time the President of the Rodeo Association issued a statement that the organization was behind the contestants 100 per cent and that they would not be black-listed by the Rodeo Association of America. He could not, however, offer any solution about the fine, for it was a ruling of the Cowboys' Association. He did, however, very forcefully bring to the front the agreement made by President Bowman, that the Turtles would never go to a rodeo and demand an increase in prize money the day before the contest opened. This cleared the air considerably, and the contest went on. The Cowboys' Association once more suffered for this unfortunate move, even though the greater number of the contestants did not favor the demands. It later became known that the Ogden Rodeo Committee had been tardy in getting out its prize lists and at the same time had grouped the prizes in a lump sum with no division of monies as to events. This, however, did not give the leaders of the Cowboys' Turtle Association the right to break the promise made to the Rodeo Association of America.

If one examines carefully the trials and tribulations which are a part of the sport of rodeo during the years of 1937 and 1939 and the disagreements between the two major Associations governing the sport, one clearly recognizes the two dominating personalities who were a part of this hectic background. Two personalities, as different as the proverbial day and night; their stations in life opposite; yet, both, and this can be said with sincerity, were striving for one thing—to achieve for rodeo a place in the sun, a place in our national field of sport and entertainment. Both men were outstanding leaders in their organizations and in their work. These two dominating personalities were President McNutt of the Rodeo Association of America and President Everett Bowman of the Cowboys' Turtle Association.

In the many controversial questions that had arisen during the three years of indecision and strife, the wisdom, foresight, and the guiding influence of Judge McNutt, (Superior Judge of San Mateo County, California), are evident throughout. It is especially noticeable in the vast correspondence that took place during these troublesome days. In analyzing his letters, one finds that his philosophy of fair treatment and his just consideration of the problems of the time are based on sportsmanship. This principle, with which he wished to imbue the sport of rodeo, is the one closest to his heart and it is the one with which he fought all those who assailed his ideals. His resignation as President of the Rodeo Association in 1940 was a distinct loss, for his guidance and sincerity had accomplished many things worth-while in the organization of rodeo.

The other dominating figure of modern rodeo, Everett Bowman, was a brilliant contestant and holder of championships in various events, as well as the All-Around Champion for several times, and he had been President of the Cowboys' Turtle Association since its beginning. Much criticism has been directed toward him. A hard worker of the "go-getter" type, Bowman is a man with a mind of his own. He is typical of the true Western breed; few men of his many qualities and abilities are found among the cowboy-contestants of today who could fill the position of president, though many feel that he held the position too long.

As head of the Cowboys' Turtle Association, he has taken many knocks, some of which have been brought about by his own lack of foresight, his stubbornness and determination, and some which would have come to any one, as the head of this Association. Everett Bowman has made mistakes but has been willing to admit his failure of vision and has tried to make readjustments. The mistakes were amplified because he was not particularly gifted in the intricasies of organization or business, nor adept or skilled in the diplomacy of business procedures. However, in spite of these possible failings, there was no one with half his ability to take his place in the Association. Everett Bowman could not be accused of failing to have the best interests of his fellow workers at heart, even though the strong armed methods he used did not at times give this impression. He was a man accustomed to get out and do things; a man of quick, but not always accurate, decision; a man for whom the words *Yes* and *No* carry more weight than a lengthy discussion *pro* and *con* on a subject.

After a brief survey of the Cowboys' Turtle Association, at present a full-fledged organization of some 1400 members, one can say, with some emphasis, that the effort expended and the difficulties encountered to bring it from its infancy to a fully matured organization have been worth while and good. In truth, through the many difficulties that the Association has passed, it has grown strong, and the original purpose of its founding has been expanded to include other worthy ventures in its scope. The original purpose of its founding, that is, the protection of the cowboy from unfair practices existing in the sport, did suffer in its infancy; however, those earlier mistakes must be classed as a sign of overanxiety on its part to do the right thing and be successful in the attempt. Many misunderstandings were often due to lack of experience, and very few were based on a malicious desire to do harm or on a flagrant dictatorial show of power.

The Cowboys' Turtle Association has not only increased the benefits of the cowboy, but it has also brought about a remarkable change in his character and appearance. This is not to be taken as a sign that the cowboy-contestant has grown soft, because he is organized and relies on the backing of an Association for protection; on the contrary, this protection has given him greater strength, but in a less belligerent manner. He has lost much of his former attitude of "going-out-and-getting" what he wants, regardless of the cost. The cowboy with the backing of the Association has some one interested in his welfare, and thus he takes a greater interest in himself and others—he has a feeling of being wanted. No longer must he go to the contests with fear and worry concerning unfair judges, timers and flagmen. If he wins, he collects the money he has honestly won, because he has met the best men in the sport in fair competition.

Another change brought about by the Cowboys' Turtle Association is noticeable in the appearance of the contestants. Because severe laws govern the cowboy's conduct at a contest, much of the rowdyism and lack of restraint, brawling, and drinking, that made up the background of the earlier days, has disappeared. Previous to the founding of the Association, the general conduct and appearance of many of the contestants was unfortunate and a sore question in the community in which a contest was held. The Rodeo Association of America did its best to encourage the boys to "clean up" and make an attempt to change the traditional and, in some cases, truthful picture of the cowboy. The contestant, previous to this time, unfortunately, had great difficulty in securing sufficient funds to keep his body and soul together, to keep a horse and to pay his entry fees, without considering the added extravagance of a wardrobe. This, however, did not excuse him from getting acquainted with soap and water, shaving, and clean clothing. The Turtle Association did much to improve and encourage the man to keep up his appearance, especially the man who had become careless because of lack of interest in his welfare.

An important rule, recently added to those of the contestants' organization, requires members pay their board and room bills and just debts incurred in a community during a contest. If a contestant fails to do this, the bills are paid by the Association and the culprit is fined or suspended, or both; his reinstatement depends on the discretion of the Board of Directors of the Association. These various aspects of the Association have given it a reputation of sound dealing, and any antagonism that had earlier been directed toward it is rapidly waning. In the minds of many people the status of the contestant has vastly improved.

The Cowboys' Turtle Association[1] is constantly working to do away with the insidious practice of false advertising. This harmful practice is unforunate for the men and very bad for the rodeo business. The demand of the contestants that the rodeo producer print a list of the purses given, not only protects the cowboy, but also does away with advertising that misleads the public to believe that the rodeo organization of a community is giving

---

[1] On March 15, 1945, at Fort Worth, Texas, the Cowboys' Turtle Association reorganized and hired as a business representative Earl Lindsey (formerly associated with Gene Autry). The representatives of the Cowboys' Turtle Association agreed to change the name of the organization to that of *Rodeo Cowboys' Association.* They also formed their own point awarding system starting January 1, 1945. Points are awarded for each dollar won in the contests. There is to be no All-Around Champion Cowboy in their point award system, but the high point winner in each event will be adjudged the champion in that event.

"Fees for joining the Rodeo Cowboys' Association point award are a minimum of $10.00 for small shows with $75.00 or less for each event; $25.00 minimum for shows of over $75.00 an event, or 1% of the prize money in the highest event, whichever is the larger.

"Membership is voluntary the first year of the reorganization, but beginning January 1, 1946, when a prize list is O.K.'d the rodeo automatically becomes a member of the R. C. A. Point Awarding System." See "Rodeo Cowboys' Association," *Hoofs and Horns* 14 (May 1945), 16.

away vast sums; that the contest will be something more than it is. Among the purses of the various rodeos throughout the country there are few that give more than five thousand dollars.

Another type of false advertising that both Associations deplore is that of calling a contest a World's Championship Rodeo. No one rodeo is the deciding contest in selecting those men who at the end of the year are the champions in their work. This is decided by the sum total of the Rodeo Association of America points (one for every dollar) won at the many contests they attend during the year. It is true that in the large final contests at the end of a year, many of the winners forge ahead to gain points that cannot be made up by other contestants at the few remaining shows; however, in the true sense of the word, they are not World's Championship Rodeos. The contests held at Madison Square Garden and the Boston Garden in the final months of the rodeo year are, perhaps, contests that might be eligible for that title. They may, more truthfully, be called Championship Rodeos because they are attended by the best of contestants in the field—the former, present, and in all likelihood, the future champions of the various events of rodeo.

The use of outstanding contestants as a means to draw a crowd to a contest is another misleading form of advertising. There is no guarantee that any one of these men will appear. Whether or not he will enter, depends entirely on the contestant. It may happen that another event of greater interest, financially as well as sporting, is scheduled at the same time, and the contestant might prefer to enter it, rather than a particular contest that has already advertised his appearance. The cowboys' decision to attend depends on the fact whether or not the rodeo is on the circuit he has planned to follow and also on the distance of the place from his planned route. Contest managers try to bring name-contestants to their shows; this is perfectly legal and legitimate. Seldom do they actually pay a boy to come because of his reputation as a performer; however, they may inform such a boy that, if he does come, his entrance fees will be paid. Usually, only the reigning All-Around Champion Cowboy is so honored.

The question as to when a cowboy is considered an amateur in the business of rodeo, and the "how, when, and where" of his becoming a professional has been an issue for many years. The first attempt to solve this question took place early in 1941 with the founding of the Cowboys' Amateur Association of America. This organization was established on the same rules as those of the Turtle Association, except that it defines who shall be considered as an amateur cowboy. It places this group of boys in their own class, and they remain there until they are qualified to join the professional organization.

An amateur is defined as a person who has never belonged to any rodeo association, and upon seeking membership, has never won more than five hundred dollars (in any one year) at rodeos. When, at the end of the year, any one member has won this sum of money, he becomes a professional. If he is to make a career of this work, he has only one thing left to do, that is to join the Cowboys' Turtle Association.

A number of members of the Amateur Organization took part in the larger shows at Madison Square Garden and at Boston Garden and won considerably more than this amount. At present there is some dissension between the professional organization and the amateur association concerning the change in plans of the latter group. The Cowboys' Amateur Association wishes to extend the winnings of an amateur contestant from five hundred to one thousand dollars before the status of the amateur is changed to that of professional.

After the years of controversy over the status of amateur and professional contestants, the issue was settled by an agreement on the part of the members of the Turtle Association to "work" rodeos at which contestants who do not make the work a career could also participate. However, if any one of these men earns more than five hundred dollars during a year, he loses his classification as an amateur and must join the Turtle Association; otherwise the membership of this organization would refuse to appear at rodeos where such a man has registered as an entry.[1]

Just where this new proposal on the part of the Amateur Association will end, is hard to say. Dissension among the contestants of rodeo work does not promote a feeling of well-being and will do considerable harm to the sport. The increase of the sum to one thousand dollars will be of great benefit to the amateur, but if one carefully checks the earnings of more than one-half of the professional contestants, he will find that this sum is a fair estimate of their earnings.

Another item concerning the Cowboys' Turtle Association and the Amateurs' Association is that membership

---

[1] Many of the non-professional cowboys are not following the rodeos for a living and to earn $500 to $1,000 extra during the year helps them considerably. A cowboy who might reach the $1,000 class may then start to follow the rodeos as a professional and try his luck at the game for a couple of years. (The figure now has been set at $2,000.)

fees in both are ten dollars per year. Half of this fee is used for running the organization, and the other half is put into a fund as a benefit to help the contestants in case they are injured, or in case of death their family will receive a death benefit of five hundred dollars. This has proved to be very worth while, for the men in rodeo are unable to secure life insurance because of the dangers and the serious aspects of the work.

The Cowboys' Amateur Association of America[1] might be classed as an organization favoring apprenticeship for a career in rodeo. The rules and regulations of this organization in comparison with those of the Cowboys' Turtle Association are identical except for those dealing with the changing of status because of earnings. There are officers, a board of directors, spokesmen for events, suspensions and fines. It is hoped that, if the association is found worthy of respect because of its contribution to the sport, it will not pass through a period of difficulties, lose its head, make superficial demands and requests harmful to itself and to the general good of the sport.

---

[1] The Cowboy Amateur Association of America voted on March 19, 1944, to change the name of the association to that of *Cowboys' Association of America*. This, again, is evidence that the cowboys do not like the word *amateur* connected with them.

CHAPTER IX

WRANGLING THEIR WAY

Cowboys go hungry, sometimes they're broke,
But often luck hits 'em a-plenty,
Then they'll give freely, without promise or note,
The limit? There just isn't any!

The man who makes a career of rodeo attends between thirty and forty contests during the year. This he must do, in order to make a fair living; the mere fact of participating in the work is no guarantee that he will succeed financially. Barring accidents and severe injury, he finds himself faced with outstanding specialists in the work. Among the fourteen hundred active participants, there are about one hundred and fifty who can be considered serious threats to anyone in the field of competition. There is always, however, the dark horse of the season—that contestant doing average work, who suddenly strikes a lucky run. Like a comet he streaks across the horizon, blazes in celestial fury, and a new star is born. There is also the contestant who runs along smoothly, piles up points at every contest during the year, reaches the enviable position of being one of the top contestants, then, toward the end of the season starts to lose as steadily as he has gathered points. There is no reason, nor is there any explanation for this change; it is simply the way of the game and happens in all competitive sports.

A contestant not only faces competition, but also considerable expense during the year. Among the men active in sports, the rodeo contestant occupies a unique position. He is one of the few sportsmen who assume all the expenses of their occupation and pay at the same time for the privilege of entering the events. He not only pays an entry fee, but participates in the work, and takes all the chances that are connected with it. Professional golfers pay an entrance fee to compete at national golf contests, the skeet shooter also pays an entrance fee to compete at such meets; however, none in this latter group follow the work as a livelihood. The point is, however, that there are no sportsmen paying entrance fees who take the chances of life and limb that the cowboys do.

The question of the entry fee is an interesting one. The contestant pays a fee for each event he enters. The fees range from three to one hundred and fifty dollars for each event, depending, of course, upon the size of the contest. At contests, running for several weeks, such as those in New York, Boston, and Chicago, the purses are large and, accordingly, the entry fees are high. As already stated, the adding of the entry fee to the purse was a point of discussion for many years. Now the fees of the contestant are, in most cases, added to the purse, and the rodeos not conforming to this rule must print in the prize list that the fees are not included.

There is no other professional sport or work in which the participant pays for the opportunity to increase his financial status and, at the same time, endangers his life while doing the work. This is as unique a procedure as the work itself and should be kept in mind by the spectators. It is quite obvious that there are many contest-

ants at a rodeo who have paid their entry fees, but because of the stiff competition, misfortune, and the innumerable things that can happen during a contest, do
not place in the money, though they have performed each
day.

In the larger contests that run from one to three weeks,
where several hundred contestants are registered, it is impossible for every cowboy to participate in one particular
event during each day. To cover just the calf roping, contestants would take an entire day, and the exhibition of
just one type of event would not be entertaining to the
spectators, nor would the action be sufficiently varied to
act as a drawing card. Thus, the go-around system is used.
A certain number of contestants perform at each performance until the entire group of men registered in that
event has been covered. In the larger contests, a single
performer does not come up every day, and his chances to
swell his finances are not so good, especially, if his luck
is running bad. However, if he places in the money, he
is "set" for the time being.

The financial expenditures of the rodeo cowboy do not
end with the expenses of the entry fees. Usually, he
travels by automobile from one contest to another. In
many instances it is a considerable distance, and he has
only some twelve to twenty-four hours, or even less, to
make the journey. The average man in rodeo travels from
thirty to forty thousand miles a year. This is no small
expense item and must be included in his expenditures.
If he is a calf roper or steer wrester and takes along his
horse, the animal is of value and must be handled with
care and properly equipped. A well-trained calf horse
has had months of training and good treatment so that

he can perform properly in the arena. The value of such a horse is about one thousand dollars in money, but considerably more in the affections of his master. This horse must be hauled in a horse trailer and given the best of care. Some men take two horses, thus doubling the responsibility.

The cowboy must eat and sleep, as well as work. Some of the men live at hotels. This is the usual life of the cowboy when he works in the large cities. Some, if married, are accompanied by their families and take furnished apartments, and, in some instances, the wife carries on the household duties of the home. While traveling from show to show on the road, many of the men, especially those with families, have a house trailer. They park their trailers on the rodeo grounds or at some nearby trailer camp and make a temporary home for the duration of the contest. Some carry with them complete camping outfits and live in tents during their summer travels.

Rooming houses, tourists camps, and private homes with rooms to rent accommodate the rest of these men. Previous to the organization of the Cowboys' Turtle Association, "back in the good old days," the cowboy often left his mark, not only on the community he visited, but in the dwelling in which he stayed. Well known in that era, is the story of the cowboy who takes a room in a private home, comes in intoxicated and falls asleep fully-clothed; then, the next morning, awakens, festooned in lace curtains because he failed to remove his spurs. The raucousness and "tearing loose" of cowboys at a Frontier

Celebration instilled fear into the hearts of many a proprietor of "sleeping space."[1]

In a discussion about the men in rodeo, mention must be made of the interesting and complicated financial arrangements that exist among them. Many a young cowboy, beginning the work, is not financially able to assume the responsibilities that are a part of the sport. If he has shown ability, talent, and is a willing worker, he is often sponsored by one of the older and more successful men and thus given an opportunity to "get ahead." These older men agree to pay the expenses on the road and, sometimes, while at the shows. They also supply a horse for the boy. In return, the patron usually receives one-half of the boy's winnings. There are many variations of this sort of deal which is found, especially, among the younger bronc, bareback and bull riders. The older man pays the entrance fee and gets one-third of the winnings; on some occasions the boy is also given an allowance of two or three dollars per day.

If the contestant is a calf roper or steer wrestler of considerable experience but does not own a horse for either of these events, arrangements are made among other contestants for the use of a horse. The calf roper agrees to pay one-fourth of all he wins to the owner of the mount. A different arrangement is made in the case of the steer wrestler. Upon securing a horse, he agrees to pay one-fourth of his winnings—one-eighth to the owner of the horse and one-eighth to the owner of the hazing

---

[1] A story that is often related by the cowboys, but as yet, there is no authentic basis for believing that it is anything but fiction.

horse. Both calf ropers and steer wrestlers have been known, at times, to pay out as much as half their winnings. However, if the contestant in the calf roping or steer wrestling events fails to win under these arrangements, he does not pay. These arrangements may be made for the whole year, for a series of shows, or, in some cases, for only one contest; all depends on the financial status of the contestant. The question of finances with the cowboy is a precarious and fickle one. Many a capable man is "caught short" because of bad luck and unfortunate breaks and, consequently, is unable to pay his entrance fees. Some of this financial juggling enables him to carry on until his luck changes.

Another form of the complicated financial maneuvering of the cowboys is "splitting." This is an agreement between two men, usually in the same event, to pool and to divide evenly all their winnings. In this way they hope that neither will run too short of money. Sometimes, the men split one-fourth of what they win instead of one-half, and the arrangement, usually made for one show, may be for a series of contests or even for the entire year. This type of agreement is also made use of when two important contests are playing at the same time and have large purses. Since it is impossible for the two to attend both contests, one man goes to one, and his partner to the other. Thus, such a plan offers them an opportunity to increase their earnings. If they are top men, both have an opportunity to win first in their event.

CHAPTER X

BIG HATS, HIGH HEELS, AND SHARP HOOKS

His sturdy old boots and copper-rivet Levis
He wears while working in chutes,
But the clothes that bring forth the feminine sighs
Are slim trousers, slick shirts, and fancy dress boots!

It has been mentioned previously that the cowboy is clothes-conscious. He is no more so than any other man, but it is obvious, upon looking over his wardrobe, that he does have a taste for good things, not only from the standpoint of the aesthetic but also of quality. Much might be written about the cowboy's garb from the aesthetic point of view, but any detailed elaboration on the topic would lead to endless discussion. However, the following are some of the interesting aspects of this habiliment. The working costume of the contestant, as observed in the arena, consists of "Levis," shirt, boots, hat, and occasionally, a scarf.

His daily work clothes are not the riding habit type of whipcord breeches, and fine, but gaudy, silk and satin shirts. If, at any time, this latter type of garment is part of his wardrobe, it is used either for the Grand Opening Parade or for dress in the evening, and, especially, for the purpose of giving the dudes "a thrill." His working clothes are assembled with the idea of utility. The tight-fitting, faded, blue denim "Levis" with the invisible copper rivets at points of stress are not only serviceable but are made of rugged fabric and are strongly reenforced in order to withstand the hard use to which they are subjected, as well as the repeated washings. The "Robin Hood" effect achieved by the fit of the trousers is not basically aesthetic, considering the various shapes of the pedal extremities of the contestants, but it is of utilitarian purpose. The explanation, as given by the cowboys, is that flapping trouser legs are often a serious cause of accidents. The belt that is worn by some of the men is purely ornamental and gives them a sense of security, but as for serving the purpose of "keeping up" their trousers, one can readily see from the fit that a surgical operation would be needed to remove them.[1]

Another piece of apparel that the cowboy is particular about in fit is his shirt. Numerous apparel shops show a number of styles and designs. Ben, the Rodeo Tailor, of Philadelphia, and Sing Kee of San Francisco, are perhaps the best-known. Sing Kee has supplied more shirts for cowboys than any other garment-maker. He is a specialist in this type of work and has a reputation for perfection of workmanship that no other shirtmaker can touch. Ben, the Rodeo Tailor, also supplies the cowboy with some very fine garments. His supply house is one of the most important. Shirts, jackets, trousers, and ensembles featured by this house are custom made to suit the exact needs of the cowboy. The garments are more or less of the luxury type; nearly every cowboy has in his wardrobe two

---

[1] Observed while traveling with the contestants. The wives of the cowboys tease their husbands for wearing such tight trousers—they say that the men are trying to show off their manly shapes and just how well they are built. "Bar flies," inhabiting the cocktail lounges of the hotels where the cowboys stay during a contest, can hardly keep their eyes or hands off these "he men" of the West.

or three of Ben's dress suits and shirts for street wear, and
for dinner and evening wear before the show and after
the evening performance. This tailor supplies the finest
fabrics, shirts of whipcord, gabardine, serge, silk crepe,
and silk satin of two weights. Suits are of worsted materials, cavalry twills and Bedford cords of light weight
and heavy weight grades, as well as serge, gabardine and
whipcord. Ben supplies the costumes for many of the
trick riders and fancy ropers, although some of the women
make their own costumes and, sometimes, also those of
their husbands and their friends. Women gifted at this
work make shirts for several of the men.

The shirt of the contestant takes the hardest "beating"
of any of his clothes. These shirts, ranging in prices from
$7.50 to $25, and even as high as $100, are an expensive
item and very often, after a contest in the arena, they have
been torn, ripped or "messed up." During a season the contestant wears out several, made of the best material.

Much has been written about the footwear of the
cowboy and it is still a source of interest. The tight-fitting
boot with the high, slanting heel serves the purpose of
holding the ankle and bones of the foot in position; it
also offers protection against severe and sudden strain
during the strenuous activity of riding and performing
in the arena. All boots have steel shanks, but about two-
thirds of the modern bronc riders sever these bands or
have boots made without them. This leaves a soft arch
which allows the rider to feel the position of the stirrups
under his feet during the ride. The heels of the bronc
rider's boots are flatter than those of other boots, and
sometimes the front edge is cut back farther, thus making
a smaller heel. There seems to be no basis in the belief that

the high slanting heel allows the cowboy, who unfortunately has had his foot slip through a stirrup, to withdraw the foot and prevent injury to himself if he is dragged. This type of heel, however, because of its small base, does allow the steer wrestler to dig his heels into the ground; it acts as a means of stopping the fast moving animal. It is also a definite aid when used in the same fashion for the unmounted roper of horses and calves. This footwear has given the man of the range and of rodeo a peculiar gait that is different from that of any other individual; often, it emphasizes the curvature of the legs and has caused much speculation concerning the bow-leggedness of the contestant. It is said that the boot has a tendency to make the foot appear smaller, yet, true as this may be, a preference for this type of footwear is hardly a point of vanity with the men of rodeo, and it is doubtful whether this is ever thought of or even considered. Cowboys have been the butt of many jokes regarding their ability to run or walk. If anyone observes the contestants entered in the wild cow milking contest, he soon realizes that such stories are unfounded. Homer Pettigrew, wearing boots, outran, in an unofficial race, the colored trackman, Jesse Owens, in a fifty-yard dash, and many cowboys can run a hundred yards in ten seconds.

Alec Alexander, negro cowboy and groom, who has been with the World's Championship Rodeo Corporation since the days when Colonel Johnson headed the organization, ran a race in Pittsburg in the spring of 1941, with Barney Willis, Olympic mentor and California track star. It was a fifty-yard race with a bet of forty dollars on the side. Alec won the race. He has appeared as the star of an all-negro rodeo in Houston, Texas, and also does some clowning and bull fighting. He is one of the unique characters in and around rodeo.

Boots are made of kid, calf, and kangaroo leather and in combinations of these leathers. Usually, the vamp is made of one leather and the top of another. The work boots are not as decorative as the dress type, but there is always some scroll work in stitching on the toe and on the top. The more elaborate dress boot is highly decorated; pinking around the top, foxing, vamp, and wing tip are not uncommon. The tops on all boots are usually piped with a different leather or, at least, some other color. Inlaid panels of colored leather in the sides of the tops are a feature of the dress boot, as well as tooling or fancy stitching of this panel. The designs used are many and varied. Boots come in many colors, of which black, brown, and tan are the most popular; the latter are antiqued for further embellishment. The very gaudy boot—orange, purple, chartreuse, etc.—is called a bull rider's boot, and the wearing of the same is an affectation on the part of the young riders in this event. Red, green, and dark blue are used in combination with the above colors and also in combination with each other. However, boots of a more colorful nature are for dress only, and, if they do appear in the arena, they are second best and are being worn out.

Another distinctive part of cowboy apparel is the hat. There are really two models—the low-crown and the high-crown types. The crowns vary in height from five and one-half inches to seven and one-half inches; the brims range from two and seven-eighths inches to five and one-half inches in width, and they are bound or raw-edged. The measurements of crowns and brims are peculiar to the styles of hats and there are numerous styles of the two models. After the hat has been worn for a time, it takes on the shape desired by the wearer. The hats, trimmed with one-, two-, three-, four-, and five-cord crown bands of braided leather and silk, may be had in black, bisque, buckskin, chocolate brown, Sudan Brown, Belgian Belly, Silver Belly and white. It is possible to tell from what section of the country the wearer comes by noting the type of crease in the crown of his hat. The cowboys from the Southwest, and particularly from Texas, affect a certain type of crease, while those from Wyoming and the Northwest have a different type. Many cowboys take pride in the distinctive way in which they crease their crowns, and this has become almost a trade mark with such men as Doff Aber, Jerry Ambler, Fritz Truan, and Carl Dossey—they all have especially distinctive styles.

Both spurs and chaps are a part of the contestants costume in his work. These two pieces of equipment are not common to all contestants, especially the chaps, which are worn usually by the bronc and bull riders and not by ropers or steer wrestlers. The spur is more essential for the cowboy who rides, while the chap is not a necessity.

Some rodeos require the bronc riding contestants to wear chaps, spurs, and a big hat; but the use of chaps at present is, more or less, an embellishment for the ride; merely adding more color and more action by flapping. Some men are in agreement that chaps aid in gripping the saddle with the legs, while others maintain that there is nothing to that theory and that they are purely decorative. All agree, however, that in case of falls, the chaps do protect the legs from bruises and burns.

Chaps are made from selected, clear and unblemished cowhides, which are costly. They may be had in many colors, such as cream, smoke, pearl, brown, and black; they are richly decorated in contrasting colors of various scroll designs such as: styled floral patterns, diamond, square, circular forms, and other geometric shapes. The belt-like band at the top of the garment is usually a decorative piece of tooled leather. Silver and nickel conchas, as well as tie conchas, add to the appearance of the wings. Chaps are cut short or long-waisted and are equipped with what is known as the "Cheyenne Leg," that is, the leather is cut away at the inside of the ankle. The type of chaps worn by the contestant is a personal selection, and there are many types from which one may choose.

The spur is one of the most interesting and characteristic pieces of the costume of the cowboy but is less conspicious. Many men take off their spurs when they are not at work; however, in the presence of groups of cowboys, one is usually conscious of an almost bell-like tinkle. The spur runs the entire gamut of artistic expression, from severe simplicity to a richly-chased design—jewel-like studies of pure silver overlay. A study of the rowel type is very fascinating. The use of sharply pointed rowels is forbidden at contests, but one may see innumerable shapes and sizes worn by men who are not contesting. Spurs are made of such metals as stainless steel, which is often overlaid with sterling silver, of hand forged aluminum, airplane metal, duraluminum, and silver steel. The heel band, heel strap buttons, and the shanks have elaborate and very decorative chasing. The selection of the type of spur to be used is one of personal preference. The bronc rider's spur is a very special item; he has difficulty in finding a pair that is exactly right in fit and balance. When such a pair is found, it is the rider's dearest possession. If a rider loses his spurs, he loses much of his confidence, for a good pair is very valuable to the contestant in action. Pete Grubb, formerly a bronc rider, lost his spurs and for two years after won very little in contests. A bronc rider is more careful of his spurs than he is of his money.

Bronc riders' spurs have various shank lengths which depend upon the individual wearing them. Some use four-, five-, and ten-point rowels, while others use the double-pointed rowel. Spurs are heavy or light in weight, depending on the need of the individual wearer. The bronc rider ties down his spurs to keep them rigid and in position, and every rider has his own peculiar way of doing this. Peculiar inventions have been devised to accomplish this; sometimes chain, wire, leather, and even string are used.

The calf roper uses a spur much lighter in weight, and it is not tied down to the boot. This allows greater freedom of action in spurring his horse to a quicker pace, in order to bring the contestant closer to the running calf.

CHAPTER XI

RODEO FOLKS

He follows the circuit and works the shows,
He's a hard-workin', square-shootin' pal;
Night time comes round an' he's all dressed up,
Lookin' for a sweet-smellin' gal!

How strenuous a life does the cowboy lead and how does it affect him? To answer this question one hundred leading performers were contacted, and the responses as to whether or not they thought their work would shorten their lives were over 90 per cent in the negative. Further investigation reveals that, in consideration of their hazardous occupation, it is surprising how few men meet death because of serious injuries sustained. Although broken bones of every nature, concussion, bad cuts, and bruises are daily happenings to these people, the injuries are rarely serious enough to incapacitate them for a very long period of time.

In the types of injuries received by the cowboy, the case history of any one individual runs the gamut of broken arms, legs, collar-bones, wrists, and ankles; head injuries, knocked-out teeth, and injuries to the eyes, nose, and ears are of the more common occurrence. Nevertheless, there are individuals who have worked in this precarious business for years, and their injuries were no more serious than those that might happen to a less-active person. Therefore, one might conclude, as in any type of work of a similar nature, that some men are more fortunate than others, and some are constantly in line for the series of "bad breaks" that this sport offers.

However, as on the stage, the show must go on. For this reason, the conduct of the performers makes some of their actions appear to the casual observer as feats of foolhardiness; however, it is a conduct that is characteristic of these people and does not spring from any self-sacrificing illusion or false bravado. Often a cowboy who is injured early in a contest is treated at once and he appears in several succeeding performances. One seldom attends a rodeo where one does not see several men limping about, with knees bandaged, ankles encased in plaster casts, shoulders strapped, arms and wrists in slings; and yet, these men carry on their part as active members, at least to the extent that their injured capacities will permit them.

Another characteristic that is especially obvious among the cowboys of rodeo is the concern about any one of their members who has been hurt. There is no unusual display of sympathy or feeling, but these boys are known to be good to "their own." Every care and comfort, the best medical attention are provided for the injured man, not only to alleviate the suffering, but also to help disperse the gloom of the sick room, and the financial business worries of the patient. An injured cowboy's friends take care of his interests, his horse, and equipment; they put his house in order before moving on to the next show and they try to leave the injured man in the good hands of interested friends in the particular city where the accident occurred.

It has been a policy of the managers of reliable rodeos to supply medical aid for contestants at performances. However, this is in the nature of first aid and, usually, does not include hospitalization; although in many contests of size, this policy of medical care is extended to include the latter service. This is not an obligation on the part of contest managers, but the practice is now becoming very wide spread, and there are sound reasons to believe that eventually it will be rule rather than exception. Many kind deeds are done by the cowboys in helping one of their less fortunate comrades out of a serious "spot." A collection made among the men for such an occasion is not uncommon, thus many an injured cowboy has been relieved of the worries that come with a protracted illness.

The rodeo cowboy has, through years of experience, learned to take care of his injuries and although there is some evidence of carelessness in this respect, on the whole, he is conscious of the fact that sane treatment and care will put him back in active duty much sooner. There was a time when, because of carelessness, the aftermath of his injuries resulted in more serious complications than the original illness. Secondary infection was an almost expected occurrence; the cowboys who did escape this very often worried because of it. The cowboy of rodeo has lost his distrust of the medical profession that was characteristic of his earlier counterpart on the range.[1] Although some of the early practices in medicine left much to be desired, the doctors, in taking care of the injured cowboy, always had better results than some of the home remedies

---

[1] Because the cowboys often did not take care of their injuries, secondary infection would set in. This came to be such a common occurrence that unless it did take place it caused wonder.

that were used. The present-day cowboy realizes that, with proper medical aid, he has a greater chance for a speedier recovery and less danger of serious complications than formerly. He returns for treatment and dressings faithfully and follows the directions of the doctor; he is less likely to turn to the various remedies recommended by those sympathetic but misleading "understanding" friends who are found in every walk of life. However, too many cowboys still fail to take proper care of sprains, bruises, influenza or, in fact, any illness or injury that leaves them active enough to "dodge" the doctor.

In the story of the rodeo cowboy there is also that very interesting personality—the wife of the contestant. These women, "rodeo wives," have made rodeo a part of their lives and follow this arduous existence wherever the work of their husbands may take them. The wives of rodeo cowboys, in most cases, are women who are thrilled by this type of life. For the most part, they are young women, utterly devoted to the sport. They realize that they are in an enviable position, one that offers an opportunity for excitement, travel, and an element of publicity; in general, it is a life which they enjoy.

These rodeo wives come from various economic and social levels. Among them are college graduates, writers, former employees of industry, dancers, teachers, secretaries, clerks, as well as country girls — sweethearts of boyhood days. In the women who have married rodeo cowboys, one is impressed by a certain well-bred, lady like, and gentle spirit. They have no starry-eyed illusions about the men they have married, they do not look upon them as knights in silver armor, nor as the romantic figures of the West who have been exploited in much of our Western literature; they do not expect these men to grow "dreamy-eyed" at their approach. This is interesting because they usually receive every courtesy and kindness from their husbands.

Because rodeo work causes these women to move rapidly from city to city and from town to town, most of their friends are the wives of the other cowboys. The majority of these women are not contestants, such as ropers, riders, or contract performers with the rodeo, and their efforts toward making a semblance of home-like atmosphere for their husbands is doubly difficult because of this constant change in abode. When they are traveling in the West during the summer rodeo season, those who live in trailers, tourists camps, and tents make a sincere and worthy effort to make this shifting existence as home-like as possible. When they go east, especially to the New York and Boston Shows of two and three weeks' duration, some take furnished apartments and continue their domestic activities. Others, on this occasion, especially those who have lived in trailers and tourist camps, take these five weeks as a vacation and live in hotels and are relieved of their regular household duties.

In general, the women who have married rodeo cowboys are not necessarily dazzling beauties, but attractive, well-groomed and genuinely sincere examples of American womanhood from every part of the country. They have a wholesome, feminine interest in lovely clothes and show excellent taste. They are fond of such sports as baseball, football, horse racing, and naturally have a very deep interest in rodeo. The majority of the wives of rodeo cowboys rarely miss a performance and, because of this constant attendance and their close relation with the sport, they are shrewd observers of every part of the business. They have a remarkable power of judgment and their observations are usually correct. They, like their husbands, have little time for that which is false or misleading. Because of a more or less informal atmosphere in their living, they have attained a certain sense of freedom of thought, action, and of courage that is most admirable.

The wives of the members of the Cowboys' Turtle Association have formed a social organization, known as the Rodeo Club. The club was first proposed and organized by Marie Messinger (formerly Mrs. Doff Aber) and meets twice a year, usually during the late winter at the show held at Fort Worth and during the Cheyenne Frontier Days Celebration at Cheyenne in July. This organization has given rodeo wives a splendid opportunity to become familiar with a group of women who are interested in and sympathetic toward one another, and, in addition, have that common interest in the work of their husbands.

The general public is of the opinion that the children of rodeo people are necessarily neglected because of the difficulties in this type of life. This is as ridiculous and untrue as some of the other false impressions of rodeo. Rodeo parents strive to give their children every attention and consideration. Besides, there are many advantages in such a life for children; an outdoor life most of the year in sunshine and healthful Western climate — away from crowded, dirt-begrimed cities; and good food, for which rodeo folks are famous. The children of the contestants are usually remarkable youngsters. Although rodeo life may be considered an unusual one for children, it can not be accused of being harmful to them. On the contrary, acquaintance with and observation of "rodeo youngsters" show that they are not only fine children, but also that they have acquired many characteristics that are most desired in children. Instead of being spoiled by the attention that is showered upon them—for the men and women in rodeo, although many are childless, have a deep affection for children—rodeo youngsters are remarkably level-headed.

It is true, they may lack the companionship of other youngsters which is part of every stationary community, but they do have a part in their parents' life which few children, under ordinary circumstances, have the privilege of sharing. There is a refreshing youthfulness beyond words, about "Mr. and Mrs. Contestant" in which they partake. Between parents and children exist not only the ties of family devotion, but also companionship, which is so very essential. This is a fine relationship in the rodeo family and is not always found in families not subject to the same circumstances.

This close family relationship and this sincere trust are due, in most part, to the women, who have loved these men well enough to marry them and follow them in this unusual life. One has great admiration for the fears, the thoughts, and reactions that must come over them and rouse their emotions when they witness the dangers which their husbands face during each performance. Either they lull the worries to rest, or because of the frequent occurrence of them, they consciously do not show any undue response during an exhibition, or in the case of sudden unfortunate accidents. It appears almost that, with time, there comes an attitude of philosophical resignation to any turn of events.

In conclusion, one might say that the man in rodeo is a hard-working individual who has chosen an unusual profession. This is a work that demands a strong body and heart, a keen eye and mind, no fear, no recklessness, a love for man and beast, a love for competition and fair play. He has raised his profession to one of dignity and usefulness; he has made it a form of entertainment for hundreds of thousands; a successful business for himself; and has given it an honesty of sportsmanship that should be indicative of this first and true American sport.

The past years of strife and stress were difficult for rodeo and many gaps appeared in the ranks of those who have been a part of this American tradition. Because the man of rodeo is only a youth, he was called upon to serve his country; because the man of rodeo has always been a free man, he went willingly to preserve freedom not only for himself, but for his fellow Americans; and because the man of rodeo began his career during the perils of war, he will now distinguish himself by riding forth again toward this new adventure with conviction, courage, and fearlessness.

Part II

BEAST

Beast, the servant of man . . .

ₒₚ

CHAPTER XII

THE INVADERS

The trails are covered with a thick, dark crust,
Thirst-stirring, sight-blinding, dry, parched dust. . . .

It was high noon. From the sky the sun washed the land with a fiery bath and reduced everything it touched to an endless repetition of form and monotony. The dust-covered lizard flattened itself to seek shelter under a protecting ledge of stone. The hare sought the thickest clump of mesquite to watch with lifeless fascination the infinite stream of red ants that moved back and forth in the shadow of a twig and transported, in portions, the bruised body of a deer-fly, crushed in the passing of the herd. The struggles of the helpless locust, caught fast in a spider web, failed to bring the fierce architect from the depths of a scarred cactus stump. Blinding in its intensity and searing in its touch, the sun drew veils of vapor from the earth and bedecked the heaven with mystical, fleeting forms. Studding the sky like jewels of jet, appeared, wheeling and soaring, great birds of shiny black; proudly they moved in the endless circle of their flight with a foreordained knowledge of their quest. With lustered eyes they looked down upon the slender, moving column, wending its way through the pathless waste stretching to the horizon.

Led by Men of God, this procession of three hundred left, some thirty leagues behind, the security and comfort of the peaceful pueblos of an ancient race. Moving westward, they approached the high mesa and the foothills of the barrier, which, foreboding and ominous, lay recumbent as some massive skeleton of prehistoric origin.

Following the Men of the Cross, rode others, with a purpose no less intent, for they were the Men of War, some garbed in the soft, rich, fabrics of the East, but now sodden and stained with perspiration of labor; others in suits of mail now dulled by a thin coat of dust. With unfaltering ambition they drove their beasts onward to the interior. The mournful lowing of the cattle, the clatter of horn against horn, the squeak of sweat-stained, dry leather, the clash of steel against steel, the groan of laboring man and beast—all added further confusion to the misery and desolation of the scene. Thus came the Children of the Sun to the land of the Southwest.

Pushing ever forward, day after day, hour after hour, they sought the riches of a fruitful but unyielding country; they sought the souls of a savage, determined, and masterful people. Every hour the sun, with its scorching breath, so seared the earth that the horizon before man and beast moved in a pulsing rhythm. Through an occasional movement of the air, hoof-churned soil clouded upward into great plumes, settled again and reduced the freshness of the landscape into a colorless haze. The lifeless banners of these Invaders leaped forward in a gay dance; then, exhausted, collapsed and strangled their supports in dust-smothered folds.

Excitement prevailed in the ranks as one four-footed invader fell and attempted to struggle to its feet. It floundered helplessly; then the flashing rays of the sun on the merciful blade of steel ended the torture of the foot-weary, thirsty beast. The dust-caked nostrils, distended for the smell of water, contracted with the first welling of blood, gushing from the severed throat. The eyes grew glazed as the great horns pitched the lolling head into the soil. High above the wings ceased their rhythm to balance as if suspended; their widening circle grew ever narrower, as they drifted silently down to the earth.

Again the column moved forward. The towering facade of the plateau in the distance, with its ever widening strip of shade, beckoned to the weary travelers. Water, forage, rest, and shade would be the prize for those surviving the ordeal. Tomorrow would take them into the high and cooler lands. Tomorrow would bring them the cities of gold, the mines, the treasurers, both spiritual and material. But Tomorow never came, for out of this haven of rest swept hordes of painted devils. They came with a clash of flint against steel, and the twang of bow strings humming a message of death; they were met with the thunder of three hundred arquebuses; they left amid the screams of hamstrung horses floundering about in grotesque patterns; the milling, careening and maddened steers impaled one another on their horns. The stampeding beasts swept out into a great arc and moved, as in a wave, to the plains. Dust, Destruction and Death were everywhere.

Man after man was dragged from his horse; armor was pierced with flint-tipped and feather-studded shafts; bodies, crumpling under the weight of falling horses, were bludgeoned, as the demons from the highlands beat the invaders into the soil. Coming, one swarm after another, their number so vast in the eyes of the attacked, they added to the confusion and fury unleashed by them. The savage onslaught took an appalling toll of both invader and defender. Survivors, able to flee the scene of carnage and savagery, fell from sheer exhaustion to lie wondering dazedly about their fate. They were ill from months of privation and hardship, they were hunted and wounded, their fate was sealed, for the vast expanse of a vicious land would take its toll.

The onslaught lessened in its fierceness, and the attackers returned to their camps to lick their wounds; yet they left a scene of desolation, typical of what was to follow for three centuries after the meeting of white man and aboriginal of this land. Smouldering wagons, debris, both animal and human, scattered in all directions; riderless horses, racing madly to and fro, returned hours later to seek their slain masters. At some distance stood small groups of cattle, cropping here and there at what ever was left of the forage after the torch had been applied. With the passing of time, some wandered from the scene of the massacre and moved from one feeding ground to another; others were driven in herds to the camps of the hill people. Horses, escaping the bloody affray, were wary of the savage and did not return, but took to their new freedom.

The heat of the day passed, as did that of the battle. The cool breeze of the highlands wafted from the summits the spicy odors of pine and hemlock, brought also the darkness of wet earth and stone, the freshness of a rushing mountain stream, as if to cover with the sweet incense of nature the dastardly deeds of man.

From under the still warm stone a lizard scurried forth with the quick, startled movements associated with creatures of the soil. The late afternoon shadows sent the scampering, nervous creature to seek protection in a still warm and blood-smeared helmet. Beady eyes gleamed, a forked tongue flicked the fly gorging itself with blood—another battle was won. The wail of the coyote, the stamping of a horse, restless for his master to rise and ride again, sent forth a startled hare; already the endless stream of tiny red ants had started their trek; the gauzy wing of a locust, caught fast on a spider web, moved gently with the fresh breeze of evening. Silently, ever so silently, from the sky came with a muffled softness the great lords of the air. With drooping heads and wings they approached the ghastly mess with a waddling gait.

The shadows lengthened as the bowl of the sky filled with the tender light of dusk. A flash of lightening in the East heralded the coming of night, which moved in on swift wings to soften the scene and complete the final struggle of natural forces. Thus came and passed the Invader.

CHAPTER XIII

THE FLEET ONES

Wild and unfettered,
Fleet-winged in their pace,
Proud heads held high,
Over prairies they race.

The era of Spanish-American occupation of the Southwest made many contributions to the development of this area. Of these, horses and cattle, the forerunners of the modern beasts of this country, were the most influential and most important. The significance of these two important contributions is obvious when one considers that the Western cattle industry was dependent upon both.

The cattle industry, certainly one of the momentous developments of this section of the country, gave the West those characteristics peculiar to it, so that the explorer, trader, trapper, missionary, miner and land-seeker, although significant, were but a passing incident of their time. Except for the last two mentioned, they left no indelible imprint on the land, animals, and inhabitants as did this truly American industry. When one thinks of the West, thoughts of breath-taking mountain scenery, of great expanses of land, of large ranches with great herds of cattle and spirited horses, and of the romance of the cowboy hold a prominent place in the mind. The Western scenic beauty, the mountains, plains, deserts, ranches, and towns make up the stage-setting; the horses, cattle, and men are the actors. Together, they created the outstanding drama of the nineteenth century of this country. So unique a drama, so vital a drama could not pass with time from this earthly stage because of the changes that come with the natural development of the new country.

The songs and poems of the West are primarily of the participants of this industry and rarely of the trader, trapper, and land seeker. The romance of this era, so varied in its interpretation, has been a source of cultural expression not only in the land itself but throughout the world.

Thus the horse and the cow, left as our heritage by the early Spanish conquerors, were factors that made possible the industry so indicative of the West. With the coming of the Spanish explorers to this hemisphere, the horse was recognized as an essential part of the expeditions. As a means of conveyance and transportation he was most adaptable to the unexplored regions which the Spanish wished to contact. The importance of cattle, as a means of supplying beef to the marching armies, was also realized, and, in all probability, cattle were imported almost as early as horses. Together, they were destined to form the nucleus from which our livestock industry has grown.

There are innumerable tales of how the stocking of this country took place. The bases of operation, those early Mexican settlements, used for the series of expeditoins that carried the Spanish throughout the entire Southwest, were of an early founding. The settlements also acted as bases of supplies from the mother country, and of these supplies the horse and a beef herd were not of secondary importance. It is not improbable that the beginnings of the wild herds of cattle and horses came from the animals that had escaped or wandered from the corrals or grazing herds on the settlements. Also, it is not improbable that the thieving Indian had a hand in the dispersion of the animals throughout the country. Raiding the Spanish cattlemen, the Indian took many of the animals into the interior. The attacks on invading armies by hostile savages also had the tendency to disperse the beef herds and thus increased the opportunity for the growth of isolated wild herds. There is also the story that the Spanish, wishing to stock the country, set free cattle and horses for this express purpose. How these two types of animals secured a foothold in this country is not an essential part of this story, but the fact that they were here and existed in great numbers at the beginning of the eighteenth century is of significance. Both types were adaptable to the climate at their point of induction, both thrived and reproduced in great numbers and thus made it possible for the industry to come into existence. The fact that both were introduced to this hemisphere approximately at the same time is significant. Had there been no cattle, it is obvious that the industry, as we know it, would never have developed. Had there been no horses, the existence of cattle and the development of this industry would have presented difficulties, which could not have been readily solved.

The use of the horse by man made the human being capable of mastering the cow of the plains. With the help of the horse man became stronger, swifter, and more daring than the cattle; he became master of the wild herds. Only with the help of the horse was man able to garner unto himself this wealth on hoof and command it.

The use of the horse as a means of transportation had allowed the Spanish to make extensive explorations, the coming of the horse to this hemisphere, and certainly to the Southwest, changed the mode of life of the native population. The hunter, formerly a man on foot, now became a swift moving threat to the animal, as well as to human life. The white man, aided by the horse, changed his status from that of a hunter to that of a cattleman.

The horse that the Spanish introduced to the Southwest was of the same breed that the invading Moors took to Spain. The horse, bred on the desert wastes of Northern Africa, had, through centuries of breeding in that dry, waterless, hot, and unkind climate, acquired certain qualities of endurance, ruggedness, wildness, and speed. This Moorish-Spanish horse of the cattle country found here the same elements peculiar to its land of birth—the rugged topography, the severe climatic changes, the parched, dry grass. Thus the beast continued its natural course of evolution until the middle of the nineteenth century when it was bred with the horse brought from the eastern part of this country. The establishing of horse ranches and the breeding of this wild animal with Eastern stock became an important occupation after the Civil War.

The distribution of horses in the West is of great interest in the study of rodeo because, while it is true that the appearance of horses on this hemisphere is found in Mexico, they moved up through Texas and became firmly entrenched in the Southwest. There is a divergence in the type from the time of the introduction of the beast until it became the horse of the cattle industry. Again, climatic conditions and environment brought about this change. The horse that moved from the point of induction northward into Texas, New Mexico, Arizona, and Colorado remained more constant to the type introduced into this country. In this section, that is, the eastern side of the mountains, the environmental conditions, as a whole, were the same. There is evidence that the horse moved from its original home northward, west of the Continental Divide into California. Here the animal met with conditions to which it was accustomed, but, upon migrating farther north, the type of horse changed because of the environment. The fertile, moist areas, with an abundance of forage, in Oregon, Washington, and part of Idaho, along with the severe winters in the interior and highlands, brought about a change in type. The wiry, hardy, and unmanageable beast, swift of foot and with the phenomenal endurance of the animals of the Southwest, lost some of these characteristics in its migration to the Northwest. The horse became a compact, huskier beast and not so rangy in build. Actually, however, there were no great differences in ability between the horses of the Northwest and the Southwest because of their common origin.

The horse of the North, known as the "cayuse," was practically the same horse of the South, the cowhorse. The name "broncho," which was applied to the unmanageable horse of the Southwest, is of Spanish origin. However, the term "broncho" has been applied to all Western horses that have bucking tendencies and it is no longer used only for those of the Southwest.

The horse of the West was bred with the American Trotter, Thoroughbred, or the Arabian horse. These breeds, still known as "bronchos," are more commonly called "cow ponies," because they are used in herding and driving cattle on the ranches and the ranges.

The original horse brought to this country was, in truth, a pony, if one considers the classification of size. All equines, fourteen hands two inches or under, are classed as pony breeds. They are characterized by a close, full-made quality. Their ruggedness is unique and is obvious in the muscular development and in the unusual bone development. The ponies had a distinct appearance; having lived the life of shifting for themselves in a land of hardship, they developed a range of abilities, rare among horses. They were sure-footed, fearless, and less scary of unknown objects; their faculties were more developed than those of the domesticated animal. The marked superiority in the constitution of the ponies was also attributed to their environment. They had better feet, legs, and wind; they could stand more hardship; they were not so susceptible to disease; they recovered more rapidly from fatigue; and they lived longer.

The western horse faced three enemies that did much to deplete the size of the herds. The first of these was the ever threatening menace, man. Whether red or white, man was a real danger; with all his faculties he worked to ensnare the wild horse and to become its master. Various methods, used to capture the beasts were: the use of the lariat, running them by means of relay until exhausted, various enclosure systems, such as blind canyons, ravines, dug pits, and corals. Firearms to "crease" the victim were also employed and often with fatal results.

A second enemy, and one just as dangerous as the first, was the predatory animals that preyed upon the wild horse. The cougar, grizzly bear, black bear, and timber wolf brought down their share of this wild horseflesh. With this group is classed the rattlesnake whose bite was fatal to the horse. The third enemy was found in forces of nature—severe climatic changes, blizzards of sleet and snow, blinding electrical storms, deep snow, floods and drought, poison streams, waterholes, bogs and quicksand.

Horses running wild under these conditions became capable beasts. Shifting for themselves, always on guard against enemies, they developed self-reliance, senses more acute, actions more resourceful and adroit. The severity of this existence made them aware of their problems and by trial and error they had to solve them. The hardship of being surrounded day and and night by danger and by severe and changing climate, allowed only the horses of endurance and natural agility, the horses of virility and strength, to survive.

At the beginning of this century the wild horse that had roamed this land was becoming scarce. It was possible now to travel days and only occasionally see a horse of this type. "Now (1901) not a mustang can be found in a day's travel, or a week's, and only an infrequent jack breaks in on the monotony of a desert ride. Ten years ago two hundred thousand mustangs were scattered over the ranges in Texas, New Mexico, and Arizona."[1] More than a century ago Captain Pike, in the year 1806, moving westward into the lands which are now parts of Oklahoma, Kansas, and Colorado, relates of the great bands of horses seen on every side.

It was the vastness of numbers that had made the horse an intruding factor, and for his intrusion he was often wantonly destroyed. The cowman, anxious to preserve what little feed he had for his stock, destroyed the

---

[1] "The Vanishing Mustang," *Current Literature* 30, (May 1901), 616.

mustang. Because he existed in great numbers, the mustang became a pest. The traveler on his horse was always in danger of losing his mount when he turned it loose for the night. There was always the danger of having his beast lured away by the bands of wild horses that came close to camp. The gentle, domesticated horse, upon coming in contact with the wild ones of his kind, overcame all restraint and fled. An attempt to recover him from this new-found freedom was considered useless.

One of the causes for the rapid disappearance of the wild horse, as expressed by observers of the time, was the fact that many thousands of ponies of the desert were surreptiously converted into canned beef and were served over Eastern tables and in army messes as the finest beef of the range.

The Western horse cannot be ignored as a contributing force in the development of the West. He was of paramount importance as a means of conveyance of the first army expeditions into the interior. He carried trapper, trader, and landseeker to regions previously inaccessible. He was essential in the first form of communication, the Pony Express, in linking together the frontier communities with the world. As a part of the cattle industry the Western horse was indispensable; he made the industry possible and set the scale by which it was carried on. With the decline of the range cattle industry in the nineties the frontier came to a close; still the Western horse was essential as a part of this industry which was carried on in a reduced area. The early man of the West owes his many achievements and successes to the wild horse of the West.

Today, although great bands of wild horses are no longer in existence, a few straggling herds are to be found.

On the rough and untenable plateaus of Wyoming, the
desert wastes of Arizona, and the mountain regions of
Idaho, Nevada, Utah, and New Mexico, one can occasionally see these sure-footed, swift, hardy horses. Their domain, which extended at one time from the Mississippi to
the West Coast and from Mexico up beyond the Canadian
Border, has shrunk; however, they are still their own
masters and lords of their land.

The Western horse made a very fine cowhorse during
the early days, but some sixty years ago the cattlemen and
stockmen began to import blooded-horses from Europe
and from the East Coast. The breeding of these refined
strains with the Western horse introduced to the West
some excellent horseflesh. The mustang was brought under
control by the breeder and horse fancier who pastured
the beasts in great enclosures, where they were allowed to
roam year after year. To this group of fence-broken horses
were introduced the blooded animals. As the years passed,
there appeared here and there a very fine example of their
crossbreeding, and every year the herds of enclosed mustangs began to show this blood.

The horse used in rodeo for the events of calf roping,
steer wrestling, and for general riding purposes by the cowboys is, for the most part, one that has been bred for speed.
Known as the Quarter Horse,[1] he is often referred to by
those who admire and appreciate his abilities as the "short
horse." The Quarter Horse, although he is often thought
of as a new breed, is one of the oldest horse types in this

---

[1] The Quarter Hourse was bred to run a quarter mile. ". . . there is about
as much resemblance between the pure Quarter Horse and an ordinary
cow-horse as there is between the Arabian and an Indian Pony." Denhardt, Robert M., "Quarter Hourse," (cited hereafter as Denhardt, "Quarter Horse.") *The Western Horseman* 5 (November-December 1940), 5.

country. Actually, the "short horse," as a breed, was discarded early in the nineteenth century when there was a greater demand for animals that could run a longer distance. The horse that was developed for greater distance is the world-renowned Thoroughbred.

Previous to the nineteenth century, during the American Colonial Period and the establishment of the Federal Government, racing in this country was not of the long-distance type. The aspects of the countryside were not suited to this particular phase of the sport of racing. At that time there were no cleared areas, no circular and oval tracks, and long distance races were impractical. Not until the beginning of the nineteenth century did this type of racing become popular, and not until fifty years later did the longest of all American races, the four-mile heat, reach its height in popular demand.

Thus, Quarter Horse racing was a colonial specialty, and there is evidence that quarter-mile racing was a popular sport in the South, especially in Virginia, at the end of the seventeenth century.

> Today when many Thoroughbred breeders are asked what a "short horse" is, they reply that he is just a bastard Thoroughbred. This, however, is not the whole truth, nor is it satisfactory. . . . Also it is no more true than if the same adjective were applied to the Morgan or American Saddle Horse, or the Standard Breed, and it could be just as well. When you stop to think about it, how many light breeds do not carry Thoroughbred blood?[1]

---

[1] Denhardt, "Quarter Horses, etc." *The Western Horseman* 7, 14.

The "short horse" lost its importance as the earliest American racing steed when the country settled and developed a taste for racing of longer distance. Because the Quarter Horse had some advocates, he was not allowed to become extinct. On the frontier and because a few of his intense admirers realized his importance as a contributing factor to the Western way of life, especially on the range, he was invaluable and his breed was preserved.

The Quarter Horse has been from the first a using horse—a horse that has been owner-bred, owner-raised, owner-trained and owner raced. His utility has not been confined to the track, and that is probably the reason for some of his weaknesses as a running horse. For some 300 years he has pulled stumps, planted cotton, headed cattle, and walked over the plantations six days a week and been raced on the seventh.[1]

The Quarter Horse is still the fastest short-distance horse in the world and is an excellent performer on the short track, the ranch, and in the rodeo arena. For quick starting, speed, and turning he is first among horses. With the added abilities of intelligent action and coolness of head he has become the ideal horse for the riders in the roping and steer wrestling events.

For several years stock magazines have been taking up the cause of the Quarter Horse, and one in particular, *The Western Horseman,* has been a great force in encouraging the breeders of this horse to continue in the work. Through the publication of articles on the Quarter Horse, *The Western Horseman* has been able to interest many people of California, Oregon, and Washington in the

---

[1] Denhardt, "Quarter Horses, etc." *The Western Horseman* 7, 14.

breed. Before this display of interest, the Quarter Horse was bred more extensively in the states of New Mexico, Oregon, Texas, and Colorado.

Today, the Quarter Horse is known best by the public as the horse used by the rodeo contestant. Fortunately, this splendid animal with his many capabilities, natural intelligence, and ability to be trained, has been ridden by the finest of America's riders, the rodeo cowboy.

The few early records in existence have been left by William Anson of Christoval, Texas. He did much to give a clue to the origin and characteristics of this horse by leaving notes which extend through the last half of the nineteenth century and into the beginning of the twentieth century. Dan Casement, Manhattan, Kansas, has added considerable information to the knowledge of the Quarter Horse. More recently, the attention of the public has been drawn to the breed by the splendid work of Jack Casement, son of Dan, and Robert M. Denhardt, College Station, Texas. Both these men have been contributing splendid articles on the Quarter Horse to several magazines, including *The Western Horseman, American Hereford Journal* and *The Cattleman*. Mr. Robert M. Denhardt has edited a book, concerning this horse, and in it he compiled the notes of William Anson.

Several successful efforts, made to obtain official recognition of the status of the Quarter Horse as a breed, show that it has not only been important for many years but is now being appreciated in breeding circles. In the spring of 1939, at the Southwestern Exposition and Fat Stock Show, Fort Worth, Texas, the first serious discussion of a Quarter Horse Association took place. During March, 1940, the American Quarter Horse Association was organized, and the following year brought forth Volume I, Number I issue of the *Quarter Horse Stud Book*. During the 1942 meeting of the American Stallion Registration Board at Chicago it was recommended and accepted that the Quarter Horse in the future be given the status of a recognized breed. Thus, to the Quarter Horse has been restored, and justly so, its place of honor among American horses of blood.

During the evolution of breeding, the Western horse lost none of its superior qualities of stamina and it improved in appearance. Among the many peculiarities of the animal, bucking or pitching was one which crossbreeding seemed to emphasize rather than eradicate. To bring these horses into such a position that they might become a part of the stock horses of a ranch, a "parada" was used. This consisted of a herd of horses, seventy-five or more, broken to the saddle, and managed by a few riders hiding at their sides. The group of wild horses was moved into this "parada," and together they were driven toward a high-walled corral of cottonwood poles. From this corralled group a selection was made for the riding stock of the ranch. Then the fate of the beast rested in the hands of man. The fact is that both beast and man faced a furious battle for supremacy, and during the next few days it was foolhardiness on the part of the gambler to call the winner. The beasts were, first and foremost, living in fear of the unknown, and this fear made them vicious. This was more desperate, because of the battle they already had faced in their existence, and the instinct of survival became very strong!

The breaking of young horses on the ranches usually took place during the summer months after the spring round-ups. This work was first carried on by the cowboys of the ranches, and no better men could be found than those closely associated with the horse ranches, but as the work took on a character of importance relative to the cattle industry, there appeared some riders of exceptional ability. In their districts they acquired the reputation of being proficient in this hazardous occupation. As their reputations as bronc "busters" grew, their services were in demand, and they were requested by the horse-ranchers to do this work. With these men this dangerous profession became a business, and eventually they began to work under contract, that is, they were paid a certain sum for each horse broken for riding. The position of the bronc "buster" placed the men in a class by themselves, as gifted and skilled technicians they were known throughout the cattle industry.

The work of breaking horses for riding did not mean that after the beast had been subjected to many humiliations he was safe to ride. A horse ridden three or four times was considered broken, but actually this horse never lost his tendency or desire to "let loose" with a few jumps and twists, even after he had been ridden for years.

The treatment received during the system of breaking might or might not ruin the temper of the horse. This ordeal, more often than not, left the horse with a hatred for and an eternal grudge against his master. Among the early professional riders of broncs were Mexicans and Negros, as well as riders from among the cowboys of the ranches. The Mexicans had a certain reputation for cruelty, and, as the business grew, their use as "busters" was discouraged. No matter what might be said of this work, it was a cruel business. Unfortunately, this cruelty was more pronounced because the time element in breaking a horse was important. The Western horse could have been brought to saddle with less trouble and ill-will on the part of both the beast and the rider, if he had been given greater consideration. This business, that is, the breaking of so many horses within a contracted time, often rushed the process, and the result was an increasing of the bad temper of both man and beast.

Plunging, kicking, stamping, biting, snorting, twisting, and whirling, the horses showed fear and fought against it. They used every known means to rid themselves of their two-legged menace. Often they had struggled against the cougar, bear, or wolf on the plains or highlands; now they were confronted not only with a similar danger, but a superior intellect, not based on instinct, but on human cunning, endurance and persistence. The lords of the plains fought a good battle for their freedom, they destroyed many of their conquerors with their flying heels and mad gyrations, but following this battle, another conqueror was ready to step forward and continue the struggle. Unlike the beaten beast, the cowboy did not turn away to sulk and lick his wounds, but rather he returned to finish his job. If this became impossible, another man was there to carry on for him. The cause of the beast was lost. This struggle for supremacy between man and beast is portrayed in the bucking bronc contests of modern rodeo.

CHAPTER XIV

THE HORNED ONES

At last he was subdued,
The Longhorn, mighty in his span,
His reign on the range was ended,
Extinguished by the hand of man.

The cattle brought by the Spanish during their conquest of the Southwest were of the long-horned type and were the progenitors of the Texas Longhorn found in this part of the country during the middle of the nineteenth century. They were the earliest "race" of cattle to inhabit our Western ranges and undoubtedly came into the country by crossing the Rio Grande from Mexico and then spread through all of Texas. The herds were more numerous in Texas and Oklahoma at first, then gradually moved into New Mexico and Arizona. The Southwest was their home and was to remain so until their extermination. The country was broader and rougher for roving than the land farther north and west.

The Texas Longhorn had certain qualities which enabled it to flourish in the wild state. The long-horned, long-legged, narrow-hipped species of cattle, having only the minimum of food and water of the Southwest for subsistence, was able to continue its existence during the times of severe drought when the stricken pastures of the West would have meant death to a less hardy beast. These cattle, equipped with long horns, were a match for the wolves, cougars, and other beasts of prey; their devotion to their young in case of attack was very manifest and brought out all their fierceness. However, the very qualities which had served them so well in the wild state were the very things that were so unfortunate for them in a state of domestication.

The tremendous spread of horns was dangerous not only to the cattlemen and horses, but the cattle themselves, on the drives or in pasture, inflicated wounds of a serious nature upon one another. The long-horned and narrow-hipped beast, that could be moved along with considerable speed toward the Northern feeding grounds and, eventually, to the terminus, ran off what little flesh it carried or was able to put on. Even after the quality of the food improved and the quantity increased, these animals tended to build up muscle and bone rather than flesh or milk. The large horns were a problem in shipping to Eastern markets. All these unfortunate characteristics and, in addition, the curtailment of grazing lands and the increase in demands for heavy beef cattle resulted in numerous experiments of breeding the Texas Longhorn with various other breeds existent in that time. The early attempts were gradually sifted down to the crossing of our native beast with that of the short-horned bulls of British breeds—Herefords[1] and Shorthorns. The result was a greatly improved stock. The hardiness of the animal of the prairies was retained, and to this were added the flesh-building characteristics of the imported animals.

---

[1] The white-faced Hereford originated in Herefordshire, England. These cattle were first introduced into America by Henry Clay of Kentucky in 1817.

Right: Texas Longhorns owned by J. W. Hammond of Cheyenne in the early 1870's.

—*Photograph by J. E. Stimson.*

Left: Grubtime at a Wyoming round-up camp near Cheyenne, 1898.

J. E. Stimson, Photographer, Cheyenne, Wyoming.

Nothing in all our Western history, with the possible exception of the life and adventures of the red man, has been surrounded with more romance than the Texas Longhorn. The movement of the Easterner and Southerner to the plains of Texas following the Civil War and the resultant growth of the cattle herds were the beginning of the range cattle industry. The primary figure of this, and the purpose of it, was the Longhorn. The first movement of great herds of cattle toward Northern and Eastern railroad termini, and later the treks to the feeding grounds of the Northern territories were the bases of much of the early history of our Western frontier; around the Longhorn have been woven tales of fact and fiction, and the great tapestry of Western literature would not be complete without it. The cattle of the plains were responsible for the development of the horse for use in work on the range and also for the birth of the cattleman and cowboy, the latter, perhaps, the first and last truly unique and American personality. The spring round-up, the great drives, the stampedé, the cowtowns—all developed from the cattle industry; all were an integral part of this frontier movement and came about because of the Texas Longhorn.

These activities, that part of the round-up which took weeks and months to achieve, consisted of driving the cattle in herds from distant points on the range to a centrally located area which had been agreed upon by the cattlemen. The cutting out of those cows already branded, the roping and branding of the calves born since the last round-up— this type of work is the action so vividlly portrayed in rodeo. The daily work of our man on the plains, and, in addition, bronc riding, steer wrestling and various roping contests are all granted an important place in the sport.

Thus, around the horse and cattle of our Western ranges grew up an important industry, which still occupies one of the most important places in this nation, even though its far-reaching activity has been reduced.

Although the Texas Longhorns had flourished on the range and were a prolific and naturally hardy race, as beef cattle they left much to be desired. In the development of the ranch the primary objective was the raising of beef. By breeding of Herefords and Shorthorn bulls with the native stock, cattlemen hoped to improve the beef quality of the cattle.

The Texas Longhorn, no longer the stock of the West, is now a zoological wonder, and the few hundred that are in existence are regarded as such. Brought to the large cities of the East and West for exhibition purposes, the remaining few are the last of a vanishing race. More rare than the buffalo, which at one time roamed the plains and plateaus, the Longhorn is now incorporated as a novelty in the Western stock shows and rodeos. With a certain dismay and apathy they stand in their stalls or corrals, or they amble about the arena and are herded together at the end of it. It is even more pathetic to see the remnants of such a noble and inspiring beast subjected to the indignity of being used for demonstration purposes. At certain rodeos, especially the indoor-arena type, under the sputtering arcs with gelatins of blue and red, they are paraded to show how the cattle were bedded down in the old days; then, an incandescent array of lights blazes forth, and the arena is suddenly filled with very beautiful and glamorous girls on horseback. These modern representatives of various Western districts propose to give a demonstration of the methods used to cut a certain animal from the herd. With well-trained horses, these beauties, by their very presence, succeed in heaping further humiliation on this lonely, unlovely, and pathetic beast.

The attempts at improvement of breed and the introduction of herds of purebred cattle finally replaced the original. Still, the difficulties of raising cattle adaptable to the environment were not overcome, for while improved stock was more acceptable on the markets, from the standpoint of adaptability to the land, it was not as good as the range cattle. They suffered severely from the heat, drought, and insects, as well as other natural enemies of the range; they were not so prolific as the original beast.

To overcome the many difficulties still existing in the improved stock, the breeders began to experiment with the humped cattle of Indian, the species *Bos indicus,* a type distinct from the cattle common to the United States, which are of the species *Bos taurus.* The Indian cattle are called Brahman or Brahma by the stockmen but are known in South America and Europe as zebus. In the true sense of the term, zebu is correct, while Brahman is derived from the name of Brahma, the Hindu divinity, who is regarded as sacred. The cattle brought to this country represented the more prominent breeds of their native land and were the Nellore, Gir, Guzerat, and Krishna Valley breeds.

The outstanding characteristics of distinction between the Brahma and the breeds common to this country are the hump on the shoulders and the large, pendulous dewlap, as well as the loose skin in the region of the navel. An additional characteristic of the purebred beast is the color of the hair. This is solid in color, although there is an occasional animal that is not uniform in this respect. The color varies from one part of the body to another, and the blending is subtle. The colors range from white to dark gray, with intermediate hues of pie-crust, tan, and a pinkish-orange; the spotted animal indicates, more or less, crossbreeding.

From available information it appears that the first importation of Brahma cattle was made in 1849, by a Dr. Z. B. Davis of South Carolina, and consisted of a bull and two cows of the Mysore breed.

In 1854 Richard Peters, of Atlanta, bought the herd of Doctor Davis and in time sold the offspring in various sections in the Southern states. About 1861 Mr. Barrow, of Louisiana, received 5 head of Brahman cattle from an Englishman who had observed the use of oxen on the Barrow farm and who had expressed a belief in improvement of native oxen by the introduction of Brahman blood. About 1866 some of the Barrow cattle were bought by Mr. Shannon and taken to his ranch near Galveston, Texas, and were purchased later by J. A. McFadden, of Victoria, Tex.

A Mr. Miller was moving to Texas in the sixties and was bringing cattle with him. A night was spent at or near the Barrow farm and one of Miller's cows was accidently served by a Brahman bull. The result was a bull calf. Later Mr. Kennedy of Corpus Christi, Tex., bought from Mr. Miller about 300 head of cattle showing Brahman blood.[1]

Thus, the stock grade Brahman cattle were spread throughout the Gulf Coast region, and in those days there was a preference shown them in the selection of range bulls.

---

[1] Parr, Virgil V., "Brahma (Zebu) Cattle," *Farmers' Bulletin* 1361, United States Department of Agriculture, Washington, D. C., 1923, 12.

In 1906 the largest importation of this type of cattle to this country was made by A. P. Borden, the executor of "Shanghai" Pierce's estate, at Pierce, Wharton County, Texas. The importation consisted of fifty-one head, and while several minor breeds were included, the majority were Nellore, Gir, Guzerat, and Krishna Valley breeds. This group of fifty-one was decreased by eighteen because of death in quarantine. The remaining thirty-three were divided into two groups; sixteen were purchased by Tom O'Connor, of Victoria, Texas, and the remainder were retained by the terms in the will of the Pierce estate. This division and the sale of the offspring resulted in the distribution of the Brahman as cattle throughout the Southern and Gulf Coast States. Eventually, the cattle were introduced into southern New Mexico, central, western, and southwestern Texas, Mexico, and Colombia, as well as the islands of Cuba and Puerto Rico.

At the opening of this century, breeding of the Brahma with the improved Shorthorn cattle of the West was attracting considerable attention in Texas and in 1906 the King Ranch of Texas began a series of experiments that have since proved to be of great importance in the development of a beef and hardy range beast.

In 1910 a half-bred Shorthorn Brahma bull was bred to purebred Shorthorn cows; the offspring resulted in the best range cattle that had ever been produced on that ranch. This new cross was observed with great interest and diligence. By 1919, after careful observation and consideration of the conditions, the breeders were convinced that their crossbred cattle, while not so consistent and uniform, were, in every case, heavier, larger, and fatter than the purebred Herefords. The experiment proved the value and importance of introducing Brahma blood into pure blood breeds.

The horses and cattle introduced to this country by the Spanish have undergone considerable change. By means of crossbreeding and the selection of blooded-animals, the livestock of the West has been improved—an improvement which is manifested in the animals seen at the stock shows and rodeos. The animals at modern rodeos are the finest to be had, for the work is of such magnitude that anything less in quality would be detrimental to the sport. The man in rodeo is a specialist in his profession, and so the animals are bred to exhibit those qualities that are essential to their part in the work.

CHAPTER XV

ASSOCIATIN'

To keep things in the groove
Through the whole confounded nation,
Came an important move—
The Rodeo Association!

The significance of the Rodeo Association of America as the guiding influence in the regulations of rodeo throughout this country cannot be overemphasized. The Association founded in 1929, was organized, "in order to insure harmony among them [rodeos] and to perpetuate traditions connected with the livestock industry and the cowboy sports incident thereto; to standardize the same and adopt rules looking forward towards the holding of contests upon uniform basis; to minimize so far as practicable conflict in dates of contests; and to place such sports so nearly as may be possible on a par with amateur athletic events. . . . "[1]

The Association—the headquarters are located in Salinas, California—is governed by a legislative body or Board of Directors; the power of making and enforcing rules is invested in this group. The Association has divided the country into fifteen territorial districts, of which the Dominion of Canada is one; the election or appointment

---

[1] *Constitution and By-Laws and Rules of the Rodeo Association of America,* (cited hereafter as *Constitution,* etc.) 1941, 3. (Permission to use.)

of one vice-president from each district makes up the governing and law-making body of the organization. Through this Board of Directors much of the success of rodeo as a sport has been realized.

To become a member-show of the Rodeo Association of America, the requirements of membership are confined to exhibitions of cowboys sports alone. Membership is extended only:

To bona fide associations or organizations in the United States or Canada holding exhibitions which may be classed as rodeos, roundups, or similar sporting events which have their major events open to all contestants and for which RAA points are given, provided however, said contestant[s] are in good standing with recognized contestant organizations and the Rodeo Association of America.

Any non-member of the RAA desiring membership may join the Association by filing with the Secretary a letter requesting membership, $35.00 application fee and a letter from the Vice-Preisdent of the District in which the rodeo operates, stating that in his opinion the rodeo is qualified for membership and in his belief will pay off the prizes offered. That said application must be filed with the Secretary in time so that the membership plus the amount of prize money paid in each event, may be shown in the RAA News at least thirty days (30) prior to the date of the membership show. The annual dues of any member shall be 2% of the amount of money paid out in purses and prizes by that member in the RAA arena events, not including mount money, and not including entry fees added to the purses. The minimum dues shall be $35.00 and the maximum dues

$150.00. The minimum dues of $35.00 from each rodeo shall become due on the 31st of December for the following year. The balance of the dues shall be paid at the time of filing results of the show with the Secretary-Treasurer. No member shall vote at any meeting unless the minimum dues of $35.00 have been paid for the current year, and if not paid by the first day of March of said year, the Board of Directors, may in its judgment, terminate the membership of the member rodeo so failing to pay. Member shows failing to report point awards in the various RAA contests within 30 days may in the judgment of the Board of Directors, be penalized by suspension or fine or both.[1]

The member-rodeos are required to place on file with the Secretary of the Association a printed prize-list or a certified statement of the total purses they are to pay in the events: bronc riding, bull or steer riding, bareback riding, calf roping, steer roping, steer decorating, steer wrestling, team roping, and wild cow milking. This statement must contain the amount of entry fees for each event, and it must point out whether or not these entry fees are to be added to the purse. This group of written statements must be filed with the Secretary of the Rodeo Association of America at least sixty days prior to the opening of the member-show. To qualify as a member-contest, the show must list in its prize-list at least four of the Rodeo Association's events.

By means of a point system the contestants are judged at the end of the season as the champions of the various events, and also by this method the All-Around Cowboy

---

[1] Article II., *Constitution, etc.*, 5-6.

of rodeo for the year is selected.[1] The points are issued on the basis of one for each one dollar paid in prizes. No points are given for money paid by member-rodeos in events not listed, nor are points given for increased prize-lists. This latter precaution is to prevent promoters from "upping" the purses in order to make their contest a deciding issue in the selection of the champion of an event. Points are not given for final monies made up of the entry fees which must be added. The question of selecting the champion of the various events by the point system is not infallible. The contestant of ability who attends the majority of Rodeo-Association-of-America contests has a better chance of winning more money and therefore more points. However, as yet, no other system has been devised that might be more successful for the purpose of making the final decisions.

The Rodeo Association of America has made every just effort to standardize the rules governing the contests held in the various districts. There is a need of some flexibility in these rules because of the variance in the state law, public sentiment regarding rodeos, and conditions in the arena. Thus the parent organization has allowed an extension of rules when the member-shows find it necessary. However, alterations are not to be made in the rules that would make the successful participation in the contests less difficult. If there is to be a variation from the standard rules, a statement of the conditions must be included in

Earl Thode	1929	Burel Mulkey	1938
Clay Carr	1930, 1933	Paul Carney	1939
J. Schneider	1931	Fritz Truan	1940
Donald Nesbitt	1932	Homer Pettigrew	1941
Leonard Ward	1934	Gerald Roberts	1942
Everett Bowman	1935, 1937	Louis Brooks	1943, 1944
John Bowman	1936	Bill' Linderman	1945
		Gene Rambo	1946

[1] All-Around Cowboys.

the prize-list of the member-show when placed on file.

The Rodeo Association of America makes a special effort to impress upon its member-shows the seriousness of the selection of the officials, judges, timers, and those men conducting the arena events. This selection is a delicate matter and one that often causes serious disagreement among contest managers and contestants. If it is not given careful consideration, many unhappy incidents might result. The officials must have knowledge of the events that they are judging and must familiarize themselves with the many rules and the annual changes that come about.

In its general rules the Rodeo Association states clearly what it expects of member-shows and what it considers the proper conduct of the contestants. All general rules of the Association become the rules of any of the member-contests. The members have the right to refuse the entry of any contestant who violates the rules, who has been dishonest in the event, or who has proved to be an undesirable character in the sport. Responsibility or liability for injury or damage, or both, the person or property of a contestant, or an assistant, or to the stock of any owner, is not assumed by the managers. Upon entering the contests, the cowboy waives all claim.

The contestant must be present or send a representative for the drawing of the horses and places that he is to have during the contest; if he fails to do this, the member-show appoints a representative to draw for the absent cowboy who must accept the results of the drawing. On the day of the contest the participant must be ready to appear when called, and a substitute is not permitted to take his place in the event. Withdrawal from an event must be made at least one day in advance except in the case of injury.

The following offenses: "refusing to contest on the animal drawn by or for him; being under the influence of liquors; rowdyism; mistreatment of stock, altercation with the judges or officials; or failure to give assistance when requested to do so by an arena director, or for any other reason deemed sufficient by the management, can result in withdrawal of any contestant's name and entry, barring him from any or all events, and withholding any money due him."[1]

The purpose of the Rodeo Association of America, with the Cowboys' Turtle Association, is to protect the rights of the member-shows as well as those of the cowboys. If a member-show fails to pay the purses won according to conditions as filed and advertised, or to appoint acceptable judges, it is suspended, and reinstatement, after meeting its obligations, is at the discretion of the Board of Directors of the Rodeo Association.

---

[1] "General Rules," *Constitution, etc.,* 12.

CHAPTER XVI

BRUSHING THE STARS

It's ridin' the broncs
That causes the thrills,
Whether they ride to the finish
Or buck off in spills.

The event of bronc riding, as seen at the modern rodeo, is related directly to the work of the early cowboy on the range in that it is a portrayal of the work of horse "breaking." There is one difference in this event which should be clarified: the horses used today are natural buckers and no attempt is made to break them. The horses of rodeo will not tolerate a human being on their backs. The wild horses of an earlier day were broken for riding and for use in the cattle industry and had rarely seen a human being; they were filled with all the fears of a wild beast coming in contact with a strange element.

The bucking horses of rodeo are not, as a whole, animals brought from the few remaining wild herds that exist in the West; contrary to popular opinion, they are not "killers," nor are they "outlaws." These two terms have been used rather loosely in describing the bucking horse, and although he displays the temper of mad or unmanageable beasts, he is not that kind of animal. The horses seen in the arena are, in most cases, halter-broken and are gentle until an attempt is made to ride them. The "killer" that one so often reads about in this sport is non-existent, and when an animal of this nature does appear, he is destroyed, because the true "killer" is a menace to himself, to other animals, and to men; therefore he has no place in the sport.

The majority of the best and the greatest number of bucking horses come from the northern and western slopes of the Continental Divide, where the grass is heavy and strong, the weather rugged, the climatic changes severe, the topography rough and unkind. Horses from this section of the country have that stout bucking heart needed by them in the work. The bucking horse was used for various types of work and its bucking tendencies have come about for many reasons, most of them unknown. Of the many animals used today, some were, and still are, broken to the plow, wagon, and various other vehicles. In some instances they were, at one time, riding horses. For some reason or other it was discovered that they were "buckers," and, as in the case of some riding horses that have been ridden for years, overnight they changed their pattern of living and became fierce, dangerous, and, usually, very sly, bucking beasts. They are now too valuable to be used for any other purpose. The reason for this abrupt change cannot be found; probably some strange inhibition or fear brings about the reaction.

Harry Rowell of Hayward, California, one of the most important stock contractors of rodeo, made the following statement regarding one of his famous bucking animals:

Horses are like men. It sometimes happens that a perfectly gentle horse will turn "outlaw"; something happens in his life that makes him declare war on the whole

FAMOUS HORSES

Upper: "Old Cyclone," most noted bucking horse of his day. Held by
Henry Isbel (1912).
—*E. A. Brininstool, Photographer.*

Center. "Long Tom" (1912).
—*E. A. Brininstool, Photographer.*

Lower: Dick Stanley on "Hightower" at Cheyenne, Wyoming (1903).
—*J. E. Stimson, Photographer.*

world. We had a Mare that we called "Tygh Valley"—
children used to ride her to school, sometimes two or
three kids on her. They got to cracking walnuts on
the horn of the saddle and after that she was one of
our top bucking horses. All you had to do to make her
an "outlaw" was to put a saddle on her. Take the
saddle off and the kids could ride her any time or any
place. She was over 25 years old when she quit bucking.[1]

The horse "Hell Bent" was a big horse—fourteen hundred pounds—purchased some time in the late twenties
by Bob Barmby, a California stock contractor. "Hell
Bent" was an excellent work horse, well-broken for the
harness, strong, willing, and gentle. However, the sight of
a saddle would send him into a frenzy of bucking. Having
given tough rides to many contestants for some twelve
years, he has earned their respect.

There are horses that buck only when ridden bareback;
others buck only when a saddle is used; and still others
that buck when any attempt is made to straddle them,
with or without saddle. One of the erroneous conceptions
in the minds of the public is that the horses are trained
to buck. This idea has absolutely no foundation.[2] However, it should be pointed out, that a bucking horse does
become conscious of the important part that he is playing
in the exciting drama. He is aware, with his limited, yet
keen, horse-intelligence, when he is going to be moved

---

[1] From Harry Rowell, stock contractor, Rowell Ranch, Hayward, California.

[2] "That stuff about the horses being made to buck is all bunk," said Mr.
Weadick. "Where people got that idea I don't know, but for the benefit
of any of the doubters, let me say that if they don't change their minds
after witnessing the performance of some of the bronks at the Stampede
I'll sure miss my guess." *Calgary Daily Herald,* (August 20, 1919), 6.

from the corral to the chute. During the saddling and preparations preceding his appearance, with the stirring music of the band and the color and confusion accompanying the contest, he is conscious of his part in the work. Waiting tensely in anticipation of his release from the chute, he, as the contestant sits astride him, quivers, breathes heavily, snorts, squeals, and with a pounding heart waits for the struggle. Who is to know whether this is fear or sheer brute anticipation of delight? Certainly, some emotional reaction sweeps through the animal, a reaction that is akin to the feeling in the human being facing competition or an ordeal. The animal does, after years of living in these surroundings, assume a certain showmanship. He is not trained to buck, but experience has made him aware of his destiny.

Very strange things happen to the bucking horse—this can be seen at almost every rodeo. One of the strangest happenings took place during the Denver Stock Show and rodeo in 1941, when "Five Minutes to Midnight," having been ridden once during the contest for a full ten seconds, quit bucking during the last performance of the show, at least five seconds before the time was up. This unusual happening gave the fans present a new thrill. Was the eighteen-year-old horse, world famous as one of the toughest bucking animals in rodeo, finished? Would he buck again or had he seen his day? The sheepish look on rider Eddie Curtis' face was a priceless example of amazement, an almost terrified suspicion in anticipation of the animal's next move. The reputation that old "Five Minutes to Midnight" had had for years could not be forgotten in five seconds. However, the fighting spirit of "Five Minutes to Midnight" had never left him; he returned on a later occasion to give a thrilling and dangerous exhibition of bucking.

This horse—belonging to the Nesbitt and Elliott string —has earned the praise of every bronc rider of note in rodeo. Over twenty years of age, he is considered by many contestants as too old to give a good ride. This opinion, however, is not shared by everyone participating in the bronc riding classic. Sitting in with a group of such notable riders as Jackie Cooper, Jerry Ambler, Burel Mulkey, Chet McCarty, and the late Doff Aber, one soon gets a very distinct impression of the respect in which "Five Minutes to Midnight" is held by these men. First and foremost, it is agreed among them that this horse must be spurred. This requirement is necessary to make a qualified ride but can be avoided, and is done assiduously by the man who sometimes desires to stay on top of the horse rather than win. Secondly, "Five Minutes to Midnight" cannot be "figured out" as to what type of ride he might give. The late Doff Aber, bronc riding champion for 1941 and 1942, gave as fine an analysis of the animal and his actions as any rider in rodeo today. Doff said:

" 'Old Five Minutes to Midnight' is one of the smartest horses in rodeo. He will bring a man out of the chute with a fast choppy movement and if he doesn't throw him on the first two or three jumps, 'Five Minutes' will slow down to an easy glide."

Both Jackie Cooper and Chet McCarty agree with Doff in these details, but hasten to add that, following this easing off, the beginning of the end is in sight.

Doff continued his description of the animal in action:

" 'Five Minutes' will turn his head around, take a look at the rider and just like this—" With three sharp snaps of his fingers, Doff demonstrated how the horse bucks a man off.

"No, 'Five Minutes to Midnight' is not through just now, his day will come but it is not yet here."

He is not an impressive horse to look at; perhaps, the smallness of this animal is his most distinctive characteristic. His color is black; he has tiny pointed ears, and everything about him suggests a typical Morgan; however, there might be some Arab in him. Ask any cowboy about "Five Minutes to Midnight"—he will agree that he has a personality of his own!

Of all the mistaken ideas, certainly the most vicious one concerning the bucking horses—or for that matter any other animal used in rodeo—is that these animals are mistreated and misused, that their vicious conduct is the result of abuse. The horse may have been mishandled originally in an attempt to break him for riding, but as has been said, this is only one of the many causes that make a horse buck and at no time has it always been the main one. The bucking horse is far too valuable a beast to mistreat or subject to cruelty at any time or in any way. He is worth in money from three hundreds dollars up, and one thousand dollars has by no means been the top price paid. Good horses with consistent bucking tendencies are rare and are sought diligently throughout the year by scouts for the stock contractors. They are the pampered animals of rodeo. Because their actions are not related to a breeding problem, it is impossible to rely on increasing their kind; therefore they are given every consideration. The horses get the very best of feed to keep them in top condition. Teeth, legs, and hoofs are kept in order; after each performance the horses are checked over for strained

FAMOUS HORSES
Upper: Earl Thode on "Five Minutes to Midnight," winner of second
place in World's Bucking Contest, Pendleton, Oregon (1931).
—*Courtesy Chamber of Commerce, Pendleton, Oregon.*

Lower: F. E. Studnick on "Midnight."
—*Courtesy Chamber of Commerce, Pendleton, Oregon.*

muscles or other injuries and are given proper attention. After a season of rodeo the animals are moved back to the ranches of their owners and turned loose into the hills on excellent pasture land. Here they recuperate during the months of the off-season. They are allowed to roam at will and toughen up for the coming season.

It seems rather ridiculous to make a statement concerning the use of injurious devices to make a horse buck. But because this is a common fallacy, it should not be neglected; perhaps one more statement to explode this idea will make an end of it sooner. Anything used so severe as to cause a beast to buck would result in injuries sufficient to harm or cripple the animal to such an extent that his valuable services would be lost. The beautiful and perfectly logical explanation for a bucking horse's action as "dreamed up" by the public, that is, the placing of a thorn, tack, burr, or a sharp instrument under the saddle, is purely imagination, and more likely, just the idea of some prankish and stupid boy. There is only one device used that has a tendency to encourage a horse to buck and to keep him bucking. This is the flanking strap, which is approved by all rodeos in all states and recognized by the various Humane Societies as non-injurious and legitimate. It is placed around the hind quarters of the horse and, as any foreign object around the rear of any other animal, has the tendency to excite, annoy, and increase his desire to rebel.

The flank strap tightens with every kick and lunge, and the horse kicks with more vigor to rid himself of the annoyance. It is on him less than twenty seconds; there is no injury, and, in fact, not even a mark to be seen. Occasionally, a horse "freezes" in a chute, and no prodding and pushing moves him from his statuesque mood. The use of a battery-charged prod[1] to break the spell is of some use; however, such moods of horses are rare and most of the contests are without such a device to be used when the need arises. The "Hot Shot" is used more often on bulls, calves, and steers. If other means do not bring the horse out of the chute, the gate is closed, and after a few minutes opened again; if the animal does not respond this time, he is unsaddled and removed from the chute.

According to contestants, the first half dozen jumps of a horse are his best efforts each time that he appears, and if he succeeds in shaking his rider loose on the first or second heave, in all likelihood he will remove the man in the next few jumps. It is said that the bucking horse of today cannot keep up his violent action for a very long time, and if a rider persisted in carrying out the ride, it is quite probable that the horse's inclination to buck would soon disappear. Considering the length of time a horse works for each performance, that is ten seconds—and no horse works every performance[2]—the care he receives during his rest period—the off-season—stimulates in him whatever wildness remains after a season of work. Most animals perform in ten to fifteen shows per season and are then ready for their rest of three or four months.

All horses do not buck alike; just as there are various types of horses, there are also various types of bucking. There are really only two distinct types of bucking, but these have many variations, peculiar to each animal. Some horses move with fast, sharp jolts and yet, barely

---

[1] Known as the "Hot-Shot."

[2] The average time of work is three performances for every contest. In time, this amounts to ten minutes a season. (Information contributed by stock contractors and bronc riders.)

leave the ground; others work with slower and more deliberate shocks but reach a greater height in their bucking. However, there are several kinds of bucking which the animal demonstrates upon leaving the chute; the most spectacular kind is shown by the horse that crouches back into a sitting squat, and when the gate is opened, springs forward with a leap on his first move. This is a dangerous break, for it causes the rider to lose his balance and often throws him on the second leap. Another horse may "come out" into the arena on a dead run, thus covering half of the enclosed area, before "digging in" to throw the rider. Another type of bucking horse that comes from the chute, wheels, twists right or left, but constantly keeps up this movement and works in a small circular area. The horse that comes out with a straight leap and hits the ground with his forefeet increases the contestant's misery by adding the extra flourish of kicking with the hind feet. The wild and fierce kicking at the highest point of the leap and the shock of the kicking beast striking the ground cause one of the toughest and roughest rides which bring down many a contestant.

The rules governing the bronc riding contest, as devised by the Rodeo Association of America, are: that the riding is to be done with a plain halter, one rein and a saddle, the latter to be supplied by the management of the rodeo. Many of the men have their own saddles and prefer to use them. The saddle must be of the recognized and accepted association gear; it is made with a fourteen-and-a-half to fifteen-inch tree and is rigged according to the Hamley design. The single rein is of braided grass or cotton rope and must not be more than one inch in diameter. No tape or knots are allowed on or in this rein; it must not be wrapped about the hand, but is held in a plain grasp while the other hand remains free.

Every bronc rider has his own rein which is fastened according to set and very complicated standards. The braiding of ropes and reins is not an accomplishment at which every cowboy is adept. The bronc rider's rein is about six feet long. It begins with a smooth end to which is attached a double-stitched strap. This strap, twenty-two to twenty-nine inches long, fastens the rein to the head of the horse. The rein itself is a four-ply braid, braided cross-type so as not to be smooth. It is braided dry and from fibers free from oil. Made of two-ply rope of twenty-four to thirty-six strands, it is started with four strands and runs up to increase gradually in diameter by the addition of more strands. This continues to a point just above the place where it is held by the rider. At this point a stop is made. This is a small loop rather than a knot and it acts as a guide as well as a means of giving a new grip, if the bucking of the horse should cause the hand to slip. Unless the bronc rider's rein is made by a capable person, it is dead, it lacks life and spring, which are so desirable in this piece of equipment. Only a few—Jerry Ambler, Stub Bartlemay, and Smokey Snyder—have the knack of this type of braiding; it is almost a lost art with the modern cowboy.[1]

The rein is the most important piece of equipment used in bronc riding. By means of it the rider gets his balance, timing, and feel of the horse. When the hand on the rein is about a foot's length back from the saddle horn, the horse "takes his head." This allows the rein-arm and the

---

[1] The method of rein braiding was explained by Smokey Snyder and Jerry Ambler.

body of the rider to get into the right position for balance, which is most essential. Because individual horses take a different head, the position of the hand on the rein, either forward or backward from the average position, is a question of inches or even less. It is interesting that some horses buck more with a left-hand rein than with a right-hand rein—as has been proved when left- or right-handed contestants have ridden the same animal.

The next most important piece of equipment to be adjusted for the bronc riding contest is the stirrup. The exact length of the stirrup is tested before each ride. This is done by placing the saddle on the ground, then the stirrup is tried by the rider. Each man has a certain length that is just right for his particular style of ride. Some stirrups are adjusted long, some short, and still others at an average or at an intermediate length.

The contestant must not change hands on the reins; both the hand and the rein must be on the same side of the horse, with daylight showing between the hand and the horse's neck as he leaves the chute. Upon leaving the chute, the contestant is required to spur the horse on the first jump and continue this action throughout the ride. From the moment the animal leaves the chute, the contestant is judged for his ride, which lasts for ten seconds and is complete when the signal is given.

A rider can be disqualified on several offenses: cheating in any manner; for being bucked off the mount; changing hands on the rein or wrapping the rein about the hand; pulling leather;[1] losing a stirrup; failing to spur

---

[1] Grabbing the saddle horn.

throughout the ride to the satisfaction of the judges, and not being ready to ride when called.

Cheating in rodeo is not a common practice and cannot be accomplished easily. There is evidence that there were forms of cheating earlier in the game—old timers mention a practice of slowing down a fiery horse by placing a block of wood under the cinch on his ventral vein. Now, the practice is unknown in the work, and, if it did exist, it would be treated severely. The Rodeo Association of America makes a point against the use of any substance or preparation on the contestant's clothing or equipment and threatens disqualification. Some cowboys, however, use rosin on their chaps and gloves. This gives a rougher surface to these worn-smooth pieces of equipment and aids the rider in gripping the saddle, stirrups, and rein. Rosin is also used on the gloved hand of the bull and bareback bronc riders. This use of rosin is a practice followed by many sportsmen for a better grip or to prevent slipping in their contests; it is considered perfectly legitimate. The practice of making an attempt to have a fair grip before starting the perilous ride should not be held against the man in rodeo. On occasions, the rider places chewing gum on the instep or in the arch of his boots to help him keep his stirrups. It is not unusual to see a lighted match applied to the gum to improve its adhesiveness. While observing a ride, one wonders if this practice might not be considered as a cowboy superstition or as a bit of wishful thinking, rather than an aid in riding. The adhesive quality of chewing gum is very familiar under certain conditions, but the rigors of bronc riding cannot be classed as one of them. Neither the use of rosin nor chewing gum is frowned upon by either the Cowboys' Turtle Association or the Rodeo Association of America; however, on rare occasions some individual judge may make a point of this use as a threat to disqualify the rider or he may mark him down for doing so.

The spurs that are used must be kept in good condition for riding; spurs that have locked rowels or rowels that will lock when used are forbidden. However, an exception is made in cases where local Humane Societies sometimes demand that the rowels of a spur must be covered with tape.

The rider and horse are judged separately, each on the basis of 100 per cent; the final rating is the total of both these percentages. Thus, a very excellent rider, having drawn poor stock, must make up the difference in the quality of his ride, for he will lose in the final rating of points because of lack of spirit in the horse. A man of fair ability, if he qualifies in his ride, often gets his own points plus those of the fine mount he has drawn. Every rider hopes and desires to get the best horse possible for his ride, in order to show his skill, for if he qualifies, the points on a fine horse are practically assured, and he is "in the money." Seldom, if ever, do man and horse receive 200 per cent, because the event is not a time contest, but judged solely on the actions of both participants.

The most controversial subject among contestants is the question of the superiority of the bucking horses, and any attempt to list the names of the greatest buckers is bound to bring vituperation on the compiler. There is no agreement among the cowboys on this question, and there are a great many opinions. It is very difficult to convince an opinionated contestant otherwise or even to discuss the matter with him in a quiet way.

A heated discussion resulted from the list compiled by the Levi Strauss Company of San Francisco. This company wished to depict, by means of a display—an advertising scheme—the world's outstanding bucking horses. The horses selected for their own peculiar merits were some of the best known in the country. "Hell's Angel,"[1] owned by the Clemans' and Colborn Organization, producers of the Madison Square Garden Rodeo, received first place; "Five Minutes to Midnight," of the Elliott and Nesbit string, was second; and "Midnight," dead since 1936, was rated third. Other outstanding mounts were Harry Rowell's "Starlight"; Moomaw and Bernard's "Badger Mountain"; Cuff Burrell's "Crying Jew";[2] and Leo Cramer's "Will James." Many others received honorable mention.

The bucking horse, "Starlight," had already gained the reputation of being one of the toughest broncs of the arena. From its earliest days this colt was impossible to break. Born about thirteen years ago in Nevada, "Starlight" was moved from the open wild areas of that state to the most coveted rodeo arenas in the world, where he retained, under the pressure of notoriety and fame, the bucking abilities so desired in this type of horse.

[1] "Hell's Angel" died in the railroad car carrying him back to the World's Championship Rodeo Ranch after having appeared at the New York, Boston, and Buffalo Shows during the fall season of 1942. The last man to ride him was Doff Aber at the Buffalo, New York Show. Doff won the bronc riding event at Buffalo in 1942. "Hell's Angel" was buried at Poplar Bluff, Missouri. "Hell's Angel," *Hoofs and Horns* 12 (January 1943), 7.

[2] "About eight years ago, Cuff Burrell, rodeo stock contractor of Hanford, California, heard of a horse that had caused a lot of trouble to his owner by kicking, bucking, and tearing up farm equipment. Burrell tried out that horse and found that he really would buck, so he bought him. The former owner was a Jew and he 'howled' so much about the damage the horse had caused that Mr. Burrell named the big bay 'Crying Jew.'" "The Crying Jew," *Hoofs and Horns* 8 (May 1939), 11.

FAMOUS HORSES

Upper: Ed. Carver on "Old Steamboat" at Cheyenne, Wyoming
—*J. E. Stimson, Photographer.*

Lower: "Young Steamboat" in action at Cheyenne, Wyoming.
—*J. E. Stimson, Photographer.*

During 1940 "Starlight" kept every cowboy, except one, Fritz Truan, from riding him. That year brought Truan his All-Around Championship. Outstanding riders with years of experience met their equal in this horse. Burel Mulkey, Doff Aber, Gene Rambo, Bob Walden, and many others found the ground in their attempts to add "Starlight's" scalp to their riding laurels.

The poll made by the Levi-Strauss and Company brought protests from everywhere in the country, principally because "Midnight" was placed third. This placement was, no doubt, due to the fact that the animal had been dead for some time; however, the memory of him and his brilliant performances of so many years was still so vivid in the minds of those who knew and had ridden him, that this placement was regarded as heresy because the contest was intended to select the world's outstanding bucking horse, dead or alive.

The following list of buckers is strictly a cowboys' list and should not bring forth too many protests.[1] These horses differ in their technique, but are considered the best and are consistently good in their work. "Home Brew," "Hells Angel," Bungalow," and "Conclusion" are the best of the Clemans and Colborn Horses; "Stork," "Harry Tracy," "Short Cut," and "Crying Jew" are the runners-up. "Ham What Am" and "Five Minutes to Midnight" are rated highest of the Elliott and Nesbitt string. "Will James," "Lee Rider," and "Hootchie Koochie" are Leo Cramer's best, and "Duster" is Harry Rowell's star. When Gene Autry was in rodeo production, before entering the Armed Forces in World War II, he offered "Calgary Red," "Top Rail," and "Trail Tramp." During the summer of

---

[1] List compiled by interviewing saddle bronc riders.

1942, the Gene Autry Flying A Rranch and the Clemans and Colborn-Lightening C Ranch (World's Champion Rodeo Corporation) combined to bring together from both ranches the world's finest string of bucking horses, rodeo stock and equipment. It was a history-making merger.

The names that are given to the bucking horses are usually expressive of their actions and are amusing as well as highly indicative of their owner's imagination. From a list of about four hundred that have been compiled the following are some of the most arresting: "Tombstone," "Satan," "Cyclone," "Commanche," "Iron Sides," "Black Widow," "Indian Sign," "Gin Fizz," "Brenner Pass," "Black Out," "X It," "Bad Whiskey," "Virginia Reel," "Yellow Fever," "Tick Fever," "Just Because," "Death Wind," "Widow Maker," "Hell to Set," "Rock and Rye," "Tragedy," "Mary's Lamb," "War Paint," "32 Below," "Pay-off," "Depression," "Cyanide," "Cloudburst," "Scene-shifter," "Typhoon," "Devils Partner," "Board and Room," "Idiot," "12 Bells," "Sunset," and "P.D.Q."[1]

Late in the fall of 1940, a horse was retired from the rodeo arena that had played his part in entertaining the vast audiences and fans of rodeo for almost thirty years. His name was "Prison Bars." He was not a particularly attractive horse, he was of a dirty-white color, weighed about twelve hundred pounds, and had a fierce temper. He was noted for being a chute-rattler and always did his bit to arouse the spectators before he was allowed to show his ability. His ability to create suspense and excitement was coupled with a peculiar way of burying his head be-

---

[1] List compiled from programs of contests, *Hoofs and Horns, The Western Horseman, Rodeo Fans, Bulletins, Rodeo Association of America, The Buckboard,* and from letters from stock contractors, Harry Rowell, Leo Cramer, Moomaw and Bernard, and Nesbitt and Elliott.

tween his forelegs; then a characteristic leap carried him and the rider from the chute on his first wild move. Appearing in the larger contests in the country, "Prison Bars" had the privilege of being one of the few bucking horses to entertain several generations of rodeo fans, as well as to throw and to fight two generations of the best bronc riders in the sport.

Concerning the bucking horses, the saddle and the bareback broncs, contestants in general concede that the saddle broncs are by far the better bucking animals. Usually there are two sets of horses for these events, and they are kept separate in the drawing for the respective events.

A bareback bronc rarely becomes a saddle bronc, unless he develops into an unusually good bucking horse. Quite often, however, a saddle bronc ·is put in the bareback string, if for some reason or other, such as age or temperament, he no longer bucks as well as he formerly did. A horse that does not respond and return to his old form remains in the bareback group permanently. Some times, this switching causes a saddle bronc to regain his old vigor and he is returned to his original status. This is, however, an exception to the rule and seldom occurs.

Often a very tough horse to ride in the saddle bronc event is put into the bareback string, especially if he shows any sign of attacking his rider. This is very unusual, but it does happen. If he tends to rear when bucking and falls over backward, the rider can get away from him more easily if he uses a surcingle rather than a saddle. A quick move is necessary to get out of the stirrups and avoid the horn, cantle, and other equipment; in a few seconds a tragedy might result if the rider is not fast enough.

The men who have ridden to fame on the backs of broncs are many, but few have achieved the crown of the champion. Since 1929, and since the selection of the Champion Cowboy of the Bronc Riding Event by means of the Rodeo-Association-of-America point system, only nine have had this honor. Some have held this honor more than once. The saddle bronc riding event is one of the high lights of rodeo; in this event the purses are high. It is accorded due honor, for bronc riding is one of the original activities of the early cowboy.

No one among the many men in modern rodeo, has offered, in a more sincere and genuine way, the fairness, the faithfulness, and the good sportsmanship for the betterment of the work than the late Doff Aber.[1] With a feeling of security and in a quiet way, he was an important figure in the sport. Knowing him, one could not think otherwise. As long as there are men of his caliber in rodeo, every honest effort will be made to keep up the high standards that are now an important phase of the sport. Doff was a top man[2] in the bronc riding class for several years, and still is rated as "high man" in the affections of all who knew him.

His most obvious characteristic was his sincere love of the game. Bronc riding was his special forte. When Doff talked bronc riding, a light would come into his eyes, and the listener wondered just what exciting memories came stumbling and crowding out of the past to intrigue and hold him to this work. His conversation, when directed in these channels, instead of growing more tense,

---

[1] Doff Aber met an untimely death in an accident on his ranch north of Fort Collins, Colorado, on May 6, 1946.

[2] Bronc Riding Champions, see p. 416.

would swing into a slower tempo; it became a well-spaced narrative.

Doff began this particular work at the age of nineteen; he had the usual bad breaks—lack of recognition of his skill, unfortunate injuries, and insufficient funds—that haunt every beginner. All of this never caused him to deviate from the course he had set; he was determined to become a first-class bronc rider. Upon witnessing his work, one may say that Doff was a born rider. With faith in his ability to succeed, and not tempted by the probability of adding to his welfare in a financial way, Doff stayed with the broncs and had the courage to prove his faith.

As early as 1935 Doff showed his great skill as a natural born rider. He proved this during August of that year at the last Tex Austin show, held at Gilmore Stadium, Los Angeles, California. This was a unique contest—there were six final horses to be ridden. The late Pete Knight, Earl Thode, and Doff were the final contestants. All had agreed to ride their last three day-money horses. However, both Earl and Pete paid boys to take their horses out. This arrangement is permissible, as long as the horses are taken out and ridden, and is not an uncommon practice when a man does not wish to ride a certain horse. Doff, however, rode his three horses, plus six final ones, making a total of nine buckers in the last three days, and a grand total of fourteen during the entire contest. The six final horses were the broncs: "Ham What Am," "Duster," "C. Y. Jones," "Crying Jew," "Five Minutes to Midnight," and "Goodbye Dan."

On the first day, Doff was first to buck off "Ham What Am" in the finals. Earl Thode bucked off the same horse the next afternoon, and Pete followed the third afternoon, even though he rode "Ham What Am" one more jump than the other two boys had. "C. Y. Jones," ridden previously, bucked him off in finals. Doff won first place, Earl was second, and Pete third. Is that riding!

In 1941 Doff attended thirty-eight contests; he placed in the finals at twenty-four of them, and established the remarkable record of placing in eighteen contests in succession.

Grandfather Aber came west from Pennsylvania in a covered wagon and settled on the North Platte river. Doff's father was at this time about three years old. During the following years the Abers developed a large ranch at Wolf, Wyoming, but this was swept away during the depression in 1929. Doff was born at Wolf and was truly a son of the Northwest which has produced so many bronc riding champions. He was never a studied or planned showman of the spectacular; in his simplicity and directness of action he always gave a good show. With a casual dignity he wore the Bronc Riding Championship Crown for 1941 and 1942.[1]

In the opinion of many people who know them, the bronc riders are the glamour boys of the rodeo, the "cream of the crop." Among these boys are those who scorn work in any other event except that of bronc riding.[2] Of the many saddle bronc riders there are only about fifteen or, at the most, twenty, who are really consistent winners in the event. As a class, they are strongly developed personalities of the rowdy, boisterous type; yet they have the generous, soft-hearted qualities that people like to see in rodeo cowboys. As contestants, they lead a tenser exist-

---

[1] Observed by the author while traveling with Doff Aber.
[2] The exception to this rule is very rare.

ence than the men of any other event, because the stock[1]
they work with is the most spectacular, and because, on the
average, there is more money in the event. The bronc
rider, with all this at stake, personifies the reckless daring
and casual charm—the chief appeal of the rodeo cowboy.
Among the ropers, Homer Pettigrew and Buckshot Sorrells are two of the outstanding wild young-bloods, but
neither one compares in daring ability with the bronc
riders, Fritz Truan, Nick Knight, Harry Knight, and
Burel Mulkey.

That mighty little man from Idaho, Burel Mulkey, has
the reputation of a bronc rider who never lets up in his
efforts to win. Boys, who have ridden tough horses carefully, have come and gone; they have not spurred them
too much, which increases the danger of bucking off. But
not Burel! Whether he rode a dog[2] or the best of broncs,
he spurred every one of them. Contestants who know Mulkey say that he has bucked off more horses and won more
big shows than any other bronc rider. He was twice winner of the R. A. A. Bronc Riding Championship and was
All-Around Champion Cowboy of 1938. As a bronc rider,
Burel does not follow the physical pattern of the group as
a whole. He is short and heavy-built, but as a personality,
he is a character. Rather homely in an attractive way, he
has the most mischievously twinkling eyes and pleasant
grin that keep his face in a constant state of animation.
Like ham and eggs, Mulkey and mischief belong together.
Mischief is his specialty, and he enjoys nothing more than
handing out tall stories and watching the listener's eyes

---

[1] There is much discussion over the dangers of bronc riding and bull riding. Advocates for both sides are strong in their convictions.

[2] A dog—a poor horse.

grow larger and larger. It may be years before one will ever find out what fun Mulkey has been having with him. Burel does not stand alone in this truth stretching business; his helper is another fine bronc rider, Nick Knight. Before either of them married, they were inseparable companions and were known in the rodeo world as the Gold Dust Twins. Many a poor innocent person, in rodeo and out of it, has listened to and believed the fantastic stories of both these men, each one solemnly backed up by the other.

A simpler set of rules governs the bareback bronc riding contest, but this event is in no way a less exciting, less difficult, or a less dangerous one. When bareback bronc riding was inaugurated as a major rodeo event, the people in rodeo knew that from the word, "go," this would be one of the fastest contests in the sport. Basically, the rules are the same as in the saddle bronc riding; the outstanding thing that makes this event essentially a hazardous and speedy exhibition of riding is that the contestant rides without a saddle. He is entirely dependent on manpower as a means to conquer the wild gyrations of a cunning and shrewd animal.

The riders of the day draw for their horses. In the chute the animal is encircled with a surcingle; this and the flank strap are the only pieces of equipment allowed in this contest. There are no reins and no stirrups; the contestant makes his hold by grasping the surcingle. He is permitted to use only one hand during the ride and must not change hands; the other arm and hand must be free of the horse and the rigging on him.

One concession is granted in favor of the rider—if it may be called a concession! If the horse falls or the rider

FAMOUS RIDERS

Upper: Pete Knight winning World's Bucking Contest, Pendleton
Round-Up.

—Courtesy Chamber of Commerce, Pendleton, Oregon.

Lower: Yakima Cannutt on "Lena," Round-Up, Pendleton, Oregon.

—Courtesy Chamber of Commerce, Pendleton, Oregon.

is knocked off at the chute, the contestant is granted a re-ride. This touch of generosity can only be taken advantage of, provided the contestant is able to ride again, or is willing to do so. In this contest, as in the saddle bronc riding event, there is a pick-up man to aid the rider who has ridden his horse to the signal. This may help to ease the dangers of the ride but seldom eliminates all of them, for a bronc does not recognize the signal as a sign to stop his bucking. Often he continues to try to throw his rider and carries on for several seconds beyond the eight-second time limit that is recognized as the length of the ride. After the signal is given, the rider thinks only of a soft place to land and a safe spot out of the way of the flying hoofs of the horse; his skillful maneuverings to remove himself from the horse draw considerable attention from the enthusiastic spectators. Those few seconds may bring painful injuries and disaster to the daring and ambitious rider.

A bareback bronc rider can be disqualified on several points which are basically the same as those in the saddle bronc riding event. The rider is judged on the skillful manner in which he achieves his ride, on the amount of spurring that he is able to accomplish, and the roughness and wildness of the horse are also considered. Here too, as with the saddle bronc riders, the desire of every rider is to draw a horse with spirit and real honest bucking ability, so that he (the rider) is assured of an opportunity to display his own particular talents of riding.

It is interesting that contestants who work in the bareback bronc riding event are specialists in the work. There are a few exceptional cases in which a bareback rider also enters the saddle bronc event; more often, however, they participate in the bull riding contests. These two events make a natural combination of work for the cowboy with this special talent.

CHAPTER XVII

GET ALONG LITTLE DOGIE

'Get along little dogie'
You're a gonna be roped,
Me and my cow pony
Got that all doped.

In skill and finesse, in smoothness and ability, the calf roping contest reveals the perfect coordination and understanding between man and horse. Because time is the important element in this contest, there is no opportunity for showmanship, save that which is always exhibited in the sheer beauty of natural, intense, and swift moving action. It is a revelation to see a man so confident in the training and abilities of his mount that he appears unaware of the fact that he is working at such a fast pace. The calf roper must be a skilled technician in handling the rope, but without his speedy, dashing, well-trained horse, this skill would be of little value.

The question has been raised concerning the fact why there are more first-rate ropers in the business than contestants in other events. The answer seems to lie in the fact that calf roping is fun. A man with some athletic ability, with one to three years of practice, can develop a remarkable skill to rope calves well. Many Westerners find more enjoyment in roping calves and steers than in participating in any other form of leisure or entertainment.

The majority of horses used by the calf roping contestants are Quarter Horses, bred especially for the fast
and furious pace of the rodeo arena; a snappy, quick-
moving and supple beast, this horse is trained in his every
move. A contestant with his hands full of reins and rope,
and his mouth full of dust and a "piggin' string,"[1] must
have confidence in the ability of his mount to bring him
close enough to rope the running calf that is twenty or
thirty feet ahead of him. Thus, the horse is of unquestionable value to the roper. The calf roping contestant can
get nowhere in the work unless he spends years in patiently
training and understanding his horse.

It is a fascinating and thrilling sight to see the roper
and horse take their places; the beast prancing, sidling, and
backing into position, working nervously and excitedly
into a stance—like a bunch of coiled springs—in an almost
sitting crouch in readiness for the first quick spurt that
will carry him and his rider fast on the flying heels of the
victim. The calf is released from the chute, driven forward across the deadline, followed almost immediately by
the roper, and—the event begins!

With increasing speed, the horse closes the gap between
himself and the running calf and draws to the right for
he anticipates the moment when the rider will toss the
whirling rope over the calf's head. Still his work is not
finished; when the stage is set for the final work, the horse
must play his part to the finish. After the rope has en-
snared the calf, the horse is trained not to stop dead in his
flight, while the rider dismounts and goes down the cord to
the calf. Rather he must ease up gently, in order not to

---

[1] Piggin' string — the cord used to tie the legs of the calf after it has been
thrown.

"bust"[1] the calf, but he must keep the rope taut enough to prevent the struggling animal from running about and adding time to the score. After the calf has been thrown and tied, the horse continues to hold the rope taut enough to prevent the animal from floundering, but not taut to the extent of dragging the calf.

This remarkable performance on the part of the horse is very exciting and is one that is not often witnessed in any other sport involving horses. A calf does not run in a straight line, but he weaves from right to left, stops dead, or hurries in the opposite direction; this type of action demands a horse of stamina, trained to know when to stop, to twist on a dime, and to keep the quarry in sight. The excitement of a struggling calf on the other end of a rope, dallied[2] or tied to a saddle, would send any other horse into a frenzy of fear or make him bolt from the scene of confusion. This is not the case of the trained calf roping horse who, after slowing down, backs away cautiously and gracefully, keeping ever tight the vibrating rope. He stands without any guiding influence until his master approaches and relieves him of the burden. Too much praise cannot be given to this horse that can be brought to such a degree of excellent behavior and understanding. This praise is reflected back on the man who has spent hours and days, weeks and months, patiently developing the hidden talents of his mount.

---

[1] To jerk a calf off its feet. This particular part of the calf roping rules applies only to those contests held in cities where the Humane Society objects to calf roping. The penalty of 10 seconds has the tendency to prevent contestants from being too much in a hurry to make time.

[2] A half-hitch around the saddle horn with the rope after the catch has been made.

The outstanding calf roper is tall, fair-haired, blue-eyed, Toots Mansfield of Bandera, Texas. In his late twenties, Mansfield was the R. A. A. Calf Roping Champion for three consecutive years, 1939, 1940, and 1941. It is difficult to describe Toots Mansfield—one really must know him to appreciate his sterling character and his absolute sincerity. One is impressed with the appearance and personality of this man. Since he is almost a legendary figure in his work, in personality he might pose for Owen Wister's "Virginian"; he is taciturn, courteous, dignified, with haunting, wistful eyes and an undeniable graciousness. He is a Texan by birth and the exact opposite of his fellow state-man, Buck Eckols, of Liberty, Texas. Runner-up for the R. A. A. Calf Roping Championship in 1941, Buck is a roper of ability, a threat to anyone competing against him. He is, like Homer Pettigrew, among the most attractive and handsome men in rodeo. He possesses the regular masculine features associated with outdoor men; there is a certain subtle mischievous sparkle in his eyes, which is combined with a lively sense of humor; Buck is a perfect companion. From the Eckols Ranch he came to New York to the Madison Square Garden Show for the first time in 1941, where his talent for calf roping placed him among the leaders of the sport.

The rules governing the calf roping event are somewhat flexible in that the conditions of the arena determine the start and the deadline rules, and they vary according to the local situations that prevail. However, the rules must be severe enough to prevent any violation of them that would bring a decided advantage to the contestant. The event is a time event, requires three time keepers, a tie or field judge, and a deadline referee; any other officials deemed necessary to conduct the contest fairly, may be appointed by the management of the contest.

The contestant is allowed two ropes; if he fails to rope his calf on a second try, he must retire from the arena and is given a rating of "no time." After the calf is roped, the rope is tied hard and fast to the saddle, the contestant dismounts and then throws the calf by hand. If the roped calf is not on its feet, it must be made to stand and is then thrown by hand and tied. Only then is the contestant allowed to signal that his work is completed. The tie, a three-leg cross tie, must hold until inspected by the tie judge, who, after inspection, gives his approval to release the calf. If, during the inspection and before the tie can be ruled a fair one, the calf frees itself, the contestant is marked no time.

The contestant, after signaling that he has completed his work, must not approach the calf, and only those persons assisting the tie judge are allowed to remove the rope from the calf and later untie its legs.

Some of the rules which the contestant with his mount must observe in order to qualify are: the loop must be released from the hand; the rope must be on the calf when the rider reaches it; a penalty of ten seconds is imposed if the roper and his mount beat or break the barrier. The contestant is allowed no outside assistance, and, if, in the opinion of the judges, the rider has "busted" the calf intentionally, he is disqualified. In some contests "busting," intentionally or not, is penalized ten seconds; if a horse drags a calf, the field judge may stop the horse and a penalty is imposed.[1]

---

[1] These last two rules are New York City rules for the Madison Square Garden Contest.

Calf roping is a fast moving contest; the time made by the cowboys is remarkable. However, no world record time can be established because every arena has different working conditions, and a standardization is impossible. However, ten or eleven seconds is considered record time anywhere. Records are kept of low time made at various arenas, and in subsequent shows there is always competition to try to lower these records.

The calves that are used in the event are from four to eight months old, weigh not more than two hundred and fifty pounds, in breed are cross-bred Brahma, White Face, Black Angus, or Longhorned Mexican. They are quick on their feet. At the present time, since the speed of the horse is being stepped up by breeding, the calf does not appear to move as rapidly as formerly.

The equipment used by the contestant is his own particular saddle, which is much lighter in weight than that formerly used by the range cowboy. His rope varies in length, depending upon the speed of his horse. Ten years ago, the average length of the rope was about twenty-five feet; now it has been reduced to twenty or twenty-one feet because the horse is speedier.

The development of the rope used by the cowboy of this country is an interesting story. It had its beginning late in the nineteenth century. Since 1824 the Plymouth Cordage Company of Massachusetts has been manufacturing rope, but primarily for marine use. Some of the rope went to farms and was also used for various other purposes ashore. The first price list showing a quotation on lariat rope was dated July 31, 1895. It is, therefore, safe to assume that this company first began making lariat about that time. Prior to that date some of the rope manufactured by this company had undoubtedly been used as lariat, although it was not made especially for that purpose.

Before the beginning of this century the Massachusetts firm made lariat of the same grade of manila fiber that was used in other manila ropes. One of the special kinds was a rope for running rigging on racing yachts. This line was called "Yacht Rope" and was made of the highest grade of manila fibers obtainable. It was creamy white in color, with a sheen almost like silk. It was stronger, tougher, and better in appearance than any other manila rope. Early in the year 1905, one of the salesmen, making a trip through the Southwest, had some samples of "Yacht Rope," which he was taking to the Pacific Coast. He showed them to the Padgitt Brothers, a Dallas saddlery firm, as examples of the finest product that had ever been made into manila rope. This Western firm requested that the Plymouth Cordage Company make some lariat out of the same kind of stock.[1] The salesman sent the order to the factory for "lariat made from Yacht rope stock." At the factory the new product was, at first, called "Yacht Lariat," and, as repeated orders followed, the name stuck to the product.[2]

When other manufacturers began to make a similar type of rope, this name was applied, preceded by the name of the individual firms. The Massachusetts firm called its

---

[1] Yacht rope is made with a very soft lay for ease in handling and free running through the blocks.

[2] In 1916 Colonel Jim Askew, who was with the Spark Show, was the first to introduce the Plymouth Cordage product to the rodeo cowboy. He had visited the company and was given a coil of rope. While there, he suggested that the company send a representative to the Sheepshead Bay Show to demonstrate the rope to the boys. (Incident related to the author by Herbert S. Maddy, J E Ranch, Waverly, New York.)

product "Plymouth Yacht Lariat." In the minds and literature of manufacturers and consumers, "Yacht Lariat"[1] came to be a grade of manila lariat.

The material used is the best grade of manila (abaca) fiber, which is grown in the Philippine Islands. This fiber comes from the stalk of the abaca tree—very similar to the banana tree—but it does not bear fruit. The better grades of fiber come from the center of the stalk of the best trees.

Originally, practically all lariat was 7/16 inch in diameter. Later some ropers wanted 3/8 inch lariat for roping calves. About 1912 or 1913 further refinements in size were required, and the Plymouth Cordage Company began making what is known as 3/8 inch "full," and 7/16 inch "full"; both of which were slightly over exact size.

Most ropers like to use one size of rope in their work. They become accustomed to a certain weight rope, as a billiard player does to a certain weight cue, and prefer not to make any change. In recent years the cowboys have been using ropes 30, 33, and 36 thread. Steer ropers use 36 thread; calf ropers use the smaller sizes, of which 27 thread is the smallest suitable for this type of work.

It is almost impossible to say how long a good rope will last. Much depends upon the roper and his horse. The careful, conservative roper may use a lariat for many months. He protects it against weather, keeps it out of the dirt, cleans and stores it in a canvas bag, when not in use. If he allows himself a little slack in roping, the life of a rope is often prolonged. A roper, not so concerned, may break a rope on his first or second catch. Bob Crosby,

---

[1] Often referred to as "Silk Manila Lariat."

who possesses the Roosevelt Trophy[1] from Pendleton, Oregon, is a roper of this type. Being a cripple, he has to bust his animal pretty hard and fast in order to to get down to it for the tie. He turns his horse fast, stops it quickly, and lets the rope take the full shock.

The product of the Plymouth Cordage Company is exactly what the cowboys want. The "lay" is just right, and the manufacturing processes are such that the rope runs a little more uniform in weight and "lay." The company has studied the product, asked for, received, and tried all kinds of suggestions made by the cowboys. As a result, the rope has been constantly improved. Plymouth Cordage Company knows the desires of the ropers, and they know the company. The cowboys are friends as well as customers.[2]

The tie rope, or the "piggin' string," used to make the three-leg cross tie has a slightly lower quality and a softer and looser "lay" than the lariat. It is about three-eighths of an inch thick. The "piggin' string" is carried coiled in the mouth or tucked under the belt, from where it can be quickly snatched when needed.

Roping horses are as famous in name and ability as the bucking ones; there are horses that have made a name for

---

[1] "Roosevelt trophy, [$4,500] an elaborate silver one, showing a cowboy on a bucking horse atop a silver globe representing the world, is presented by the Roosevelt Hotel of New York. For permanent possession it must be won three years in succession at the Cheyenne Frontier Days and at Pendleton's show.

"The trophy was first offered in 1923; Yakima Canutt winning it. Paddy Ryan won it in 1924 and Bob Crosby [in 1925]." [He won it the second time in 1927 and the third time in 1928.] East Oregonian (September 1, 1929), 1.

[2] Interview with Harry A. Taylor of Plymouth Cordage Company, manager of Southern Division Office, Houston, Texas, at Cheyenne, Wyoming. Correspondence with J. S. Bradford, Advertising Manager, Plymouth Cordage Company, North Plymouth, Mass.

themselves and their masters in the sport and have brought fame to both, because of the intelligence and understanding that they have shown. The roping horse is not so spectacularly named as his more rampageous, and belligerent kin, the bucking horse; nevertheless, he has carved a niche for himself.

Some of the better-known names of the well-trained and skillfully performing horses are "Comet," "Dogie," "Nord," "Roany," "V H," "Sadie," "Bartender," and "Streak." "V H" and "Streak" died in similar accidents about four years apart; the trailers carrying them overturned or broke loose and the animals were injured so seriously that they had to be killed. The loss of a fine horse, that has been a part of a cowboy's daily life and work, is felt as keenly as the death of a dear and close friend.

Perhaps the most famous roping horse of the arena today is "Baldy." He was four years old in 1936, when he started his rodeo work under the tutelage of that well-known cowboy, Ike Rude. Baldy was born near Claremore, Oklahoma, on the Dawson ranch and was purchased, at the age of one year, by R. Mason of Nowata, Oklahoma. Four years of his life were spent under this master; then he was purchased by Ike Rude. Thereafter, his life was changed. The brilliant performance of this man and his horse in 1936 was overshadowed by a most unfortunate accident. In the move from a Canadian contest to another rodeo, "Baldy's" trailer caught fire, and before his plight was discovered, he suffered serious burns. He still has scars from this accident on his left front leg. Rude, at that time, seriously considered disposing of "Baldy," but after he had consulted a veterinary, the horse was saved by understanding and sympathetic treatment.

Although the injuries were severe and there were difficulties in handling him, "Baldy" was pronounced cured early in the following spring and carried Ike to the pot of gold sought by every cowboy of the arena. His recovery was remarkable, and the men in rodeo were amazed that he could still be useful in this high tension work.

When "Baldy" performs in the calf roping event in some of the classic contests of the country, the spectator has a thrilling moment. He was recognized as one of the most active and skilled horses in rodeo; he and his master parted company in January, 1942, when he was purchased from Rude by Clyde Burk for the sum of twenty-five hundred dollars![1] The spring of 1942 found "Baldy" and his new master "standing" the people in the aisles in performances on the Eastern circuit of the new Flying A Ranch Stampede. Before summer arrived, Clyde and "Baldy" made a name for themselves among the many fans of rodeo in several large Eastern cities.[2]

Among other excellent roping horses are Juan Salinas' "Honey Boy" and Buck Sorrell's "Bill," also known as "Pound." "Pound" is a small horse and is especially good in an indoor arena, because he has a great deal of speed for a long score. He is called "Pound" because he tries so hard to catch his calf; he runs doggedly after it as fast as he can, but the calf seems to be running much faster than the horse.

Clay Carr of Visalia, California, has a fine horse known as "Jay." He is also known as "Set-em-Up." He is one

---

[1] This amount is the highest on record ever paid for a calf roping horse.

[2] Clyde Burk was fatally injured at the National Western Stock Show and Rodeo, Denver, January 21, 1945. He was hazing for Bill Hancock in the bulldogging event when the horse he was riding stumbled and rolled on him. Clyde Burk died the next morning without regaining consciousness.

of the few roping horses with sense of his own but does not always use it properly. Upon carrying the rider close to the calf, and, after the rider has twirled his rope a couple of times, "Set-em-Up" figures the calf is caught; then he stops hard and fast, whether the roper has caught the calf or not. Sometimes the rider has not even thrown his rope. He is a difficult horse to ride because of this thinking power; he stops so quickly that he has thrown Clay Carr and John Bowman, both Rodeo-Association-of-America All-Around Champions, and several other cowboys who have tried to ride him.

And Clay Carr! He, Everett Bowman, and Louis Brooks are the only men who, up to the present time, have won twice the R. A. A. All-Around Cowboy Championship. Clay, holder of the Jo Mora Salinas Trophy, is a strange man, difficult to meet and extremely hard to get acquainted with. He is, without a question, one of the great cowboys of the age; a man of many complexes, one of which is inferiority; yet he is one of the smartest, shrewdest, and cleverest individuals in rodeo. He has an air of indifference toward the desires and opinions of others, and appears to lead a rather lonely life, perhaps, because he has a very suspicious nature. In spite of this, Clay has the respect and admiration of everyone in the business and is regarded as a very tough customer in a business deal, fight, or a poker game.

One does not try to figure out this man of moods, but rather accepts whatever friendship he offers; one is flattered by any politeness, consideration, interest, or attention he may show. He seldom goes east to contest, but in the West and particularly at the California shows, he is a master and can "take," in his own inimitable way, most of the boys competing against him.

Irby Mundy, one of the oldest cowboys still contesting, formerly owned a horse by the name of "Hap." He was one of the few horses that died with "his boots on." During a steer wrestling contest, when Irby was hazing a steer for Bill McMacken, who was riding "Hap," the horse stumbled and fell to the ground with his rider under him. In the pile were Bill and the steer. When they were finally untangled, it was discovered that "Hap" had collapsed in the run and had died of heart failure.

"Rowdy," another famous horse, is owned by Andy Jauregui of Newhall, California. "Honest John," a steer wrestling and calf roping horse, carried Harry Hart to the Steer Wrestling Championship in 1939. He was hurt in an accident and died at the age of seventeen years. "Chico," Gene Ross' horse, carried his master three times to the coveted position of steer wrestling champion. Among the old-time contestants, Bob Crosby heads the list with two very fine animals, "Bullet," his steer roping horse, and "Comet," his calf roping horse. "Comet" is so well reined that Bob often shows him in exhibitions, guiding him with only a wire around his neck—no bit, no bridle.

A good roping horse is seldom used in steer wrestling, unless it be for the purpose of hazing. This does not seem to do any harm. But the very best roping horses are not, as a rule, used in any event except in roping. The steer wrestling horse must learn to carry his rider along side the steer, close enough to allow the rider to jump on the steer. A roping horse must stay right behind the calf or steer in order to give the roper every opportunity for the right kind of throw. A few horses have occasionally been used for both events, but this tends to confuse them, and spoils them for both events.

A good roping horse is very hard to find; many of the very best ropers are willing to pay a fourth of whatever they win to the man who owns a good horse and will permit them to ride him. It is said that Toots Mansfield, the World's Champion Calf Roper for three consecutive years, hunted a long time for a roping horse that suited his needs. However, all are very glad to rent their horses to this champion, and his good fortune is theirs.

In checking over the names of the many men participating in the calf roping event and in the steer and team roping contests, one finds a duplication of names. Even more obvious is the fact that the outstanding men and the champions for the past twelve years are men from the Southwestern states of Texas, Arizona, New Mexico, Nevada, Oklahoma, and California. Roping has always been a necessity on the ranches. The contenders for this crown of modern rodeo are men from these various states. The names of Toots Mansfield, Bud Spilsbury, Bob Crosby, Dee Burk, Clyde Burk, Carl Shepard, Hub Whiteman, John Bowman, Roy Lewis, Jess Goodspeed and his brother Buck, Buck Eckols, Homer Pettigrew,[1] Ike Rude, Dave Campbell, John Rhodes and his son, Tommy, Buckshot Sorrells, Juan and Tony Salinas, Everett Shaw, and Hugh Bennett, are very prominent in this particular phase of rodeo work.

Closely allied to the calf roping contest, but rarely seen at rodeos, are the Single Dally Steer Roping and Dally Team Roping contests. Seldom does one see both these

---

[1] 1946 Calf Roping Champion (I. R. A.)

events on the same program with calf roping, and seldom do they appear outside of the Southwestern states. One of the above contests occasionally appears with calf roping in the Northwest and in the East, and it is always a privilege to see this type of roping. However, the calf roping contest, although not so spectacular as other roping events that use larger animals, does give the audience the opportunity of seeing the animal roped and tied, while these other two events are roping contests only.

Both the single dally and the dally team roping contests are conditioned by the arena, and this in turn determines the start and deadline rules. As in the calf roping contest, there are three timers, a deadline referee, a tie or field judge, and other officials considered necessary for conducting the event.

A contestant in the single dally steer roping is allowed one loop. If he fails to make his catch, he is retired from the arena. If the steer is roped, the contestant must dally to stop the steer, for a tied rope is an infringement on the rules. The catch must be made by placing the rope over the head or the head and one horn of the animal. Should the roper succeed in catching the head or horns and one front foot, he is penalized five seconds; any other type of catch means disqualification. Should there be any question concerning the catch, the decision of the judges determines the matter.

The event is timed from the moment the steer crosses the deadline until it has been roped and the horse has brought the animal to a stop and faces it with the rope taut. The contestant is penalized ten seconds for beating or breaking the barrier; he is disqualified, if in the opinion of the judges, he has intentionally handled the animal roughly.

In the dally team roping contest each man is permitted only one rope but is allowed two throws. When the animal crosses the deadline, he belongs to the roper, regardless of what happens. He must first be roped by the head or horns, or head and one horn. If the animal is caught by the head or horns and one front foot, the roper is penalized five seconds; other catches mean disqualification. One partner of the roping team is required to rope one or both hind feet; however, a penalty of five seconds is imposed if only one hind foot is caught. If the steer is allowed to back into a loop, the roper is penalized or disqualified. In this event, as in the former, the rope must be dallied and not tied.

Under no conditions must the steer be thrown. The timing of the event is not complete until the steer is stopped and both horses are facing the beast in line with ropes tight. Penalties and disqualifications are the same as for the single roping event.

These events need a combination of well-trained horses and fast and skilled ropers with strong ropes. The strength and weight of the steers may very quickly ruin the well-made plans of the contestants, for a broken rope almost always ends the drama. However, the strength of the animal is recognized by the judges, and if the ropes have been properly placed, under certain circumstances, allowances are made by the officials for broken ropes![1]

During the annual convention of the Rodeo Association of America held at Colorado Springs, Colorado, in January, 1942, it was decided to include the events of

---

[1] It is entirely within the discretion of the judges of the contest.

Single Steer Tying and Team Tying with those already recognized and receiving Association points. Both these contests have been long in coming about, not because of an insufficient number of interested participants for the events, but because there is much criticism if they are not carried out exactly according to rules. Steer tying is perhaps the wildest event in rodeo; only about five shows offer it as a contest—Cheyenne, Wyoming; Pendleton, Oregon; Safford, Arizona; and one or two others. Excitement reigns high when the cowboys "bust" those big steers and tie them as if they were calves! "Busting them" is done by turning the horse at an angle to the steer after the catch and by running him off fast enough so that the steer is jerked around, off his feet, and stunned slightly when he hits the ground. This is known as "taking a trip" and also as "laying it behind 'em." The rules governing the arena and the number of officials selected for judging these two events are the same as those for other roping events.

The single steer contest allows the participants to have two ropes. If, in roping the animal, the first attempt is not a qualified catch, the second rope may be used; however, only if the first rope is free from the steer or free from the saddle, for in this event, the rope is *tied* to the saddle when the roper proceeds to tie the steer.

In roping the steer, the qualified catches are: around the horns, over the head or half of the head, or around the neck. The loop may include one front foot. Should the animal be caught in any other fashion, the roper must not attempt to throw the steer, for any catch other than those listed is designated as a foul, and the roper is signaled to retire from the arena, if he attempts to throw his animal under these conditions. After making a disqualified catch and releasing the rope, the contestant may use his second rope. In a qualified catch the steer is thrown and tied with a three-leg cross; then the roper signals that his work is completed. After giving the signal, he brings his horse forward to give slack to the rope, while the tie is being examined by the judge. Should the steer be able to get to his feet before the judge has determined whether or not the tie was a fair one, the roper is allowed no time on that steer.

Some confusion results in the rules governing the single steer tying event and in those governing the dally steer roping, because they are often combined. They must be carefully observed and kept separate. Any change in this procedure results in failure to conduct the contest properly; it allows criticism on the part of the contestants participating in the event, and also on the part of outside agencies that are not sympathetic towards roping contests.

Another roping contest, that of team tying, has been recognized recently by the Rodeo Association as a rodeo event. Points are given so that, eventually, the participants will be granted the championship at the end of the season.

> [The] team [is] allowed only two loops at the head and should they miss with both loops, [the] team must retire from the arena and will receive no time; after steer is properly roped by the head, the other partner has two loops at the steer's hind feet and should he miss both loops, team will receive no time. If either roper ropes [the] steer after judge's signal "no time," the team will be disqualified in all events for the rest of the contest.[1]

---

[1] "Team Tying," *Constitution, etc.,* 19.

The first catch must be made by the head, half head, or horns of the animal, while the second catch is made on one or both hind feet. Should the steer fall before the second catch is placed on the hind foot or feet, he must be allowed to stand and regain his footing. Before the tie is started, both ropes must be properly and securely placed on the animal, and no part of the catch ropes may be used to make the tie; only then may he be tied by both legs below the hocks. The steer may be thrown by means of tripping, stretching, or "tailing down." The tie is then examined and passed on by the judge, whose decision is final. There is the usual ten seconds' penalty for beating and breaking the barrier.

Both these events, so recently recognized by the Rodeo Association of America, will no doubt bring forth some new names in the rodeo world. It will be of interest to note whether or not this recognition as major events will make them popular and important phases of rodeo sports. Because of the similarity, it is not probable that these four roping contests will be included in one rodeo, but if there should ever be a competition of roping activities alone, it would afford a great opportunity to witness these very skillful cowboy actions. A contest of this nature with worthy purses, held in the Southwest, where roping is still the work of many of the people in the cattle country and an activity very dear to them, would bring out the finest men and create widespread interest.

An occasional roping-match is worked up between two outstanding contestants; such contests attract people from far and near. Such a match has been carried on for several years between Bob Crosby of Roswell, New Mexico, and George Weir of Monument, New Mexico. The two men,

single handed—according to the rules—rope and tie ten
steers for a one-thousand-dollar prize. In recent years the
contest has gained importance because it has become very
well known. The title of Champion Steer Roper has moved
from Bob Crosby to Carl Arnold of Buckeye, Arizona,
who, in turn, was challenged by King Merritt of Cheyenne,
Wyoming. From five to six thousand fans attended the
exhibition. These men show rare talent and ability, and
the contest is looked forward to as an annual event.

CHAPTER XVIII

THE MODERN URSUS

Here's to the bulldogger!
—He may tear his pants—
As with the tough steer
He wrestles and rants.

Of all the various contests in rodeo it is said that bull-dogging or steer wrestling[1] offers the greatest amount of eye-appeal to the spectator. For dash, daring, and audacity on the part of the contestant, the handling of the tough, wild, vicious brutes creates a tremendous thrill. People who know and follow rodeo cannot decide whether this spectacular display of strength is more sensational in its appeal or in the exhibition of finesse and skill. There is always the possibility, in an evaluation of dangerous activities, of mistaking a reckless, fearless, and daring action

---

[1] "Pendleton rodeo and annual scene of the greatest cowboy show of the west has received advice from England that 'bulldogging' is not 'bulldogging.'

"That great rodeo event in which a cowboy grapples with a wild steer and throws him for the count, is called 'bulldogging,' but it is a misnomer, recites the British complaint.

"It is pointed out in the complaint that the English bulldog evolved in the bullfighting days of the tight little Isle. That's why the bulldog has a turned up nose. After sinking his teeth in the velvety nose of a bull he could continue breathing.

"Now a cowboy bites a bull's nose during a bulldogging exhibition but he cannot sink his teeth in the animal's lip until the beast has been thrown. Therefore, the British suggest that this bull versus man event be given some other name." *Sun Star,* Merced, California (November 1, 1926).

for skilled training, and to allow the former to overpower and dazzle the sense of values—that is, to permit the danger element to overshadow the true worth of skill. It is generally conceded among contestants that steer wrestling does involve great danger,[1] but the man of strength and fearless nature can, without years of practice, achieve greater results in less time in this event than can the bronc riders and calf ropers in their respective fields.

There are two opinions as to when and where steer wrestling first originated. One holds that this great sport was introduced by the Mexicans, and later taken up by the American cowboy to overcome the belligerent calf or steer that resisted the rope and fought the branding iron. The other holds that steer wrestling was never a part of the actual work of the cowboy on the round-up, but became a rodeo feature through the daring performance of a colored cowhand of southern Texas, named Bill Pickett. The latter contention seems to be the more acceptable.

The fascinating story that lies behind this first appearance of steer wrestling, early in this century, (1910), reveals the reckless, "devil-may-care" attitude of the performer of an act which is still considered one of the most spectacular in the rodeo arena. As the story goes—based on tradition and hearsay, and elaborated upon in repitition—Bill, upon failing to drive a steer into a corral, became angry and leaped from his horse to the steer's head and proceeded to wrestle the animal to the ground. There

---

[1] "Amazing pluck was exhibited by Ray McCarrell, in the bulldogging contest at the Stampede Friday. When he was handling the steer it turned on him and ran a horn from the back of his knee through to the kneecap, which was displaced. The pain must have been terrific, but he stayed at his task until he finished, and then limped to the stand and watched the rest of the contests, meanwhile calmly smoking a cigarette." *Calgary Daily Herald* (September 2, 1919), 11.

Upper: Bulldogging a steer in "The Old Days."
—*E. A. Brininstool, Photographer.*

Lower: Woman Steer Roper (1910).
—*Courtesy Chamber of Commerce, Cheyenne, Wyoming.*

are many versions of the original tale; one, especially, adds considerable color. It relates that the colored cowboy, as he twisted the head of the animal, grasped the lower lip between his own teeth and held the beast in this position until he succeeded in causing it to fall to the ground. This method of biting the lower lip of the steer brought about the term "bulldogging," because, if a bulldog were set upon a steer, the running beast would lower its horns to fight off the dog. Thus, the bulldog could sink its teeth into the steer's lip. The dog would pull back; the pain of the hold on the lip, together with the added momentum of the yanking, would cause the steer to fall. There are various interpretations of this struggle, and, although the details differ, essentially the story carries the same theme.

The fame of Bill's feat spread, and he was hired to appear at rodeos to demonstrate his skill for a rather meager fee. Later he joined a Wild West Show and traveled throughout the country. He was injured while performing with the Miller Brothers Wild West Show at the Jamestown Exposition in 1907, and Lon Seeley, a half-drunk cowboy with the show, substituted for Pickett and became the first white bulldogger. Thus, eventually the cowboys took up Bill's trick and mastered it; now steer wrestling is one of the major features of nearly every rodeo. Bill Pickett has passed from the scene of his triumph, but his name has not been forgotten and is woven into the legends of the sport. The name Pickett is still carried on in the sport by his nephew, Joe Pickett, popularly known as "Lucky Boy" Williams.

The contest of steer wrestling is governed by arena conditions, as are also the start and deadline rules. For this contest there are three timers, a deadline referee, a field judge, and other officials appointed by the managers of the rodeo.

The contestant must furnish his own horse and one hazer to work with him. After being released from the chute and after crossing the ten-foot head start line,[1] the steer belongs to the wrestler. With a quick pace the contestant and hazer work, one on each side of the running animal. The position of the contestant depends on which side he wishes "to take" the animal. The hazer must keep the steer moving in a straight course until the cowboy is prepared to leap from his mount to the head and horns of the beast and must then later pick up the cowboy's horse. After catching the steer, the wrestler must bring him to a stop and he accomplishes this by swinging his body forward, using his heels as a brake. In a cloud of dust the plunging animal is stopped; then the work of twisting him down begins. Should the animal be knocked down or thrown[2] by the impact of the hurtling body of the man, or should it be thrown by the wrestler driving the animal's horns into the ground, the beast must be allowed to get up on all four feet, and then be thrown. A steer is not considered thrown until he is lying flat on his side with all four feet out and head straight.[3]

---

[1] This distance varies according to the size of the arena and is known as the *score*. When there is no *score*, the contest is called "lap and tap."

[2] Hoolihaning — The act of leaping forward and landing on the horns of the steer in bulldogging in such a manner as to knock the steer down without having to resort to twisting him down by twisting the head and neck. This is barred in recognized events. It does happen, however, accidentally.

[3] Pegging — The act in which a steer wrestler sticks the horns into the ground to aid him in twisting the head of the animal, causing it to fall. This is barred in recognized contests.

There is a time limit of two minutes in this contest; if the wrestler has not caught and thrown the steer in this time, he is retired from the arena and given a rating of no time. Penalties are imposed on the contestant for interference by the hazer and for beating or breaking the barrier. Although there is no penalty listed for breaking a horn of the animal, if this should happen, the beast is usually released, and the contestant given no time. Undue abuse of the animal and tampering with the steers or chutes mean disqualification. It does not seem possible that a beast of 700 or 750 pounds could possibly be abused by any actions on the part of a man weighing 180 to 200 pounds. Because of the criticism directed against the steer wrestling event, these rules are observed very strictly.

Among the bronc riders there are men such as Fritz Truan, Chet McCarty, and Bill McMacken who also make a specialty of steer wrestling. Both Fritz and Chet are known as riders of tough horses and are as different in personality as any two men can be. Chet is a quiet, rather shy, gentle man; most people think of him as belonging in a Will James story. He spends a good deal of his time running the B Double A Ranch, near Tucson, Arizona, but he manages to attend most of the larger contests in the country. Since 1939 he has been a contestant at the Madison Square Garden Show and in 1941 won the Bronc Riding event at that contest. With a low time of 4-2/5 seconds in steer wrestling, he is a threat to the best of contestants. Chet has a quiet, natural, friendliness about him that endears him to his friends. He was born in Bowe, Washington, and is another of the great bronc riders from the Northwest.

In contrast to the serene and gentle Chet, the fabulous Fritz Truan[1] was one of the wildest, most "hell-raising" youths that ever hit the rodeo world. Proud of his capers and escapades—whether it was poker playing, driving a car, or getting tight—he did everything in a most spectacular way. He was twice winner of the R. A. A. Bronc Riding Championship, 1939 and 1940, and in the latter year also became the All-Around Championship Cowboy. Born in Ceile, California, not far from Mexicali, he began "rodeoing" at the age of nineteen, and this bronc riding, steer wrestling cowboy, who had a weakness for Scotch melodies, was one of the brightest stars of rodeo.

Steer wrestling as an event is not well-received in all districts; especially not in the state of California and in Canada where the event undergoes some minor changes. There it is called Steer Decorating, a less spectacular, but none the less dangerous, variation of the original event, and especially so for the man in the case. The event differs in that the contestant, upon leaping from his horse to the head of the steer and while the animal is going full speed,

---

[1] The author last saw and visited with Fritz Truan in Boulder, Colorado, 1944, during the Pow Wow Celebration. Fritz was traveling with his wife, the former Norma Holmes, and some friends. They had just come from Cheyenne Frontier Days where Fritz contested and were attending the Boulder contest before returning to the West Coast. Fritz was to be reassigned to new duties in the South Pacific.

We sat under the end gate of a truck to escape the hot sun pouring down on the rodeo grounds. Fritz was quiet and reticent, and seemed greatly changed. From his conversation, one knew he had seen plenty of action and he was anxious for the war to be over. At this time he had over-stayed his leave but these few weeks of rodeoing had given him a great deal of pleasure and happiness. Fritz Truan is one of the boys that did not come back.

"Sgt. Fritz Truan, United States Marine Corps, of Salinas, California, R.A.A. World's Champion Cowboy, 1940, was killed in action in Iwo Jima, February 28, 1945, according to word received by Mrs. Fritz Truan of Henryetta, Oklahoma." "R.A.A. Bulletin," *Bulletin, Rodeo Association of America* 9 (April 1945).

places around the nose a rubber band or puts a band decorated with ribbons on a horn. The decoration to be used and the place of application is decided upon by the managers of the contest. Another change in the contest is that, if the contestant misses his steer, he is allowed to take the hazer's horse and continue; however, the time limit of one minute does not often offer this opportunity.

The steer must be on all four feet when decorated, and the breaking of a rubber band or shortening of ribbons disqualifies the cowboy. There is also a penalty of ten seconds for beating or breaking the barrier.

The steer wrestling horse used by the cowboy is usually of the Quarter Horse breed and is especially trained to bring the rider close enough to the fleeing beast to enable the cowboy to make his leap. The sport is strictly a man's sport; a few women have entered the work—but from the standpoint of exhibition rather than competition.

Among some of the well-known horses of this work that have earned fame for their riders are "Little Hog Eyes," "Stranger," "Silver," "Blue Boy," "Sport," and "Crutches." A mare by the name of "Biddy," formerly owned by Bill McMacken, is considered one of the fastest of all cowboy horses. Used in the steer wrestling contest, she is chiefly valuable as a hazing horse. "Biddy" also has a reputation as a roping horse; she was formerly used in this event by John Bowman and was considered by him as one of the best. Occasionally when Bill was roping at smaller contests, "Biddy" seemed more than willing to cooperate.

Dick Herren's bay stud, "Hardtack,"[1] was also a very

---

[1] "Hard Tack" died of pneumonia while Dick was serving in the armed services as a Marine.

fine bulldogging horse and with him Dick succeeded in getting his steers. "Coon Dog," owned by Everett Bowman, and the horses "Roany" and "Speedball," belonging to Mike Fisher and Charles Colbert, are also worthy of mention in the naming of outstanding horses of the rodeo arena. The latter, "Speedball," is now considered by steer wrestlers as the top horse in this event. He is a very beautiful animal and shows considerable intelligence when put to test. All these animals are known for their ability to perform and offer their riders every advantage for success.

In 1933 a very remarkable record was established in steer wrestling at the contest held in Sidney, Iowa. A contestant of some years standing by the name of Shorty Ricker brought his ox to the ground in 3-4/5 seconds— then the world's record[1] time. This record, however, was broken some four years later at the Salt Lake City Rodeo. There, in the summer of 1937, Dave Campbell lowered the time for this event by reducing the record time 1/5 of a second; the next day in the same event, Hugh Bennett, of Arizona, tied the Campbell record, and the world's record time in steer wrestling is still held by these two men at 3-3/5 seconds.

One seldom finds among a group of men in any type of work so unique a personality as that of Dave Campbell. His personality is as expansive as his physique, and there is a "lot" of Campbell. He, with Gene Pruett, Bill Mc-Macken, Howard McCrorey, Toots Mansfield, and several others gives one the impression of walking among the lofty

---

[1] The question of world's record time is a delicate one because of the various start and deadline rules and also because of the type and weight of steers. However, Ricker's record was recognized as the best made at that time.

aboreal giants of northern California. Dave is not only great of stature, but great of heart and mind. He is a man not only skilled in his work, but also a roper and wrestler of words and idealogies. Well read, gifted in elucidation, and with a world point of view, he is at his best when tossing verbal loops with his friend, Gene Pruett.

Among the other prominent men in steer wrestling are Bill McMacken, Homer Pettigrew, and Chet McCarty. Bill, at one time, (1935) was co-holder with Ricker of the world's record time, and is at present the holder of the best time at Pendleton, Oregon—a very difficult arena— with the time 9-8/10 seconds established in 1941, after breaking his former record of 10-3/10 seconds in the same arena. Bill is a South Dakota boy, born at Pierre, but is better known as from Trail City of that state. His father owned and operated a cattle ranch. The youngest of a family of seven, Bill was fourteen when he began to tag along and follow in the footsteps of three older brothers, Joe, Fritz, and Bud, who had made names in the sport. Since 1936 Bill has been riding saddle broncs; he has a natural ability for this sport, although he is well known as a steer wrestler. Twice winner of the five-thousand dollar Jackson Trophy offered at the Pendleton Show, dark, handsome Bill has "rodeoed" through the country and was selected as one of the members of the American Team to go to Australia in 1939. The trip to that continent is one of the highlights of his life. People like Bill. Spectators are enthusiastic about him, for in appearance he is the epitome of the work. He has the look, the personality, and the ability of the ideal Western character.

Another interesting and talented chap in the steer wrestling game is Homer Pettigrew of New Mexico. As one of the most consistent winners, he is always hard to beat, no matter how bad his luck is running. A sturdy, husky lad, Homer is perfectly coordinated physically and can stand the hardships of the arena, as well as the strain of night-life and social activities—which are many! As All-Around Champion Cowboy of 1941, Steer Wrestling Champion of 1940, with a low time of 3-3/10 seconds, Champion Steer Wrestler for 1942, 1943, 1944, 1945, Homer has a flare for handling steers. He has an enviable record in this event in rodeo as well as in calf roping. At the age of twenty-six he had the honor of being top man in rodeo.

The speed and efficiency of the steer wrestler seem amazing, and while everyone does not have the opportunity to witness such breath-taking, record-breaking time, it is not unusual for one to witness steers thrown in five seconds. The fleeting instant of a second does not become important until a contest based on this unit of time is observed.

One of the difficulties faced by local managements of rodeo contests has been to prove to the Humane Societies that rodeo is not cruel to animals. This has required very delicate handling on the part of the promoters, and their sincerity and genuine effort to prevent any misunderstanding in this respect have been creditable.

There is no desire on the part of the rodeo officials or the contestants to harm the animals they own or use in the work. The animals not only have a monetary value, but are valuable because their characteristics are suitable for this work. Thus, an injured animal is a loss from both standpoints, and in this sport the care of the stock is an important financial saving that is uppermost in the minds of the contractors. The rules of the Rodeo Association of America and of the member-shows are made to protect the animal in every way possible. Upon examination of the rules, one can readily see that the beast is given consideration over the contestant.

In spite of all the protective measures, there has been an occasional flare-up over the treatment of animals in rodeo. In addition, there are the various interpretations of the matter by newspaper and magazine writers who have no knowledge or background of the sport. It is unfortunate that any misunderstanding between a contest-committee and the Humane Societies over the treatment of the animals cannot be settled by the two parties concerned without undue protestations from people who are incapable of judging the matter. Usually, any difficulties that may arise between the two organizations are settled satisfactorily in a very short time—long before the national publicity of the occasion has even had a good start. Thus, a minor incident and misunderstanding develop with no justifiication. If rodeo is cruel, then hunting, fishing, bull fighting, fox hunting, and pig sticking are barbarous.

Rodeo has had several close calls in having legislation discriminate against its activities, as became evident especially in California. In 1937 a bill was put before the State Senate which was so formulated that there was a possibility of prohibiting roping at rodeos, or might have been used, at least, as a wedge against the contests. The bill was directed at the motion picture industry to prevent cruelty to animals used in the business, but it could have been interpreted to include rodeo, if the legislation had been effective. Rodeo has always made a special effort to be in complete accord with the Humane Societies of that state. The managements of the California contests united at this time and brought their case before the legislating body, and the bill failed. Promoters of rodeos held in Los Angeles have made a practice to work with the Society for the Prevention of Cruelty to Animals rather than against them, and have made a request that the society, before attacking them publicly, come to the management and make a request for a change in conduct.

In 1939 the Great Western Rodeo at Los Angeles Union Stock Yards was "in for" much trouble, when, during a first performance, a group of women staged a demonstration inside the stadium. They were booed from the arena by most of the spectators. The next day a warrant was issued for the arrest of the promoter who was released on a one thousand dollar bond. When brought to court, he entered a plea of "not guilty," and the case was set for a week later. Upon hearing the case, the judge urged the jury to bring a verdict of "not guilty," since there was no evidence presented to corroborate the charge of cruelty. It is interesting to note that several representatives of the Humane Society agreed to testify that there had been no cruelty at this contest. These same demonstrators had also caused similar disturbances at Tucson and Phoenix, Arizona; however, without results.

Previous to these two attempts to accuse the rodeo of harboring cruelty to animals, the most famous attempt to blacken the name of the American sport was made in England in 1924. During the rodeo in London, newspapers and periodicals discussed this matter at great length.

The British public protested against the cruelty inflicted upon the steers in the steer roping event and thought that this American sport was as bad as Spanish bull fighting.

Some writers mentioned the great disapproval demonstrated by the spectators in regard to the event and expressed the hope that there would be an end to such performances in England; however, they admitted that rodeos were well attended and even popular in Canada and Australia. Other writers took an opposite view and stated that rodeo was healthy and no one would be the worse for attending.

On one occasion in London, the contestants were arrested on a cruelty to animal charge. A United Press dispatch said:

> After the rodeo defense had produced twenty witnesses Monday attempting to prove that steer roping and wrestling were not cruel, the trial of the American cowboys whose show at the Empire Exhibition was stopped was adjourned a week. . . . Laughs abounded when the Counselor for the defense asked the S. P. C. A. inspector who had declared steer roping cruel, "Have you ever been at the Grand National polo matches or at the Steeplechase?"[1]

---

[1] *Denver Post,* (July 1, 1924), 9.

"An amusing comment was made by Mrs. F. W. Swanton, general manager of the Humane Society of Oregon. After seeing the Pendleton Round-Up of 1927 she said:

" 'Most of the steers are accustomed to it, and roll over like cats as soon as a cowboy grabs them,' she declared. 'The Round-Up isn't perfect by any means. There are a great many bruises at the end of the program, but the society is glad to know that most of them are suffered by human beings who take part of their own volition, rather than by dumb animals, which have no say in the matter.'

"Mrs. Swanton has been assigned to be present at the Round-Up, and she will protect cattle and horses from possible cruelty. In regard to the bucking horses, she continued:

" 'As a matter of fact, most of the horses enjoy the bucking contests more than do the riders. I have seen some of the so-called outlaw horses actually smile after they have unseated a cowboy.' " *East Oregonian,* Pendleton, Oregon (September 18, 1927), 1.

Some ten years later, in 1934, Tex Austin, having taken a rodeo to London, was arrested on the same charge; the matter was settled amicably, when the calf roping event was eliminated for the duration of the show.

It is not the purpose of this study to point out that the citizens of other countries participate in sports in which our standards of cruelty are shocked, for there is no justification in our actions in maligning the activities of others that we do not understand, nor is there any need to justify the actions of rodeo when dealing with the animals that are used in the sport. Rodeo stock is the best fed and cared for stock of any in the world; the unfortunate accidents that do occur in relation to the stock are few in comparison to sports of a similar nature.[1]

---

[1] At the 49th Annual Cheyenne Frontier Days a woman carrying a large placard walked among the paraders. The card read: "Rodeo Sport is Savage. It Breeds Crime."

CHAPTER XIX

BULLS AND BUTTOCKS

The Brahma bull's the one to fear,
Great to watch—but not too near!
Never know what the bull will do—
His next target might be you!

A highlight event of the rodeo, from the standpoint of thrills for the audience, is the bull riding contest. In spite of the fact that this contest is seldom given the publicity that it rightly deserves as a thrilling attraction, it does offer a type of emotion to the spectator which continues to bring him back when other events will fail to do so. The bull riding contest offers the spectator a thrill based on the expectation of seeing a contestant thrown, gored, and tossed on the horns of an ugly, humpbacked, vicious bull, usually of the Brahma breed. While this is not a pleasant thought, still it is possible to pack stadiums and arenas with thousands of sensation-seeking people, 90 percent of whom attend the contest with the idea of seeing a contestant succeed in his ride or be thrown. Seldom does the average spectator take into account or appreciate, in the full sense of the word, the riding ability, skill, and years of practice needed for success as displayed by the man in rodeo. The spectator is aware of only the contestant being successful in the work or failing to make the grade, he passes judgment by seeing a man thrown or fall without considering that he has made a good ride or performed his duties with skill. Thus, in the mind of the spectator the element of danger plays an important part in the concept of the success of the event. This is not an attempt to say that the majority of spectators in the rodeo crowds wish to see a man injured; however, close calls, the almost serious injury, the precarious slips, that are a part of the bull riding event, titilate the senses. This is a thrill, created by expectation of a terrifying sight which the spectators hope will not happen. They are not anxious to have anything happen, but if it should, they want to see it!

No other event in rodeo offers to the senses that same emotion, for the bull riding contest is unique in that one-half of the performing element is a murderous beast. The dangers in every other contest of rodeo are doubled in this particular one. A man may be injured by a fall or a kick from a horse, steer, or calf, but this injury does not come from the vicious actions of a treacherous animal wishing to show his hatred of man by attacking him on the first opportunity. Another thrill that the audience experiences in the bull riding contest arises from the ever-present feeling that the beast is conscious of the crowd and would attack if possible. This feeling pervades the spectators and either gives them a sensation of being akin to the daring cowboys, a sense of fearlessness and bravery, or a fascination created by the sheer danger and horror of what could happen if the beast were able to get among the crowds. A bull, having been freed of the rider, circles the arena and stares intently at the spectators, as they sit securely behind the wire barrier, which separates them from about seventeen hundred pounds of nasty bull.

The Brahma bull has several characteristics that make it one of the most dangerous beasts to be associated with in any manner. It has the universal characteristic of a bull of any breed, that is the attacking of unknown, moving objects not akin to it. A person who ventures on foot into an enclosure holding Brahma bulls is taking a serious risk. A man on horseback is not safe unless there is sufficient space for him to move his mount out of the way of the animal's charge. It is said that the Brahma bull charges with his eyes open, thus making the attack on the victim more accurate and vicious. This particular bit of information was not gathered by first hand experience, but its authenticity cannot and will not be challenged.

During the Fort Worth Show of 1937, a Brahma bull got loose, jumped a nine-foot fence, and proceeded to leave the building by the front entrance. He was met by a group of policemen—Texans by birth—who took no chances with a bull "on the loose." They shot him forty times; besides the bull as a target, several automobiles were included, not to mention several scared pedestrians who sought to get out of the animal's way. He was eventually downed, and to end his misery, it was necessary to cut his throat.

Another characteristic of this breed of bull is that it is not content with throwing the rider, but invariably, after ridding itself of its burden, it turns and fights, and woe to the man who is too slow or unable to get away from the vicinity of the beast. This is evidenced by the actions of the "hands" helping in the arena when a Brahma "on the loose" swerves their way. They make the fastest move credited to a cowboy and seek the highest possible point out of reach of the animal's horns. Like clinging monkeys at the side of a cage, they wait at the top of the chute gates and wire barrier enclosing the arena until the animal has moved away. The cross-bred Brahma bull is not an animal to be taken casually, nor is it wise to underrate his ability to be tough.[1]

While these animals are not the recipients of names as often as the bucking horses are, there are some that have been labeled with surprising accurateness. The names of "Yellow Fever," "Double Trouble," "Spillum," "Yellow Jacket," and "Black Widow" show remarkable sense-fitness for the occasion. "Wasp," "Buzzard," "Cyclone," "L'il Abner," "Aggravation," "Bad Dreams," "Deer Face," "High Noon," "Arkansas Traveller," "Tiger," "Tom Collins," and "Shimming Sam" do not miss their mark; as bulls, they have a reputation of being able to "turn on" the misery for the riders. Among the bucking bulls, "Sonora Red" has a reputation for piling the boys in the dust, and not satisfied with this, he continues to buck until removed completely from the scene of action and returned to the stock corral. During the 1940 season "Sonora Red" was

[1] Observed by author while attending rodeos, 1940-1945. "Probably the highlight of the rodeo was the bullriding event. The bulls turned out of the chutes were Brahma celebrities exclusively and were headed by such devastating bovines as Double Trouble, who is reputed never to have been ridden the 8 seconds to the whistle by any contestant at any show. The jovial Brahma did not content themselves by turning on the riders after they were thrown, but were determined to roister among the newspapermen and news photographers, whom they either put to flight or scattered hither and yon with abandon and insouciance. And when the bull throws a newspaperman — that's news!" "Round'Up th Paster," by Stan, *Hoofs and Horns* 10 (April 1941), 8.

"The notable indoor Tulsa rodeo got its name from the fact that during the show there three years ago, a big Brahma bull hopped the arena fence, climbed the stadium steps and circled the top deck of the spacious Tulsa fair grounds enclosure a couple of times. The resultant antics of the several thousand spectators then on the same side of the fence with the Brahma, causes this to be the Third Annual 'Stampede,' comin' up." Vincent, B., ed. Oklahoma, *Herdsman*, Tulsa, Oklahoma, *Hoofs and Horns* 10 (April 1941), 8.

Upper: Mrs. Riordan, the only woman rider of her day who rode bucking broncs, using a side saddle.
—*Photograph by E. A. Brininstool, 1912.*

Center: "Sharkey," the Belgrade Bull, Pendleton, Oregon, 1912.
—*E. A. Brininstool, Photographer.*

Lower: Tillie Baldwin doing the Roman Stand, Pendleton, Oregon, 1912.
—*E. A. Brininstool, Photographer.*

able to unseat every cowboy save two, who still remained seated on the signal of the finish of the ride.

In the bull riding contest the cowboys and animals are selected by the management of the show for each performance. The stock is numbered and drawn for by the selected performers. If a man has already worked on the animal he draws in this particular event, he must draw again. When the animal is placed in the chute, his front quarters are encircled with a loose rope that is fastened in such a manner that upon completion of the ride it will fall off. Knots or hitches to prevent this are forbidden. This rope must have a bell attached; without this no time is given. The animal is also equipped with a flank strap similar to that used on the bucking horses for the same purpose.[1]

The ride is for eight seconds[2] and is timed from the moment the animal leaves the chute. If a rider is knocked off at the chute, or if the animal falls in the enclosure, the rider may be granted a re-ride at the discretion of the judges. The riding must be done with one hand; the other must be kept in the air at all times. It is of interest to see how the rope is wrapped about and grasped in the hand, and how, with the violent actions of the animal, the grip becomes tighter because of the peculiar placement of the rope in the palm of the hand. The beast must be spurred satisfactorily.

The contestant may be disqualified for cheating in any manner, for bucking off, for not being ready when called to ride, for touching the beast with his hat or free hand, for

[1] The flank strap has a tendency to make the bull buck.
[2] Ten seconds in Canada.

using sharp spurs or spurs with locked rowels. The animal must not be spurred in the chute.

Some years ago, a form of cheating known as "sweating a steer" was practiced. A particularly vicious and fiery beast could be excited and disturbed by pulling the flank strap tight, so that when the time came to leave the chute, the animal would be tired and not give such a tough ride. This practice, in addition to that of spurring the animal in the chute to excite him before "the turn-out," is forbidden.

In the bull riding event the animal is given every opportunity to throw his rider. Many a good contestant must leave the back of a bull because of the annoying practice of the animal to run along a wooden or wire fence or to run headlong toward the barrier and stop short and pitch the man over his head. Even worse is the habit of turning away from the fence to slide sideways, thus crushing the contestant's leg or body against the fence. There are no pick-up men or any particular aid for the cowboy bull rider except the action of the clowns. From the moment the bulls are run into the chutes until they leave the arena, this contest is packed full of every sort of thrill imaginable.

Among the prominent bull riders, the names of Smokey Snyder, Gene Rambo, John Schneider, and Dick Griffith are perhaps the best known. Some of these men have held several times the championship crown for the event. Smoky Snyder, five times holder of the World's Champion Bull Riding event and that of Bareback Bronc Riding twice, is a specialist in bareback events. A talented bull man but also a rider of broncs, he demonstrated his skill conclusively in 1932 at the Calgary Stampede when he won both these events.

Smokey is in his thirties and appears as a short, slim, but well-built man. He has been part of rodeo since 1923, when he first began riding; he is a great favorite in any crowd before which he appears. Making the most of his height, sticking out his chest and walking with a swagger, Smokey gives the impression of being a tough, but this belies his true nature. He is a gentle and kind fellow, rather solemn of face, but with twinkling eyes and easy speech; his slight build masks a body of muscle; in riding the beasts, he gives everything his body and mind are capable of for a magnificent performance. Smokey, when asked what he thinks about while on the back of a heaving beast, said in his quiet, easy way, "Lots of things"; and when pressed further, he answered laconically, "Ah don't dare tell!"

He has appeared in every important show in the country, and was one of the selected few to be asked to join the Tex Austin Show that went to London. His name will always be remembered in the sport, for not only has his career been brilliant and consistent, but he also has the confidence of everyone in the work. His advice to the younger riders in the bareback events is something to be heeded; they listen to "that man named Smokey" with respect and appreciation. It is a privilege to say, "Smokey is my friend."

Other men who have distinguished themselves in the bull riding contest are George "Kid" Fletcher, Carl Dossey, Jim Patch, Gerald Roberts, Paul Gould, George Mills, and Bob Estes—all men of courage and ability.

A discussion of bull riding is not complete without some comment upon that hero of the arena, the rodeo clown. He takes every known chance every time he steps into the arena; 90 per cent of his work is devoted to making fun of the cowboys, kidding about their falls and spills, their failures to make a ride, their lack of success in roping a scampering calf. In general, the clown appears to be making a nuisance of himself. Sometimes he has a spot on the program for his special nonsense, and with the aid of a remarkably trained horse or mule he puts on a show that endears him and his brand of humor to the spectator. It is, however, during the twenty or thirty minutes that it takes to run off the bull riding contest that the rodeo clown shows the "stuff he is made of." During this time he is constantly placing himself in every precarious position, letting himself wide open to meet eternity in a very sudden and thorough way.

His work during this contest is planned work, and although it gives the appearance of being all fun and nonsense, the illusion is too successful to be convincing that it is anything but hard and dangerous. The playful slaps on the rump, the tantalizing pulls on the tail of the animal, the "razzle dazzle" gridiron tactics from left to right, the ducking and diving in and out of the wooden barrel, which is the clown's only protection from the animal—all seem to be just so much joyous living. Contrary to belief, they are all well-calculated moves to keep his coat-tails from being parted over a twenty-inch spread of skull and horn. The rodeo clown is the best friend of the bull riders. Many a time he must step in at the right moment and take every chance of losing his own skin, to draw, by his clever trickery, the attention of an ugly beast upon himself and away from the prostrate form of an unfortunate cowboy. It is this split-second action and timing of the clown that make him a great performer or, upon failure to function at the right moment, a dead hero.

Some wives of rodeo contestants have said that, if ever their husbands should take to bull riding, there would be a divorce. One wonders what might be the form of rebellion of the wife whose husband should suddenly feel the urge to try his hand at clowning! There must be some unusual kind of emotion—either one of genuine recklessness or one of imagination—that will induce a man to face, without adequate protection, a beast of some seventeen-hundred pounds with murder in his heart and the look of a demon in his eyes.

The bull with his rider comes hurtling from the chute, and while eight seconds of riding is a lifetime, the next five or six minutes may mean eternity for the clown. As soon as the contestant is thrown, or has made his ride and upon signal takes leave of the animal, the clown rushes in to distract the animal's attention away from the cowboy. Seldom is the contestant able to get off without a fall, or at least a moment of juggling insecurely on his feet. At this moment of danger the bull seems to sense the insecurity of his foe and he wheels and charges. In just that instant the animal accomplishes his disastrous work. Also, at this moment of danger the clown becomes all important, and his work begins. By his clever maneuvering, he brings the animal forward and away from the rider and gradually works the infuriated animal to the exit. Sometimes the beast wheels away from his tormentor and moves about the arena, as if looking for a means of escape. Again, he takes any direction but that of the legitimate way out. Some animals, lacking fight, appear anxious to leave the arena and make a dash for the exit after being relieved of their rider. If this should happen too often, the clown steps in and puts on a show of bull fighting; the beast may stay to give a genuine battle, and the exhibition often has unscheduled thrills for the spectator.

Many are the tales of narrow escapes, reckless fighting, severe injuries; many skins have been saved by the quick thinking of the rodeo clown. From nearly every contest come stories of the magnificent behavior of this personage who so often steps forward at a critical moment and helps his friends and comrades out of a tough spot.

Among the men who make a specialty of clowning and lifesaving at rodeos, are several who have made an exceptional name for themselves in this hazardous occupation. Jasbo Fulkerson, George Mills, Hoyt Hefner, John Lindsey, Homer Holcomb, Elmer Holcomb, and Jimmy Nesbitt are only a few who have carved a place in this work. Years of experience as active contestants in the many contests of rodeo have given them a sincere appreciation of what is expected of them. This knowledge of what the cowboy contestant experiences in active participation makes these men acutely aware of every serious and dangerous moment. During the bull riding contest the clown must be constantly wide awake and aware of what is happening, for his work demands a clear head, a strong heart, shrewd observation, and an unfailing sense of timing.

Mingled with the very serious and unhappy aspects of the work are those elements of humor that constantly brighten the scene and relieve the tension of the entire sport. One of those bits of rare humor that might have taken a more serious trend was witnessed at the Colosseum of the Louisiana State University at Baton Rouge. It was a thrilling sight to see Jim Patch, a cowboy from Miles City, Montana—a small, husky lad—coming out on the back of the famous bucking bull "Yellow Fever." Jim was riding the beast with a skill rarely seen among older and more experienced men, and was doing a fine job. Turk Greenough, one of the judges, moved in for better observation of the ride, distracted the animal, and the beast took after him. Climbing for a high spot, Turk was knocked off his perch, only to fall directly on the back of the animal and to take Jim with him to the ground. At this moment Jimmy Nesbitt took the cue; he dashed in to bring the bull away from the tangle of legs and arms of the men rolling in the dust, to save their lives—and to save this humorous incident from turning into a harrowing experience.

Jimmy Nesbitt is famous for his clowning; to see him work with his famous straw-stuffed dummy is a "hair-raising" experience that one seldom finds in any other sporting activity. In the same show at Baton Rouge, Jimmy tangled with that tough bull "Spillum" of the Leo Cremer fighting stock. While Jimmy was less fortunate than the contestants of the previous exhibition, this occasion afforded perhaps one of the greatest displays of clowning and bull fighting that has ever been seen by the followers of rodeo. The big bull had thrown his rider and started for Nesbitt who whirled away, seeking safer pastures—his foot slipped and he went down to be tossed some feet up in the air by the beast. Catching the falling man on his horns, "Spillum" tossed him again. The clown rolled like a ball and after a few hazy moments gathered himself together to go back and give that bull and the audience a taste of real courage and "slap-happy" fearlessness. He used his straw dummy as a shield, and there was hardly a spot where he did not whack that animal with the flat of his hand. The spectators screamed themselves hoarse in horror and sheer delight over his daring. It is said that Jimmy was a sore boy for days from the pounding he took from this treacherous animal. Jimmy has clowned at some of the leading shows of the country; he is an old favorite of the fans in Madison Square Garden, where he has been a repeater for many years. Any show at which Nesbitt clowns is bound to offer in thrills all the average fan can wish for—or take!

Jimmy taught George Mills to fight bulls. Once when Jimmy was injured so severely that he could not perform, George stepped in and did the work. It is now a case of George, the pupil, surpassing the master. Jimmy and George are the only clowns who, when fighting bulls, go into the arena without a cape.

It is commonly conceded that George Mills is beyond a doubt the best bull fighter in the game. He seems to be almost fearless and often allows a bull—one without horns —actually to toss him into the air and butt him along the ground just for the fun of it. He takes more chances than any other clown. George Mills is not only a clown and bull fighter of excellence; in 1941 he won the R. A. A. Champion Bareback Riding event. He is a bull rider of ability. Riding bulls and experiencing their various actions, he knows how to help the other riders out of the tough predicaments they get into.

Another man who has made a business of following the rodeo in the precarious occupation of a rodeo clown, a man who because of his ability in the work need not "take a back seat" for anyone, is Homer Holcomb. He was form-

erly a world's relay riding champion and all around contestant; in his seventeen years of being "funny man" for
rodeo, he has earned a reputation of fearlessness that few
possess. Homer's talent for comedy is brilliant; sad-faced
out of make-up, he is hilariously pathetic in the arena. One
of his favorite tricks and a feature at any contest is that
of riding a chariot hitched to a Brahma bull. This act
nearly brought an end to his successful career, when well-
formulated plans, that had many times worked so well,
failed. The bull, on becoming belligerent, was released
from the chariot, but on this particular occasion the gadget
failed to work, and Homer found himself faced with an
infuriated animal. The beast proceeded to turn about and
butt the vehicle into the fence. Not satisfied with this turn
of events, the animal succeeded in overturning the chariot
and thus trapped the clown beneath it. For a time there
was a possibility of the bull attacking and goring the
trapped man. Homer, upon freeing himself, made tracks
for the fence, the bull close on his heels.

During the seventeen years of clowning he suffered innumerable injuries and he wears the scars of his daily
battles with justifiable pride and satisfaction, for he has
done a good job. There are plans "in the air" for his retirement to less hazardous pastures; in anticipation of that,
he is giving his brother, Elmer, all the experience of his
many years in the work, in order that the name may be
carried on. Homer Holcomb with his trained mule has
been a welcome sight to the patrons of rodeo. With his
spirit of gaiety and fun he has relieved the tension and
overwhelming excitement—so conspicuously a part of
every rodeo.

CHAPTER XX

HOME ON THE RANGE

With any rodeo, to make a big hit,
There have to be men to keep the stock fit.

In the early days the ranchmen owned practically none of the land on which their cattle grazed, for it belonged to the government and was classed as public domain. The vast areas of unfenced range were open, and the cattle roamed free. With the encroachment of civilization, great changes have come over the cow country, and the cattlemen have been crowded from their grassy plains by the homeseeker into the high mountain districts. The farsighted stockmen, realizing that ownership of land was necessary for successful continuation of the livestock industry, acquired large holdings of grazing land, thus preserving, on a diminished scale, the method of the early range existence.

Hundreds of ranches in the West are devoted to cattle raising, but not more than fifty are raising stock to be used in the sport of rodeo. In most cases the raising of rodeo stock is a sideline of a greater ranching activity, that of raising cattle for market. While this phase of business, that is, raising and supplying stock for rodeo, has proved to be lucrative, the percentage of livestock contractors is small,[1] and these ranches are so scattered that practically every state west of the Mississippi River has several devoted to the business.

Some of the major rodeo stock ranches are those owned by Leo Cremer, Harry Rowell, Moomaw and Bernard, Nesbitt and Elliott, and the World's Champion Rodeo Corporation. The largest of these is that of Leo Cremer. It has about 55,000 acres with a run of 10,000 head of sheep and about 500 head of cattle, is located, approximately, a hundred miles north of Yellowstone National Park and thirty miles from Big Timber, Montana. Cremer, who supplies stock for rodeos throughout the West, has been in the business of stock raising for thirty years.

While studying law at Notre Dame University, he went west to Montana for a vacation and there had his first taste of ranching and witnessed his first rodeo. His interest in the work grew until he is at present one of the undisputed leaders in the business. Some of the toughest bucking horses in rodeo are from his ranch; he introduced to rodeo the large bucking horse. Formerly the smaller cayuse was the typical arena horse, but, when Cremer put into practice his theory that "all other things being equal, a good big horse is better than a good little horse," he proved his contention. It is said that, when the bronc riding cowboys first saw the Cremer draft-type of horse,

---

[1] List of Rodeo Livestock Contractors: J. L. Case, Lone Wolf Ranch, Sutherland, Nebraska; T. Thompson, Bell Fourche, South Dakota; Lem Carmin, Douglas, Wyoming. M. H. Barbour, -C Ranch, Klamath Falls, Oregon; S. Anderson and J. Connelly, Kildeer, North Dakota; Beutler Brothers, Beutler Brothers Ranch Co., Elk City, Oklahoma; J. C. Sorenson, Flying U Ranch, Camas, Idaho; Tooke Brothers, Tooke Ranch, Ekalaka, Montana; R. H. Foos, Gendive, Montana; Jim Heir, JMH Ranch, Morris, Minnesota; Earl J. Anderson, JX Ranch, Grover, Colorado; Fred Lewis, Lewis Ranch, Browning, Montana.

which Cremer proposed to use in the arena, they expressed considerable glee. Also, this glee changed to surprise after the first contact of cowboy with this type of animal.

Leo Cremer, known as "Leo the Lion" by the cowboys, offers, as his contribution to rodeo, about one hundred and fifty saddle broncs and forty bareback broncs. "Lee Rider," "Hootchie Kootchie," "Hell to Set," "Merry Widow," "Widow Maker," "Mexico," "Sad Face," "Bald Hornet," "Tim Buck Two," "Melrose," "Sure Shot," and "Andy" are his most outstanding animals.

Stock for a rodeo is moved from the ranches by various means, depending upon the distance and location of the contest. For nearby contests, or those within two hundred miles, the stock is usually trailed to its destination; for contests at a greater distance it is trucked or shipped by means of baggage car. While being moved to the contests, the stock is treated in the same manner as that in a fine group of race horses. While traveling in baggage cars, it is cared for by a professional handler who makes every effort to relieve the strain and difficulties of the trip. Upon arrival, it is exercised daily until the contest is ready to be run. On the days when the animals are being used in the arena, they are watched and cared for with even greater diligence. They are watered early in the morning, are fed twice daily, and after having appeared in the arena, they are properly cooled and again fed.

About fifteen miles south of the Canadian border and near Tonasket, Washington, is located the twenty-two thousand acre cattle and rodeo stock ranch of Leo Moomaw and Tim Bernard. They have supplied stock for rodeos for two decades and have had such enviable contracts as Cheyenne Frontier Days, Pendleton Round-Up, Lewiston,

Ellensbug, Fort Worth, and numerous others. Every year they scout the Western section of the nation and Canada to find the finest bucking horses of which they have heard and add them to their already well-known and growing string of broncs. Both these men are stockmen and have participated in rodeo as contestants. Intensely interested in the sport because of their love for the work and its close relationship to the cattle industry, they strive to keep the stock for the contests in a first-class condition, both in action and in appearance.

As is the custom of other stockmen on their scouting trips, they take with them a rider to make a test of the bucking abilities of the horse that they intend to purchase. A horse of the Moomaw and Bernard string must not only be a bucking horse, but must show, in action, qualities that are indicative of showmanship and persistent bucking. While many of their horses are not wild in the sense that they have just been removed from a habitat of complete freedom—they are used for draft work on the ranch during the off season—they can, with constant care, be made to retain and improve their bucking tendencies. If a good bucking horse appears to be turning "sour," he is given considerable encouragement for improvement if he is allowed to buck off several riders. This return of confidence often encourages him to use even more energy in throwing the rider who is trying to stay on.

Such attempts to improve the horses for rodeo make the stock of this Washington ranch well remembered by the contestants. Moomaw and Bernard's "Badger Mountain," "Black Out," "Blue Blazes," "Dinimite," "Black Widow," "Y Four Silver," "Jack Wade," "Social Security," "Levi

Strauss," and "Iron Sides" are horses whose abilities to buck are not readily forgotten.

This firm is also one of the few rodeo stock ranches that raises Brahma bulls for the sport. By crossing the Brahma with the White Faced Herefords, these men have produced a very superior bucking animal. Contestants say that bull riding, as a contest, is now one of the greatest bucking events, because it is possible to breed bulls that provide this action, while among horses it is not a problem of breeding. With the development of a better type of bucking bull, one wonders whether, eventually, this contest might not supersede, if not replace, the event of bucking horses because the scarcity and rarity of the latter animals is becoming evident.

The Nesbitt and Elliott Ranch of Johnstown, Colorado has supplied animals to the leading contests in this country as well as in England. These men, pioneer stock contractors, have been important in rodeo for twenty-five years. For eighteen years the ranch was known by the name of McCarty and Elliott—Ed McCarty of Chugwater, Wyoming, was then a partner. Since 1940, when McCarty's interest was purchased by Don Nesbitt of Snowflake, Arizona, the ranch has been under its present name.

They supply stock for the Fort Worth Fat Stock Show, the Pendleton Round-Up, Cheyenne Frontier Days, National Western Stock Show at Denver, and the Arkansas Livestock Show. They have had such enviable contracts as the Madison Square Garden, Yankee Stadium, Soldier's Field, Los Angeles, San Antonio, and were co-directors with Billie Rose at the Fort Worth Frontier Centennial of 1936.

Stock from this ranch was used for the first cowboy sports taken to the old Madison Square Garden in New York by Tex Rickard in 1926. In 1924 they supplied the stock for the first Tex Austin Show that was taken to London, and their bucking horse list at that time included such stars as "Headlight," "Deerfoot," "Overhall Bill," and "Invalid." Ten years later they again supplied the stock for the second Austin contest in London; their string of broncs included the fabulous "Midnight," "Five Minutes to Midnight," "Invalid," and "Broken Box." The last named horse is still bucking today.

As owners of two famous and legendary bucking horses, "Midnight" and "Five Minutes to Midnight," Nesbitt and Elliott have always occupied a unique place in rodeo as stock contractors. They own from four to five hundred head of stock, which includes some of the best bucking, parade, and arena saddle horses, as well as bulls, steers, and calves; consequently they are well able to supply every need for a contest that will be well remembered.

How "Midnight" and "Five Minutes to Midnight" were discovered and brought to this country is a tale of great interest to anyone who follows rodeo. Both animals were purchased by Colonel Jim Eskew in the fall of 1929, at Toronto, Canada. They were owned originally by Peter Welch, and were purchased at a sheriff's sale. At one time Colonel Jim owned nine of the Welch string of broncs. In 1930 "Midnight" and "Five Minutes to Midnight" were purchased by McCarty and Elliott. The horses then were not so well known; their ability and national fame were developed after that time. It is said that the purchase price of these horses was approximately two hundred and fifty dollars for the two; however, their unusual talents warranted carrying insurance of five thousand dollars each.

"Midnight" died in 1936 and is buried on the Nesbitt Elliott Ranch. His grave is marked with an appropriate stone with an inscription eulogizing the greatest bucking horse that ever lived. The inscription reads as follows:

To Midnight

Under this sod lies a great bucking hoss;
There never lived a cowboy he couldn't toss.
His name was Midnight, his coat was black as coal,
If there is a hoss-heaven, please, God, rest his soul.

By a Cowboy[1]

Today "Five Minutes to Midnight," as dean of the Nesbitt and Elliott string of bucking horses, heads such animals as "Ham What Am," "T Joe," "Wildfire," "20 Below," "Double Trouble," "Screamin' Hi Ki," "Blue Bonnett," "V 8," "Slingin' Sam," "Devil Dog," and "Rompers." The best bronc riders agree that this ranch has had, and still does have, some of the finest "buckers" in the country.

At the head of Dublin Canyon near Hayward, California, are about eleven thousand acres of foothills devoted to the raising and pasturing of rodeo stock. This is Harry Rowell's Ranch and its location is ideal in every way to freshen and bring back the jaded appetite of rodeo animals. A man of keen insight and years of practical experience, Harry Rowell offers quality stock to rodeo. His bucking horses are among the best. "Starlight," "Lee Overalls," "Duster," "Sad Sam," "Felix," "Tombstone," "Calvert," "Sceneshifter," "Brown Bomber," and "Pale Face" are

---

[1] The grave was visited by the author at Johnstown, Colorado.

nationally known both as individuals and as part of a string. He has a great reputation as a friend of rodeo and of those who take part in the sport. He is a firm believer in and a sponsor of everything that is typical of the days of the "old West"; he deplores sham and insincerity. He expends all his energy to maintain a good program of cowboy activities and has absolutely no interest in a program that includes the various events so often found in the "thrill circus" type of contest.[1]

Occasionally, one hears about some very interesting stock deals in which a large organization, such as the World's Championship Rodeo Corporation, located at Dublin, Texas, contracts for the best stock of another ranch. Late in the year 1941, this Texas ranch made such a deal with Grabner-Bedford Incorporated, of Prairie City, Oregon. The latter organization is widely known and has an outstanding reputation in the West for owning some of the finest stock used in rodeo. Through this deal, the World's Championship Rodeo Corporation added such horses as "High Skip," "Colonel Dean," and "Conclusion" to its already unsurpassed group of buckers and has now one of the finest groups that has ever been assembled. This arrangement enabled this Corporation to take a collection of horses, such as is rarely seen in Eastern contests, to the Madison Square Garden and the Boston Garden Shows, for which it supplies stock. Deals of this type are not necessarily rare, but usually a contractor, having horses of such caliber, does not dispose of them to a rival organization, even for a considerable amount of money.

---

[1] Information offered by Harry Rowell, Rowell Ranch, Hayward, California.

CHAPTER XXI

TUMBLEWEEDS IN THE EAST

I ain't a gonna rodeo no more,
I'm gonna sit home in the shade,
An' let my horse just roam around,
While I drink lemonade!

In a discussion of the stock contractor in rodeo one should not overlook the important place occupied by the J E Ranch of Waverly, New York. The organization is headed by Colonel Jim Eskew, who, assisted by his two sons, Junior and Tom Eskew, has built up a record in the northeastern part of this country that cannot easily be equaled by older established organizations of the West. The J E Ranch has the reputation of putting on some of the finest shows in rodeo. Colonel Jim's policy is to give a show of cowboy activities; he has little patience with fluff, foolishness, and folderol that have been incorporated in many contests as the basis of entertainment. Colonel Jim Eskew has a deep and sincere appreciation of showmanship, but this gift and talent are expended only in relation to the improvement of true rodeo sports.

He was born in Tennessee and, as a youngster, visited his uncle's ranch in Texas. On this ranch Jim grew to manhood and eventually acquired his own outfit. The reputation to know and the ability to understand cattle, horses, and men, is perhaps, the outstanding characteristic of this man, who has spent the greater part of his life in bringing the joys and thrills of the West to thousands of people in the East.

A rider of bucking horses, he eventually joined Buffalo Bill's Wild West Show and became closely allied with Tom Mix. His admiration for this friend is evident in the fact that he named his youngest son, Tom Mix Eskew. Some years later, he and Mix worked on the 101 Ranch and spent their summers contesting at rodeos. These early experiences with the first of Wild West Shows to be seen in this country aroused in young Jim Eskew that latent appreciation of the dramatic phases of our Western heritage and awakened that hidden talent of showmanship which has carried him to the position of the foremost producer of rodeo sports east of the Mississippi River.

After he had tasted the excitement and the thrills and had become aware of the hard work that is part of the business of producing, he started his own show. It was a wagon-show at first which he moved from place to place throughout the states of Kentucky and Tennessee. His traveling enterprise grew until it eventually became a railroad show, and is now one of the largest traveling rodeos in the world. Colonel Jim Eskew has the distinction of being the man who introduced the famous bucking horses, "Midnight" and "Five Minutes to Midnight," to this country. That alone would stamp him as a leader in his work!

There exists, more or less, a gentlemen's agreement between the Eskew organization and others of a similar nature to the effect that the J E group is to work in the eastern and northeastern section of the United States in staging rodeos for cities, towns, state and county fairs, and in supplying an entire show or just the stock and featured contract performers. The season in the East opens early in April and takes this organization into Connecticut, New York, Ohio, Pennsylvania, Delaware, Maryland, and Virginia, with shows running from six to ten days at a time.[1] The World's Championship Rodeo Corporation handles the New York and Boston contests because of the magnitude and scale involved.

The location of the J E Ranch at Waverly, in the south-central part of New York State, has created a tremendous interest in rodeo sports in the East. The efforts to bring the ranch to its present location were, for the most part, due to the persistence of Edwin J. O'Brien of that city. O'Brien was brought up on a farm; was around horses all his life, and as he grew older, his love for horses turned to the Western type of animal, to cowboys, and to rodeo. He first met Colonel Eskew in the fall of 1938, at the Elmira Fair. They discussed the possibilities of having Eastern headquarters, and Colonel Jim visited Waverly and looked at several locations. One of the most important features of Waverly is its central location; with three railroads, the traveling show could easily be moved in any direction.

However, Colonel Jim did not plan immediately to locate at Waverly. In the winter of 1938, he had almost decided to make his headquarters in Missouri. O'Brien was persistent; by letters and telegrams he portrayed to the Colonel the advantages of the New York State location. In the spring of 1939, he received a letter

---

[1] In the past year (1946) this organization expanded its territory and staged rodeos in Saint Louis and Chicago to capacity crowds. Roy Rogers, cowboy film star, is co-producer. See Chapter XXV., p. 307.

from the Eskew organization inquiring whether there was a large barn nearby so that the rodeo could "lay over" for two weeks between shows. O'Brien located the barn in Tioga County, which is the present J E Ranch barn, and with the aid of Herbert Maddy, Eskew's general representative, brought the Colonel once more to Waverly. This time O'Brien was ready for the head of the rodeo. Colonel Eskew was entertained by the Mayor, by several prominent people of the city, and by the Board of Trade. As a further inducement to bring the rodeo headquarters of the J E Ranch to Waverly, O'Brien, backed by the Board of Trade, played his trump card. To push the establishment of the home ranch near this city, the Board of Trade offered to give three hundred acres of rolling country and foothills to the organization, if it would guarantee to stay three years and agree to put on a rodeo once a year for the citizens of the city. The Board of Trade, made up of a group of young and enterprising men, gave every assistance and encouragement to the development of the project. The success of the venture has been almost fabulous, and it has been possible for the J E Ranch to reimburse the Board of Trade each year.

The ranch at Waverly is an ideal location to winter the stock and, at the same time, is a centrally located headquarters in the rodeo-conscious East. The venture has brought considerable publicity to that little city of six thousand inhabitants, which is located five miles north of Tioga Point, the link between the historic waters of the Chemung and Susquehanna Rivers of Indian fame. Now well-known as the "Rodeo Capital of the East," Waverly, New York, is fast becoming the mecca of Eastern rodeo sport and activity. The ranch is beautifully located in the rolling foothills of the Allegheny Mountains, about two miles from the city, and the original three hundred acres have since grown to six hundred. The ranch has not only grown in acreage but also in housing facilities; the original building—a barn standing on the property—has been augmented with a ranch house, several guest houses, corrals, arena, and a grandstand for the annual rodeo held there on the Fourth of July.

The owners of the ranch hope that it will not only be headquarters and home for the J E organization, but also that it will become a game reserve. The surrounding country is abounding in wild life; the topography is ideal for a reserve. Within the boundaries of the ranch are about eighteen springs, and three or four natural hollows which could be scraped and made into shallow lakes. If it were planted with rice and grain, it would suggest a stopping place for migratory fowl, as well as a natural feeding ground for pheasant, partridge, and woodcock. It is not an uncommon sight to see deer come from the surrounding wooded area to join the cattle and horses in feeding. No hunting is allowed; therefore, it is possible that eventually the area will be restricted and recognized as a State Game Reserve.

At one time, during the off season, in the month of January, when the author had the privilege of spending some time in the congenial and enlightening surroundings of the J E Ranch, it was stocked with one hundred and ten head of horses and from eighteen to twenty steers and bulls. Before the spring season opened, about sixty additional animals were to be added and were at that time being selected from Western stock. The calves used during the previous season had been sold and would be replaced

for the coming season with new stock. The opportunity
to visit the ranch during the off season was perhaps more
advantageous to the visitor than during the excitement and
confusion of the rodeo season. He enjoyed such excellent
company as that of the late Herbert S. Maddy, that remarkable little man of rodeo and show business for so
many years; of Joe Pickett, nephew of the fabulous Bill
Pickett; of Smoky North, a bull rider of no mean repute,
and of Curly McCall, rider and trainer of jumping horses,
who was formerly a rodeo contestant and now with his
family, farms and trains horses within the shadow of the
J E Ranch.

The author was a novice in discussing rodeo with the
able general representative of the J E Ranch, Uncle Herbie,
whose personal experience, innumerable associations, and
vast knowledge of everything concerning the sport date
back to its very beginning. In 1899, Herbert S. Maddy
had been associated with the Ringling Brothers Circus as
a press agent, and later joined, in the same capacity, the
Wild West Show of Colonel W. F. Cody. Thus, his
energies were for many years divided between circuses and
the many Western Shows that were appearing at that time.

He was born at Muncie, Indiana, in 1875; because of
ill health he was sent to his uncle's ranch, the Craig outfit of southern California. On this ranch he developed
considerable skill as a relay rider and also tried his hand
with the broncs. Upon his return to Muncie in 1891, he
remained only a short time and then went to St. Louis
where he secured a position on the St. Louis Press as a re-
porter. During the Spanish-American War he represented
this press as a war correspondent, but the war was over
before he had an opportunity to get to the battle front.

His career took him through the West, and among the many friends he made there, are numerous members of the Crow, Pawnee, and Blackfeet tribes. Time has removed those great Western characters who were his close friends, Buffalo Bill and more recently Major Gordon W. Lillie (Pawnee Bill).

In 1933 Herbert Maddy joined Colonel Jim Eskew and took over the important position of general manager of this organization. He was known far and wide throughout this nation by the many people participating in rodeo and by all fans of rodeo. He had a reputation for telling the "tallest" stories, which appeared in his column, "Eastern Rodeo Chat" in *Hoofs and Horns*. His concise, informative, and pertinent remarks about rodeo activities and personalities made it one of the most popular columns of this monthly magazine. Uncle Herbie died in the spring of 1942 and is sincerely missed in rodeo. At that time, Colonel Jim Eskew suggested to O'Brien, who had contributed much in establishing the J E Ranch at the present location, and who is also the originator of the copyrighted saying, "Waverly, New York, Rodeo Capital of the East," that he become the author of the column of Eastern activities in *Hoofs and Horns*. For a time, O'Brien did this but now he is no longer active in the work.

Also associated with the J E Ranch is Fog Horn Clancy, one of the best-known characters of rodeo today. He has been in the game in various capacities for nearly half a century. He grew up on a ranch in Texas, and took part in his first rodeo on July 4, 1898, at San Angelo, Texas; the events at that time were known simply as riding and roping contests. Clancy not only entered the competition but also "called" the events, an activity which since has been elevated to the title of "announcing." It was not long until Clancy stopped entirely the rough work of contesting in the arena and devoted his time to announcing, and soon, as an official announcer, he was traveling throughout the country.

Before the advent of the public address system, Clancy was America's most widely-known rodeo announcer. He traveled throughout the United States, into Canada, and sometimes took a jaunt into Mexico; everywhere he followed the business of giving the rodeo spectators the necessary information to help them enjoy the performance. In 1916 he was the official announcer of the Cheyenne Frontier Days; from there he went to New York to hold the same position at the New York Sheepshead Bay Speedway, and from New York to Kansas City for the same position at the Kansas City Round-Up.

Fog Horn is known as America's only rodeo handicapper. Having seen all the present crop of rodeo contestants come up in the game, he knows their ability in the arena. With this advantage, coupled with his knowledge of the bucking prowess of practically every bronc in the country, he is able to foretell in advance, as soon as mounts are drawn, which contestants are headed for the top money prizes and which ones are riding for a fall. The forecasting which he does in a number of daily papers during a rodeo show has added great interest to the performances for the spectators. He is considered by many people as the greatest living authority on rodeo and Western personalities. At the present time, besides his connection with the press department of the J E Ranch Rodeo, Fog Horn

Clancy is also associated in the same capacity with the Rodeo Corporation of America. In addition to these activities he writes many short stories about the West and rodeo characters for a number of Western magazines.

Part III

DUST

. . . and to the dust they shall return.

ⴷP

CHAPTER XXII

CELEBRATIN'

The town was bedecked with banners,
Buzzing excitement rode high,
They came from all corners a-riding,
For a Glorious Fourth of July!

The first ray of light streaked the sky from east to west, as men on horseback moved into a brash little town, nestled in one of the great natural hollows of the Divide. Still wrapped in the deep slumber that follows a night of complete abandon, the frontier post presented a picture of peacefulness and solitude. The shouting and clamor of the inebriated, the thick blue-grey vapor of burning tobacco, the heavy odor of sweating, sticky bodies, the restless stamping of saddle horses, the disonance of tone-weary musicians, the brassy, hoarse laughter and wilted finery of the ladies—all the diversions of the night had disappeared with the freshening of the scene that comes with the dawn. The very dawn, which some hours earlier had swept in from the great ocean in the East, brought to the distant cities the anniversary of the birth of the nation.

In the West this day already gave promise of a renewal of all the enthusiasm present at its nativity. It was a day of the first week of July during the last decade of the nineteenth century. The only holidays that the early frontiersmen were certain to celebrate were Fourth of July and Christmas, and this day was the Fourth of July.

279

The spring round-up had just ended and the men were drifting along the trails homeward. This holiday was the big day of the year, the one most apropos of their existence. It was their opportunity to return home for a while before starting back on the trails with the herds toward the Northern markets.

Thus, with the dawn of the day and for many days preceding it, home-coming cowboys swelled the population of an already overcrowded town. Already in the early morning there appeared on the horizon riders, riding at full gallop on a crest of light sandy dust. Wheeling and twisting their mounts, darting among fearless pedestrians, they shouted and called with husky, dust-laden voices in recognition of friend and kin; they were greeted with heartfelt cheers by both young and old—those loved ones left behind during the months of their trek.

Preparations for the day had been going on for some weeks. It was a case of the "butcher, the baker, and the candlestick maker" all lending their efforts to make it a grand occasion. Some days earlier, a site, now hallowed by former celebrations, had been selected and cleared of a year's florid growth. This site was located on a small stream that looped and twisted about the town. Nearby, in a grove of cottonwoods stood a rough wooden platform, which, with the falling of dusk, would resound to the clatter and stomp of leather sole and heel and the tinkle of metal spurs.

As the sun rose higher in the sky, the places of business with their flamboyant wooden false-faces disgorged their habitues into the confusion of the crowded street. The weather-beaten buckboards with nervous teams stood axle-deep in dust and were loaded with baskets and blankets; the air was split with the shrieking and screaming of delighted youngsters. In one vehicle sat a rough built gangling woman, with the reins resting lightly, but taut with hidden strength, in her scarred hands; beside her was a young mother in calico dress and bonnet, who busied herself with her child and listened to the venerable gentleman at her side. His eyes were clear and sharp, but filled with memories of a younger day, as he vividly related his yearly reminiscences to his youthful guardian and charge.

Men from the trails, men from the ranges, men from the ranches, men from the town—astride their mounts, they led the cavalcade to its destination. A more daring and rampageous generation of boys and girls raced among the moving vehicles and jockeyed one another for a more favorable position in the procession. Because it was the Fourth of July, the "ladies of question," in all their brittle finery, were permitted to join the celebration. Ogled by wishful-thinking young blades and smug in their knowledge of conquest, they ignored, with haughty grace, the stares and whispers of the envious matrons. Mingled with this heterogenous group were the plumed and bedecked first citizens of the land; with a quiet fierceness, not yet aroused by the flames of drink, they rode on their painted ponies with effortless ease and a suaveness of lineage.

The churning wheels and the endless beat of hoofs raised the pulverized soil, which engulfed the shouting celebrants following the procession, as it turned from the road to the green-blanketed pasture land, the main ground for the celebration. From this oasis of green the air already carried a relieving freshness; with an onrushing surge the procession broke into units, each one seeking the more desirable spots under the trees. Here, greeted with jeers, cheers and laughter, they came upon the early-comers, who generously shared their plunder.

Men stood about in groups and talked excitedly of the opportunity to display their skill before their boasting friends; others rode off to herd up from the foothills the grazing cattle of some willing and generous rancher. Huge horned animals, gaunt, long-legged beasts, quick to run and quick to stop and fight—these were the animals for the sport of the day. An occasional wild bronc was brought up close for inspection, and after careful study bets were made. On the back of the steed a youthful and daring cow hand tried his luck, and frequently, this man and beast, together in a struggle, were united with their common origin—dust. Disappearing from the sight of the spectators, bronc and rider moved out across the plains, and were followed by the other riders who would witness the struggle in all its finality.

Ropes were unlimbered, whirled, twisted, tested; on speedy and panting horses the men tossed their loops which settled like sinuous serpents around the heads of the struggling cattle. Money exchanged hands as both the fortunate and unfortunate exhibitors displayed their skill in seriousness and fun.

Then the day had passed; the lengthening shadows and early evening breeze brought to the hungry the acrid odors of burning campfires, scented heavily with the rich aroma of strong coffee. The womenfolk busied themselves emptying baskets and boxes of food, very unlike that of the chuck wagon vintage. They ate their meal in silence, as the last glow of the day faded.

Here, there, and everywhere appeared, as if through the power of some wonderful jinnee, the steady glow of lanterns. The younger children had grown weary of the long hours; sleep now touched their eyes, as their stomachs grew round and their blood became saturated with fresh air; they were rolled in saddle blankets and placed in safety away from the marauding night prowlers and exuberant celebrants.

From somewhere came the first gentle twang of a guitar, the whine of a violin mingled with the clatter of baskets being repacked, and scuffling feet moved toward the dancing space. Laughing men and women joined together and shuttled back and forth, around and through, weaving the endless pattern of their joys. The wail of a baby called a young mother from the moving tapestry; her partner sought another lady who was less occupied, but with eager eyes the gentle madonna of the West watched their every move, while the infant gurgled at her breast. The hours moved too rapidly, the rows of lanterns surrounding the area began to flicker for want of fuel and, encrusted with charred insects, they lost their gleam.

The wild and hysterical neighing of frightened horses brought the frivolity to an end. What rapacious denizen of the night, animal or human, had come from the highlands to prey on this gathering? Loud and boastful curses filled the night, as the men moved to seek out the disturber of their peace. But the pungent, sickening stink of a pole cat scattered this brave posse with greater ease than a more formidable foe could have done; laughing from sheer relief, both men and women, now weary from pleasure, prepared for the journey home. They awakened the less rigorous brothers who had been rolled to the edge of the platform to sleep off their weakness; with much prodding and pushing they hoisted them into the saddle or into buckboards with the children. The moon rose high, as the exhausted procession moved toward the comforts of home and weeks of happy reunion.

Rodeo was born in such simple homelike picnics and annual celebrations. Local cowboy activities and sports were the basis of the national entertainment which, on this holiday of the year, the Fourth of July, is still honored with great gusto throughout the East and West.

CHAPTER XXIII

FOURTH OF JULY AND THE GRAND CIRCUIT

Eagerly on the circuit's trail,
South and north and west they go,
Little towns, big towns making ready
To welcome the annual rodeo!

There still exists a sentimental relationship between cowboy activities and sports and the Fourth of July. It is the single great day of the year for rodeos and especially in the West. Because of this early association, many communities choose this date for their annual rodeo. There is perhaps no finer or more significant way of celebrating the day than by an exhibition of a truly American sport; however, it is unfortunate that so many contests of this type take place on the same day. Even if one does not consider the many contests of Rodeo-Association-of-American membership that occur on the Fourth of July, there are still far too many contests of the non-member type that also use this holiday for their annual rodeo. This problem of competition has now been remedied to some extent. The officials of the Rodeo Association advise their member-shows of the difficulty involved in supplying adequate talent, livestock, and contestants, as well as those professional touches that are needed to prime a contest and which help make a fast, well-organized entertainment. Because the Rodeo Association of America has no legal or advisory right to keep non-association shows from making this mistake, the problem has grown immensely, so that now it is almost impossible to guarantee a show on this date, which will be worthy of being rated as a first-class rodeo.

Because of this lack of foresight, on this one day of the year rodeo is not only in competition with other types of entertainment, but is in serious competition with itself. This is truly serious because it attempts to spread itself, in order to meet the demands of the various contests; the talent of both contestants and livestock thus becomes inferior; and the public becomes more conscious of the lack of quality, especially if the community is staging the contest as a means of drawing the outsider to the show. Although, seemingly, there are enough professional contestants to supply the needs of the rodeos held on the Fourth of July, it must be remembered that it is their privilege to go to contests of their own choosing. It is quite natural that the men who follow the sport as a means of a livelihood will attend those contests offering the greatest purses, and, in most cases, these are Rodeo Association of America member-shows with contest points.

It is always difficult, and often impossible, to secure contract talent and feature acts for this day. Because of the great demand for this specialized type of work on this particular day, the price for talent increases in proportion to the position the performer occupies as an artist.

Apparently, there is no special remedy for this undue complication, unless the managers of the many contests will realize that this overtaxing of the facilities of the sport is harmful, not only to their particular contest, but also to the sport itself. Throughout the country, the many important contests on the Fourth of July have drawn visitors from every walk of life. Among the better-known events and those that are sure to have outstanding contestants during the two and three days of celebration for this holiday are: Livingston Round-Up, Montana; Spud Rodeo, Greeley, Colorado; Mandan Rodeo, North Dakota; Black Hills Round-Up, Belle Fourche, South Dakota; Red Lodge, Montana; Willits Rodeo, California; Reno, Nevada; Buckeroo Days Rodeo at Klamath Falls, Oregon. A rodeo no less important than those mentioned above, and one of national renown, is the Prescott Frontier Days Celebration at Prescott, Arizona. It is a non-professional show and is not a member of the Rodeo Association of America. It has gained national fame because it is the oldest rodeo in existence and—a fact which makes it very unique—it is a rodeo for the range cowboy. The Calgary Stampede and Exhibition, which usually takes place the week following the Fourth of July, and the Black Hills Round-Up are perhaps, with the Prescott Rodeo, the most significant at this time of year, not necessarily because of purses, but because of their age and the reputation of giving the finest exhibition of cowboy sports.

In rodeo, as in other fields of entertainment, the participants follow a circuit of contests. Because of the magnitude and the extent of the sport, it is not possible for any one contestant to attend all the rodeos of the country. The season extends from the second week in January until the middle of December. Formerly, the month of December was the only month without a contest; however, a show held at San Francisco in the year 1941 broke that long-established record.[1]

---

[1] See Chapter XXIX., p. 368.

The season is inaugurated by the Denver Stock Show and Rodeo that takes place shortly after the first of the year. This is followed by such contests as the Fat Stock Show and Rodeo, at Houston, Texas; the Rodeo, at Phoenix, Arizona; and *La Fiesta de los Vaqueros*, at Tucson, Arizona. The Fort Worth Southwestern Exposition and the Fat Stock Show and Rodeo at San Angelo, Texas, are two of the most important events. They are the early spring contests of the Southwest and are attended by many cowboys who make their living by contesting.

The large contests, which end early in March, are followed by a divergence of the rodeo cowboys—some move westward to California for a series of shows held on the West Coast until the end of June; others move eastward to Cleveland, Ohio; Pittsburg, Pennsylvania; Washington, D. C., and Baltimore, Maryland. These Eastern shows are indoor-arena contests. Thus, by the first of July the rodeo cowboys are scattered far and wide throughout the nation. This makes it possible to have a representation of talent throughout the country at many of the Fourth of July contests. Following this important date, many of the men work their way, by means of attending smaller events, toward that outstanding and celebrated contest, the Frontier Days Celebration, Cheyenne, Wyoming, which is usually held for five or six days during the third week of July. However, simultaneous with this contest, two others, some five hundred miles away, bid as strong contenders for the presence of major contestants. They are the Covered Wagon Days Celebration at Salt Lake City, and Ogden Pioneer Days, held at Ogden, about forty-five miles north of the Mormon Capital. Although both these cities in Utah stage contests at the same time as

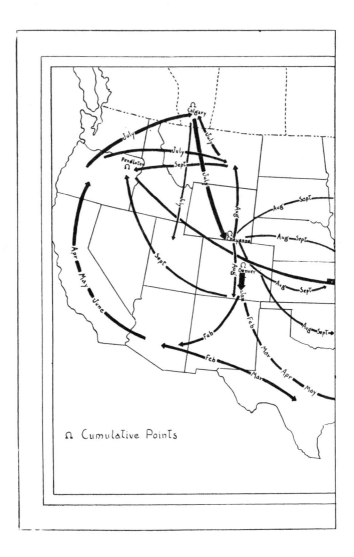

Ω Cumulative Points

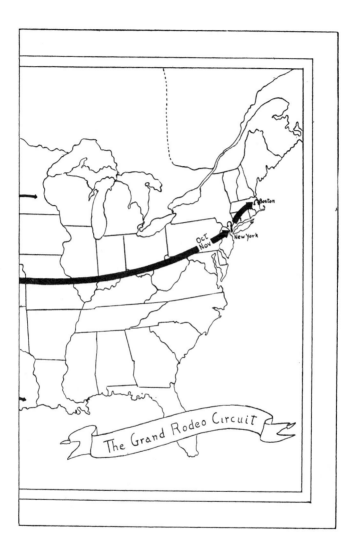

Boston

New York

Oct
Nov

The Grand Rodeo Circuit

Cheyenne, their combined purses do not quite equal that of their rival—the nationally known Cheyenne Frontier Days Celebration.

Following the converging of practically all the major performers at three outstanding shows within an area of five hundred miles, this grouping of talent breaks up once more, and there are three general directions of migration.

The Northwest move—to Montana, Idaho, Washington, and Oregon—which includes shows held at Billings, Great Falls, Omak, Sun Valley, Missoula, and Tremonton. The second shift is toward the Middle West—to South Dakota, Iowa, Nebraska, Kansas, and Oklahoma—where The Days of '76; Iowa Championship Rodeo at Sidney; Sheridan County Rodeo; Kansas Championship Rodeo; Firemen's Annual Rodeo, Ada, Oklahoma; Elk's Rodeo, Woodward, Oklahoma; Will Roger's Memorial Rodeo, and Vinita, Oklahoma, are some of the more important. The third move is south of Cheyenne—Colorado, New Mexico, and Texas—here are held, in Colorado, the Boulder Pow Wow Days; Monte Vista, Ski-Hi Stampede; Durango Spanish Trails Fiesta; Colorado Springs Rodeo; Colorado State Fair, Pueblo, Colorado; the Annual Cowboy Reunion at Las Vegas, New Mexico; the Beaumont Rodeo, and the Midland Fair Rodeo in Texas. The Cowboys' Reunion is a forty-seven year old institution; it was first staged by Theodore Roosevelt's Rough Riders and is now a three-day contest sponsored by the American Legion.

This carries the season through August to about the first of September, when there is a great trek northward to three very important contests of the Northwest—the Ellensburg Rodeo, Washington; the Pendleton Round-Up, Oregon, and the Lewiston Round-Up, Idaho. The three shows take up, in time, almost the first two weeks of September, and here gather the elite, the great and near-great of the rodeo world, preparing "to polish off" the Western season in anticipation of the contests *de résistance* which follow some three weeks later—the Chicago Rodeo at Chicago, the Madison Square Garden Championship Rodeo at New York City, and the Garden Rodeo at Boston, Massachusetts.

A contestant, who follows rodeo as a profession over a period of three years, can get into practically every state of the union, if he should choose to change his circuit. It is, however, natural for him to follow, with his friends, those contests in which he has been financially successful in the past.

This was the normal trek of the rodeo contestant until the entrance of our country into World War II. Then, the spring of 1942 brought with it not only the gloom that prevails during a national crisis, but also the desire for victory and a just peace. Rodeo felt the heavy hand of the effects of war and made considerable changes in the scheduled and planned contests, especially on the West Coast.

At first, in order to prevent any unforseen catastrophe that might occur when a nation is at war, there was a movement whch forbade the gathering of citizens in large groups. However, shortly after this movement, there was a tendency to allow the nation to continue with its pastimes and sports as a psychological good during time of stress. Many rodeos planned to cancel their contests for the season but reversed this decision and held the events; some, however, canceled their programs for the duration of the war. This was a rather severe blow to the contestants, especially from the standpoint of reducing their opportunities to contest and thus reducing their earning power. This was somewhat compensated by the introduction of the Flying A Ranch Rodeo, a show owned and promoted by the motion picture star, Gene Autry. In the spring of the year 1942, the show went on the road two months, and the circuit brought the contestants from the precarious West Coast zone eastward to six large cities; Cleveland, Ohio; Pittsburg and Philadelphia, Pennsylvania; Washington, D. C.; New Haven, Connecticut; and Providence, Rhode Island. The combined purse of $30,000 plus the addition of entrance fees offered an advantage that came at the opportune time.

CHAPTER XXIV

BIG TIME AND "BIG SHOTS"

Indoors, outdoors, city or town,
Roundups, Stampedes, or One-day Shows,
Wide-open country or arena-hall,
Follow the crowd, wherever it goes!

Rodeos may be produced in auditoriums, indoor arenas, armories, or in any large building that has adequate space for spectators and the scheduled events. The indoor arena has proved to be a boon to the sport for it allows the contests to be carried on in any part of the country and at any time of the year. During the late winter the Southwest, which in all reality is the winter home of rodeo, is able, by means of the enclosed arena, to hold such contests. In this particular section of the country rodeo is introduced as an added attraction and, usually, as the featured sport and entertainment of the Fat Stock Shows of Colorado and Texas. There are, however, several outdoor contests in the winter, such shows as those held at Phoenix, and Tucson, Arizona, where the climate is more conducive to outdoor activity.

The use of the indoor arena has permitted, with considerable more success, the introduction and the exhibition of cowboy activities to the large cities of the East. Rodeo contests of the large scale type are held on the Eastern coast, in most cases, during the late fall and early spring;

from the standpoint of weather, both times are unseasonable for outdoor entertainment, and for this reason the rodeo producer might become very discouraged, if he were obliged to stage a contest in the open. Thus, the use of the indoor arena eliminates one of the many worries that are connected with the work—the canceling of performances because of inclement weather.

Contests held in an enclosed arena, as a whole, offer to the spectator considerable comfort and advantages that are not to be realized in outdoor events. The seating in a modern sports arena is comfortable, easily accessible, and at the same time affords a splendid opportunity to witness the contest in its entirety. Absent from the indoor arena —and this is no loss—are those great clouds of dust that are whipped up from the ground and dropped like a smothering veil over the spectators; they not only obscure the action of the contestants but prevent the spectators from actually opening their eyes to see, if there is anything to be seen at that time. Dust at rodeos has been a problem for the managers of the contests as well as for the spectators.

Various means and methods have been suggested and used to eliminate this distracting and annoying hazard, but still, nature will not be misled to conduct herself in any other manner than that to which she is accustomed. In a large, plowed-up area, subjected to heat-laden and drying winds, dust, on the slightest provocation, can be the only result.

One other important advantage of the indoor arena is that the action of the contest is confined within a certain fixed area, not too large. One can always observe the contest, even if he does not occupy the best seat. The arena is surrounded entirely by seats, there is no race track around the performing space; one of the most distracting and annoying features about many of the outdoor arenas is the fact that the spectators are so far from the scene of action that they loose much of the thrill.

To hold a contest with the above advantages in the very heart of a great Eastern city has stimulated the interest and enthusiasm of the Eastern fan for rodeo. Upon attending the spectacular indoor-arena shows, one becomes amazed at the ardent following that this sport has acquired. These contests, with purses ranging from $5,000 to $100,-000, with entry fees added, are an attraction that has brought to the larger cities the finest talent—animal and human—and has laid at the feet of the people of the East the very best that rodeo has to offer.

Enthusiasm runs high when one witnesses the one time humble and unlovely everyday work of the cowboys and sees how the courage and daring of these men brings thousands of shouting and approving spectators in sophisticated and staid Boston to their feet. Rodeo cannot fail to pull at the heartstrings and arouse the emotions of everyone present; it stirs up in the spectators youthful memories that are a part of young America and lifts them out of everyday cares.

What rodeo has achieved and will continue to achieve for the America of the East, it has already accomplished for almost half a century for the America of the West. One cannot help being envious of this heritage. The vastness of the country, the natural wonders and beauties, the personalities that have developed from the environment—all this is to be felt in rodeo.

If the Western outdoor rodeo fails to offer the many comforts that are demanded by Eastern followers—and these refinements are also sought in some Western contests —there are several important aspects which are part of every outdoor event that cannot be incorporated in the enclosed arena contest. God-given sunshine—and rain—and dust—are a part of rodeo. Magnificent backdrops of snow-capped mountains; endless vistas of plains and rolling hills; breath-taking natural amphitheatres formed eons ago by a restless earth; tall, dark, green pines standing as silent and mysterious sentinals—all are canopied by a sky of blue. No producer of scenic effects can or dares compete with the Master Designer of this planet. Rodeo in the open air has no equal, be it a local contest working diligently and patiently to build up a contest worthy of rank among those of note, or be it the large, historical celebration based on years of successful operation with a following that comes from every section of the country.

Those summer contests held in the East, in the foothills of the Alleghenies of Pennsylvania, in the Blue Ridge Mountains of Virginia, or on the undulating land of Connecticut and New York State, have that element of nature that is necessary for the creation of the spirit of rodeo. Perhaps, they lack the vastness of background, the clarity of atmosphere, the vicious and violent moods of nature that are typical of the West, yet there is an openness that allows an expansion of heart and mind which enables one to appreciate the true significance of the sport.

The size of a contest, the amount of prizes, the historical significance of the event—these are not the criterion of success of an exhibition. No single element, nor a combination of many, is a guarantee of success;

however, a good show is evident when they are present. Any number of small local contests might not bring to the arena the "names" of the rodeo world; nevertheless, they put on a contest that can rightfully be classed with the best to be seen. In these small contests speed, efficiency, and simplification of presentation are the envy, and rightly so, of the larger and more spectacular shows. Local talent performing for its own profit and pleasure, as well as for the glory of the community, is not to be despised; for, while the rodeo contestant today is called professional, and his skill as a performing member on a range might be questioned, in almost every case the individual began as a local exhibitor and performer. The names famous in rodeo came, for the most part, from small Western communities and were first recognized by these communities.

During the last decade the small community or local rodeo, particularly in the West, has fortunately been under the direction of groups of civic-minded citizens. There are various local organizations—the Chamber of Commerce, the Junior Chamber of Commerce, the Elks, Rotary, Firemen's and Policemen's Benevolent Associations, and American Legion Posts—that have sponsored rodeos. Some organizations have held contests of several years' standing and have built permanent arenas on the outskirts of their respective towns.

The membership of rodeo committees is composed of local merchants and prominent men and women interested in furthering the welfare of their city. They make the various arrangements for the contest and they have proved to be more satisfactory than the importation of a producer or a promoter of such contests. This takes years of experience; while there is often much to be desired in some of these local contests, usually they offer a good show, and the spectators, contestants, and managers are well satisfied. Although the contest is small and the returns are negligible, the entertainment needs of the community are satisfied. At first, these local rodeo committees feel unable to become members of the Rodeo Association of America because of the additional expense involved, but with growth and success they, in most cases, join the Association as soon as possible. Worthy of mention here is the small contest with proper equipment and fair purses; if planned for a favorable time, it is never neglected by the rodeo contestants.

Cowboys have always "stood by" contest-committees who have treated them fairly, and there is no reason to believe that they will fail to do so because of the size of the contest, for these people are doing their best to put on a good show. The cowboy-contestant realizes that the small, community show, coming along every few days, is a definite aid in keeping an even financial keel between the less frequent, larger contests. He realizes that these small community contests, if given the opportunity, will, in time, increase their scope and thus their prizes, which in the end will be of benefit to the contestant.

It is quite natural that various unscrupulous promoters of entertainment have taken, and unfortunately in a few cases, still do take advantage of the fine reputation that rodeo has built up for itself over a period of years. Not so many years ago one could read, from time to time, about such actions of the fly-by-night or "suitcase" promoters. Appearing in some small town and approaching the various local organizations of the village, they offered to stage a contest for a certain sum of money and promised to assume all responsibilities and worries that are connected with this work. The setting for the event was laid by means of a wide advertising campaign which infected the community and the surrounding districts with enthusiasm in anticipation of the contest, and thus, everything would appear in readiness for the occasion. Local money was expended for the equipment, stock was rented, and a printed and mailed prize list was circulated among the contestants. Invariably, the promise to bring outstanding cowboys to the event was a further inducement to loosen the purse strings of local, civic-minded citizens of the community in question. These promoters did not attempt such an ordinary thing as merely skipping town with a suitcase filled with gate receipts and entry fees, but because of their subtlety they held the community to a signed contract regardless of the final results of the show, either in quality of entertainment or in financial returns.

Among these promoters were those who did not fail to "walk out" when the "going was tough." Very often the community was left with endless legal attachments. There were bills for lumber used in the construction of chutes and the corral, for loan of stock used in the contests, for advertising and publicity campaigns to put the show before the unsuspecting public, and for numerous incidental items that appear insignificant but pile up and become enormous when added to the general expenditures. Often too, they were unable to pay the purses advertised; consequently, when this problem was worked out on a percentage basis, with as little as twenty-five cents on a dollar, the resultant feeling was not one of pleasure between the contestants and the local managers. The feeling of strained relations was increased when, in some cases, the horses and equipment of the cowboys were attached by the "closing in" on the part of the various firms to which the contest was indebted, because the animals and equipment were on the grounds of the show.

The cowboys had paid entry fees for the privilege of working; the purses were reduced to a percentage of the original sum; with the added troubles of having their property confiscated, these cowboys often expressed their wrath by taking the matter into their own hands. While such action was justifiable, it was an unfortunate situation, for many lads ended up in the local jail to cool their heels and only added to their many troubles the further misery of fines and payment of damage.

Added to these conditions of hoodwinked local committees and cheated cowboys was the attitude of a dissatisfied crowd, that had paid good money and had anticipated a quality performance. The failure of the committee to produce a good show did not increase the desire among the spectators to patronize future rodeos. The unscrupulous promoters did much harm not only to those directly affected by their trickery, but also other communities were discouraged from having anything to do with rodeo, whether legitimate or not, when this information and unfortunate situation received publicity.

Through the organization of the Rodeo Association of America and the Cowboys' Turtle Association, the activities of the "suitcase" promoters have been curtailed. The cowboys refused to attend events unless there was a bank guarantee of the purses, and the Rodeo Association of America exposed the name of the promoters and their shady dealings. This did much to rid the country of their kind.

More recently the Better Business Bureaus of many communities have taken it upon themselves to investigate thoroughly any offers by promoters of shows. They have discouraged the citizens of the communities from having dealings with the outside promoter. It is unfortunate that the Better Business Bureaus find themselves unable to prevent or, actually, to prosecute the shady promoter; this is a difficult procedure in any court of law, unless it can be proved that such a transaction was carried out intentionally. The protective bureaus have, however, helped to create an unhealthy situation for anyone dabbling in crooked promoting.

The problems of rodeo were not so easily settled simply by putting such individuals out of business. Further causes of discomfort and annoyance for the genuine rodeo promoter were a number of Wild West Shows, Thrill Circuses, and out-door arena entertainments which were advertised as rodeos, or at least publicized as exhibitions of contests relative to cowboy activities. True, there is no objection to such forms of entertainment including the various rodeo events; however, unless they are a major part of the show, the entertainment should not be classed as rodeo, nor should the word *rodeo* be used so prominently as to convey the idea that the event is strictly rodeo.

Many of the 'Thrill Circuses" are chock-full of "hair-raising" events, running the entire gamut of dare-devil stunts. They include auto races, auto crashes, big-top aerial acts, jitter-bug contests, dog-races, high-diving, and wire-walking acts. There is also evidence of incorporating important "name" orchestras in the shows. All this does not imply that these are cheap or dowdy shows; however, it is misleading to call entertainment of this type "rodeo"—

a dozen head of cattle and perhaps as many so-called cowboys make such a title even more ridiculous.

Several of these Thrill Circuses have had excellent patronage; there is no question that they have an appeal for the public. There is no objection to this particular type of entertainment; the managers of legitimate rodeo contests might well learn a lesson in the procedure of advertising, because they do rightfully advertise full-fledged rodeos.

This Thrill Circus type of entertainment has been refused membership in the Rodeo Association of America and rightly so. This entertainment should not be deplored; however, if it were to receive membership in the Association, the horizon of the Rodeo Association would have to be expanded so as to include the many other sporting activities such as horse-racing, polo, et cetera; the true purpose of the organization would be lost in the welter of detail that would result from such an expansion. The Rodeo Association is for rodeo alone; it intends to devote its entire strength and energy to the development of this one particular sport.

Thrill Circuses have appeared in Los Angeles, California; Tulsa and Oklahoma City, Oklahoma; Buffalo and Albany, New York; Chicago, Illinois, and Cleveland, Ohio. In the two latter cities serious accidents to the spectators have resulted because of the lack of proper facilities to protect them from the animals in the events. Similar accidents might occur at a rodeo; however, as yet, none have been reported. During the Cleveland show a trained bull broke through the enclosure surrounding the arena and climbed into the grandstand. As a result about seventeen spectators were injured, and as many lawsuits were brought against the City of Cleveland, because the stadium was owned by the city.

During the latter part of August, 1941, a similar accident occurred in Grant Park, Chicago; a bull leaped into the crowd of spectators and again several persons were injured. The aftermath of both these shows resulted in a general distrust in the abilities of such promoters, and the City Fathers were discouraged from having anything to do with rodeo or any related entertainment. Thus, again, the unthinking, incapable and unscrupulous impressario brought discredit to the honorable name of rodeo. In Buffalo, New York, during the late summer of 1942, the promoters of a Thrill Circus ended in jail for trying to cheat the performers out of their wages.

Early in the spring of 1941, an advertising and promotion agency in Washington, D. C., proposed to organize the sport of rodeo into an association. It was to be called National Rodeo Incorporated and planned to make a business of staging Championship contests. After this brief announcement, nothing more was heard of this organization, and at this time nothing tangible in this respect has been developed.

CHAPTER XXV

MEN WHO DIDN'T SCARE

Stream-lined rodeo—smooth-singing teams,
Horses and stars from Hollywood screens.

In contrast to the unscrupulous promoters, are the many fine men who have spent a lifetime devoted to the promotion and production of modern rodeo. Among these men who have made a career of the work and have brought credit to the sport and also achieved fame throughout this country, no one is better known than Colonel W. T. Johnson, who was one of the first to bring rodeo with its true Western spirit to the large eastern cities of New York and Boston. He came from the West in 1925, bringing this American cowboy sport with its full flavor, and produced the annual show in New York until 1937, when he retired from rodeo. Before his retirement he had added Boston and several other cities to his circuit. Having once produced a rodeo for a city, the genial Texas Colonel never failed to receive a contract for each succeeding year.

His entire stock and equipment were purchased by the two well-known cattlemen, Mark T. Clemans and William J. Clemans, Jr., of Florence, Arizona, who were financed by a banker of that state. The transaction included about three hundred head of horses, half of which were bucking animals and the other half, parade and arena animals. Included in the purchase were Brahma steers, bulls and calves, and riding gear. The purchase of the Colonel's show, which was considered the world's largest rodeo outfit, involved a sum of approximately $150,000. The purchasers and owners of the Lightening C Ranch organized the new enterprise into the World's Champion Rodeo Corporation with headquarters at Dublin, Texas. The management of this ranch was placed in the very able hands of Everett Colborn, who came from Blackfoot, Idaho, to take over the position. Having had years of experience as a co-partner of the organization, known as "Colborn and Sorenson, Rodeo Producers," and as arena director for the Johnson Shows at Madison Square Garden, New York City, Everett Colborn had the ability to assume this responsibility. The World's Championship Rodeo Corporation is regarded with respect as is evidenced in the fact that both the New York and Boston contest-contracts have been awarded to it each succeeding year since its beginning.

Colonel W. T. Johnson, upon retiring from active participation as a rodeo entrepreneur, devoted his energies to the general supervision of his five ranches. All are located in Texas, one each at Van Horn, Eagle Pass, and Lobo, and two at Spofford; these ranches are stocked with thousands of head of cattle and sheep, all carrying the famous and well-known brand of Six Bar. To aid him in carrying this tremendous responsibility, Colonel Johnson was assisted by his son, Thomas Johnson, Jr. Colonel Johnson brought the Western cowboy and his work into the limelight of the nation's greatest city, and since his retirement each succeeding annual performance is a monument to his foresight.

The most recent rodeo entrepreneur is Gene Autry of screen and radio fame. Having appeared two years as the guest star of the Madison Square Garden and Boston Garden Rodeos, Gene was occupied during these years in organizing one of the largest and most complete traveling rodeos of all times. He has spared neither expense nor energy in gathering together the finest collection of horses, cattle, and equipment, and he included the necessary costumes and props to stage successfully this most American of spectacles.

Before any attempt was made to organize the traveling show, the necessity of establishing headquarters was imminent. Gene purchased a ranch of twelve hundred acres, located near the small town of Berwyn, Oklahoma, and then made public the plans of his traveling rodeo. The citizens of this little town were so impressed by their distinguished neighbor that on January 1, 1942, the name of the town was legally changed to Gene Autry, Oklahoma. On this ranch the consummation of his plans for the Flying A Ranch Stampede came about. The many years of preliminary work gradually took shape so that by February of that year the show opened for its world premiére as the feature entertainment of the Houston Fat Stock Show and Livestock Exposition.

The Stampede, headed by Gene and his renowned horse, "Champion," had approximately one hundred and twenty-five leading rodeo contestants and made a two months' tour through five states. The performances were six- and seven-day stands in Cleveland, Ohio; Pittsburgh and Philadelphia, Pennsylvania; Washington, D. C.; New Haven, Connecticut; and Providence, Rhode Island. In every engagement the Flying A Ranch maintained a Rodeo

Association of America membership with contest points for the participants in each recognized event. In addition to the purse of $30,000 plus entry fees, the Flying A Ranch Stampede offered $2,000 in prizes to the cowboys attending all six contests and winning the most points in each event. The All-Around Cowboy of the Stampede received seven hundred and fifty dollars, while the champions in the five recognized events received two hundred and fifty dollars each.

With horses of such reputation as "Top Rail," "Red Bluff," "Calgary Red," "King Tut," "Mill Stone," and "Dear John"; with tough fighting bulls and steers, and rampageous calves; with magnificent parade and arena horses—all lending their skill, beauty, and spirit to the show—it was bound to be a success. Costumes treated with fluorescent dyes, the Grand Entry and the Finale, as well as a Country Square Dance—these features of the show became a blaze of hidden color when the incandescent lights were extinguished and the costumed performers were subjected to violet ray lamps. This rather theatrical aspect, used intelligently, enhanced those typical features of rodeo and lent that touch of glamour and the spectacular which are so dear to the heart of the rodeo fan.

Closely associated with the Gene Autry rodeo is John Agee, the man who has trained more famous screen and circus performing horses than any other individual. He began his work with the Ringling Brothers of the circus fame, continued with them for thirty-six years and became equestrian director of the circus. He has a natural knack for handling horses, which has brought him in contact with the greatest shows of this type in the country. He has helped train practically every horse of the many cowboy heros of the screen and show world.

After leaving the combined circuses of Ringling Brothers and Barnum and Bailey in 1923, he was associated with Tom Mix and worked on that screen star's horse, Tony. In 1940 he joined Gene Autry, who entrusted him with the training of the two famous Autry horses, "Champion" and "Champion, Jr." John Agee has the satisfaction of knowing that the horses he has trained have carried the outstanding men and women of the entertainment world to the pinnacle of fame.

After witnessing the two appearances during a performance, one no longer questions the fabulous personality of the owner of the Flying A Ranch Stampede. Gene Autry is one of the most outstanding Western personalities appearing either on the screen, or on the dirt and sawdust of the rodeo arena. It may be said quite sincerely that his clean-cut, regular-habit, All-American personality is not one that is only donned for his public appearances.

Another "new-blood" in rodeo-producing, also via Hollywood, is Roy Rogers, Republic Pictures' singing cowboy star. Roy has a captivating personality, a true Western spirit, and, like Gene Autry, attracts millions of fans. In the past he appeared as guest star, with his famous horse "Trigger," at the Eastern contests. Now, as has been mentioned, (see footnote, page 270) he is co-producer of the Eskew show. With this group he has just completed a very successful circuit of spectacular performances before millions of rodeo enthusiasts. These shows are "smooth and stream-lined," similar in their elaborate features to those of Gene Autry and his Stampede.

Roy Rogers also brings the Sons of the Pioneers, a musical ensemble of two guitars, a violin, a bull-fiddle, and several excellent voices. This group of men and their music was one of the hits of the 1942 contests in New York City, Boston, and Buffalo, New York. The Sons of the Pioneers, led by Bob Nolan, composer of *Tumbling Tumbleweeds,* offer a new type of music—a new interpretation of Western lore, rich and full of understanding. In their inimitable way, the Sons of the Pioneers have created a new appreciation of Western music.

In motion pictures these two men, Roy Rogers and Gene Autry, portray the ideal Western hero—the idol of many American youngsters; on the radio, their melodious voices have all the lilting loneliness of that unique American character, the cowboy; now to rodeo, they bring their sparkling personality, talents, and an endless heartwarming appeal.

The uninitiated, or those spectators attending a contest for the first time, are apt to be in a state of happy confusion in this—their first contact with rodeo. From the very beginning of the contest, the movement of the events is fast and without let-up. The color, rhythm, music, and the uniqueness of costume have a power of fascinating the spectator to such an extent that he loses sight of much of the action. After witnessing a show for several times, one becomes conscious of the smoothness and ease with which the contests are run off, and he appreciates the fine points of the action rather than the more obvious rough and tumble aspects of the show. One becomes more interested in the "how" of the events; how soon a calf is roped and tied; how a ride is evaluated; what makes a qualified ride; how a steer is thrown. In this way the knowledge of these phases of the sport increases and adds much to the enjoyment and understanding of the contest as a whole.

A contest is usually opened with a Grand Entry, a parade of fifty to one hundred horsemen and horsewomen. Led by the Color Bearers, the parade moves rapidly; racing at full gallop, the procession circles the arena and returns, weaving back and forth in a serpentine fashion, through the center. The horses are richly caparisoned, and their riders are dressed in colorful riding costumes of gabardine and of satin. The larger the show, the more elaborate the costuming; the arena becomes a sea of undulating, rhythmic color. Grand entries in California are miles long; everyone who owns a horse or can steal one participates. Much silver mounted equipment is in evidence, and the contesting cowboys are very inconspicuous.

Following this colorful opening of the show, comes the introduction of the judges and officials of the contest. At this time the spectators become familiar with the names of the various personalities who are acting in the capacities of arena director, field timers, referees, and judges. The selection of capable men for these positions is an important consideration, and they are the best to be found in the work; usually they have been, or still are, active contestants.

Many contests, especially those of a community nature, invariably have, as a feature which is introduced early in the show, a young lady who has been selected as Queen of the Rodeo. Dressed in flashing regalia, suitable for the occasion, she is accompanied by two ladies-in-waiting. It is a sought-for honor by the belles of the town; the chosen ones enjoy this honor and popularity and have much attention showered on them for the duration of the contest.

After the Grand Entry and the introduction of the presiding officials, the actual contest, as far as the rodeo contestants are concerned, gets under way. Anyone of the various cowboy activities may lead off, but the usual procedure has been that the bareback bronc riding contest is the first event. The various contract acts are interspersed among the actual rodeo contests. The trick riding and fancy roping exhibitions follow the bareback bronc riding. This is an exhibition of roping skill rather than a contest and it displays the best exponents of the art of roping.

A number of contract performers are a part of every large rodeo. They perform in such acts as the trick and fancy roping and riding exhibitions—open for adults as well as juveniles—and a horse-back quadrille in which about twelve contestants take part. If there is a guest star, this performer is usually some popular Western star of the screen or of a defunct Wild West Show business, who with the aid of a well-trained horse offers the spectators an exhibition of fancy tricks.[1] The skill of both the performer and horse is readily seen in the ease of performance, in the lack of delays in the execution of the tricks, in the animal's response, and the patience of the performer. A part of every contest are the clowns with trained mules, horses, or donkeys; ten to fifteen minutes are devoted to their hilarious nonsense. The clown, however, is seen throughout the program and is especially welcome and useful during the bull riding event.

In addition to the above groups of events, which are commonly a part of the greatest number of rodeos in the

---

[1] The Guest Star is usually found only at the larger contests. The rodeo clown is a part of every rodeo and is found in the arena from the beginning to the end of the contest.

country, are the novelty trained-animal acts. These are: trained Brahma steers and buffaloes, high school horses, teams of horses with rider standing Roman style hurtling automobiles, Australian whip cracking and boomerang throwing, exhibitions of horse shoe pitching, and shooting the bow and arrow by the champions.[1]

These various contract acts are found on almost every program and are used not only because of the interest they have for the spectators, but also to fill in those gaps that exist between the events while the chutes are being prepared and filled with animals needed for the regular rodeo contests. The saddling of the horses and the arrangement of equipment for the riding events take time, as does the setting up of the various devices needed for the calf roping and steer wrestling contests. After these preparations have been made, the events move along without a hitch or delay. If a horse, steer, or bull should cause trouble while being prepared for exhibition, this added action lends many more thrills to the show; a contract act in progress at the same time loses its grip on the spectators if an animal should climb from the chute into the announcer's stand. All this sideline and back-of-the-scene preparation and excitement are a part of the show. The veteran rodeo fan always keeps one eye open for this additional and unforeseen drama that may come at any moment.

Depending upon the size of the rodeo and its location, additional features may be offered. The large cities of the East have attractions, such as a mounted basketball game— a thrilling, rough and tumble spectacle. More shirts are lost during the scramble than points are made by the con-

---

[1] There are numerous trained animals and also specialists and champions of various skills and sports.

testing teams. The cowboys' wild cow milking contest, which now receives Rodeo Association of America points, adds to every rodeo a zest and a bit of robust humor which invariably brings howls of approval and laughter from the crowds.

A cow is roped by one member of a team of two cowboys, the rope is dallied until one cowboy gets hold of the animal. It is released when both cowboys reach the bellowing animal. One man holds the head of the cow while the other proceeds to milk, catching about ten drops of fluid in a soft-drink bottle. Upon securing the milk, he races back to the judges but dares not cross the finish line until his partner has removed the rope from the cow. It is a timed event. In large rodeos the combined purses are about twenty-five hundred dollars.

Another contest, mirth-provoking in nature and a strenuous exhibition, is the wild horse race. Three men compose a team. The horses, with only a halter and a rope rein, are turned loose into the arena. Two members catch a horse and hold it while the third partner saddles and mounts it, then rides it across the finish line at the opposite end of the arena. This contest offers a purse of considerable size, and although it is not a Rodeo-Association-of-America point event, it is one of the most exciting to be seen in the arena.[1]

In the Southwest one is likely to see more roping contests—team roping, single, roping, as well as the regular featured calf roping contest. In the Northwest there are bucking and riding contests, which have no equal anywhere in the country. Both sections of the country have

---

[1] A contest which is one of the best. It is seen in the West more often than in the Eastern contests.

their Indian tribes represented in dances and riding races; in addition, there is always the pageantry of the many historical celebrations that are the theme of the contest.

Incorporated into Western rodeos, and possible because of the preponderance of outdoor arenas, are the many novelty races. They are added for humor, fun, and excitement. The pig race, figure-eight stake race, relay race, chuck-wagon race, potato race, are only a few of the many amusements. There are prizes for the winners, who are usually local men entering for the sport and fun of the contest.

Also depending on the location of the contest, there may be an exhibition of breed-horses of Arabian and Palomino blood, and cattle of the show type. Much of this type of entertainment depends on the willingness of exhibitors to show their stock and on the management of the contest to allow time for such an exhibition. When the rodeo is a featured entertainment of a Stock Show, it is, of course, only one part of a very elaborate exhibition of stock and is secondary to the main objective of the show, i.e., the exhibition of fine breeds and the purchase of those for sale.

A contest of several days' duration with a sizeable purse usually features the drawing of the bucking horses for the final determination of the champion riders of that particular show. The men, four to six, who have been the winners and have not bucked off in the event, draw the horses they will ride in the final day of the show. The bucking horses, the best of the string, are paraded before the spectators and are then prepared for the ride. In the meantime, the victorious riders draw the names of the horses they are to ride. Much suspense and excitement is created;

everyone is on edge, betting and "pulling" for his particular rider. The purse for this final ride is made up of the entrance fees; although no R. A. A. points are awarded to the winner, the prestige, the purse, and usually a trophy —a saddle, plaque, or cup—are of great importance to the winner.

The indoor contest usually ends its performance with some spectacular historical or patriotic theme in order to bring the rodeo to a quick, but colorful and exciting conclusion. Frequently the Finale of a contest features some important figures or events indigenous to the locale.

CHAPTER XXVI

FAR FROM THE HOME RANGE

Over the border and across the sea,
They thrilled the crowds in each country.

Rodeo is no longer confined to the United States. Its popularity has taken it to Canada, Australia, Venezuela, England, and recently also into the theatres of war. In Canada, interest in the sport has been particularly in the southwestern part of the Dominion in the Provinces of Alberta, Manitoba, and Saskatchewan. There has also been some interest in the sport in the eastern part, especially in Toronto. The development of rodeo in Canada has been an outgrowth of the same background that stimulated its activities in the western sections of the United States. The basis of all rodeo, no matter where it is found, is the cattle industry. Although there is little information regarding the sport in Canada before the beginning of this century, it is believed that in the early nineties there was evidence of cowboy activities in the frontier town of Calgary, in the Province of Alberta. The earliest mention made is found in the *Calgary Weekly Herald* of May 16, 1893. It says:

> In connection with the mid-summer fair there will be a series of interesting cowboy sports. Mr. Geo. Lane, of High River, is making all the necessary arrangements. The first event will be a roping contest by the crack

315

ropers of the Northwest. Wild steers will be driven in from the range and each competitor will have an animal selected for him by the judges. A watch will be held on him from the start, until the steer is tied down with three feet. The man who performs this feat in the shortest time is the winner. The first prize will be a $75 saddle presented by Messrs. Carson & Shore; second prize a silver mounted bridle and spurs from the society. Another event will be a cowboy race—600 yards with three turns around the post. The first prize in this will be a $75 saddle presented by Messrs. Hutchings & Riley; second prize the same as in the roping contest. This is the first thing of the kind ever attempted in Calgary and should prove one of the most attractive features of the fair.[1]

The last sentence of the above quotation leads one to believe that this was the real beginning of cowboy sports in Calgary. The midsummer fair at Calgary was held on June 20-23, 1893; it opened with a Ladies' Day and contests of horse and man for supremacy. According to the *Herald,* the contest would "no doubt prove of the greatest interest to the citizens and the many visitors expected in by the Train."[2]

Several days after the conclusion of the fair, the *Herald* commented on the cowboy activities which evidently had impressed the spectators. The *Herald* says:

The exhibition was entirely new to probably a majority of those present and they watched the sport with the keenest enjoyment. The horses bestrode by the

---

[1] *Calgary Weekly Herald,* (May 16, 1893.)
[2] *Ibid.,* (June 19, 1893.)

cowboys were important factors in the contest. The hardy little brutes seemed to be possessed of human intelligence and the manner in which they performed their allotted parts was a revelation.

The roping of range cattle by the cowboys—genuine cowboys straight from the roundup—is a new feature in the exhibition and one that cannot fail to attract visitors from all parts; it is one, too, that is characteristic of the Northwest especially, and will be particularly interesting not to strangers merely but to our own people as well, since so few of residents of towns really know anything of range life.[1]

The cowboy contests which made their first appearance at this fair at Calgary, in 1893, evidently were roping events and did not include bronc riding activities, such as might have been found on the ranches at that time. However, this latter activity was added to the list of contests at the fair the next year, for the *Herald* of July 13, 1894, says:

Such western sports as cowboy and Indian races promise to be interesting as will, no doubt, be the riding of the bucking broncho, where the man sitting the straightest and closest to the saddle takes the first prize.[2]

A week later the *Herald* says:

The riding of the cowboys was a feature of the day's sport and although the horses did not pitch very badly some good riding was done and the men could have

---

[1] *Ibid.*, (May 27, 1893.)

[2] *Semi-Weekly Calgary Herald and Alberta Livestock Journal*, (July 13, 1894.)

stood it a great deal harder. Mike Herman was awarded first and Billy Stewart second.[1]

The first date recorded for a rodeo in this section of Canada is the year 1901. An event of this nature was staged in honor of the visit of the Duke of York, who, after the death of his brother, the Prince of Wales, was heir apparent to the English throne. This man later became George V of England. Little is known about the contest which was staged by the citizens of this little Canadian town, nor of the results of this auspicious occasion, but evidently, interest in the activity had not yet been crystallized—at least, not to the extent of making it an occasion to attract people to this city. The fact that rodeo was still a novelty and a curiosity and had not yet reached the proportions of a sport and business might have been a deterrent to the citizens of Calgary in making an annual affair of such an exhibition.

Not until about ten years later is mention made of an attempted revival of interest in this sport in Calgary. About 1911 two men from the United States went to Calgary with the express purpose of staging a rodeo, but their efforts failed. This must have been discouraging, but it is interesting to note that evidently their interest did create such a strong impression that one of them, who remained there, was able to interest the people of Calgary in the project, so that in 1912[2] a rodeo was staged. These two men were Guy Weadick and Tom Mix. Tom Mix re-

---

[1] *Ibid.*, (July 20, 1894.)

[2] "The 1912 Stampede will remain an outstanding historical event because of the bulldogging and steer roping events, items which are now prohibited. The record bulldogger that year, Senor Clemento of Old Mexico, threw and held his steer in 7½ seconds, on the final day." *Calgary Daily Herald,* (July 15, 1924), 11.

The "Big Four."
(Program Cover).

turned to the United States, and Guy Weadick remained in Canada to see their dreams eventually come true.

Through the strenuous efforts and farsighted vision of this American, Guy Weadick, rodeo was brought to this small town in western Canada. To him, Calgary and the northwest part of Canada can give credit and thanks for the world-wide publicity which the city has since received. By sincere persuasion Guy Weadick secured the financial backing necessary to promote what he called "The Stampede"—a title used for the first time for a cowboy contest —and now recognized as first-rate wherever rodeo is is known. Weadick secured this financial aid from four wealthy Canadian ranchers, Pat Burns, George Lane, A. E. Cross, and A. J. McLean—known as the "Big Four"—each of whom gave him $100,000 to put on the contest. A purse of $20,000 for six performances attracted the cowboys, and Weadick offered to the world a contest that made rodeo history. This was the beginning of big purses in rodeo. This first important Canadian contest was a six-day rodeo and attracted some of the best-known men of that day. Weadick not only exhibited the talented riders[1] of Canada, but also those of the United States; in addition he brought many expert and experienced ropers[2] from our Southwest.

---

[1] Important Contestants of Stampede of 1912: Mrs. H. McKenzie, Mrs. Aubrey, Miss Fanny Sperry, Bertha Blancett, Nip Van, W. S. Bunnell, Will McBryde, Alf Vivian, John Glenn, Bert Weir, Mike Harmon, Art Accord, Add Bradshaw, Frank Bajorquez, Harry Tipton, Geo. Webster, Charles Vesper, Henry Webb, Bert Kelly, Doc Pardis, and B. C. Red. *Calgary Daily Herald*, (September 2, 1912), 2.

[2] Trick Ropers: Florence La Due, Bertha Blancett, Lucille Mulhall, "Tex" McLeod, Stanley Whitney, J. Welsh, W. Woolf, Esteven Clemento, [sic] Senor Magdalana, [sic] Senor Randon. *Calgary Daily Herald*, (September 3, 1912), 2.

The Stampede of 1912 was honored with the presence of a royal visitor in the person of His Royal Highness, the Duke of Connaught, Governor-General of Canada. He and his party arrived on September 5, 1912, and the Calgary *Herald* says of his visit:

> The presence of the duke at the Stampede will confer a distinction upon the proceedings that will give them tone and significance. Never before has such an opportunity occurred in Canada, for any royal party to witness the sports of the range, and as we have the finest gathering of riders and ropers ever got together, the governor general shall witness a celebration unique in the history of the Dominion. The duke has graciously consented to partake of a typical "round-up" breakfast, which will be prepared and served by men who have been in this country ever since the days of the open range.[1]

Evidently the presence of the duke caused some of the more enterprising officials of the Stampede to take advantage of his visit, for two days later this headline appeared in the *Herald*:

"Citizens are 'soaked' a dollar to see the Duke inspect cadets, scouts, veterans and other military organaizations."[2]

"The Duke of Connaught is himself a soldier—is he to be made part of a Stamped attraction."[3]

The following day, the *Herald* printed the following democratic outburst:

---

[1] *Calgary Daily Herald,* (September 4, 1912), 1.

[2] *Ibid.,* (September 6, 1912), 1.

[3] *Ibid.,* (September 6, 1912), 1.

The management of the Stampede may be congratulated on the ability with which the affair was organized. It cannot be congratulated, however, either on its demeanor towards the public or its treatment of the public on several occasions. In fact, if there is anything of which Calgary feels a little bit ashamed today it is the management of the Stampede itself. As the days passed the impression became prevalent, and events appeared to justify it, that those who had the affair actively in charge were out after the money, and did not care much for anything else, as long as they got it. They broke faith with the public on several occasions. They turned thousands of people away from the grounds one day without giving them more than a few minutes of a show, and without endeavouring to return them their money. They charged an admission fee to the Calgary Cadets honored by the Governor-General of Canada, thus making a circus spectacle of a public event for their own pecuniary benefit.[1]

Following this successful and inspiring exhibition in Calgary, Weadick ventured a similar event and purse the next year, 1913, at Winnipeg, Manitoba. He had, by this time, established himself as one of the outstanding producers of cowboy sports in the Canadian Southwest.

Following his two important successes, a period of four years of war intervened before "The Stampede" was brought back to Calgary. In 1919 the same four ranchers, who had shown their faith in his original venture, induced Weadick to stage the contest again, "The Victory

---

[1] *Ibid.*, (September 7, 1912), 1.

Stampede," in Calgary. This time the purse was increased to $25,000.

In 1922 the management of the Calgary Exhibition Corporation approached Weadick and asked him to unite his show with that of the annual fair held in that city. With his characteristic hard-working approach to a problem, Guy, in the next ten years, increased the attendance from ninety-odd thousand to the fabulous figures of 258,469 in 1929.[1] The part that "The Stampede" played in this enormous increase was not insignificant, not to mention the managerial skill displayed by this American. In 1932, because of an economy measure, the committee backing the Exhibition and Stampede dispensed with his services. This was a severe blow to a man who had devoted so many years to the development and growth of his inspiration.

Today, the Calgary Exhibition and Stampede is truly a monument to the genius and hard work of that one man, Guy Weadick. As the leading contest of Southwestern Canada, it is an annual event held the second week of July. It draws the same group of followers annually with an attendance of approximately 267,000; it is both a professional and amateur contest. Here are represented the various cowboy events as listed by the Rodeo Association of America, but the outstanding single feature is the Chuck-Wagon Race. This contest also holds two bronc and two calf roping events, the North American Championship and the Canadian Championship events respectively. To be winner of the North American Bronc Riding Champion-

---

[1] 1944—attendance 285,458. From the office of the General Manager, J. Charles Yule, Calgary Stampede, Calgary, Alberta, Canada. The largest daily attendance was Friday, 1944, 68,336.

ship, is one of the greatest honors of all rodeo sports and almost equals, in magnitude, the honor of winning the title of All-Around Cowboy.

The outstanding event at Calgary is, as mentioned above, the Chuck-Wagon Race. It is considered one of the most colorful features of "The Stampede" and has received the highest praise as the most thrilling and exciting event of that rodeo. The rules governing this event are many and elaborate, they cover every possibility of preventing misunderstanding and dissension. Each unit or outfit consists of a wagon drawn by two teams, a driver, and four mounted outriders. All are attired in cowboy costumes. The wagon must be a regulation round-up wagon and outfitted completely with all the equipment needed for such a unit, with the exception of food, to establish itself and exist on the range. The equipment includes a regular stove, canvas cover, poles, guy ropes, stakes, and other necessary paraphernalia.

The camps are set up opposite the judges' stand in such a position that all are given fair opportunity to get an equal start in the race. When the flag is lowered, the members of each outfit strike camp. Throwing a fifty-pound stove into the wagon, they are off. The drivers, before starting out on the track, cut a figure eight around two barrels placed before each camp, each of the drivers passing his barrels on the right side. The driver cannot be given any assistance by any other member of his team and he must drive his wagon alone. The four mounted men are required to stay behind the racing wagon so that they may not hinder other teams from passing their outfit. When the drivers have completed the figure eight around the barrels, they move on to the track, go around it once, and finish under the wire.

Time is taken as each lead team passes under the wire. Because of hazards, it is important that the lead team, as part of a four-horse team, be attached to the wagon with the driver still holding the reins. Time is taken on each wagon. The seven outfits having the best time each day receive, respectively, the day's purses ranging from ten to seventy-five dollars. The total time for the first four days of the contest is recorded, and on the fifth day the finals are run. The twelve outfits having the best total time are allowed to race and share the final money ranging from three hundred and fifty dollars for the first prize to twenty-five for twelfth place.

Because this is a race displaying the skill of the driver and outriders, and the speed of the teams, penalities of seconds are imposed for offenses committed. Penalities are imposed for: outriders helping the driver after the team starts; outriders interfering with other contestants; losing part of equipment; hitting the barrels; failure to cut figure eight in manner designated; failure on the part of all outriders to finish the race with the wagon. The races lose none of their interest or excitement for the spectator because of the gory spills and pileups that take place frequently.

Calgary has been the scene of some of the greatest contests of all rodeo, and Canada has produced a number of outstanding rodeo cowboys. Among them are the Linder brothers, Herman and Warner, experts at riding, roping, and steer decorating.[1] Herman has been the winner of the

---

[1] Steer Decorating is a Canadian form of steer wrestling.

All-Around (North American) and Canadian Championships on several occasions and has placed in the North American and Canadian bronc riding events. Jack Wade of Halkirk, Alberta, has also made a name for himself as the All-Around Champion.

At the Calgary Stampede the outstanding bronc rider of the thirties, the late Pete Knight came into prominence. In 1927 he took the North American bronc riding contest and between 1927 and 1932 won the Canadian Riding Championship three times. He was the outright winner of the famous Prince of Wales Trophy, and among his many honors was the Rodeo Association of America Championship for bronc riding for 1932, 1933, 1935, and 1936. In 1936 he traveled to London with the Tex Austin Rodeo; later that year he went to Australia and New Zealand. Before his death, Pete Knight knew, saw, and experienced every phase of rodeo. He was considered one of the greatest riders of all times. Pete was an Easterner by birth—Philadelphia, Pennsylvania, his birthplace. In his childhood days his family moved to Oklahoma and later to Crossfield, Alberta. This latter address is often given as his birth place; however he was a citizen of the United States. Pete met an untimely death in the spring of 1937, while contesting at the Hayward Rodeo, Hayward, California.

Another man who has been closely associated with the Calgary Stampede and who was a close friend of Pete Knight, is Harry Knight of Banff, Alberta. He began rodeo work early but did not become well known until about 1926, when he appeared at the Stampede, won the Canadian bareback riding contest and placed in the North American event. Harry Knight is not of great stature

nor of great weight but attained a certain free style, a
perfect balance, and a knowledge of timing. Much of his
hidden strength and ability lies, it is said, in the extraordinary development of his legs. In his younger days
he had considerable experience as a dog-musher and eventually went into this form of racing. He has won the dog
derby twice, a run between Calgary and Banff, and also
appeared in such races in Washington and Idaho. This
type of sport causes much strain on a man's legs; it has
much to do with their muscular development.

Harry Knight is one of the few people in rodeo who
possesses true sophistication and much charm which are
entirely independent of any effort on his part. He knows
how to do things in the grand manner without ostenta-
tion. He has a knack of making money and an even more
remarkable knack of getting rid of it fast! He has many
friends in every walk of life and is at home with the blue-
bloods of New York as well as with the poorest ranch
hands in Arizona and Texas. Harry is blunt to the degree
of being almost insulting; his contacts with people make
them feel flattered that he noticed them at all.

Harry Knight won such important Northwestern contests as Ellensburg, Pendleton, and the 1928 Amateur
Riding Contest at Cheyenne. He also participated, with
creditable success, in the events of calf roping and steer
wrestling. A severe injury at the Chicago World's Fair in
1933, almost cost him his life. The following year he
was on his way to London as a judge with the Austin
show. The next year, 1935, he was again riding as a
champion and was overshadowed only by his best friend,
Pete Knight. Harry has now retired from active participation; however he still acts in some official capacity

related to cowboy sports and occasionally appears at rodeos of importance.

Among the many important rodeos in Canada the best-known ones are at Black Diamond, Raymond, Macleod, Cardston, Bassano, Alsak, Brooks, Pine Lake, Stony Indian, Czar, and Carstairs. The first four mentioned are two-day events; the others are one-day contests only.

A part of any Canadian rodeo, regardless of size, is the introduction of the many colorful and intriguing Indian tribes, most of which are indigenous to this section of the country. Many of them partake in the contests and lend much atmosphere through their presence at and their encampments around the rodeo grounds. The natural setting of great scenic beauty, the participating members, as well as the contest itself, afford the spectator the opportunity of seeing rodeo in its true nature.

It might be said that rodeo reached the position of being a tournament on an international scale when it was made an important feature, equal in size to the other exhibits, of the Royal Agricultural Society of New South Wales, Australia. In 1938, M. A. W. Skidmore and Thomas B. MacFarlane, representatives of the Royal Agricultural Society, made an extended tour of Canada and the United States to visit the leading agricultural shows, exhibitions, and rodeos, in order to observe the talent available, as well as the methods of running rodeos. After making this tour, Mr. Skidmore and Mr. MacFarlane were able to stage the biggest and most successful contest ever seen in Australia. In 1939 there appeared, at the Royal Easter Show held in Sydney, two teams of American and Canadian cowboys and cowgirls, as well as eight Indians from Canada—the group totaling twenty-two members from North America.

This group met in competition with the best Australian cowmen to stage one of the largest rodeos in the Southern Hemisphere.[1]

The beginning of rodeo in Australia, goes back some thirty years and was known at first as "Bushmen's Carnivals." The major event of these early Carnivals was the contest known as Campdrafting. This event offered good purses as well as the opportunity of many side bets among the contestants and spectators.

Campdrafting consists of about 50 to 80 fast steers put into a corral with an open gateway about 40 feet wide. The competitor mounted on his camp horse is shown a steer by the judges and he is required to work that animal from the mob taking the steer through the gateway. On getting the animal into the field; the cowman drives the animal forward for about 100 yards, he is required to circle a peg. Moving the animal another 100 yards, he must circle a second peg but in the opposite direction from that of the first. On accomplishing this the man is required to move the steer forward another 100 yards and circle a third peg, in the same manner as the first one.

The time allotted for this contest varies from 1-1/2 to 2 minutes. A good rider and horse, as soon as he gets his steer from the mob will keep him on a straight course to the first peg, where the horse will move forward and shoulder the steer round the peg, straighten up the steer to the next peg where the horse will move forward again to the opposite side and shoulder the steer

---

[1] Letter from Thomas B. MacFarlane, Councillor and Assistant Honorary Ringmaster, Royal Agricultural Society of New South Wales, December 7, 1941.

round the peg. The same procedure to the 3rd and last peg. If at the completion of the course the competitor has any time left he will exhibit to the judge his horsemanship and the skill of the horse in shouldering and working the steer. Should a steer cross the boundary line, he is "lost" and no points are awarded. Points are awarded as follows: Cut Out, 26; Course, 4; Horse Work, 79.[1]

At the early carnivals, as many as sixty horses competed in these Campdrafts—a maiden draft, an open draft, and a consolation draft. Usually two or three days were required to complete the carnival, and the contest ended with what was known as a Buckjumping[2] Championship event.

One of the foremost judges of rodeo and the campdrafting contest in Australia at the present time is Roley Munro, who, about thirty years ago, attended several of these carnivals with three horses and backed himself to win $10,000. He also held the fastest time for throwing and tying steers. This was before the days of bulldogging when steers were thrown by the tail. The early "Bushmen's Carnivals" were at that time confined to northern New South Wales and Queensland.

The first modern rodeo was staged in Australia in 1929. The contest consisted of Campdraft, Buckjumping Championship, and Bullock Riding Contests. It was given considerable publicity and was the first rodeo to be broadcast throughout the continent. It was successful, both from the standpoint of finances and entertainment, and

---

[1] *Idem.*

[2] Buckjumping—bronc riding.

from within a radius of hundreds of miles came many people who camped in their cars near the contest grounds. The following statement by Mr. MacFarlane is one piece of evidence concerning the success of the show:

> One incident remains fresh in my memory. We refused a tender of $20 from the local Hotelkeeper for the Publicans booth on the Rodeo Ground. We guaranteed another Hotelkeeper $125 if he would take on the booth and he made $1750 profit in one day.[1]

Mr. Thomas B. MacFarlane, Merriwa, New South Wales, was one of the three organizers of this rodeo. After he had persuaded some of the Councillors of the Royal Agricultural Society to see this rodeo, he finally convinced them that it would not only be a great success as entertainment, but also a financial one, if such a contest were held in conjunction with the Royal Easter Show. His powers of persuasion proved to be potent; from that time on he had charge of organizing the rodeo events each year for that national institution.

Since 1929 rodeos have been staged in many places in New South Wales and in Queensland. In 1935 the Melbourne Centennary Show staged a Stampede which was a failure. This show was attended by many American contestants who had been imported for the occasion. From this contest John Schneider, Ned Winnigar, George Marcielle, and Alice Greenough were hired and later taken to the Sydney Contest during the Easter Show. During their appearance, these American men taught the Australian cowboys the art of steer wrestling.

---

[1] Letter from T. B. MacFarlane, December 7, 1941.

The Australian public was thrilled by the performance which resulted in such crowds that it is now impossible to accommodate all the people who patronize the Royal Show and Rodeo. In 1938, Sydney's one hundred and fiftieth anniversary, the Royal Easter Show and Rodeo drew an attendance of over a million people. In 1939, when the International Tournament betweeen Canadian, Australian, and American Teams took place, the attendance reached around 900,000; in 1940 and 1941, (war years) around 750,000. Rodeo has taken such a hold on the people of Australia and has reached such importance as a form of entertainment that there has been formed an Australian Bushmen's Carnival Association which is similar to our Rodeo Association of America. Its purpose is to further the development of this fascinating sport and entertainment. This Australian organization was fortunate in having for its first president, Mr. MacFarlane, who has devoted so many years to the betterment of the sport. He has seen rodeo spread throughout eastern Australia.

Because the climate is favorable, rodeo is staged in outdoor arenas. Next to the contest staged by the Royal Agricultural Society, those in the order of merit are Rockhampton, Warwick, and Goondiwindi in Queensland; Scone, Willow Tree, Tamworth, Wingen, and several others of more recent origin in New South Wales. World War II prevented year-round contests from North Queensland to Southern New South Wales. In the spring of 1942, the Royal Easter Show was canceled for the first time in years.

Among the names of past and present contestants in Bushmen's Carnivals and Rodeos, the following are the most prominent: R. F. Munro, R. Atthow, R. Grace,

C. Hassett, A. Trott, H. Burgess, F. Perrett, C. Pearce, J. Palmer, A. Hayden, A. Winter, A. Bowd, L. McNamara, Jean Burgess, Jessie and Jean Stirton, May Wood, May and Bessie Scott, Gwen Duncan, Beryl Curr, and Vera Carpenter.

The following American and Canadian cowboys and cowgirls were taken to Australia by the Royal Agricultural Society of New South Wales to compete in its annual contest: John Schneider, Ned Winnigar, George Marcielle, Clay Carr, Fox O'Callahan, Milt Moe, John Bartram, Joe Burrell, Alvin Gordon, Clark Lund, Herman and Warner Linder, Frank McDonald, Jack Wade, Jack Sherman, Jerry Ambler, Bill McMacken, Shorty Creed, Ted Elder, Jasbo Fulkerson, Mel Stonehoise, Hank Mills, Cecil Jones, Harley Walsh, Waldo Ross, Doris Haynes, Alice Greenough, Gene Creed, Ivadel Jacobs, Alice Van, Trixie McCormack, and Tad Lucas.

Because the war had made it impossible to import contestants from Canada and the United States for the 1941 Easter Contest, much regret was expressed by the managers of the show, as well as by the contestants. However, since World War II has now come to an end, there is every reason to believe that rodeo in Australia will once more assert itself as an important sport and entertainment. As a sport it has proved suitable and agreeable to the people of that country. As an entertainment it has been so outstanding that no other sport has been able to compete with it in attendance. In all probability, rodeo is in Australia to stay!

Credit must be given to the late John Van "Tex" Austin for the introduction of genuine cowboy activities and rodeo to the people of Great Britain. Tex Austin brought this American sport to London, England, during the early summer of 1924, and again, ten years later in 1934. This event was held at Wembly Stadium. Having promoted rodeos in New York's Madison Square Garden, in the Boston Garden, at Soldier's Field, Chicago, and in Hollywood, California, Tex Austin, with this experience, was capable of producing for the English people a rodeo composed of outstanding contestants, livestock, and equipment. Tex Austin was a Westerner by birth—born at Victoria, Texas, in 1888. In 1908 he moved to New Mexico and was a resident of that state until his death in 1938. His early association with the Southwestern cowboy remained with him throughout his entire life and served as an inspiration which made him one of the best-known promoters of large-scale contests.

His first rodeo in England in 1924, was staged during the British Empire Exposition at Wembly. This rodeo broke all existing records of that time for attendance; during this contest the managers had difficulties with the Royal Humane Society over the treatment of the animals in the calf roping contest. In the spring of 1934, Tex again took a rodeo outfit to England; the contest opened early in the month of June and continued four weeks. The contest purse was approximately ten thousand dollars; in addition, the entire proceeds of one show were presented to the contestants as a gift. Again, during this show, as had happened ten years previous, the rodeo received considerable notoriety when Tex Austin was arrested for the same charge of cruelty to animals. Aided by fanatics on this side of the ocean, the Royal Humane Society brought up the matter. After undue legal action, the case was settled amicably when the authorities agreed not to prosecute, if the roping events were eliminated from the show. This was done, and the contest continued without further difficulty.[1]

Rodeo as a sport or entertainment does not have such an appreciative following in Great Britain as it does in this country, Canada, and Australia. Great Britain never experienced a cattle industry of such scale or nature or on a free range basis as was the case in these other countries. Consequently, there is not the interest in nor the glorification of the characters and activities of a frontier society which is foreign to the greater number of the inhabitants of an older land. Thus, it cannot be expected that a sport or work of this nature would create among the English any interest other than that of curiosity. It is interesting, however, to note that two members of this great Commonwealth of Nations have, because of enviroment, as deep an appreciation of rodeo as our own country.

Just as rodeo has not been successful in a sense of establishing itself as a permanent entertainment in England, some other countries have not been enthusiastic about accepting it. Rodeo had been attempted in Hawaii with little success;[2] late in 1937, there were rumors of a fully organized Wild West Show and Rodeo being taken to Germany to play for some eight or ten weeks in the larger indoor arenas. Several rodeo promoters were approached by a well-known booking agent of New York concerning this movement, but the expansion program of the Third Reich cooled the ambitions of anyone willing to take such a risk at that time.

---

[1] Information offered by Smokey Snyder.

[2] More recently rodeos have been successful in Hawaii and they now seem to be a part of the entertainment and sport of the Islands.

Early in 1942 arrangements were made for a three-weeks contest in the bull arena of Caracas, Venezuela. The contract was made by a New York promoter and a Señor Martinez, of Venezuela, aided by several backers from that country. Some livestock, such as saddle horses and bucking horses, were furnished by an Eastern dude ranch; while the greater portion of the stock—steers, bulls, calves, and horses—were furnished by the stockmen of that South American country.

About thirty-two American contestants agreed to sign up for the expedition; among them were such well-known men and women as Mr. and Mrs. Dick Herren; Mr. and Mrs. Andy Curtis; Mr. and Mrs. Paul Bond; and Mr. and Mrs. Jack Jackson; Bob Estes, Mike Hastings, Bill Hancock, Howard McCrory, George Yardly, John Williams, and the Riding and Roping Ramsey Family, which is composed of several performers. These contestants looked forward with pleasure to this early spring tour, but unfortunately it turned into the most unhappy fiasco in which people in rodeo had ever been involved.

Before embarking on this unhappy journey, the cowboys were given round trip tickets and one week's salary; however, upon sailing, they found that they had been given steerage accommodations. The work of the cowboy may give the impression of crudeness, but one should by no means assume that this fixes his standard of living. The rodeo contestant of today has had the opportunity not only of experiencing, but also thoroughly enjoying the comforts of the largest cities of this country; therefore he should not be expected to accept anything inferior, simply because of the character of his work. A cowboy and his family enjoy good living and are quick to make known the lack of it. It was revealed later that the promoter of this rodeo and his party enjoyed first class accommodations. An argument ensued, and by the time of debarkation a feeling of ill will existed among the entire party.

During the first week, the performances drew good attendance from the citizens of Caracas, but the second week, when interest waned, the Venezuelan backers decided to cancel the show. This unfortunately caused the funds to be retained by one of the banks. One dispute led to another, until the usual characteristics of annoyed and cheated cowboys became evident. Several of the men became involved in fights with the backers and were placed in jail. After several hours the American consul managed to have the promoters released, and in the meantime Shorty McCrory, one of the contestants, succeeded in drawing the attention of the President of the Republic to their plight, and this brought about action. The cowboys were released after twenty-four hours in jail.

Conditions did not improve in spite of this presidential beneficence. The stock was not fed and suffered considerably in eighteen miles of rugged terrain, while being moved from Caracas to the port. Also, there was no money for transportation. The trip was made overland through mountain trails by the men and the stock; several animals died because of their weakened condition, caused by lack of food.[1]

The contestants, upon their return to this country, were not particularly sad, but certainly wiser. Most of them recall with a certain degree of pleasure, that comes to those who have had exciting if not lucrative adven-

[1] Information obtained from Mr. and Mrs. Dick Herren, Bob Estes, and Herbert S. Maddy.

tures, those harrowing days of uncertainty in a strange country. On the whole, foreign adventures have no special appeal for the rodeo cowboy, except those that have already been experienced with success. Nevertheless, there is no doubt that if and when such opportunities arise again, many cowboys will want to participate. It is part of the cowboy's nature to prefer adventure to a life of serenity and security. He likes the element of chance.

World War II depleted the ranks of rodeo, but the cowboys in the service of their country did much to spread this interesting sport in every theatre of war. These boys, as members of the armed forces, introduced rodeo as a means of entertainment for troops and natives in various countries. Rodeos were held in France, Italy, China, England, India, South Pacific Islands, and several were held in Honolulu, Hawaii. Much credit must be given to these boys for their ingenuity in making use of the animals and equipment that were available. In 1944, Fritz Truan participated in a rodeo held in Honolulu and won the bronc riding contest. At a rodeo, held almost a year later in Honolulu, May 2-6, 1945, a memorial service was held in tribute to Fritz. *Hoofs and Horns* for July, 1945, says:

This year's show was dedicated to Sgt. Fritz Truan who was here last year and afforded the crowd many thrills by his performance. On the first night of the rodeo the crowd of 6,000 persons paid silent tribute to this fine cowboy who lost his life in the battle of Iwo Jima. A bautiful stallion which Fritz rode last year to win the bronc riding was led into the stadium with the saddle empty and stood spotlighted while a Marine bugler sounded taps. The announcer said: "The man we honor is not with us tonight. He planned to compete for you in this show as he did last year. This horse with its empty saddle is a reminder, not only of him whose memory we honor tonight, but every cowboy who has died that we may enjoy in peace and happiness the sport they [sic] loved best."[1]

[1] "Honolulu Rodeo," *Hoofs and Horns* 15 (July 1945), 13.

CHAPTER XXVII

PROGRESS AND PROBLEMS

Count your points, watch technique!
If Lady Luck 'don't' let you slip,
You're ridin' high and handsome
Toward a World Championship!

Ten years after the organization of the Rodeo Association of America, another rodeo association made its appearance in the southwestern part of the country. This organization, known as the Southwest Rodeo Association, was formed in 1938, primarily to give the contestants[1] from that region, and those who, in most cases, work in that section, an opportunity to win special prizes offered in rodeo. This was to be an encouragement to those men who did not include the Northwest and California in their circuit, where the Rodeo Association of America was principally represented at that time. The new association became the center of distributing awards for the Southwest at the end of the rodeo season.[2]

The Southwest Rodeo Association was not proposed with the idea of competing with the Rodeo Association of America, nor did it advocate that the member-shows relinquish membership in the Rodeo Association of America

---

[1] Outstanding calf ropers and steer wrestlers originate in and come from the Southwest.

[2] Information offered by C. A. Studer, secretary-treasurer of the Southwest Rodeo Association.

and join this Southwest organization. The Southwest Rodeo Association encourages membership in both associations; the contestants whose activities take them into both areas have the advantage of receiving greater remuneration. It is possible for contestants to win first place in both organizations, but this is a rare occurrence.

Membership in the Southwest Rodeo Association has this advantage: it permits small contests in this particular area—and they are numerous—to become members and to have benefits otherwise denied them, since the fee for membership is only half as much as that in the Rodeo Association of America. There is an additional advantage in being a member-show of an organization which has a greater representation in the Southwest than the R. A. A.

The Southwest Rodeo Association is in complete accord and cooperates in every way with the Cowboys' Turtle Association. One of the directors is a member of the Turtle Association. Further evidence of this cooperation is found in the fact that no member-shows are permitted "to work anyone" except members of the Cowboys' Association and amateurs who have not been placed on the black list. Local cowboys, actually working on ranches, may participate in any of the member-shows provided they have not been blacklisted by the Turtles.

The Southwest Rodeo Association Round-Up is the bulletin of the association and, in character, resembles the organ of the Rodeo Association of America. The various shows are listed; purses, contestants, and their respective positions are all included in the monthly survey made by the bulletin. It also includes short notes about various contests and rodeo personalities. This bulletin is reprinted in *Hoofs and Horns* Magazine.

In awarding points for the championship of the South-west area in the six recognized events—calf roping, steer wrestling, saddle bronc riding, Brahma bull riding, bareback riding, and single steer roping—the number of points is uniform in each contest, so that all contestants have an equal opportunity to win the All-Around Title. In calf roping and steer roping the entrance fee is considerably larger than in the other events, and if the Southwest Rodeo Association should give points on the basis of dollars earned in the calf roping and single steer roping contests, as is the case in the R. A. A., the contestants in these events would probably be the top men for the All-Around honor. The Secretary of the Association made the following statement as an illustration:

No matter how much money is given in the various events, if there are four day monies in calf roping, three in saddle bronc riding, and two in steer wrestling; the points are doubled up in the last two named events to correspond with that of calf roping. As a general rule the points are awarded on the basis of 40-30-20-10 for each day money and 80-60-40-20, for each final money.[1]

The season begins and ends with the calendar year; the annual convention, at which the awards are made, usually takes place about the middle of December. During this convention, awards in cash and merchandise are given which amount approximately to three thousand dollars. This tends to encourage the cowboys to remain in the terri-

---

[1] The purse allotted for the day is divided into four percentages for the first four winners. Purse for the final day is usually made up of the entrance fees; percentages are greater for the winners on the final day. Information offered by C. A. Studer, secretary-treasurer of the Southwest Rodeo Association.

tory and to compete at the local shows. Practically every town with a population of at least one thousand has a rodeo, stock show, or some similar attraction during the year. The membership of this Association is drawn from the states of Oklahoma, Texas, New Mexico, and in some cases from Kansas, Missouri, Arkansas, Louisiana, and Colorado; at the present time about fifty member-shows belong. Since March, 1942, this association has been known as the National Rodeo Association, at which time the directors of the organization voted for a change in the name.

The Southwest Rodeo Association has, since its beginning, in no way impinged upon the assumed powers of the Rodeo Association of America. It has caused the managers of local contests to realize the advantages of being a member of a large association. Through its efforts it has encouraged the contestants not only to participate, but to keep alive the cowboy activities that were originally indigenous in this part of the West. Many communities would suffer for want of talent if this organization did not exist. The Southwest Rodeo Association offers opportunities not only to the contest committees but also to the cowboys. To the regular rodeo contestant it offers a worthy compensation and localizes his efforts within a not too large area. To the regular range cowboy, who does not care to make his living by following the work, it offers an opportunity to participate and to increase his earnings without traveling great distances.

The set-up, as presented by the Southern Organization, offers rodeo as a whole an opportunity to become a sport and to be recognized as such. If, under an association such as this one, there were developed several area associations— Midwest, Northwest, Pacific, and Eastern Rodeo Associations—this would be the initial impulse toward the development of this work into a better-organized competitive sport, involving group or team spirits. The various contestants would belong to the area organization and would be allowed to contest at any rodeo they wish; there would be no interference in regard to their moves or their opportunities to win money and points. At the same time, the contestants would bring credit points to their league or area organizations.

The winning contestants in the two or three leading areas and the associated member contestants would participate at a final World Series Rodeo for such titles as, The American Rodeo Championship for the winning district, All-Around Champion Cowboy for the individual contestant, and the Championships in the contest events for the winning men. There would still remain the personal element of every cowboy working for himself, but at the same time he would be permitted to contribute his points as credits to the area association of his choice. A contestant might be permitted to work for one area association one year and change his affiliation the next year. No attempt would be made to regiment a contestant into membership in a certain association. The possibility of one association offering compensation for the credit points of a good contestant would, in many cases, cause dissension; nevertheless, this would not differ from the "swapping" of the services or the "buying-up" of contracts of good men, as is practiced in the big league baseball teams and other professional sport activities.

If rodeo wishes to become a recognized sport, there should be a sublimation of some of the personal aspects that are rampant within it. A team spirit must prevail.

Until there is a feeling of unanimity among the individuals concerned, rodeo as a sport will remain highly individualized, and the public will fail to understand it as a sport rather than mere entertainment.

Considering the important place that rodeo occupies in our national entertainment life, it is surprising that it has received so very little notice by sports writers, commentators, and feature writers. The publicity which the sport has received, has come from those writers directly associated with the contests, people who are more interested in building up their particular celebration than in disseminating knowledge of the sport as a whole.

Sports writers have kept aloof from much, if any, discussion of rodeo in their columns, because they have maintained that, as yet, it is going through a formative stage. These writers agree that it is a great sport and should be recognized; however, there are so many grades and levels of contests that it is impossible to unify the sport into a contest that would put it on a sound basis for judgment. The formation of leagues, based on size of contests, purses offered, and skill of various contestants, might be a unifying factor; however, as long as a contestant pays for membership in the Cowboys' Turtle Association and also entry fees for the privilege to contest and is allowed to compete with the poorest and the best men, rodeo will remain in the nebulous stage—half way between sport and entertainment. This is no attempt on the part of the author to promote discussion that might cause a trend one way or another; it is simply a statement of facts as they exist. Rodeo, in the true sense of the word, is a sport, but, as yet, it cannot or has not been conducted and guided according to the standards that are prevalent in the sport world. The

Rodeo Association of America acts as a commission of guidance; nevertheless, it is unable to reduce the greatest obstacle in the way of a general unification, that is, the number of promoters. The majority of promoters are good *per se* in the field of entertainment, but if rodeo is to be a sport, it must be removed from the influence of so many different opinions.

There is one important deterrent factor in publicizing the rodeo, and this is reflected both on those who publicize and those who receive the publicity. It has already been stated that the rodeo cowboy is "poor copy." Among all entertainers and sportsmen contributing to our national pleasure, he is the least known. The reason for this is not because he is unwilling to allow himself to be discussed and commented upon, nor is there any unwritten law requiring him to remain the great, silent man of the West, but rather because of an open rebellion against the misinterpretation and ignorance on the part of those people who write about rodeo and the contestants without sufficient information.

The cowboy can appreciate a lack of knowledge concerning his work and life but he deplores a flagrant abuse of his willingness to give information; an abuse of his confidence and constant misinterpretation of him and his work cause him to avoid publicity. He has no desire to be made the ridiculous figure which is evident in the works of so many writers. He has little faith in the ability of these people to put into words his feelings, emotions, and experiences.

Unfortunately, the general attempt to bring the cowboy to life in prose has taken two directions. Authors have persisted in making him either an imbecile or a "wise guy"; they rarely give a true picture of our Western rodeo cowboy as an ordinary man—an intelligent, hard-working, fun-loving American.

After an interview with a writer, the cowboy is never sure as to what words might be placed in his mouth or just which one of the two above-mentioned niches he will occupy in the finished product. Actually, his type of work and the fact that he pays for the opportunity to work make publicity for the cowboy unnecessary. It is not necessary that he be a publicity-seeker, such as one finds among people in the entertainment world; he needs no press agent to dream up exciting, exotic formulae to "put him across" to the public. His very life involves more drama and excitement than that of the outstanding characters of stage or screen—more experience than would be realized in a lifetime. He needs no "build-up"; he can afford to ignore the publicity agent and reporters, who are sent out to get a story. By refusing to comment, he prevents the spread of misunderstanding and misleading information. However, sound publicity does help the cowboy and it pleases him, even though he may not admit it. It induces contest managers to pay his entrance fees to bring him to their shows; it brings advertising contracts— both of which aid him in a financial way. At one time it was very fashionable among contestants—but this is becoming less so—to scorn those in their group who get publicity. The entire issue could be relieved if writers would not think in terms of getting a story but rather would consider the fact that any phase of the cowboy's work and life would be good reading. Thus, at the same time, they would interpret the information truthfully, without embellishment or detractory statements.

The Eastern writers might be guilty of failure in analyzing the situation and in many cases might be cold-blooded gatherers of information; on the other hand, the writers of Western fiction have drawn a picture of the cowboy that is now accepted as the characterization of the man. It is unfortunate that some of the Western novelists have taken the very thing which is so close to their hearts and have misused it unwittingly. With a group of stock phrases, illiterate sayings, and so-called Western jargon, they have, first, created the language of the cowboy and then, they have characterized him, adding so-called humor, personal experiences, and reactions.

The majority of Western stories and novels, that are accepted by the reading public as typical of the Western people, by no means give a true picture. A more deplorable situation exists in the fact that a great many Western stories and articles are written by authors of the West who still persist in wrapping the entire section of the country west of the Mississippi in a cloak of sentimental naiveness. They are, perhaps, more guilty of misleading the public than any other group. They glory in the fact and make it known at every possible opportunity, that they were born in the West, lived on a ranch, and placed a rope over half a dozen calves. They wreathe their entire life and that of many unsuspecting cowboys in an aura of impossible and ridiculous fiction which, as fiction, is bad, but as truth, is a form of slander.

Note: A new development took place on April 28, 1946. This was the merger of the Rodeo Association of America and the National Rodeo Association into an organization to be known as the International Rodeo Association. This is a significant move, for it shows the trend toward the uniting of similar organizations.[1]

On March 16, 1947 a committee composed of R. J. Hoffman, E. N. Boylen, IRA Officials; Harry Rowell, Bob Barmby, and James Millerick, Stock Contractors; Monte Montana and Vern Goodrich, Contract Performers; Bill Linderman and Earl Lindsey, RCA Officials, met in Stockton, California. They made an agreement on nine points which promised to be of definite advantage for rodeo. The most significant change seems to be in the first point:

Rodeo contests shall be "OPEN" to all contestants who wish to enter, whether they are members of the R.C.A. or not, with the understanding that anyone who is on the R.C.A. blacklist or who are undesirable to managements, shall not be permitted to participate. Rodeo managements to notify R.C.A. of any contestants who have made infractions of general Rodeo Rules.[2]

---

[1] "Colorado May Be Headquarters of Merged Rodeo Association," *Rocky Mountain News,* April 29, 1946, 18.

[2] "Earl Lindsey, Bus. Rep., and Bill Linderman, Director of RCA, met with Western and Northwestern committees," *The Buckboard* 2 (May 1947), 23. "Agreement," *Hoofs and Horns* 16 (May 1947), 18.

CHAPTER XXVIII

OUTSIDE, LOOKING IN

Cowboys, as all others,
Like stuff written-up,
They know who's in the lead,
And the runners-up.

An important "mouthpiece" for rodeo and rodeo contestants is the monthly magazine, *Hoofs and Horns,* published at Tucson, Arizona. It is devoted entirely to rodeo
and portrays, in good taste, the spirit of the sport and
those active in it. It contains official information about
the Rodeo Association of America, the National Rodeo
Association[1] and, until recently, the Cowboys' Turtle Association;[2] the news in it is authentic and worthy of consideration.

Hoofs and Horns first appeared in July, 1931, as a
weekly cattle paper and, as such, lasted until April, 1933.
In the fall of 1933, it was purchased by Mrs. Ethel A. Hopkins, who since that time, has been publishing it as a
monthly magazine. Mrs. Hopkins, the editor, has worked
diligently in the editing of this magazine. At one time it
was associated with a publishing group known as Wild Life

---

[1] Formerly the Southwestern Rodeo Association.

[2] The Cowboys' Turtle Association is now known as the Rodeo Cowboys'
Association. See "Cowboy Organization Makes Change," *Hoofs and
Horns* 7 (May 1945) 16. "Editorial Comment," *Hoofs and Horns* 7
(September 1937), 3.

Section, which was sponsored by the Arizona Game Protective Assocaition. In 1937, when this association began to publish its own magazine, *Arizona Wild Life*, Mrs. Hopkins devoted her energies to make *Hoofs and Horns* an authentic publication of rodeo activities and personalities. The purpose is stated as follows: "Our aim is to help the cause of legitimate rodeos in every way possible and particularly to gain recognition of sports writers of this fine American sport."[1]

The aim, a worthy one, has been pursued faithfully, and today *Hoofs and Horns* has a remarkable following among contestants and rodeo fans. It is not a pretentious publication, the simplicity of make-up and contents is typical of its sincerity. It contains short but accurate comments by the editor in a column known as "This and That." Among the contributors is Fog Horn Clancy, publicity writer and press agent for some of the important rodeo promoters in the country. Clancy's column, "Memory Trail," contains not only the nostalgic memories of the early days of rodeo, but also a unique interpretation and evaluation of facts—past and present—of the sport. In a lighter vein was the column "Eastern Rodeo Chat" by the late Herbert S. Maddy, the veteran press agent and veritable encyclopedist of rodeo information.

Chuck Martin, Bruce Clinton, Walt Coburn, authors of some of our "hair-raising" Western literature, are regular contributors with articles suitable for the magazine. More informative for the fans of rodeo are the reprinted *Bulletins* of the Rodeo Association of America. These give a complete account of all member-contests, re-

---

[1] Information offered by Mrs. Ethel A. Hopkins, editor and owner of *Hoofs and Horns*, 1942.

sults, and winners of the events, as well as the monthly standings of the cowboys in relation to the Rodeo Association points for championships. With this information it is possible to follow the actions of friends in the work or those contestants in whom one has a particular interest. The *Bulletin* usually has a commentary on some phase of the sport by the secretary of the association.

Formerly a column was devoted to the actions and members of the Cowboys' Turtle Association, and one section was devoted to the activities of the Rodeo Fans of America. Thus it was possible to keep a complete check on all activities of the sport. In 1942 a section known as "Western Corral" was introduced which reviews Western literature. This is an excellent and important addition to the magazine. Interspersed throughout are short stories and articles by various interested people who, through their comments, add to the pool of general information which is assembled every month.

Besides *Hoofs and Horns,* several other publications have sections devoted to rodeo. One of the best of this group, *The Western Horseman,* offers not only fine articles on rodeo, but gives a wealth of excellent information relating to all types of Western horses. *Ranch Romances* and *Billboard,* the latter known as the world's foremost amusement weekly, also contain sections concerning the cowboy sport. Previous to the appearance of *Hoofs and Horns* as a rodeo publication, two other attempts were made to publish a magazine of this type. *Wild Bunch* was published in 1917 by a man named Homer Wilson; a later attempt was *Cow Country* by Fay Ward. Because rodeo in those days was still a Western entertainment without the national following of today—it was before the time that men and women followed the game as a living—both these earlier publications failed.

At the present time, *Hoofs and Horns* and *The Buck-board* are unique in that they are strictly about rodeo. Since the sport has taken a hold on the American public, it is surprising that some enterprising publishing house has not attempted to bring out a competitive magazine. A magazine of photographic pictures would have consider-able following among the fans of rodeo.

In March, 1945, at Fort Worth, Texas, about 100 mem-bers of the Cowboys' Turtle Association met to make changes in that organization. One of the innovations of the new organization was the founding of the bulletin, *The Buckboard,* which is now the official organ of the as-sociation. The first issue of this bulletin, which publishes news of the Rodeo Cowboys' Association, appeared in July, 1945.

In February, 1941, two men were sitting in a dental office in Endicott, New York, and were discussing the social activities that had centered around a number of rodeos during the previous season. One was Dr. Leo Brady, a well-known dentist and rodeo enthusiast, who had been attending contests as often as his practice would permit, the other was Fog Horn Clancy.[1]

During the conversation Dr. Brady remarked that, since there were so many people throughout the country who liked and enjoyed the sport of the cowboys, some kind of social organization should be formed—he had in mind the Circus Fans of America and suggested the name, Rodeo Fans of America. This conversation was the initial

---

[1] Information offered by Dr. Leo Brady and Rev. Roy Cuddy, Endicott, New York, 1941, 1942.

impulse; a week later a meeting was held in Dr. Brady's home in Endicott, and the plans for the organization were completed. The organization to be known as "Rodeo Fans of America," was incorporated under the laws of the state of New York; in May, 1942, the National Arena, or headquarters, was moved to Waverly, New York, and at this time the business of making it a nation-wide organization got under way.

The object of Rodeo Fans of America is to keep alive the fine traditions of the old West, to help perpetuate the sport of the cowboys, and to increase the social relationships among all those who admire the contestants and enjoy the sport. Thus, the organization makes every rodeo more than just an entertainment—it is in reality a social gathering of people who have a common hobby. The idea was immediately taken up by several close friends of Dr. Brady and was, of course, endorsed by such well-known personalities of rodeo as Fog Horn Clancy, Mrs. Ethel A. Hopkins, and the late Herbert S. Maddy.[1]

The plan had national publicity in *Hoofs and Horns* and other Western publications, and shortly after applications for membership came from all parts of the country. It is interesting to note that the membership reveals an excellent cross section of people in various occupations. It includes government officials, bankers, doctors, lawyers, merchants, and business people.

Since the birth of the organization the officers have developed a monthly publication. At first, this paper was called the *Stirrup;* now it appears under the title *Rodeo Fans.* A bucking horse insignia makes the relationship to

---

[1] Information obtained from Herbert S. Maddy, Edwin J. O'Brien, Colonel Jim Eskew, J E Ranch, Waverly, New York.

the sport obvious. In the first half year of existence, the Rodeo Fans of America made much progress, which was evidenced by the splendid representation of members at the Madison Square Garden Rodeo in October, 1941. During the second week-end of the New York Show the new club held its first convention. A block of good seats was reserved for those attending. Every courtesy and consideration was shown the members by the management of the contest—thus, *Rodeo Fans* was launched.

During the first convention a banquet was held and attended by such well-known figures in rodeo as Gene Autry, Fred Alvord, and John Agee, in addition to about seventy fans. Thus, *Rodeo Fans of America* was introduced to the largest contest in the world; with this impressive beginning it has many hundreds of rodeo fans. Members display their Rodeo-Fans-of-America membership card at a rodeo and are shown special privileges. In addition to this advantage, a feeling of friendship, extending across the country, is developed among the followers of rodeo. They have a sincere interest in the sport, which, in many cases, is the outgrowth of a youthful longing to know about the West. One seldom hears a heated argument among the fans of rodeo about a contest or a personality in the sport, as is often the case among the fans of other sports. Rather, Rodeo Fans find their fun and enjoyment in reminiscing about the rides, the spills, the thrills, the cowboys and cowgirls of the past and present, the contests from Montana to Massachusetts, from New York to New Mexico.

Rodeo Fans plan to have units of the national organization throughout the country. The various units are now known as corrals, line-camps, or chuck-wagons, and each club is to be named after some well-known Western character, now deceased. These clubs are to hold their own meetings and social affairs; meet with other clubs or corrals at rodeos; and hold state and national conventions.

Children, naturally, have a great interest in rodeo and because of this, Rodeo Fans of America formed a Junior organization. The idea of Junior Rodeo Fans was first conceived and put into effect by Edwin J. O'Brien of Waverly, New York, the man who has done so much to bring rodeo to the East as a permanent thing. Likewise, the children have their own local clubs, enjoy social activities similar to those of the grown-ups and find in the monthly magazine a section devoted to them and their interests. Thus, they feel that they are members of a really worth-while national organization.

In a discussion about people and businesses associated with rodeo, various prizes, trophies, and awards are interesting and worthy of mention. Upon paying his entry fee, every contestant has an opportunity to win, according to his placement in the various events, part of the day money as well as the final money. Although the purses are one of the most important sources of revenue for the cowboy, they are not the only means of remuneration. However, two conditions affect the greater number of contestants and prevent them from partaking in these added opportunities: they must be among the outstanding men in their work and they must also win. Besides the combined purses of rodeos which rang from $1,000 to $100,000, there are additional awards of money and trophies to the champions and to the runners-up in the various events.

The best known group of money awards and trophies is the series of gifts donated by firms and private individuals to the Rodeo Association of America. These prizes are to be awarded on the completion of the rodeo season and usually are presented during the annual convention during January of the following year.

For many years the Levi Strauss Company of San Francisco, makers of "Levis," the champion overall, has headed the list of donors of prizes and trophies. Their contribution of five hundred dollars in cash and a gold and silver belt buckle is the top award given to the All-Around Champion Cowboy. Formerly, an additional award was made to this lucky man, such as a five hundred-dollar silver-mounted saddle presented by the Garcia Saddle Company, Salinas, California. However, now an effort is made not to shower the All-Around Cowboy with additional awards, but to give some credit to those men who are runners-up for this national honor. There are second, third, fourth, and fifth places for the All-Around Championship, and those men who are fortunate enough to win these places are presented with gold and silver buckles donated by the Porter Saddle Company, Tucson and Phoenix, Arizona. This company has been a donor for some years; besides contributing to the above event, it has also given one hundred dollars in cash to the Champion Calf Roper of the year. On former occasions it has presented belt buckles to the six closest contenders in the event. Some donors distribute their awards among the different events; however, their important award is usually designated for one particular event, such as the bronc riding contest, steer wrestling or calf roping event. In some cases, for a number of years they have retained the position as donor for the same Rodeo Association contest.

Harry Rowell, stock contractor of Hayward, California, has been giving two hundred dollars for many years to the Champion Bronc Rider; the World's Championship Rodeo Corporation, Florence, Arizona, offers one hundred dollars in cash to the man in second place for this honor. Since 1939 Montgomery Ward and Company, Chicago, offers $400 in cash to be divided into $200, $125 and $75 for the Champion Bull or Steer Rider, and second and third runners-up respectively. This prize was formerly donated by the West Holliday Company, San Francisco, California, which has now turned its prize money to other events. The All-Around Champion Cowboy for 1941, Homer Pettigrew, was sponsored that year by Montgomery Ward and Company and he reaped the many benefits that come to the holder of this honor and distinction in the cowboy sports.

H. J. Justin and Sons, Fort Worth, Texas, manufacturers of boots, also contribute important prizes for the champions. Their awards go to Team Tying contestants. For several years the Hamley Saddle Company, Pendleton, Oregon, has offered one hundred dollars to the cowboy attaining twenty-fifth place in the All-Around standings; Charles S. Howard, Buick automobile dealer and owner of "Seabiscuit," has been a donor of one hundred dollars for the Champion Steer Decorator and fifty dollars for second place in this contest. The maker of the famous Stetson Hat, John B. Stetson Hat Company, Philadelphia, Pennsylvania, has also been a donor of long standing and presents the Champion Steer Wrestler with a cash award of one hundred dollars. In 1942 three cash awards of one hundred dollars each were added by Gene Autry's Flying A Ranch Stampede, in the Bronc Riding, Steer Riding, and

Calf Roping contests—the money to be given to the winner of the first place in each event. Among the very reliable donors for years are Salant and Salant, manufac-
urers of Uncle Sam Work Shirts, New York City, who
favor the runner-up in the Bronc Riding event.

Although there have been changes in the donors of the
Rodeo-Association-of-America prizes and trophies, the
firms and individuals mentioned above have, in most cases,
held their respective positions for years. It should be emphasized that these prizes are awarded only to those men
who have reached the top in their work. The majority of
contestants receive only the remuneration that comes from
winning in the contests which they enter.

Besides the cash awards and gifts, such as inscribed
belt buckles, innumerable merchandise prizes are given by
local firms of a community in which the rodeo takes place.
These prizes are many and various: wrist watches, ten-
gallon hats, jackets, shirts, trousers, boots, gloves, scarfs,
tie and scarf pins, cigarette cases, lighters, ropes, embossed
saddles, silver-mounted brides, chaps, and spurs. Frequently the All-Around Champion of the year and other
well-known cowboys pose as models for riding apparel for
such firms as Montgomery Ward and Company Sears-
Roebuck Company, and also endorse cigarettes and
smoking tobacco. The merchandise awards, being numerous, are distributed among a greater number of contestants than the more important cash awards. Thus, a cowboy may not be a top-ranking contestant, but it is possible
for him to collect a number of these prizes as he moves
from town to town.

Money awards and merchandise prizes are of considerable interest to and are deeply appreciated by the rodeo

cowboy, but among the top-flight contestants, there is genuine interest in having a permanent memento of their honor. Sculptured trophies, plaques, and loving cups are as dear to the heart of the man in rodeo as to the sportsman in golf, tennis, or any other athletic endeavor. Rodeo does not differ from these other sports—cowboys, like other sportsmen, are born collectors and though money awards are welcome, they are transitory. Thus, the trophy has a great appeal for the rodeo cowboy.

The Calgary Stampede and Exhibition, Canada, in addition to the regular money prizes offers the greatest number of sculptured trophies to winners of contests. Among them is the G. A. Gaherty Trophy, a bronze model of a bucking horse. This goes to the winner of the North American Bucking Horse event. A similar trophy was to be awarded in this contest each year up to and including the year 1942. The Edward, Prince of Wales Cup is a Challenge Trophy for the Champion Canadian Bucking Horse Rider; it is retained by the committee for safekeeping. A sterling cigarette case, suitably inscribed, is awarded to the winner as a memento of the occasion.

The winner of Steer Decorating, which takes the place of Steer Wrestling, is presented with "The Greyhound Trophy," donated by the Western Canadian Greyhound Lines Limited. The trophy, sixteen inches high, depicting the early aristocrats of the range, is a bronze model of a longhorn steer. This was won and a duplicate trophy was awarded in this event each year up to and including the year 1945.

The Canadian Western Natural Gas, Heat, Light and Power Company, Limited, donated a most pretentious trophy, known as the Gas Company award. It is an action model in bronze, depicting a chuck-wagon with two teams and a driver. A metal replica, in the form of a plaque, is given each year to the winner in this event. When it has been won three times by the same team, it becomes the permanent possession of the winner.

The A. E. Cross Memorial Trophy, donated by the Calgary Brewing and Malting Company, Limited, is given to the Canadian Champion All-Around Cowboy. This bronze trophy shows a calf roping scene and is about twenty-two inches long and seventeen inches high. The trophy is in duplicate and will be awarded to winners of this honor for several years. All these sculptured trophies are the work of Charles A. Beil, Banff, Alberta, a well-known and distinguished cowboy artist of Canada.

The awarding of prizes to the contestants has an amusing side, especially in the amateur contests in small communities. These rodeos always open with a street parade which arouses interest in and draws attention to the contest of the afternoon. Numerous parade and contest prizes are offered as an inducement to bring the local cowboys out to ride, as well as to add an element of good-natured humor and fun to the festivities. Most of these parade-prizes go to local people and to the visiting dudes. The prizes are worth while, neither particularly elaborate nor especially valuable. However, they serve their purpose, for they create a feeling of fun among the visiting and local cowboys and the local townsmen, especially the prize-donating merchants.

Among the amusing prizes offered have been: three Victor records for the loudest cowboy in the parade, a pint of whiskey to the best-looking cowboy, a shampoo and finger wave to the first cowgirl to place in any event, one case of beer for the homeliest cowboy, one Fitch's Shampoo to the male contestant with the curliest hair, a seven-dollar mattress to the cowboy with the largest family, and five dollars in merchandise to the orneriest cowboy. Such prizes are not a financial strain on the contributors; in donating them, business proprietors have an opportunity to become active participants in the development of their local contest.

CHAPTER XXIX

PRESCOTT TO PENDLETON

Old timers remember 'way back when'
The show was just beginning,
They fondly recall those 'good old days'
And the cowboys who did the winning.

One of the romantic periods of man has been, and still is, the era of the Westerner—its history is a saga of human endurance, resourcefulness, daring, and courage—all of which are significant characteristics and form the basis of all human achievement. Men who possess these attributes are leaders, not followers. They have urged mankind on; their efforts in constant striving have left the unquestionable mark of progress. If in the future generations there should be a retrospective picture portraying the men who carved a nation out of this wilderness, the American cowboy will be prominent in that composition. It was the cowboys who, with their thoughts, deeds, and skills, moved into the great waste and through their determination and bravery created from it a flourishing empire with a unique industry and an unusual personality. The cowboys have produced a drama of color and glory which equals that of any previous momentous era.

American rodeo dramatizes that phenominal development of an unknown country and the important cattle industry which for three decades ruled the area. The genius of the cowboy made this movement possible. Thus, in the story of the rodeo contests of America it is fitting to consider, as the introductory event, the first-known public event of that kind.

Twelve years before the turn of the century in the hills of Yavapai County, Arizona, in a frontier town by the name of Prescott, the world's first active rodeo was held. On July 4, 1888, cowboys from the surrounding ranches gave, as an entertainment for the people of this town, an exhibition of ranch activities and cowboy sports. The details of the contest have been obscured because of time, but one important record is left in the form of a trophy. It is a silver engraved plaque with an inscription stating that the individual honors were won by Juan Levias. This relic and a few remaining pioneers are all that is left of the important occasion. However, although almost sixty years have passed, on the Fourth of July, Prescott, Arizona still stages a contest as the annual entertainment for the people of that city and the surrounding districts.

Prescott is known as the "Cowboy's Capital of the World," and its contest has assumed such spectacular titles as "America's Greatest Non-Professional Show" and the "Grand-Daddy of 'em All." The contest attracts the active range cowboy and has the honor of being the oldest rodeo still in existence. This Prescott Frontier Days Celebration is a non-profit, civic, recreational, and educational enterprise, which is held for four days on the grounds and in the buildings of the Northern Arizona State Fair Association. For the cowboys who work the year round on the ranges, the show provides an opportunity to contest and to exhibit their skill in this specialized form of work and also to better their financial status.

It is important to note that the contest is *not* a professional show and is *not* attended by the professional rodeo cowboy. Anyone may enter any event in which he, during the past three years, has not won as good as second place in the finals of a major rodeo or cowboy contest which give points toward national and world championships. The men who perform at the Prescott Frontier Days are professional in that they display the skill of their profession— that of range cowboy. From the ranks of this Arizona show came many nationally-known contestants who rose to the top in rodeo and are now professional in the sense that they are earning a living by attending contests. From this group came, also, many of the originators of the Cowboys' Turtle Association.[1]

There has been considerable discussion about the word "professional." The members of the Cowboys' Turtle Association resented the implications when it was used in the sense that they were capable of performing only in the arena. The range cowboys resented its use when they were classed as "amateurs" and not professionals in the sense that they were not genuine cowboys or were amateurs at their work. The word must be used with the understanding of what the cowboy is actually doing for a living —ranch work or rodeo work. Both groups are composed of men worthy of being called cowboys; both are composed of specialized workmen—one for endurance and the activity of the range, the other for skill, speed, and the activity of the arena. However, the ordinary cowboy is an

[1] Information from the secretary of the Northern Arizona State Fair Association.

amateur when he competes in the arena with a rodeo top hand.

Actually, Prescott had attained fame before it closed its events to the rodeo cowboy and made them for the range cowboy. It maintains that it is not a closed show—it is not a closed show for the range cowboy and is open to all of them as a national sporting event, with only one restriction—they must be range workmen. Many rodeo cowboys have ranches and are workmen on them during certain times of the year; however, this contest is closed to them.

This Arizona contest, as a show of range workmanship, has gained considerable publicity and fame. It has brought world-wide attention to Prescott and Yavapai County; during the four days of showing it has an attendance of approximately fifty thousand. One of the features of this contest, besides the regular events of rodeo, is the Sheriffs' Roping Team. County sheriffs from all parts of the state participate in this event. Because it is an open contest, the entrance for the events is large—between two and three hundred contestants apply for admission. In order to run off the roping events, some of the men are required to appear as early as seven o'clock in the morning.

During the celebration the cowboys take possession of the town. Besides the regular rodeo events, parades are held and other forms of entertainment are provided for the visitor—if he has need of entertainment other than that of watching cowboys from the entire West "make merry" during this widely-celebrated Western holiday! For the edification of the visitors as well as a gesture to the cowboys, the merchants offer many prizes that are not only of monetary value but also amusing. The Prescott Show is one of the most exciting and truly Western contests—if you can take it! It is a four-day fling with all that still remains of the Old West in the full spirit of that era.

Several other Arizona contests are worthy of mention. The Phoenix Championship Rodeo and *La Fiesta de los Vaqueros* held in February are the best known. The Phoenix contest takes place about the second week of that month and has been in existence about twelve years as such, although rodeos had been held there previous to that time. There is no historical reason for the celebration; it is an entertainment for the many winter visitors who come from all parts of the United States to revel in the celebrated climate of this Southwestern state.

Because it is a late winter contest and one that offers excellent purses of about one thousand dollars for the four days of contesting, it attracts many cowboys who attend the many winter contests and Fat Stock Shows of the Southwest. It is a splendid show with the finest stock and contestants to be seen anywhere. A special feature is the very fine souvenir program. It is well-planned, very artistic in design, features pictures of the contestants and the events—in all, it is really worthy of the name—"souvenir program."[1]

The contest at Tucson, Arizona, *La Fiesta de los Vaqueros,* which comes immediately after the Phoenix celebration, covers the Washington's Birthday holiday and is a three-day show. The contest offers a purse of approximately ten thousand dollars and draws its stars directly from the previous show. It includes, with the regular rodeo

---

[1] Information offered by the secretary of the Phoenix Championship Rodeo.

events, an Indian celebration and is staged as an entertainment for the winter guests of this well-known resort. Featuring a Brahma bull scramble, and a Sheriffs' steer roping contest, as do the Prescott and Phoenix rodeos, this contest is one of the really good ones of the Southwest. It draws capacity crowds. The city is crowded with visitors from many lands because it is world famous as a playground for winter tourists and is equally famous as a health resort.[1] Both the Phoenix and the Tucson contests inaugurate the spring rodeo season.

Rodeo has taken a very definite hold in the state of California, and during the summer and fall months contests are in progress up and down the entire length of the coast. However, there is a feeling that rodeo as a sport does not hold the affection of the people of the West Coast as it does of those in the inland areas of the West. Rodeos are found especially in those areas east of the Sierra Nevadas and the Cascade Range—the eastern and western slopes of the Continental Divide.

Perhaps, California with its diversified opportunities for outdoor life, its wide range of entertainment and the fact that it has so recently attained the status and complexion of the older Eastern seaboard, is not yet ready for a return to the simple and direct forms of entertainment that are a part of its heritage. Nevertheless, many fine rodeos are held in California and they have a following of both contestants and fans. Prominent towns and cities holding contests on the Pacific Coast are Salinas, San Bernardino, Hanford, Newhall, Cambria, Victorville,

---

[1] Information from the office of *La Fiesta de los Vaqueros,* Tucson, Arizona.

Bakersfield, Red Bluff, and Sonoma. Los Angeles has been the scene of several very successful rodeos.[1]

In the late fall of 1941, a very successful rodeo was held in San Francisco during the Grand National Livestock Exposition, in this city's new two-and-one-half-million dollar exhibition building known as the Cow Palace. Rodeo was used as a means to draw people to the World's Fair held in the city during the years 1939 and 1940. In December, 1946, San Francisco reinaugurated the rodeo, and staged a contest with large purses and played to capacity crowds.

Farther north on the Pacific Coast, but inland in the states of Oregon and Washington, are several annual contests. Lakeview, Bend, Klamath Falls, Molalla, and Pendleton are in the former state; Tonasket, Chelan, Kennewick, Colfax, Omak, and Ellensburg in the latter. The rodeos held at Ellensburg and Pendleton are famous Northwestern contests and are the two west-slope shows which the followers of the sport never miss. They are as prominent in that section of the country as the Cheyenne Frontier Days show is on the east slope and the surrounding plains' area.

The Ellensburg contest is a three-day event and takes place during the Labor Day holiday. It has been in existence over twenty years; it is a Rodeo-Association-of-America member-show and favors the members of the Cowboys' Turtle Association; however, some years it adds to the regular events those that are "non-professional" and open to all. Through many years of successful work the managers of this contest have built up rodeo equipment, an arena, and grandstands valued at about

---

[1] Information from the secretaries of rodeo committees of contests of California.

Aerial View: Pendleton Round-Up.
—*Courtesy Chamber of Commerce, Pendleton, Oregon.*

fifty thousand dollars. This contest attracts the best rodeo cowboys and particularly the saddle bronc riders, most of whom are Northwesterners. One of the very interesting features of the rodeo is the Stage Coach Race, depicting as a contest the mode of travel of the pioneer. The Squaw Race, Indian War Bonnet Race, Indian Pony Relay, and the Cowboy Pony Express are featured performances which, from the standpoint of entertainment, prove to be excellent racing attractions.

Southeast of this Washington contest and following about one week later—usually the middle of September— is the world-famous Pendleton Round-Up of Oregon. The beginning of the Pendleton Round-Up goes back to the year 1908. In that year the Pendleton Baseball Club was in debt to the extent of six hundred dollars. The management of the team was taken over by a committee which signed a note with a bank, in order to secure sufficient funds to finish the season.[1]

At this time, a group of cowboys planned to give an exhibition of cowboy sports which included roping, bull-dogging, and bucking contests, as well as other wild-west stunts. This exhibition was to be held at the ball park. These cowboys included the following:

> Charles Buckner, a colored man whose people lived south of Pendleton on Stewart creek on a ranch; Joseph Cantrell, living near Adams; Melvin Buck, a noted bronco twister and wild horse rider of those days; Jimmy Ghangrow, a fine rider of Adams; Mack Marcus, an Idaho Indian, familiary known as "Salmon River"; Lee

[1] Trent, Rupert, "How Pendleton Round-Up Started," (cited hereafter as Trent, Pendleton, etc.,") *The Live Wire,* Pendleton, Oregon, (September 11, 1913).

Caldwell of Pendleton, known as "Babe" because he was so young; Guy Hayes of Pendleton; "Wild Bill," a Umatilla Indian and a crackerjack rider, and Glen Bushee of Pendleton, famous all over the Northwest as an impersonator of the Indian.[1]

The new managers, Henneman, Tatom, and Bond, persuaded the cowboys to hold their exhibition in conjunction with the ball game, thereby to strengthen the attraction for the baseball team. They offered the cowboys five dollars each and arranged to pay for the expenses of bringing in the horses. The managers also secured a saddle from James Crawford and E. I. Power, saddle manufacturers, for the winner of the bucking contests. The cowboys gave a two-days' show.[2]

The next year, at the end of the season, a similar contest was given for the benefit of the baseball team.

Shortly after the 1909 show, Glen Bushee was coming up from a trip to Portland and met Roy Raley on the train. Bushee got to talking with Raley regarding the 1907 and 1908 exhibitions, and Raley asked him if he thought that such a show, on a big scale, providing it were financed by the "right people," and good prizes were offered, would "go."

---

[1] Melvin Buck was later sentenced to prison for horse stealing, but escaped and never has been captured. He dropped out of the public view much to the regret of those who love fine riding. Trent, "Pendleton, etc." *The Live Wire.*

"Salmon River," met a gruesome fate. After he left here, the bodies of himself and his brother were found in the Snake River bound together with barbed wire. The murder of "Salmon River" caused much regret in the bucking circles. He was one of the cleverest, most daring and most reckless riders ever seen in this country. Trent, "Pendleton, etc.," *The Live Wire.*

[2] *Ibid.*

Bushee told Raley that he believed such a show would be a success "if it was pulled off by good people."

When Raley got into Pendleton, he started to "work up" the idea. It "took" instantly because of the success of the cowboys' benefit exhibitions for the baseball club in the two previous years. The substantial elements of the community got behind the project and pushed it to final organization. Stock was issued originally at $10 a share and the citizens generally subscribed and also gave donations for a fund to finance the first "big show." The name "Round-Up" made a hit and was selected as the title of Pendleton's frontier exhibition.[1]

This city is the home of the internationally known Hamley and Company, manufacturers of saddles and distributors of cowboy outfits and equipment. They are also the makers of the accepted Association saddle used in the Rodeo-Association-of-America bronc riding event.

The annual Pendleton Round-up has a standing of many years and is eagerly looked forward to by the rodeo contestants. It is a member-contest of the Rodeo Association of America; it is a four-day show, offering as a purse the sum of approximately four thousand dollars. At Pendleton, the visitor has an opportunity to witness not only the best cowboy sports, but also one of the outstanding gatherings of Northwestern American Indian tribes. Featured as part of the Round-Up, are the well-known and publicized Indian Parade and the full-blooded Indian ceremonial and war dances. Woven into this spectacle and colorful tapestry of four stirring days, are about two thousand In-

---

[1] *Ibid.*

dians—tribes represented by the Umatillas, Yakimas, Walla Wallas, Chemawas, Chipawas, and Cayuses. They camp in tepees on the grounds of the contest—the largest congregation of natives ever assembled at one time for a rodeo. In richly decorated costumes of beads and buckskin, with headdresses of feathers and carrying war implements, this Indian cavalcade moves on magnificent ponies swathed in colorful trappings.[1]

Since the founding of the Pendleton Round-Up in the year 1910, Hamley and Company have contributed at least one saddle each year to the amateur bronc rider and steer roper; in addition, they supply two or three saddles to be presented as prizes at the contest. The saddles range in value from $225 to $550 and "the first saddle that was given in the year 1910 is still in use and is in good condition for it was in the shop not long ago for a little bit of service and oiling."[2]

Hamley and Company have been contributors to various shows throughout the country and, in former years, have furnished prize saddles for the Madison Square Garden Rodeo. In more recent years, these saddles have been presented by other donors, but were manufactured by this Oregon firm. The company gives one hundred dollars to the holder of twenty-fifth place in the R. A. A. Cowboy standings. It has an added fine reputation in that it devised the Association saddle—the original rodeo committee saddle—which was adopted as standard equipment by every large contest in the country. It is recognized as "the original and logical bucking contest saddle."[3] At rodeo

---

[1] Information offered by Oren Allison, secretary, Chamber of Commerce, Pendleton, Oregon.

[2] Information from a letter from David Hamley, Hamley and Company, Pendleton, Oregon, 1941. Visited the firm, 1945.

[3] *Idem. Hamley's Cowboy Catalogue*, No. 41.

Sam Jackson Trophy, Pendleton Round-Up.
—*Permission to use, Chamber of Commerce, Pendleton, Oregon.*

contests in this country the bucking saddles invariably bear the trade mark of this firm—the Circle H brand.

Among the many awards and prizes offered at this contest to the cowboys is the five thousand dollar Jackson Trophy. It is a very coveted award, second only to that of the Annual All-Around Championship of the World. The Jackson Trophy must be won three times before it becomes the permanent possession of the winner. It has been awarded twice to Bill McMacken, Ike Rude, and Everett Bowman.

In comparison to other contests of major importance, the Pendleton Round-Up is listed among the best rodeos to be seen. It draws the finest performers; the competition is heated and furious; every man works to do his utmost, not only to reap the benefits that come to those who win, but because many a national reputation is made in this arena. Here the spectator finds every phase of rodeo at its best and, as a visitor, a cordial welcome to the city. The Pendleton Round-Up is a "must" contest for every rodeo fan—at least once during his life. This Oregon Show, and those at Ellensburg, Washington, and Lewiston, Idaho, are the three Northwestern rodeos that practically every rodeo contestant makes a sincere effort to attend. The Lewiston rodeo is a follow-up of the Pendleton Round-Up and offers a three-day contest which rates, in excellence, with the other two.

CHAPTER XXX

CHEYENNE, DENVER, AND THE FALL
ROUND-UP

They say that 'East is East and West is West,
And never the twain shall meet',
But rodeo from coast to coast
Fills every doggone seat!

No contest has received more world-wide publicity, from the standpoint of being a big event of the West, than the celebrated Cheyenne Frontier Days. Known as "The Daddy of 'em All," it has now had a half century of national and international success and fame. With five days and nights spent in re-living the times of the early West, this southern Wyoming celebration offers to the nation, each year during the last full week of July, thrills, glamour, headaches and fun—all of which have been a part of this one-time frontier town on the edge of a rugged wilderness.

Cheyenne, the capital and largest city of Wyoming, was at one time surrounded with an atmosphere of adventure and romance. This atmosphere still clings to it; Cheyenne was the center for all the famous personalities of the West, including bad men—both red and white— scouts, hunters, vigilantes, builders of railroads, cattlemen, and finally, land seekers. It began as a shanty and tent town, but by 1867 it was the western terminus of the

Union Pacific Railroad. Because of its position, Cheyenne became one of the most important centers of the cattle industry. Besides the diversified industrial trends, which include railroading, aviation, cattle and sheep industry, one finds also the retail and wholesale business of which this city is now a center. The name of Cheyenne, Wyoming, with eighty years of historical background, still conveys to impressionable minds all that made up the early history of the West. The mere mention of its name never fails to bring to mind that it is the home of the most important rodeo in the world.

The Cheyenne Frontier Days is an annual celebration and was first staged in the year 1897. It was held for a number of years at Pioneer Park, but is now presented in Frontier Park, in the northern part of the city. During the early contests there was no charge for general admission; a fee was taken only for seats in the grandstands. It is no longer a regional contest; it has grown to such an extent that it is recognized as the greatest Western contest of the country and is attended by the premier contestants and noted visitors.[1]

The beginning of the Cheyenne Frontier Days Celebration is mentioned in a letter written at Denver, Colorado, August 29, 1897, by Mr. F. W. Angier, Passenger Agent of the Union Pacific, to Mr. E. A. Slack, editor, *Sun-Leader*, Cheyenne, Wyoming. It says:

> Immediately upon my return I called upon Mr. Winchell relative to rates upon Cheyenne and Northern Line and he will gladly arrange for his line. Have taken

[1] Information from the office of Robert D. Hanesworth, secretary, Chamber of Commerce, Frontier Days Association, Cheyenne, Wyoming.

matter up with Mr. Lomax and will advise what he says
regarding main line points as soon as I return from
Cripple Creek where I go tonight. I have talked with
some of the people here on the subject of Frontier Day
and they all say that Cheyenne can get up a day that
will take the people. The attraction which can be made
with the cowboys alone is something that few people
here have ever seen, and if they will arrange for handling
cattle and horses and give exhibitions of their riding,
throwing rope and doing fetes that [sic] are common
to them, mounting wild horses and things of that sort,
it will make something novel and exciting yet having
no expense attached to it. It will be sort of wild west
show; have it at the fair grounds and charge 25 cents
admission, if necessary to raise the money.

Those that I have talked to think that such an
entertainment at Cheyenne will make it the banner day
of the year and as interesting as anything that can be
shown at the festival of mountain and plain at Denver.[1]

The letter is of significance for three reasons. It reveals first, the interest of the Union Pacific Railroad in
encouraging and helping to build up the Frontier Celebration. Secondly, it reveals that cowboy activities are

---

[1] *Daily Sun-Leader*, (August 30, 1897).
Fifteen years later one finds the following item in the *Wyoming Tribune*.
It says: " 'The Stampede' at Calgary, Canada's wild west show; 'The
Rodeo' at Salinas, California's wild west show, 'The Round-up' at
Pendleton, Oregon's wild west show, and a dozen other imitations of
Frontier Days, have representatives here observing events, signing performers, and observing ideas. 'The Stampede' is new and therefore an
unknown quantity, but there are present persons who have witnessed all
other performances and it is unanimous opinion that none rises above
the dignity of a feeble immitation of the festival which made Cheyenne
famous. Frontier Days is the one 'big show' of wild western celebrations." *Wyoming Tribune*, (August 17, 1912), 3.

not as common a sight in this area of the country as is generally supposed. Thirdly, it shows that a bit of jealousy existed between Denver and Cheyenne, and that the success of the Festival of Mountain and Plain provoked Denver's northern neighbor. It should be noted apropos, that the suggestions for both celebrations, the one at Denver and the one at Cheyenne, were made by the Passenger Agents of rival railroad lines: Major S. K. Hooper of the Denver and Rio Grande, and Mr. F. W. Angier of the Union Pacific.

On the evening of August 30, 1897, a meeting was held at Cheyenne in the office of Riner and Schnitzer, which was attended by "the representative business men of the city manifesting a great and commendable interest in the novel celebration of 'Frontier Days' as proposed and talked of in the last few days. . . . "[1]

A committee of seven men was appointed to solicit funds and make plans for the celebration. It was decided that the scale of the celebration would depend on the funds donated by the citizens. Plans were also made to have on the day selected for the event, "all the cowboys, bull whackers, and old frontier characters available, and the committee solicit correspondence from all the cowboys."[2]

By September third, the committee had secured one hundred and fifty dollars from various citizens who had been interviewed regarding the anticipated celebration.

---

[1] *Daily Sun-Leader,* August 31, 1897.

[2] Frontier Day Committee, 1897; Warren Richardson, J. A. Martin, E. W. Stone, J. H. Arp, G. R. Palmer, J. D. Freeborn, and D. H. Holliday. *Daily Sun-Leader,* (August 31, 1897.)

Plans to advertise the event were urged by the *Daily Sun-Leader*. It says:

> Do not allow any mail to leave Cheyenne before September 23 without being enclosed in a Frontier Day envelope. Advertise Wyoming's Day all you can. Fancy envelope and paper to match at Sun-Leader office.[1]

Representatives of the committee went to Denver to advertise the event and sold almost twelve hundred tickets. To impress the visitors with Cheyenne, an effort was made to improve the appearance of the city.

> For several days past Marshall Proctor has been at work with the "chain gang" cleaning the streets and alleys of the business portion of the city and will put Cheyenne in as presentable condition as possible for Frontier Days. Old cans, bottles, paper and, in fact, all old rubbish is being raked up and hauled away to the city dump.

> The Frontier Day committee will arrange to have all cans, dry goods boxes, barrels, etc., which now occupy conspicious places on the sidewalks in the business section of the city, temporarily removed and gotten out of sight for Wyoming's first celebration of Frontier Day.[2]

Concerning the celebration, the *Sun-Leader* says: "There was no disorder of any kind and everything went off in a fine manner." However, it contradicts itself later and says: "The crowd was so large that fences were torn down and property destroyed."[3]

---

[1] *Ibid.*, (September 9, 1897.)

[2] *Wyoming Tribune*, (September 22, 1897.)

[3] *Daily Sun-Leader*, (September 23, 1897.)

Following this first celebration there were compliments and criticisms regarding the event. The Wyoming *Tribune* says:

Probably the wild horse race offered more exciting features than any of the other events. The horses were halter broken only, had never been ridden or even saddled before and there was a wild time for fifteen minutes in front of the grand stand. When the word was given the dangerous experiment of saddling was begun and carried out with indifferent success. One or two of the less vicious animals were saddled and ridden around the track before the others had felt the drawing of the girth. Some bucked horribly and then laid [sic] down, and there were a number of narrow escapes, both in the crowd and among the broncho "busters."[1]

The editor and manager of the *Tribune*, Frank Bond, commented on the success of the venture, particularly in view of the late start in organization. He seemed to fear that the visitors might get the impression that the activities, as seen during the celebration, were, at that time, still a part of every day life in Cheyenne. He criticized some of the features and asked for a more varied program for the next year. The editor also deplored the fashion in which the crowds were handled. He says:

It was providential that no one was seriously hurt, for the narrow escapes were numerous. It is a curious and inexplicable thing, the unaccountable desire of dozens of ladies to stand on the race track, totally oblivious to the extreme novelty and danger of their

[1] *Wyoming Tribune,* (September 24, 1897.)

position, and while it was a relief to see them grab their petticoats and safely get away from the deadly feet of wild and crazy bronchos, the spectacle was not edifying, and should be dispensed with next year.[1]

Mr. Bond felt that the Frontier Day celebration while not elevating in character, was not harmful to any extent.

In commenting on this first gala occasion, the *Daily Sun-Leader,* in 1900 says:

I remember that two lone representatives of the noble red man graced the procession, and did a war dance later in dishabille duet in front of the grandstand. The committee had neither time nor funds to obtain the genuine article, from the interior department, and had worked over two commercial tourists in distress, to fill the bill. One of them—a son of Erin—did a bit of high class Irish jig during the war dance act—forgetting evidently the character he was representing and doubtless more or less enthused by a quart of firewater which protruded from a gap in his breechclout and dripped from the corners of another and larger gap in his face.[2]

Thus, Cheyenne Frontier Day was introduced fifty years ago, and those who doubted that it would become a permanent institution in Wyoming were fully persuaded. "The skeptical man is no longer to be found."[3]

---

[1] *Ibid.,* (September 24, 1897.)

[2] *Daily Sun-Leader,* (August 17, 1900.)

[3] *Ibid.,* (September 6, 1895.)

With spirits gay, on Frontier Day
I came with all my dough;
In bed I lay, I'm not so gay,
My head is swelled you know.[1]

The *Daily Sun-Leader*, September 6, 1898, under the heading, "Our Second Celebration," says:

Since early yesterday morning, teams have been coming into the city, bringing people from the country by the hundreds, from distances of fifty to seventy-five miles. Every incoming train has been loaded down with passengers, over 2,500 coming from Colorado points. . . . Buffalo Bill's big outfit added over 600 to the crowd, and never in the previous history of the town, have the streets presented so animated an appearance as they did this morning with crowds of cowboys, emigrants, Indians of the Sioux, Arapahoe and Shoshoni, and thousands of well-dressed people.[2]

In the year 1903, the Union Pacific came to the aid of the harassed officials of the Frontier Celebration when accommodations for the visitors became a problem. They turned over to the committee one hundred and fifty cots which were installed in public buildings for the use of the visitors.[3] Four years later a representative of the Frontier Day Committee was sent to Denver to place a rush order for one thousand cots, which were to be used in public halls and other available places.

A very interesting letter dated June 5, 1912, was received by the Secretary of the Frontier Days Association

---

[1] *Ibid.*, (September 7, 1898.)

[2] *Ibid.*, (September 6, 1898.)

[3] *Daily Leader*, (August 24, 1903.)

from Warren T. Spalding, Secretary of the Massachusetts Prison Association. It says:

> I have recently run across a newspaper clipping, dated August 17, 1909, telling of one feature of the Frontier celebration of that year. As the story goes, it had been customary to have a hanging, using a dummy for the purpose, but in that year there was to be a real man used, one having been found whose neck was so constructed that he could pass through the experience without injury. I am writing to ask whether there is any truth in the story about that man (whether the hanging came off), and also whether the fake hangings took place in previous years. I shall be glad of any printed matter regarding your celebrations, which must be very interesting.[1]

The committee disclaims that there were ever any hangings—of a human being or of a dummy—however, one year, at the time when Tom Horn was waiting to be executed, such a proposal was made. The committee said that a such proposal was jokingly made to the effect that the execution take place at the Frontier grounds on one of the show days—an event which would increase the crowd. "The rubber-necked man mentioned in the letter has never visited Cheyenne, and the committee has so advised the inquiree," says the Wyoming *Tribune* for June 8, 1912.

However, research has revealed the following item in the *Tribune*, September 18, 1897.

---

[1] *Wyoming Tribune,* (July 23, 1907), (July 8, 1912.)

He Wants To Be Hanged

A Fort Russel [sic] Man Will Appear

A Frontier Day Gratis

Fort D. A. Russel, [sic] Wyom., Sept. 17.

Editor Tribune:—Notice your advertisement in The Tribune for men to be hanged, shot, buried, etc., on Frontier Day, the 23rd inst., you would greatly oblige me by putting my name on your list of applicants for any of the above named parts. I have played in private theatricals a number of times at this post, with the Buckley Ministrels, and am very desirous of seeing Frontier Day a successful event. Hoping you will favor my application, I am, sir, Very respectfully yours,

J. Buster Keefe

P. S.—Kindly answer at your earliest convenience to give me time in order to prepare for my part. Will appear gratis.

J B K
Care of Knapsack[1]

Six days later, on September 24, 1897, in the same paper, The Tribune, the day after the first Frontier Day celebration, there appears the following statement:

Two of the events on the program were stirring reminders of early days to a good many of the old settlers in Wyoming who witnessed them yesterday. One of these was the vigilante committee, masked and armed to the teeth, who took hold of Bill Root of Lara-

---

[1] Wyoming Tribune, (September 18, 1897.)

mie and rushed him through the crowd toward a high pole across the race track. Bill dodged into the basement story of judge's stand and a horrible dummy was substituted in his place. The latter was hauled up and riddled with bullets.

Evidently this type of local advertising and fun-making eventually reached the eyes of the Secretary of the Massachusetts Prison Association and caused him to write his letter. It is quite evident that advertising was one of the ways in which the committee "put across" the early Frontier Day celebrations. In the early spring of 1910, the committee, through Senator Warren, sent a cable to ex-President Theodore Roosevelt in Africa asking him to be a guest at the celebration and to express his preference as to the date when he would be able to attend. Colonel Roosevelt replied, saying: "Accept Pleasure Invitation Cheyenne End August."[1] Upon his arrival in Cheyenne, on August 27, 1910, he said he was "dee-lighted"[2] to be there and when asked how he enjoyed the celebration he said, "It's bully."[3] Thereafter, for many years, both these comments were used to advertise the contest throughout the country.

At the celebration was also presented the equally well-known Frontier Days Parade, which is a spectacle featuring the complete history of transportation from the year 1860 up to the present day. To the original parade of costumed riders and visiting horsemen, have been added magnificent floats and old vehicles, portraying the Pageant of Transportation. One seldom has an opportunity to view a finer collection of rare and outmoded conveyances than

---

[1] *Ibid.*, (March 28, 1910), 1.
[2] *Ibid.*, (August 27, 1910), 1.
[3] *Ibid.*, (August 29, 1914), 3.

Right: Cowboy riding down Seventeenth street at Cheyenne Frontier Days, 1907.
—*J. E. Stimson, Photographer.*

Left: Theodore Roosevelt and Buffalo bill at Cheyenne Frontier Days, 1910. Left to Right: Theodore Roosevelt, Buffalo Bill, party unidentified, Charles Irwin. —*Courtesy Chamber of Commerce, Cheyenne, Wyoming.*

is to be seen in this parade. In addition to the color, drama, and memories of the past, as featured in the parade, the five days are crammed full of the excitement, danger and thrills of rodeo. During the evening a spirit of informality, fun and gaiety prevails, and every effort is made to reproduce life as it was lived during those raw days of this one-time frontier town.

The Cheyenne contest is a member-show of the Rodeo Association of America and offers purses ranging from $1,000 to $1,600 for each contest. All entrance fees are added to the purse; they range from ten to one hundred dollars (steer roping) depending upon the importance of the event. In addition to the regular events of the rodeo, other features are listed to amuse the spectators. These are: an Amateur Bucking Contest, a Denver *Post* Cowgirl's Relay Race, a World Championship Cowboy Relay Race, a Cowgirls' and Men's Half-Mile Cowpony Race, a Wild Horse Race, and the Cheyenne Frontier Derby, which is run on the last day of the contest.

Immediately after this large contest, a smaller one is staged in Boulder, Colorado. It is known as the Pow Wow celebration and originally was not a particularly important one, as far as rodeo is concerned. However, it is, year after year, increasing in popularity and importance. It is a three-day celebration, featuring a rodeo and horseshow for two days, and—until the advent of World War II—a rock drilling contest for the world's championship. This latter contest relates directly to those historical days when this Colorado city was one of the important mining centers of the West—a position which it still occupies today but on a smaller scale. The Pow Wow Days-celebration begins on the final day of the Cheyenne contest, and its rodeo opens on the following day. This plan enables the managers of this small contest to obtain the services of some of the very best rodeo cowboys who are moving southward from Cheyenne to the larger contests at Monte Vista and Colorado Springs, Colorado, and to the late summer events in New Mexico and Texas. The rodeo at Boulder does not attract all the top men, for there is a splitting of this group at Cheyenne; some go on to the northern Wyoming and Montana shows and remain there until September offers the Washington, Oregon, and Idaho contests. However, the men moving southward do compete in the Boulder show. The result is that in recent years the Pow Wow rodeo has become a "crackerjack"—superior in many ways to the larger, longer established, and more prosperous contests. Because, from a financial standpoint, the Boulder contest is still, to a certain extent, in its infancy, and because many people do not know that the best men in rodeo compete at this show, it is not always a spectacular or a financial success, but, as a rodeo, it is the real thing!

A personal element and intimacy exist between the spectators and the contest as a whole, which the author has never witnessed at any other show. The explanation of this lies, perhaps, in the size of the contest. It is not large in scale; the events are held in an arena which, although small, is adequate for performances. There is no race track around this arena, and the spectators are able to sit —well-protected behind a sturdy fence—close enough to the performers to see every move closely. The advantage of the absence of a track around the arena is certainly obvious in this Boulder contest.

At first, the Boulder show was unable to offer very large purses, but the entry fees are added and each year the purses have been increased. The cowboys feel that this is a very worth-while amount, and they like, particularly, the contrast—a small, intimate two-day contest after the strenuous days (and nights) in Cheyenne.

The Boulder contest stages a rare exhibition of one of the finest groups of Arabian stallions and mares in the country. These horses are brought from the L. W. Van Vleet, Lazy VV Ranch, picturesquely located in the high country, about twenty-one miles northwest of Boulder. Breeding these horses in a high altitude has been the fascinating enterprise of Mr. Van Vleet for some years, and his ranch is now the fourth largest of its kind in the country. On his ranch one sees blooded horses—grandsons of the world-renowned stallion, "Skowronek." "Kabar" and "Rifage" are both grandsons of this stallion, for whom the Russian government at one time offered Lady Wentworth of England one-quarter of a million dollars. From the Van Vleet ranch comes the world's tallest Arabian stallion, "Barek," standing sixteen hands and one-quarter inch. The purpose of Mr. Van Vleet in establishing his Arabian horse ranch is to "improve breeds of all other light horses all over the world. . . .[1] The Arab is used to produce half-breed or quarter-breed stock horses of superior quality. Infusion of Arab blood also yields wonderful saddle horses." For the past five years Mr. Van Vleet has held, during the summer months, regular Sunday morning exhibitions of his horses. People—native and tourists—flock from miles around to attend the show,

---

[1] *Boulder Daily Camera,* (August 16, 1941), 3.

which is free. A corral was constructed and also a grandstand to accommodate the people. The attendance, at first, was small, but the popularity of the exhibition has grown to such an extent that a second stand has been built and over a thousand people attend a single performance. The opportunity to present the Van Vleet horses at the rodeo during the Boulder Pow Wow Days is indeed a proud one for the committee. Rarely does a community enterprise of this size have such a wonderful opportunity; it is equally rare that the average tourist should see such a fine string of horses.

Farther south in Colorado and on the western slope of the Continental Divide is the city of Montrose. For a number of years it has held an annual rodeo in July, which is also a classic example of a small show that attracts the best in rodeo showmanship. Montrose maintains that it is the first outdoor contest in the world to use an electric timer in all events. In this novel method of timing, a dial, eight feet in diameter, is so placed that all the spectators may see it during the show. Naturally, the electric timer has caused much interest in the rodeo world. Montrose claims as native sons: George Mills, one of America's ace rodeo clowns and bull fighters, and his brother, Hank Mills of bareback bronc and bull riding fame, who at one time was a well-known jockey in the racing world.[1]

Rodeo is a popular form of entertainment throughout Colorado, and during the summer and fall months contests are held from North to South in the state. The rodeo season opens in January with the contest held in conjunction with the annual Stock Show at Denver.

---

[1] Information offered by the secretary of Montrose Rodeo Committee.

The story of cowboy sports and rodeo in relation to Denver is an interesting one. There is evidence that cowboy exhibitions were held in this city in the early years; however, as full-fledged contests, they were not successful until a much later date. While preparations for the first Festival of Mountain and Plain[1] were in progress an interesting account concerning a cowboy contest appeared in the newspapers. In the *Rocky Mountain News* for Monday, September 30, 1895, appears an item about a Western character by the name of "Arizona" Charlie, who was arrested for cruelty to animals. The *News* says:

> The show, as was advertised, consisted of exhibitions of rifle markmanship, riding of bucking bronchos, chariot races, feats in the saddle and other similar acts, but the crowning effect of Arizona Charlie's was to show his proficiency in lassoing bulls and throwing them.

"Arizona" Charlie's show was stopped at both performances by the secretary of the Humane Society of Denver. Both times Charlie was freed and finally, several days later, the charge of cruelty was dismissed by the judge. Charlie ran into difficulties several weeks later with the Humane Societies at Leadville and Pueblo, Colorado. These incidents finally involved, in nation-wide publicity,

---

[1] The idea of a festival for Denver was first suggested by Major S. K. Hooper, Passenger Agent for the Denver and Rio Grande Railroad. *Rocky Mountain News,* (August 25, 1895), 6.
"One citizen protested the use of the word 'carnival' and that the carnival idea was unappropriate and un-American. He suggested that the harvest be the motive of the celebration." *Denver Republican,* (September 7, 1895), 1.
"The celebration was named the Festival of Mountain and Plain by Mr. I. N. Stevens after many names were suggested and after a $10 prize had been offered for a name." *Denver Republican* (September 12, 1895), 1; *Rocky Mountain News* (September 14, 1895), 8; *Rocky Mountain News,* (October 16, 1895), 12.

several state officials—Governor McIntire,[1] Sheriff Bowers of Colorado Springs, the Mexican Consul, Lieutenant George J. Byram of the United States Army, William H. Ballou, vice-president of the American Humane Association, and President J. G. Shortell of that organization. The Governor was exonerated of showing " 'timidity and indifference' in not stopping bull fights in his state."[2]

Thus, rodeo or cowboy sport in its infancy received a jolt in Denver which did not encourage promoters of the sport to produce shows in that city. Instead, Denver turned its interests to the Festival of Mountain and Plain which was held October 22, 23, and 24, 1895. The program consisted of a historical and industrial parade, Indian races, dances, and sports, and ended on the last evening with a grand masked ball of the Silver Serpents, which was attended by the elite and socially prominent of Denver. There is no evidence that the cowboy and his activities were any part of this first celebration.

During the next five years the Festival of Mountain and Plain was held annually, but in the last two years, 1898 and 1900, complaints were registered concerning the need of new ideas in the festival. The new blood to be infused in the Festival of 1901 was a "broncho-busting tournament."[3] "The announcement spread like a prairie fire, and the cowboys made arrangements to see city life and show

---

[1] *Ibid.*, (October 9, 1895), 8.
"Governor McIntire declares that he had the State militia in readiness to raid the arena, but that the sheriff of the county refused to call upon him for assistance under the circumstances, only by a gross usurpation of power, which would have rendered him liable to impeachment." *Rocky Mountain News.* (October 14, 1895), 1.

[2] *Ibid.*, (October 14, 1895), 1.

[3] *Ibid.*, (October 1, 1901), 9.

the thousands what they consider amusement."[1] The trophy offered for first place in this contest was a five-hundred-dollar belt; also one hundred dollars cash and six prizes in gold. The belt was "subject to challenge and competition once only each year, preferably at the festival in Denver. If the holder doesn't defend it, he loses possession. Any person winning the belt three times shall become permanent owner thereof."[2]

John M. Kuykendall and George D. Rainsford were responsible for the new idea in the festival. Mr. Rainsford was so enthusiastic about this first cowboy contest in connection with the Festival of Mountain and Plain that he said:

> I think that in years Denver will be the scene of an international rough riding contest which will parallel the importance of the Yacht races. It is the American pastime, and that is why the American people will take hold of it with great energy. I myself will make an effort to get some of the best Cossack riders in St. Petersburg and several expert Italian riders to come here and compete next year. Nothing will stop it from becoming a great event. There will be so many horses and riders entered that it will take fully three days to hold the contest.[3]

M. Thad Sowder was the first winner of the belt.[4] In the contest of the year 1901 the prizes for "mean" horses

---

[1] *Ibid.*, 9.

[2] *Ibid.*, 10.

[3] *Ibid.*, 1.

[4] Contenders for the belt: S. E. Shuster, Palace Routt County, Colo.; W. H. Rider, Dunkley, Colo.; Joseph Harris, Westwater, Utah; W. M. Craver, Cheyenne, Wyo.; J. F. Farrell, Cheyenne, Wyo.; and M. T. Sowder,

were the same as for the best riders; $150, $125, $100, $75, $50, $25. The first prize was won by "Peggy,"[1] a big bay mare, owned by J. M. Kuykendall.

Concerning the Festival of Mountain and Plain of that year, Vincenzo Monti, a retired glass merchant from Rome, Italy, who was, at that time, at Hotel Metropole, Denver, said:

> But some of the very prettiest features of our carnival are missing in yours. But we have nothing to compare with your—What do you say? Broncho busting? It that it?—that I saw a few days ago.[2]

Under the heading "All Ended Well" in the *Rocky Mountain News*, the tenor of the occasion is well stated in some of the following comments. The *News* says:

> As the programme contained nothing of special interest to miners, the attendance from Colorado mining camps was small. Wyoming sent a large delegation on account of the broncho riding contests and it is claimed many mountain towns would have been liberally represented if the proposed drilling contest had been carried out. . . . [3]

Another citizen proposed that a great musical festival be given the following year instead of the Festival of

---

Cheyenne, Wyo. *Rocky Mountain News*, (October 1, 1901), 11. Prize winners: First prize and the belt for the world's championship, M. T. Sowder; second, A. W. Vaughan; third, Duncan Clark; fourth, W. N. Craver; fifth, B. F. Stone; sixth, Walter McCool. *Rocky Mountain News*, (October 4, 1901), 1. *Denver Republican,* (October 4, 1901), 8.

[1] "'Peggy' the wickedest broncho of the Festival was returned to the Kuykendall ranch to rest and then be put to work. Her avocation is bucking for she strongly objects to a saddle. 'Peggy' could be harnessed and used to draw a buggy." *Denver Republican* (October 8, 1901), 3.

[2] *Denver Republican,* (October 5, 1901), 3.

[3] *Rocky Mountain News,* (October 5, 1901), 8.

Mountain and Plain. Major S. K. Hooper, the originator of the Festival, suggested that the festival and carnival features be eliminated, and that the celebration be one to display the industries and agricultural products of Colorado, Wyoming, Utah, and New Mexico.

The retired glass merchant from Rome, Italy, mentioned above, also expressed his views when he said:

"One thing that surprises me very much is the commercial spirit that seems to prevail in the management of the festival. I see by the papers that there is talk of abandoning the carnival, because the visitors do not spend enough money."[1]

The Festival of Mountain and Plain ended in the year 1901 with this question: "Will there be another Festival?"[2] The Festival was held the next year, but according to the newspapers the cowboy activities were the most important feaure of the celebration, and the masked ball of the Silver Serpents was of secondary importance. Thad Sowder again won the belt, but the decision of the judges was severely protested by the spectators and several of the cowboys.

The Denver *Republican* gives an idea of the feeling toward the Festival held in 1902:

The Festival of Mountain and Plain has been going on in Denver for three days. So surreptiously has it been

---

[1] *Denver Republican,* (October 5, 1901), 3.

[2] "Merchants Failed to Derive Expected Benefits From Outside Visitors and Trade Was Slack." *Denver Republican,* (October 4, 1901), 1; 12.

"J. S. Appel, made a point of the idea that the commercial spirit of the festival was injurious to it and proposed a week of holidays. He pointed out that the newspapers were spreading that Denver used the annual festival to 'fleece' the rural population." *Denver Republican,* (October 6, 1901), 26.

carried on that comparatively few of the people have given it a thought, and as for those outside of town, they never know of it. Low rates and all, not more than 2,000 people above the ordinary travel came into the city in the three days. . . .

The apathy of the public of the city and state is explained by the fact that not a single new feature was offered this year. The festival was crystallized around the hangover of last year's popular feature—the bucking contest. . . . This was the third bucking contest in the city in 12 months.[1]

The following year, 1903, cowboy sports were held under the rules of the Festival of Mountain and Plain Association but there was no festival. Thad Sowder was there to defend his title, and the main contest was held between him and William McNeerlan of Virginia Dale, Colorado. Each of these two men brought a horse, and they exchanged horses for the ride. Sowder brought "Bald Hornet" which was assigned to McNeerlan, and the latter brought "7-X-L Outlaw" which Sowder was to ride. The purse was one thousand dollars. The event was held at the Denver Wheel Club Park, on August first, but no decision was reached by the judges. It is of interest to note that this program was enlarged to include a dummy race, exhibition riding, cowgirls' race, potato race, stake race, and a rough and tumble race.

By 1904 the Festival of Mountain and Plain and organized cowboy activities were, as far as Denver was concerned, a thing of the past. The Rocky Mountain *News*

---

[1] *Denver Republican,* (October 10, 1902), 1.

gives the following account concerning an interesting event:

M. Thad Sowder,[1] who twice won the world's championship rough riding contest at Denver, arrived in the city [Cheyenne] to-day, and entered in the championship contest. This is the first time that he has been an entry since the belt contests were transferred to Cheyenne.[2]

This is conclusive evidence that Cheyenne, with its Frontier Days Celebration, won out as the home of cowboy sports. Although there had been no obvious friction between the two cities, as to where the center of cowboy sports was to be located, Cheyenne newspapers made constant reference to the fact that Denver was trying to "muscle" in.

Nothing more is heard of the Festival of Mountain and Plain until the year 1912, when plans were made to revive it. The following comments in the Denver *Republican,*

---

[1] The following interesting statement was made in the Cheyenne *Daily Leader.* It says:

"The principal feature, of course, of the entire celebration will be the bucking and pitching contest for the *champion belt,* championship saddle and championship of the world. The belt is now held by Thad Sowder, who will be here to defend the title. The $200 saddle offered by the Union Pacific is held by Elton Perry and he, too, will be here to ride against all comers. Both of these trophies will go to the winner of the contest this year." (Italics by the author.) *Daily Leader,* (August 6, 1903.)

Later one notes in the *Leader,* for August 28, 1903, that there was a mistake about Sowder's entry in the contest. It says:

"Thad Sowder, in an interview in the Denver Republican, stated that the reason he did not come to Cheyenne to participate was because the judges were partial and had already decided upon the winner and in any event the contest was not official. These two charges were palpably false as the man referred to as the winner selected was Elton Perry, who did not even qualify in the finals."

[2] *Rocky Mountain News,* (August 30, 1904), 2.

August 18, 1912, once more show Denver's interest in the success of Cheyenne's Frontier Days Celebration. The *Republican* says:

> Denver could do as much with her Mountain and Plain Festival. Denver could show the methods of today. Denver could have throngs every fall as Cheyenne has them every August, and by the Mountain and Plain festival Denver could build up for herself a reputation of having a fall carnival that smacks—not of empty ribaldry—but of great things, as does the carnival of the sister city, and shriek the bigness and broadness of the West.

Denver had its fall Festival of Mountain and Plain in that year, 1912, but this was the end of the festival idea as an important celebration and certainly the end of cowboys sports and rodeo in that city. In January, 1931, in connection with the Silver Jubilee of the National Western Stock Show, rodeo was once more brought to Denver as a part of this annual affair. It is now firmly entrenched as a feature of the Stock Show and has grown each year in size and attendance. The rodeo held in connection with the National Western Stock Show officially opens the season of rodeo after the first of each year.

Immediately after the holiday season, the cowboys, who have spent several weeks relaxing after the strenuous New York and Boston Shows, begin to appear in Denver. The majority of them take up residence at the various hotels. Several days before the opening of the Show, they drift in, singly and in groups and the hotel lobby becomes a colorful and lively scene. The boys gather in groups, shout their greetings to one another, swap stories, catch up on the latest rodeo gossip, and discuss the coming show.

Besides the contests already mentioned, well-known names of other popular events in Colorado are: Ski-Hi Stampede, Monte Vista; Spanish Trails Fiesta and Rodeo, Durango; "Spud" Rodeo, Greeley; and Cattlemen's Days, Gunnison. Contests are also held at Meeker, Canon City, Estes Park, Loveland, and Brush. One is held at Pueblo in connection with the State Fair, and the county fairs at Sterling, Rifle, and Hotchkiss also feature contests.[1]

There are several unusual types of rodeo. A very unique one is the Kids' Rodeo at La Junta, Colorado. All contestants must be under sixteen years of age. A similar contest has been staged at El Paso, Texas; both are annual events and are constantly increasing in size and popularity.[2] Colleges have also "taken up" rodeo. A good many Western colleges have rodeo clubs; however, intercollegiate rodeos have been held only at the University of Arizona at Tucson and at Victorville, California.[3]

A very unusual, and at the same time very worth-while type of rodeo is held in the State prisons of Texas and Oklahoma. This is an annual event in the Texas State Prison at Huntsville. It is held on four successive Sundays during the month of October; unusual arrangements are made in order to cover all the entrants as well as to accommodate the the interested public. It is an amateur contest

[1] Information obtained from questionnaires sent to secretaries of the Colorado contests, 1941-1942.

[2] See *Hoofs and Horns* 8 (November 1938), 11.

[3] See *Hoofs and Horns* 8 (April 1939), 20; 9 (March 1940), 15; 19 (January 1941), 14.

because the participants are all inmates; about three thousand prisoners attend, the majority from several prison farms in southern Texas. About one hundred fifty inmates take part in the show as active contestants, and about four hundred and fifty work in some other capacity relative to staging the contest. For several days before the contest the contestants are allowed to rehearse and practice for the events. This is necessary to allow the show to move with speed and to allow those men who are not able to do this type of work every day to get into good form for the show.

A similar contest has been held at the Oklahoma State Reformatory, but this institution is perhaps better known for its cowboy band. Under the leadership of Frederick Pike, one of the better known Western band leaders, this musical organization has made a name for itself throughout the Southwest playing for parades, rodeos, and other sport events.

Rodeo has played, and is continuing to do so, its part in a rehabilitation program of the men who are looked upon as social outcasts. It ranks with the sports of football, baseball, tennis, and basketball, and has much to offer to these unfortunate men.

The historic city of Deadwood, South Dakota, holds an annual Western contest known as the Days of '76. Located in the Black Hills, the city of Deadwood was once the scene of frontier America—in its turbulent infancy and its bloody youth. It was at one time the haunt, and is the last resting place of many faublous Western personalities—"Wild Bill" Hickok, Jack McCall, "Clamity" Jane, "Poker" Alice, and "Deadwood" Dick. Situated in a long gulch in the heart of the northern Black Hills, Deadwood, as a Western town, was one of the most vivid communities that "sprung up" along a placer stream. This vividness of its birth and the drama of its growth are portrayed anew each year during the second week of August when a four-day celebration takes place.[1]

This celebration—Days of '76—is staged under the auspices of the Chamber of Commerce and is now (1947) in its twenty-third annual showing. The round-up and rodeo sports are combined with the more personal and local historical pageantry of this city and area. A three-mile historical parade is presented on the mornings of the first three days of the contest. During the evening, typical entertainment of the early gold rush days is a part of the program, and the special feature is a staging of the historical "Trial of Jack McCall for the Murder of 'Wild Bill' Hickok," produced by the Whisker Club of the city.

The program, as devised by the committee members of the Days of '76, is both educational and entertaining and holds wide interests for all visitors. Because of its diversification, the celebration gives a clue to the trends in Western civic entertainment. Basically, it rests on the particular interest or origin of the community. The entertainment varies because of the different historical backgrounds. Deadwood, born in a great gold rush, has considerable affection for the miner and his activities; ranch activities were evident in the early days of this town, but the miner and his work were far more important, thus the celebration centers about his life. The rodeo events that are a part of this South Dakota holiday are not the major attraction in the re-enactment of the history of Dead-

---

[1] Information from the office secretary, Chamber of Commerce, "Days of '76," Deadwood, South Dakota.

wood, but they are an important part of the entertainment.[1]

Northwest of this city is celebrated one of the outstanding Fourth of July Rodeos in the country. The Black Hills Round-Up at Belle Fourche is less conscious of its historical background than its southern neighbor, but after a quarter century perpetuating the ranchman's work on the range, it has developed a contest of high standing.

This contest is billed as "The Event of the West" and certainly has worked out one of the most elaborate publicity campaigns that has ever been seen in advertising the sport. The publicity and advertising directors of the Round-Up have spared no efforts in informing the citizens of that part of the country that a contest is taking place in Belle Fourche, South Dakota.[2]

For many years, it has been a problem to bring a great number of people to a place which is sparsely populated. That it can be done, has been beautifully and conclusively illustrated in this show—through the concentrated efforts of a well-planned campaign of the advertising committee. They use every possible means of advertising; some very novel ways of attracting the visitor are used — illustrated wax wrappers on bread for distribution in surrounding communities, match folders, and scenic booklets distributed in all the local stores. In addition, there are the usual billboards, window cards, pamphlets, road maps, stickers, bumper strips on cars, radiator cap signs, windshield stickers, newspapers, magazines, motion picture theatres, and the radio. Although the publicity is

---

[1] *Idem.*

[2] Information from the office of J. F. Koller, secretary-manager, Black Hills Round-Up, Belle Fourche, South Dakota.

intensified in the home county, it is also spread with considerable emphasis throughout the tri-state region of Wyoming, Montana, and South Dakota, from which states come not only spectators but also the rodeo cowboys and range workmen.

The contest features a historical parade, rodeo events, United States Cavalry maneuvers, cowboy and cowgirl races, pig races, lamb chases, and hide races, and attracts, in its three days of celebration, about twelve thousand people.

The Black Hills Round-Up, supported by annual subscription from the businessmen, is not a financial success. However, it brings to this section of the country thousands of tourists who spend money which is of local benefit to the places of business in the Black Hills district.[1]

The Round-Up was started in the year 1918, as a war-time Red Cross and Service Organization Benefit. The first contest, in a star attraction, brought together Sam Brownell and the bronc "Tipperary." Sam Brownell had been the world champion bronc rider of the Cheyenne Frontier Days in the year 1917. "Tipperary" had never been ridden before and in this 1918 contest he again won. In the year 1921, Yakima Canutt, the world champion bronc rider, was brought to the show to ride "Tipperary" and is said to have been the only cowboy who ever made a qualified ride on the horse. There is a difference of opinion concerning this. It is said that Canutt lost a stirrup during the ride, and this automatically disqualified him, although under the circumstances, it is granted that he did ride the horse. In the year 1926, "Tipperary,"

---

[1] *Idem.*

owned by Charles Wilson and Art Richie of Buffalo, South Dakota, was ridden for the last time in a contest. He died in the year 1932.

The Black Hills Round-Up usually has one outstanding attraction. The managers are always "on the lookout" for an event that will create wide-spread interest and draw to their contest visitors from every part of the country. In the year 1940, at the close of a night performance, the Round-Up featured the Grand Opera singer, Maud Runyon, American-English mezzo-soprano, singing love songs in Sioux Indian language. It was considered a triumph of that year's Round-Up.[1]

The Belle Fourche show has a reputation of being one of the outstanding contests of the country on the Fourth of July; it certainly equals any one of the number of similar events throughout the year. Each year it attracts rodeo cowboys—to be sure not all the best ones—but year after year, some of the world's champions of the various Rodeo-Association-of-America events enter the contest. It is remarkable that a contest of such size can be put on by a fifty-year-old cow town of about twenty-five hundred inhabitants. This fact shows the determination of spirit that exists in many of our Western communities striving to keep alive the traditions of our early American frontier.

A similar situation exists in the town of Sidney, located in the southwest corner of Iowa. With a population of about twelve hundred, this small community stages a contest known as Iowa's Championship Rodeo. This has been the custom for over twenty years. It is held for four days and four nights and is considered the premier con-

---

[1] *Idem.*

test of the central West. It is a member of the Rodeo Association of America and of the National Rodeo Association, and draws the cream of rodeo contestants—in fact, a program of participating contestants at this show might be the first one hundred of the rodeo world. To Sidney, during mid-August, come some of the most important contestants in rodeo; the contest offers everything that can be seen at the more spectacular and larger shows in the East and the West. The show is owned and controlled exclusively by the Williams-Jobe-Gibson Post, Incorporated, American Legion, in Sidney, and pays a purse of about seven thousand dollars. In addition to a good-sized arena and race track, it has two covered stands and bleachers, which surround the entire contesting space. The Iowa Championship Rodeo at Sidney is a contestants' rodeo; they like it and class it among one of the very best of the season.[1]

With the first sign of fall weather, rodeo gradually moves eastward, and by the first week of October everyone has shifted his interest to the contest of contests—the tournament of cowboy sports held in New York City. The men, who have worked hard all spring and summer, make the trek to the Madison Square Garden Rodeo, which is usually held during the month of October. Here they compete against about one hundred and fifty experts in the work. Performances are held every evening and twice a week as matinees for the largest assembled rodeo audience in the world.

It is a great thrill to see the recognition given the one-time humble, daily work of our cowboys. The New

---

[1] Information from the office of the secretary of Iowa Championship Rodeo, Sidney, Iowa.

Yorkers welcome them with open hearts; for the duration of the show, rodeo is practically the supreme entertainment of this sophisticated, yet genuinely interested populace. In spite of the many forms of sports, activities, entertainments—cultural and otherwise—that exist in that cosmopolitan city of the East, rodeo, year after year, never fails to attract hundreds of thousands of new followers, and adds them to its millions of fans throughout the country.

The Madison Square Garden Rodeo is a contest with the largest purses and entry fees and is the longest in duration. It is an exhibition of keen competition and hard fighting for supremacy in the events, as well as for the monetary compensations that this position brings to the winner. This contest is held in the most important sports arena in this country; yet, at no time do the size of the contest, the number of the contestants, the purses at stake, and the vast crowds seem to overpower the rugged nature and vital personality that are a part of rodeo. The spirit of this American sport is not diminished because of scale nor because of location; it retains all the vigor, the excitement, and daring that are seen in any of the Western contests. Although it is an indoor show, in which the natural features of the outdoor arena are lacking, the contest is not weakened because of the fact that it is staged in the very heart of a large Eastern city. The untiring efforts of the promoters to stage this contest—with the best men, animals, equipment, and featured performers—as the greatest and largest rodeo in the world, overshadows and overpowers any aesthetic elements that might be lacking. These elements are of great importance to the Westerner, but the lack of them does not lessen the enthusiasm of the city-bred individual who has not experienced them.

In the arena of Madison Square Garden, rodeo reaches its climax in staging, drama, color, and thrills. Not unlike the ancient Roman games, but with less brutality and cruelty, the contest is presented to the people as rodeo in all its glory. It has never been rejected by the people of that city, and obviously, it never will be. Modern rodeo, as seen in the New York Show, never experiences a lack of interest. It offers an entertainment that is different—one that is sincerely thrilling and genuine—and immediately captures the fancy and devotion of the city. Only in a city of this type can a competition of this magnitude be held with success.

The advent of the rodeo to New York City, for its annual show in October, is looked forward to as eagerly as the various festivals of drama, dance, and music that are a part of the entertainment and cultural scheme—it is an accepted and welcome fact. The cowboys and their wives look forward to it also, for it is the climax of the rodeo season in every way—socially and financially.

During the last twenty years, in which rodeo has fascinated the minds of the Eastern people, it has moved into that bulwark of American tradition—the city of Boston, Massachusetts—and to the larger Midwestern city of Chicago, Illinois, more recently also, to Saint Louis, Missouri. Apparently, the people of Boston are not so imbued with their historic lineage that there is no appreciation for a tradition that is as glorious as their own. Rodeo has gained a hold on Boston and is now an established institution—immediately after Madison Square Garden, the very same men and women open in Boston for a two-weeks show. The New York and Boston contests are now considered as the highlight events of the Eastern rodeo season.

During the fall of 1941, a new Eastern show was opened for the first time at Buffalo, New York. It took place about one week after the Boston Garden contest and was held in the Memorial Auditorium of this western New York city. This was the first time that the people of Buffalo had the opportunity to see a real rodeo. Before this contest, two or three attempts had been made to interest the citizens, but unfortunately, the contests were really not rodeos. Intermingled with circus acts and thrill performances, the various rodeo events were lost to the spectator.

The contest gave the people of Buffalo an opportunity to see a thrilling exhibition, which they accepted with considerable enthusiasm and appreciation. Under the skilled management of Frank Moore, who manages the Madison Square Garden Rodeo, it was "off to a good start." The stock and equipment were furnished by the J E Ranch of Waverly, New York, and the contest attracted most of the contestants who had appeared at Boston and New York City. The following year the rodeo was again brought to Buffalo, but it failed to draw sufficient crowds to make it a paying proposition. At present it is not included in the Eastern circuit.

The development of rodeo as a sport or spectator event fits into the pattern of the rise of sport which follows the Civil War. Previous to the war, recreation, popular amusement, leisure time, and sport followed the ideas of the colonial era. In most cases they were looked upon with disfavor. It is true that frontier occupations such as hunting, fishing, and riding of the range did offer moments of pleasure, competition, and exhileration, but work and the hardships of the time were more predominant. Many of the pioneer aspects of life were present during the first half of the nineteenth century, and there was neither wealth nor leisure to permit the American people to indulge in spontaneous play. As long as the people were occupied with the open frontier—the settlement of land and the exploitation of natural resources—America remained a serious-minded nation.

America's interest in sport and recreation appeared with the vanishing of the frontier, with the rise of industry, and the urbanization of the population. This great change in the life of Americans—formerly an out-of-door people—a change to industrial work and living conditions in crowded cities led them to seek leisure in amusement and sport activities.

People had shorter working hours and longer vacations. They turned enthusiastically to recreational activities. This trend encouraged the building of auditoriums, arenas, stadiums, and grandstands to accommodate the people who now had leisure time to witness competitive sports and games. The people who did not enter into the sports as active participants, as professionals, or as amateurs joined the millions of interested spectators. Earlier, prize fights and football games had converted the public into a spectator crowd.

The new elements found today are the varieties of sports and games, the large scale publicity and advertising schemes to attract the public, the ever-increasing interest of the people in the activities, and the commercial aspects of enterprising firms who have increased their sales by exploitation of sport. In addition, newspapers reflect a popular interest in sport. Newspapers and magazines show great concern in sport news and devote sections and pages to the results of competitions, the teams, the championships, and champions, and the personalities of the sports and games.

The development of the work of the range cowboy in the cattle industry into an American sport and competitive contest—rodeo—is not unlike the change of the early pioneer occupations of hunting and fishing into the various sports and competitions of today. These three activities had in their original form, without question, elements of recreation, sport, amusement, and competition, and among the many sports and sporting spectacles in existence at the present time, these have grown directly out of frontier occupations. Rodeo attracts fewer people who enter as active participants than many other sports, but its position as an important spectator sport cannot be denied.

Rodeos are found in all parts of the United States. They are no longer the sport and entertainment of the West; they are now a part of the sport and entertainment world of our whole nation. During the entire year they are held throughout the country and range from small one-day celebrations in some little Western towns to a large contest of several-weeks duration, such as takes place in Madison Square Garden in New York City. Already in the year 1913, this sport was recognized as one of magnitude. The *World* for December 17, 1913, published in Aberdeen, Washington, says:

> From a seating capacity in 1910 of 2,500 and a production cost of $3,500 the Round-Up of Pendleton has jumped to a seating capacity in 1913 of 31,000 and a

production cost of $35,000. Staged in a small city of the semi-arid region of Eastern Oregon where the population is sparse, it has today reached that point of renown where it attracts almost as many spectators each day of the three days' exhibition as witnessed the world series championship baseball games in New York and Philadelphia this year. Newspapers reported 40,000 people at the Polo Ground in New York, while 32,000 people witnessed the finals in the Round-Up at Pendleton on Saturday, September 13, 1913. New York City alone has a population of over 5,000,000. Pendleton has a population of less than 6,000; the entire State of Oregon has a population of less than one million, and the entire population of the three States of Oregon, Washington and Idaho is less than two and one-half million or not one-half of the population of the city of New York alone. And comparing the attendance at the Round-Up with the population the ratio is the greatest of any event in the world, the famous Passion Play of Oberamergau [sic] not excepted.[1]

Rodeo, at the present time, is still growing rapidly in popularity—both as a sport and as a paying, big-time business. Statistics show that it is second only to baseball in attendance. Because of this tremendous and unexpected growth, accurate figures for the year 1946 are not available. However, over two hundred cities and towns staged rodeos, and it is estimated that almost two thousand cowboys—professional and amateur—performed. Gate receipts totaled almost ten million dollars and over two million dollars was given in prize money. While the majority

---

[1] *The World,* Aberdeen, Washington, (December 17, 1913), 1.

of these cowboys do not fall in the high income bracket as a result of their financial success at rodeos, many of them, especially the top-ranking ones—champions and runners-up in the various events—have earned between $15,000 and $25,000 in one year.

Thus today, rodeo takes its place among the great sports of America. Throughout the country — east to west, and north to south — it attracts millions of spectators. Its fame abroad—in Canada, England, Australia—and, during World War II, its introduction as a means of entertainment in various theaters of war have helped considerably in keeping alive this sport which originated in the pioneer days of our country's making.

CHAPTER XXXI
EMPTY CHUTES

Gone are the cowboys,
Leaving imprint of boots,
Weary banners falling . . .
And . . . empty chutes.

As the last spectator turned his back toward the great oval arena, arc lights, partly dimmed by a haze of smoke and dust, glared down upon a scene of disturbed splendor. Here and there, as if scattered by the careless hand of a giant, lay crumpled programs, crushed containers, trampled newspapers, empty coke bottles, moist straws, and torn ticket stubs. The endless bowl of empty seats presented a picture resembling that of furrows made awry by the upheaval of thousands of migrants. There was scraping of shifting feet on concrete—the swaying mass of humanity had retreated into the dimness of the labyrinthian channels leading from the heart of this amphitheatre to pour out into the already crowded streets of a huge Eastern city.

Inside, still remained the evidence of their presence. Strong odors of moist soil and sawdust, and the stench of beasts persisted; mingled with them were odors of stale tobacco, cosmetics, food, damp concrete, and clothing. Emptied of its milling thousands, the great arena rests exhausted. The movement of a boy leading horses across

411

its moist bosom is like the last struggling effort to respond again.

As the great arcs, one by one, were thrown into darkness, they glowed and gleamed for the moment like threads of scarlet, only to disappear into nothingness. There was an intense silence after the lights were dimmed—the final darkening was followed by the cracking of contracting superheated metals. From the basement came the lowing of cattle; the restless movement of horses echoed and re-echoed as the hours passed; the blackness was broken only by the dim circle of the torch carried by the watchman on his hourly shuffle through the building. . . .

Dusk had fallen over the small university town north of Denver; as the fading rays of a gaudy sun drifted into the dull tones of an early evening sky, there appeared the first glow of lights in the homes of the community. From the crest of the foothills, backed by the eternal ridge reaching from north to south, the moist, cool air from the clouds that crowned the frowning ridge, swept across glacial snows into the valleys—only to rebound and to drop down into the numerous canyons and flood the city with wave after wave of crystalline snow.

Winter moved early from its lofty heights, and this late October evening found the town, looking from the shadows of the mountains eastward to the plains, strewn with the first snow of the year. Drifting lightly, swirling in a graceful dance until it moved into the warmer currents of air hugging the ground, it finally fell sullenly and dispiritedly. It disappeared almost as rapidly as it came —the roads gleamed in the fading light, mirror-black.

In the arena, on the outskirts of the city, the furrowed soil, now hardened into sunbaked knolls, was frosted with ermine snow. The gleam of lights of an approaching automobile streamed down the road in a silvery path and flooded the arena in an eery glow. It swung away with the sudden movement associated with youth, and, with its ruby eye, disappeared up a side road. Again the arena was drenched in darkness except for that ever-present reflected light from the drifting clouds.

The night air still persisted, bringing with it snow. Dashing against the high wire fence surrounding the denuded area, it set into motion the knotted, grey-white rags tied at spaced intervals. Fluttering, tiny flags, they waved a gay salute to their mission. Parading in grotesque patterns in the background, stood the white-washed faces of chute gates. Clattering and creaking with every on-rush of an increasing wind, they waited in all their harlequin loneliness for the day when, again, there would be a test of their knotty strength.

Gone from the scene are the rows of grey planks that had formed the seats for crowds of happy, holiday-seeking people; gone are the men on horseback in faded blue "Levis," large hats, and colorful shirts; gone are the vendors of novelties and food; gone the amplified voice of a word-weary announcer; gone are the clouds of dust, the drenching rains, the burning rays of the sun; gone are the cattle, horses, trailers, and tents—the rodeo. Yet, there still remained that symbol of American entertainment—the empty arena—standing in its familiar pattern, now fast losing shape, as the mountain storm moved in with pelting rain, sleet, and snow. Morning found it blanketed in crusty white, awaiting in anticipation its days of glory to keep alive those sacred traditions of the West. . . .

The evening performance of a small community rodeo on the Pacific Coast was just beginning. It had been one of those hot days that so often settles in to bear down on both man and beast in a final effort to assert its supremacy before giving way to the crispness of atmosphere that comes with late fall days. As yet, the welcome chill of the season had not been able to overpower the persistent heat and drought. The grass was greyed into a monotonous hue, and as the sky darkened into a deep sable, the first light of the rising moon and the fierce glare of arcs gleamed on the foliage encrusted with beige crystals of dust. Months of being sun-drenched and days of shriveling heat had not discouraged the coatless citizens from gazing into the depthless sky, night and day, in anticipation of rain.

On this evening, as if to escape the heated cubicles of their homes, they moved in an endless procession from their parked cars to the Community Fair Grounds for the annual contest of cowboy sports. They came, wearing every type of garment suitable for comfort—loose cotton dresses and suits, slacks, and shirts, open at the throat. Already their presence was keeping the purveyors of ices and cool liquids busy, and the more they consumed, the more uncomfortable they felt.

Busy ticket takers and impatient, weary ushers urged them to their seats in order to keep the perspiring group from blocking entrance and aisles. Programs, grasped in sticky hands, soon lost their crispness and became wilted fans, as the crowd increased and was packed into well-organized strips of uncomfortable humanity. As the grandstand filled, their restlessness became more audible; they amused themselves by waving and smiling to nearby neighbors. With envy and pride they watched the dashing boy on horseback as he rode by and practiced throws with a rope; the chutes filled with trembling, excited, treacherous broncs; the contestants were shooed from the arena—the rodeo came to life.

Already the band had finished its introductory medley, and a slim, dark, weatherbeaten man came to the microphone—the contest was ready to begin. For an instant the arena was plunged into darkness; off in the distance, over the mountain tops, a flash of lightening streaked the sky. All this was lost to the crowd, for at that very moment the arcs again flooded the arena; across its powdery surface came the Grand Entry Parade lead by the Color Bearers; the band gave voice to the national anthem. The crowd rose as one, and the voices, in patriotic fervor, sang praise to this country, to its men of vision, and to "that inalienable right"—to live as free people.

CHAMPIONS

All-Around Champions

1929....Earl Thode	1938....Burel Mulkey
1930....Clay Carr	1939....Paul Carney
1931....J. Schneider	1940....Fritz Truan
1932....Donald Nesbitt	1941....Homer Pettigrew
1933....Clay Carr	1942....Gerald Roberts
1934....Leonard Ward	1943....Louis Brooks
1935....Everett Bowman	1944....Louis Brooks
1936....John Bowman	1945....Bill Linderman
1937....Everett Bowman	1946....Gene Rambo

Champion Bronc Riders

1929....Earl Thode	1940...Frtiz Truan
1930....Clay Carr	1941....Doff Aber
1931....Earl Thode	1942....Doff Aber
1932....Pete Knight	1943...Louis Brooks
1933....Pete Knight	1944...Louis Brooks
1934....Leonard Ward	1945...Bill Linderman
1935....Pete Knight	1946....Jerry Ambler R.C.A.x
1936....Pete Knight	I.R.A.xx
1937....Burel Mulkey	x Rodeo Cowboy's Association
1938...Burel Mulkey	xx International Rodeo Association
1939....Fritz Truan	

Champion Bull or Steer Riders

1929....John Schneider	1938....Kid Fletcher
1930....John Schneider	1939....Dick Griffith
1931....Smokey Snyder	1940....Dick Griffith
1932....Smokey Snyder ⎱ tie	1941....Dick Griffith
1932....John Schneider ⎰	1942....Dick Griffith
1933....Frank Schneider	1943....Ken Roberts
1934....Frank Schneider	1944....Ken Roberts
1935....Smokey Snyder	1945....Ken Roberts
1936....Smokey Snyder	1946....Dick Griffith I.R.A.
1937....Smokey Snyder	1946....Pee Wee Morris R.C.A.

Champion Calf Ropers

1929....Everett Bowman	1939....Toots Mansfield
1930....Jake McClure	1940....Toots Mansfield
1931....Herb Meyers	1941....Toots Mansfield
1932....Richard Merchant	1942....Clyde Burk
1933....Bill McFarlane	1943....Toots Mansfield
1934....Irby Mundy	1944....Clyde Burk
1935....Everett Bowman	1945....Toots Mansfield
1936....Clyde Burk	1946....Homer Pettigrew I.R.A.
1937....Everett Bowman	1946...Royce Sewalt R.C.A.
1938....Clyde Burk	

Champion Bareback Riders

1932....Smokey Snyder	1940....Carl Dossey
1933....Nate Waldrum	1941....George Mills
1934....Leonard Ward	1942....Louis Brooks
1935....Frank Schneider	1943....Bill Linderman
1936....Smokey Snyder	1944...Louis Brooks
1937...Paul Carney	1945....Bud Linderman
1938....Pete Grubb	1946....Bud Linderman I.R.A.
1939....Paul Carney	1946....Bud Spealman R.C.A.

Champion Team Tiers

1942...Joe Bassett	1945....Tom Rhodes
1943...Gordon McFadden	1946...Manerd Gayler
1944....Tom Rhodes	

Champion Steer Wrestlers

1929....Gene Ross	1938....Everett Bowman
1930....Everett Bowman	1939...Harry Hart
1931....Gene Ross	1940....Homer Pettigrew
1932....Hugh Bennett	1941....Hub Whiteman
1933....Everett Bowman	1942....Homer Pettigrew
1934....Shorty Ricker	1943....Homer Pettigrew
1935....Everett Bowman	1944....Homer Pettigrew
1936....Jack Kerschner	1945....Homer Pettigrew
1937...Gene Ross	1946...Dave Campbell I.R.A.
	R.C.A.

Champion Steer Decorators

1931....John Schneider	1939....Ray Mavity
1932....John Schneider	1940....Jack Wade
1933....Frank McDonald ⎱ tie	1941....Frank McDonald
1933....Howard Brown ⎰	1942....Jimmy Wells
1934....Leonard Ward	1943....Arnold Montgomery
1935....Leonard Ward	1944....Padgett Berry
1936....John Schneider	1945....Floyd Peters
1937....Art Lund	1946....Bud Spence
1938....Warner Linder	

Champion Steer Ropers

1929....Charles Maggini	1938....Hugh Bennett
1930....Clay Carr	1939....Dick Truitt
1931....Andy Jauregui	1940....Clay Carr
1932....George Weir	1941....Ike Rude
1933....John Bowman	1942....King Merritt
1934....John McIntyre	1943....Tom Rhodes
1935....Richard Merchant	1944....Tom Rhodes
1936....John Bowman	1945....John Bowman
1937....Everett Bowman	1946....John Bowman

Champion Team Ropers

1929....Charles Maggini	1939....Asbury Schell
1930....Norman Cowan	1940....Pete Grubb
1931....A. Beloat	1941....Jim Hudson
1932....A. E. Gardner	1942....Vern Castro ⎱ tie
1933....Roy Adams	1942....Vic Castro ⎰
1934....Andy Jauregui	1943....Mark Hull ⎱ tie
1935....Lawrence Conley	1943....Leonard Block ⎰
1936....John Rhodes	1944....Murphy Chaney
1937....Asbury Schell	1945....Dr. Lane Falk
1938....John Rhodes	1946....Led Englesman

Wild Cow Milking

1944....Everett Shaw	1946....Gene Rambo
1945....Choate Webster	

Single Tying

1945....Amye Gamblin	1946....Cotton Lee

ADDENDUM—CHAMPIONS

The previous list names RAA champions from 1929 through 1944 and other champions for 1945 and 1946. To clarify the categories for those last two years, there is some overlapping in this Addendum.

RCA All-Around World Champion Cowboys

1947	Todd Whatley*		1961	Benny Reynolds
1948	Gerald Roberts		1962	Tom Nesmith
1949	Jim Shoulders		1963	Dean Oliver
1950	Bill Linderman		1964	Dean Oliver
1951	Casey Tibbs		1965	Dean Oliver
1952	Harry Tompkins		1966	Larry Mahan
1953	Bill Linderman		1967	Larry Mahan
1954	Buck Rutherford		1968	Larry Mahan
1955	Casey Tibbs		1969	Larry Mahan
1956	Jim Shoulders		1970	Larry Mahan
1957	Jim Shoulders		1971	Phil Lyne
1958	Jim Shoulders		1972	Phil Lyne
1959	Jim Shoulders		1973	Larry Mahan
1960	Harry Tompkins		1974	Tom Ferguson

PRCA All-Around World Champion Cowboys

1975	Tom Ferguson	
1976	NFR Champion**	Tom Ferguson
	PRCA Champion	Tom Ferguson

*Named after the end of the season

**In the years 1976, 1977 and 1978, the so-called sudden death system was used in connection with the National Finals Rodeo. Two sets of champions were named, the PRCA Champions being those who had won the most money up until the NFR, and the NFR Champions, based solely on winnings at that contest.

1977	NFR Champion	Tom Ferguson
	PRCA Champion	Tom Ferguson
1978	NFR Champion	Tom Ferguson
	PRCA Champion	Tom Ferguson
1979	Tom Ferguson	
1980	Paul Tierney	
1981	Jimmie Cooper	
1982	Chris Lybbert	
1983	Roy Cooper	
1984	Dee Pickett	
1985	Lewis Feild	
1986	T.B.A.	

IRA All-Around World Champion Cowboys

1945	Bill Linderman	1950	Gene Rambo
1946	Gene Rambo	1951	Del Haverty
1947	Bud Linderman	1952	Buck Rutherford
1948	Gene Rambo	1953	Casey Tibbs
1949	Gene Rambo	1954	Casey Tibbs

RCA Saddle Bronc World Champions

1945	Bill Linderman	1960	Enoch Walker
1946	Jerry Ambler	1961	Winston Bruce
1947	Carl Olson	1962	Kenny McLean
1948	Gene Pruett	1963	Guy Weeks
1949	Casey Tibbs	1964	Marty Wood
1950	Bill Linderman	1965	Shawn Davis
1951	Casey Tibbs	1966	Marty Wood
1952	Casey Tibbs	1967	Shawn Davis
1953	Casey Tibbs	1968	Shawn Davis
1954	Casey Tibbs	1969	Bill Smith
1955	Deb Copenhaver	1970	Dennis Reiners
1956	Deb Copenhaver	1971	Bill Smith
1957	Alvin Nelson	1972	Mel Hyland
1958	Marty Wood	1973	Bill Smith
1959	Casey Tibbs	1974	John McBeth

PRCA Saddle Bronc World Champions

1975	Monty Henson	
1976	NFR Champion	Mel Hyland
	PRCA Champion	Monty Henson
1977	NFR Champion	J. C. Bonine
	PRCA Champion	Bobby Berger
1978	NFR Champion	Joe Marvel
	PRCA Champion	Joe Marvel
1979	Bobby Berger	
1980	Clint Johnson	
1981	Brad Gjermundson	
1982	Monty Henson	
1983	Brad Gjermundson	
1984	Brad Gjermundson	
1985	Brad Gjermundson	
1986	T.B.A.	

IRA Saddle Bronc World Champions

1945	Bill Linderman	1950	Casey Tibbs
1946	Jerry Ambler	1951	Deb Copenhaver
1947	Jerry Ambler	1952	Casey Tibbs
1948	Carl Olson	1953	Casey Tibbs
1949	Casey Tibbs	1954	Casey Tibbs

RCA Bull Riding World Champions

1945	Ken Roberts	1960	Harry Tompkins
1946	Pee Wee Morris	1961	Ronnie Rossen
1947	Wag Blesing	1962	Freckles Brown
1948	Harry Tompkins	1963	Bill Kornell
1949	Harry Tompkins	1964	Bob Wegner
1950	Harry Tompkins	1965	Larry Mahan
1951	Jim Shoulders	1966	Ronnie Rossen
1952	Harry Tompkins	1967	Larry Mahan
1953	Todd Whatley	1968	George Paul
1954	Jim Shoulders	1969	Doug Brown

1955	Jim Shoulders		1970	Gary Leffew
1956	Jim Shoulders		1971	Bill Nelson
1957	Jim Shoulders		1972	John Quintana
1958	Jim Shoulders		1973	Bobby Stiener
1959	Jim Shoulders		1974	Don Gay

PRCA Bull Riding World Champions

1975	Don Gay	
1976	NFR Champion	Don Gay
	PRCA Champion	Don Gay
1977	NFR Champion	Don Gay*
		Randy Mager
	PRCA Champion	Don Gay
1978	NFR Champion	Butch Kirby
	PRCA Champion	Don Gay
1979	Don Gay	
1980	Don Gay	
1981	Don Gay	
1982	Charles Sampson**	
1983	Cody Snyder	
1984	Don Gay	
1985	Ted Nuce	
1986	T.B.A.	

IRA Bull Riding World Champions

1945	Ken Roberts		1950	Harry Tompkins
1946	Dick Griffith		1951	Jim Shoulders
1947	Wag Blessing		1952	Jim Shoulders
1948	Harry Tompkins		1953	Billy Hand
1949	Jim Shoulders		1954	Jim Shoulders

*Won the championship in a ride-off.
**The first black RCA/PRCA world champion.

RCA World Champion Calf Ropers

1945	Toots Mansfield	1960	Dean Oliver
1946	Royce Sewalt	1961	Dean Oliver
1947	Troy Fort	1962	Dean Oliver
1948	Toots Mansfield	1963	Dean Oliver
1949	Troy Fort	1964	Dean Oliver
1950	Toots Mansfield	1965	Glen Franklin
1951	Don McLaughlin	1966	Junior Garrison
1952	Don McLaughlin	1967	Glen Franklin
1953	Don McLaughlin	1968	Glen Franklin
1954	Don McLaughlin	1969	Dean Oliver
1955	Dean Oliver	1970	Junior Garrison
1956	Ray Wharton	1971	Phil Lyne
1957	Don McLaughlin	1972	Phil Lyne
1958	Dean Oliver	1973	Ernie Taylor
1959	Jim Bob Altizer	1974	Tom Ferguson

PRCA World Champion Calf Ropers

1975	Jeff Copenhaver	
1976	NFR Champion	Roy Cooper
	PRCA Champion	Roy Cooper
1977	NFR Champion	Jim Gladstone
	PRCA Champion	Roy Cooper
1978	NFR Champion	Dave Brock
	PRCA Champion	Roy Cooper
1979	Paul Tierney	
1980	Roy Cooper	
1981	Roy Cooper	
1982	Roy Cooper	
1983	Roy Cooper	
1984	Roy Cooper	
1985	Joe Beaver	
1986	T.B.A.	

IRA World Champion Calf Ropers

1945	Toots Mansfield	1951	Chuck Sheppard
1946	Homer Pettigrew	1952	B. J. Pierce
1947	Buckshot Sorrells	1953	B. J. Pierce
1948	Buckshot Sorrells	1954	Dean Oliver
1949	Homer Pettigrew		

RCA Bareback World Champions

1945	Bud Linderman	1960	Jack Buschbom
1946	Bud Spealman	1961	Eddy Akridge
1947	Larry Finley	1962	Ralph Buell
1948	Sonny Tureman	1963	John Hawkins
1949	Jack Buschbom	1964	Jim Houston
1950	Jim Shoulders	1965	Jim Houston
1951	Casey Tibbs	1966	Paul Mayo
1952	Harry Tompkins	1967	Clyde Vamvoras
1953	Eddy Akridge	1968	Clyde Vamvoras
1954	Eddy Akridge	1969	Gary Tucker
1955	Eddy Akridge	1970	Paul Mayo
1956	Jim Shoulders	1971	Joe Alexander
1957	Jim Shoulders	1972	Joe Alexander
1958	Jim Shoulders	1973	Joe Alexander
1959	Jack Buschbom	1974	Joe Alexander

PRCA Bareback World Champions

1975	Joe Alexander	
1976	NFR Champion	Chris LeDoux
	PRCA Champion	Joe Alexander
1977	NFR Champion	Jack Ward
	PRCA Champion	Joe Alexander
1978	NFR Champion	Jack Ward
	PRCA Champion	Bruce Ford

1979 Bruce Ford
1980 Bruce Ford
1981 J. C. Trujillo
1982 Bruce Ford
1983 Bruce Ford
1984 Larry Peabody
1985 Lewis Feild
1986 T.B.A.

IRA Bareback World Champions

1945	Bud Linderman	1950	Jim Shoulders
1946	Bud Linderman	1951	Casey Tibbs
1947	Carl Mendes	1952	Jim Shoulders
1948	Sonny Tureman	1953	Harry Tompkins
1949	Jim Shoulders	1954	Casey Tibbs

RCA World Champion Steer Wrestlers

1945	Homer Pettigrew	1960	Bob A. Robinson
1946	Homer Pettigrew	1961	James Bynum
1947	Todd Whatley	1962	Tom Nesmith
1948	Homer Pettigrew	1963	James Bynum
1949	Bill McGuire	1964	C. R. Boucher
1950	Bill Linderman	1965	Harley May
1951	Dub Phillips	1966	Jack Roddy
1952	Harley May	1967	Roy Duvall
1953	Ross Dollarhide	1968	Jack Roddy
1954	James Bynum	1969	Roy Duvall
1955	Benny Combs	1970	John W. Jones
1956	Harley May	1971	Billy Hale
1957	Willard Combs	1972	Roy Duvall
1958	James Bynum	1973	Bob Marshall
1959	Harry Charters	1974	Tommy Puryear

PRCA World Champion Steer Wrestlers

1975	Frank Shepperson	
1976	NFR Champion	Rick Bradley
	PRCA Champion	Tom Ferguson
1977	NFR Champion	Tom Ferguson
	PRCA Champion	Larry Ferguson
1978	NFR Champion	Tom Ferguson
	PRCA Champion	Byron Walker
1979	Stan Williamson	
1980	Butch Myers	
1981	Byron Walker	
1982	Stan Williamson	
1983	Joel Edmondson	
1984	John W. Jones, Jr.*	
1985	Ote Berry	
1986	T.B.A.	

IRA World Champion Steer Wrestlers

1945	Homer Pettigrew	1950	Bill Linderman
1946	Dave Campbell	1951	Dan Poore
1947	Homer Pettigrew	1952	Hank Mills
1948	Barney Willis	1953	Ross Dollarhide
1949	Homer Pettigrew	1954	Ross Dollarhide

RCA World Champion Steer Ropers

1945	Everett Shaw	1960	Don McLaughlin
1946	Everett Shaw	1961	Clark McEntire
1947	Ike Rude	1962	Everett Shaw
1948	Everett Shaw	1963	Don McLaughlin
1949	Shoat Webster	1964	Sonny Davis
1950	Shoat Webster	1965	Sonney Wright
1951	Everett Shaw	1966	Sonny Davis
1952	Buddy Neal	1967	Jim Bob Altizer
1953	Ike Rude	1968	Sonny Davis
1954	Shoat Webster	1969	Walter Arnold

* John W. Jones, Jr. is the son of 1970 champion John W. Jones.

1955	Shoat Webster		1970	Don McLaughlin
1956	Jim Snively		1971	Olin Young
1957	Clark McEntire		1972	Allen Keller
1958	Clark McEntire		1973	Roy Thompson
1959	Everett Shaw		1974	Olin Young

PRCA World Champion Steer Ropers

1975	Roy Thompson	
1976	NFR Champion	Charles Good
	PRCA Champion	Marvin Cantrell
1977	NFR Champion	Guy Allen
	PRCA Champion	Buddy Cockrell
1978	NFR Champion	Kenny Call
	PRCA Champion	Sonny Worrell
1979	Gary Good	
1980	Guy Allen	
1981	Arnold Felts	
1982	Guy Allen	
1983	Roy Cooper	
1984	Guy Allen	
1985	Jim Davis	
1986	T.B.A.	

IRA World Champion Steer Ropers

1945	John Bowman		1950	Choate Webster
1946	John Bowman		1951	Choate Webster
1947	Clark McEntire		1952	Buddy Neal
1948	Everett Shaw		1953	No award; Ike Rude probable winner
1949	Choate Webster		1954	Jim Snively

RCA World Champion Team Ropers

1945	Ernest Gill		1960	Jim Rodriguez, Jr.
1946	Chuck Sheppard		1961	Al Hooper
1947	Jim Brister		1962	Jim Rodriguez, Jr.
1948	Joe Glenn		1963	Les Hirdes
1949	Ed Yanez		1964	Bill Hamilton
1950	Buck Sorrels		1965	Jim Rodriguez, Jr.
1951	Olan Sims		1966	Ken Luman
1952	Asbury Schell		1967	Joe Glenn
1953	Ben Johnson		1968	Art Arnold
1954	Eddie Schell		1969	Jerold Camarillo
1955	Vern Castro		1970	John Miller
1956	Dale Smith		1971	John Miller
1957	Dale Smith		1972	Leo Camarillo
1958	Ted Ashworth		1973	Leo Camarillo
1959	Jim Rodriguez, Jr.		1974	H. P. Evetts

PRCA World Champion Team Ropers

1975	Leo Camarillo	
1976	NFR Champions	Bucky Bradford,*
		Ronnie Rasco
	PRCA Champion	Leo Camarillo
1977	NFR Champions	David Motes,
		Dennis Motes
	PRCA Champion	Jerold Camarillo
1978	NFR Champions	Brad Smith,
		George Richards
	PRCA Champion	Doyle Gellerman
1979	Allen Bach	
1980	Tee Woolman	
1981	Walt Woodard	
1982	Tee Woolman	
1983	Leo Camarillo	
1984	Dee Pickett, Mike Beers	
1985	Jake Barnes, Clay O'Brien Cooper	
1986	T.B.A.	

* The ropers competed as teams of two men.

IRA World Champion Team Ropers

1945	Dr. Lane Falk	1952	Vic Castro
1946	Led Englesman	1954	Bobby Jones
1950	Claude Henson		

IRA Champion Steer Decorators

1945 Floyd Peters
1946 Bud Spence
1947 Tom Duce

IRA Champion Team Tiers

1945 Tom Rhodes
1946 Manerd Gayler
1947 John Rhodes

IRA Wild Cow Milking

1945 Choate Webster
1946 Gene Rambo
1947 Vern Castro

IRA Single Tying

1945 Amye Gamblin
1946 Cotton Lee

IRA Single Steer Stopper

1946 John Bowman

AFTERWORD

By Kristine Fredriksson

Clifford P. Westermeier's *Man, Beast, Dust: The Story of Rodeo*, published in 1947 by the World Press in Denver, was the first scholarly work to appear among the more than 125 books on rodeo that have been issued to this date. Its Library of Congress classification was SF, i.e., animal culture. Two later books, published in 1982 and 1985, the only other serious studies to date, were designated as GV, i.e., recreation. It would appear that rodeo has not yet, formally at least, found its way into the American history category. Only in the last few years has it been accepted as a subject at sessions of scholarly conferences, and that augurs the beginning of its eventual incorporation into the mainstream of American culture studies.

The concluding date for the material in *Man, Beast, Dust* is 1945. That year turned out to be an important one for the sport of rodeo in terms of change. The following pages will deal with those changes during the forty years since the publication of the book.

By the spring of 1945, the active membership in the Cowboys' Turtle Association (CTA) had risen to more than fourteen hundred, as a result of new recruits and men returning from the Armed Services. A conflict of attitudes in the membership became apparent, with the more progressive individuals making a stronger case for change. At first, it was simply an expression of dissatisfaction with the association's name, which had been the butt of jokes over the years. At a board of directors' meeting in Houston, Texas, in February 1945, the decision was made to reorganize and to change the name to the Rodeo Cowboys Association (RCA).[1] A new slate of officers was chosen, in a few weeks Earl Lindsey was hired as business manager at a $7,500 annual salary, and a national office was set up in the Sinclair Building in Fort Worth.[2]

The older CTA members felt these steps to be extravagant, the sentiments being totally in keeping with the traditional attitudes of western men, aptly expressed by CTA's president Everett Bowman, who had resigned even before the transition to the RCA organization had been completed: "I always felt that any time we had to go outside of the Cowboys to get someone to run the business, the thing was sunk."[3] There would appear to be little doubt that new leadership ideas brought in by returning servicemen had a good deal to do with seeing the changes implemented. It marked the beginning of a time when those with a more broad-minded outlook would lead the sport on to its glory days in the second half of the twentieth century.

Along with these changes came the establishment of a monthly magazine, *The Buckboard* (see p. 352), published by the RCA itself. It was to be superseded in 1952 by the semimonthly tabloid, *Rodeo Sports News*. *The Buckboard* replaced, as far as the association was concerned, *Hoofs and Horns* as its official organ. That had been the mouthpiece of the CTA since 1936, earlier in which year it had also begun to represent the notices of the Rodeo Association of America (RAA), the scheduling organization of rodeo committees, which was operational by 1929. At that time, the RAA had established its own point-award system, giving one point per dollar won to determine the champion, or high-point winner, each year in each event and all-around, that is to say, a contestant competing in two or more events. The RCA adopted the same system to arrive at the highest annual money winners, including, for a few years, the events of wild-cow milking, steer decorating and team tying.[4] This point-award system was to be retroactive to January 1, 1945. However, the RAA and its own guidelines continued to exist, as well as those of a third organization, the National Rodeo Association (NRA) (see p. 342), formed in 1942 out of a regional group.[5]

After a few years the need for a consolidation of the RAA and the NRA became evident. When the RCA entered into the picture, the problem grew even more apparent. Within days of the RCA's organization, a meeting was held to work out the dilemma. Negotiations were, however, delayed an entire year until, in the spring of 1946, two of the three groups, the RAA and the NRA, combined to form the International Rodeo Association (IRA).[6]

Its purpose was to seek nationally known companies to donate support, and in that effort it foreshadowed a trend of later decades, but the partial consolidation did not solve the problem. Both the remaining associations were in a position to sanction rodeos. While the RCA remained firm that its contests would be limited strictly to the professional cowboys, the IRA allowed anyone to enter some of its larger rodeos.[7]

Late in 1947, after the season was over, the RCA named its first all-around world champion at the request of the Levi Strauss Company, a national trophy donor.[8] The nomination only added to the already existing confusion since there would now be two all-around champions as well as two in each of the specific events. Not until 1955 was the matter resolved. The IRA had quietly decided to drop the word *champion* while still awarding checks to the highest money winners. It was finally the RCA's top cowboys who became the exclusive holders of the world championship titles.[9]

In the late 1940s and the early 1950s, average Americans participated far less actively in sports than they do today. They were more likely to be passive followers of sporting events, including rodeo. Rising attendance figures were accompanied by greater coverage by national publications. In turn, this increased public awareness attracted to the sport, as competitors, a number of young men, not necessarily from a rural background, who were to become the focus for rodeo's so-called Golden Age.[10] Their names were publicized like those of other famous athletes. National magazines and television game shows began to feature these cowboys.

Among them were some veterans of the Armed Forces who had gone back to college on the G.I. Bill. These mature young men were instrumental in the formation of the National Intercollegiate Rodeo Association (NIRA) in 1949 and played an important role in placing rodeo in the mainstream of American sports. Scholarships were made available as rodeo took its place among athletics at several western institutions. Today the NIRA has a membership of 2,435, representing 130 colleges and universities in about thirty states.

Eager to give the sport a favorable image in the press, the RCA formed, in 1955, the Rodeo Information Commission (RIC). It was a collaborative effort of contestants and rodeo committees, each contributing from their dues and purses, respectively, to the operation of the new arm of the RCA. Its function was to produce materials to educate reporters about rodeo in order to gain the same kind of coverage that other sports already received. [11] In this endeavor the RIC was the first of the forerunners of the present-day Rodeo News Bureau, which was established in 1973 as a fully staffed department devoted exclusively to the news and publicity of the sport.

Although some contests had begun to be televised on a network level, and successfully so, the RCA curiously did not perceive TV coverage as a benefit to the sport. Rather, the belief was that attendance would go down as a result of on-the-air exposure. In this notion the association actually set a limit of network telecasts to two per year. [12]

The key factor that kept rodeo from achieving full national prominence was thought to be that it had no end-of-season event like baseball's World Series and hockey's competition for the Stanley Cup. Even though champions were named each year, there was no public event to draw attention to their accomplishments. To remedy that situation, the RCA created in 1958 the National Finals Rodeo Commission, a corporation whose duty was to be "to produce and direct an annual National Finals Rodeo on behalf of the sport as a whole in order to bring national attention to rodeo and to win for it long deserved public recognition as one of America's leading spectator sports." [13] Dallas, Texas, was chosen as the site for the first three years of the Finals, in which the top fifteen contestants in each event were eligible to compete. CBS won the rights to televise the first year's contest in the Livestock Coliseum. [14] On this occasion television was thought to be an asset.

In accordance with the plan to relocate every three years, the NFR was held in Los Angeles from 1962 to 1964. It proved to be less effective as a host city than Dallas, and it was only in the first year that the general public really showed an interest in the event, although media attention actually did increase over time. [15]

Oklahoma City became the third location for the Finals, a position it retained for twenty years. The first NFR in that city, in 1965, coincided with the dedication of the National Cowboy Hall of Fame and

Western Heritage Center, which through 1982 continued as a major sponsor of the event.

As rodeo entered the 1970s, it came to include another element, one that was to change its image further and give the sport even more visibility. Contestants referred to as "the new breed" began to join the ranks of the earlier membership. These young men, usually from an urban background and college educated, chose rodeo for the athletic rewards it had to offer. They attracted the attention of reporters and photojournalists who saw in the new breed of cowboy an interesting subject for coverage, not just of the actual contests but of the behind-the-scenes routines, the agonies, the triumphs, and the lifestyles as the contestant went down the road. Kieth Merrill's Oscar-winning documentary, *The Great American Cowboy,* released in 1972, featured the two world champions, Larry Mahan and Phil Lyne. In that year, too, no less than four feature films with rodeo backgrounds appeared: *J. W. Coop, Junior Bonner, When the Legends Die,* and *The Honkers.*

A number of the new cowboys had received their training in rodeo schools, a phenomenon that had had its modest beginnings in the 1930s but that did not really begin to develop until the 1950s. The first regular school was offered in 1962 by five-time all-around world champion Jim Shoulders, who has a total of sixteen world championships to his credit.[16] From the 1970s on, rodeo schools were not just places to learn new skills but also a means by which a champion could earn additional income as instructor to a new generation of rodeo cowboys. It even became respectable for a full-fledged rodeo contestant to attend a session in order to improve his technique.

In all, this training resulted in a greater sense of professionalism. It was increasingly important to the cowboys as well as the association to gain for rodeo public acceptance as a bona fide American sport. In fact, the RCA added the word *Professional* to the front of its name in 1975, to become known henceforth as the PRCA — the Professional Rodeo Cowboys Association.

Rodeo did not exist without opposition from those who felt disadvantage fell to the animal participants. Protests had been raised since the 1870s. Beginning in the 1930s, various states had introduced legislative measures, designed to curtail rodeo activities and other public events involving animals. In the 1970s, a decade in which rodeo enjoyed unprecedented growth, the strongest criticism to date came from a variety of animal-welfare organizations. As early as the 1950s, the then RCA had begun a collaboration with the American Humane Association (AHA) in an effort to establish regulations, agreed upon by both organizations, to protect rodeo stock from possible injury or mistreatment. These rules appear as part of the text in the PRCA rule book, which is updated each year. In the eyes of the PRCA as well as the AHA, the campaigns by other humane interests are engineered in such a way as actually to use rodeo as a springboard in fund-raising efforts.[17] However, the protests received have made the PRCA realize the need to educate the public about the rules of competition and the treatment of livestock if rodeo is to continue to grow as a spectator attraction.

Over the years an increasing number of corporations have contributed end-of-season prizes to professional rodeo or special awards at individual contests. Large-scale national sponsorship of the sport began in earnest when, in 1971, the R. J. Reynolds Tobacco Company approached the RCA about a $105,000-a-year program, to be known as the Winston Rodeo Awards. This was the first in a series of awards programs designed to benefit more contestants and demonstrate the association's growing concern that the general membership and not just the top cowboys should profit from bonuses offered. In the next several years, a number of programs were developed to this end with the Joseph Schlitz Brewing Company, Justin Boot Company, Frontier Airlines, Heublein Corporation, Adolph Coors Company, Nestlé Company, and Blue Bell, Inc., among others. As the 1970s ended, the yearly earnings of top cowboys could be seen to increase markedly, inching toward the $100,000 range. Earnings of the less successful rose significantly, too. Offsetting this raise were higher travel costs for contestants and the cost of competing at more rodeos in order to remain high in the standings.

In nearly all the cases, the awards programs grew in dollar amounts over the years and began to take in larger segments of those involved in the sport, such as the stock contractors, the clowns, and high-school-level contestants, from whose ranks future members will be drawn.

The Justin Boot Company has shown important support through its Justin Heeler Program, begun in 1981. Under that program, a fully equipped mobile medical center provides aid and preventive treatment to cowboys at various major rodeos each year. The emphasis on sound medical care of rodeo injuries has gained full acceptance among today's contestants. A previous generation might have scoffed at the sophistication and resorted to a variety of self-medications.

Consistent with the expansion of the sport and the interest it was receiving from the corporate world, the PRCA in 1977 formed a revenue-producing subsidiary to be known as Professional Rodeo Cowboys Association Properties, Inc. It enables the association to negotiate with sponsors of the sport in the licensing of products to bear the PRCA seal of approval as well as other endorsements.[18] In addition, PRCA took over the publication of *Prorodeo Sports News,* so renamed in that year.

In the early 1980s, the growth of the sport and the concern for the largest number of contestants continued. In-house-produced television broadcasts, begun in conjunction with John Blair and Company of New York City in 1978, continued to bring the sport before large national audiences. In 1982, the PRCA formed its own TV production company, PRCA Productions, bringing to that endeavor the support of corporations already sponsoring the sport, as well as others that additionally contributed to the prize money of the televised rodeos. In the format of Rodeo ProTour U.S.A., five rodeos plus a Rodeo ProTour Finals I were broadcast to the nation in the company's first year.

In the mid-1980s some significant changes were made that were to steer the association in a different direction. The 100-rodeo rule went into effect in 1984. Free to enter as many contests as he wishes, the contestant selects one hundred rodeos in one year from which his earnings will count toward championships. This is said to result in a guarantee of larger profits for the cowboy while limiting his expenses. At the same time, it would appear to take away some of the freedom that historically the cowboy has enjoyed.

Another scheme seemingly that might do the same began in that year also. Known as the TriPro Divisional Rodeo, it was designed to allow a contestant to compete in one or more divisions in accordance with his "goals and abilities." An additional benefit was seen to be the development of recognizable sports personalities, to which the association has been increasingly devoted for decades.[19] However, the TriPro concept comes across merely as an updated version of the Schlitz-sponsored Circuit System of the 1970s.

The PRCA has taken great pains to assure its membership that each new venture is designed in such a way as to retain the age-old characteristic of the cowboy, couched in phrases such as "controlling our destiny" and "taking care of business." Yet, to be part of the various programs, the cowboy cannot help but relinquish some of the personal privileges—independence, freedom, and desire for short-term planning—that often made his earlier counterpart chose rodeo as a way of life in the first place.

Continuing its efforts to gain greater recognition for rodeo and its contestants, the PRCA in 1985 introduced yet another new concept, the Winston Tour. This comes as close as possible to the idea of team rodeo, which the association fought vehemently and defeated in the late 1970s, laying itself open to charges of monopoly. In an annual draft, the top cowboys in each event are to be chosen as one of eight members of eighteen outfits, or teams, each sponsored by a national corporation. In four-day, tournament-style competitions, these athletes were showcased at six exhibitions in the first year. The concept was declared an immediate success in terms of spectator attention, media coverage, and contestant enthusiasm.[20] The scheme took away important support for the majority of contestants, however, giving exposure only to 136 of rodeo's top competitors. The National Finals Rodeo moved to Las Vegas, Nevada, in 1985, after twenty years of enormous growth enjoyed in Oklahoma City. The change was not without debate and criticism among cowboys and fans alike.

The Winston Tour predictably also drew criticism from most of the PRCA membership, who objected to the fact that the large sums of money won at the tournaments by the drafted 136 would count toward championship standings. A compromise was reached in an eleven-hour board meeting in early 1986. The Tour concept was revised to restrict the outfit members from competing in more than 125 other rodeos for rough-stock contestants or 100 for timed-event contestants. Furthermore, the bottom twenty-five percent of the participants are to be replaced each year to enable more to enter the select group. Another concession was to make the annual draft open to the entire PRCA membership instead of to the top twenty-four in each event.[21]

A surprising development occurred early in 1986. After fifteen years of building up sponsorship and concern for growth and public recognition, a retrenchment was called for. PRCA Properties is to be dissolved by the end of that year, along with its subsidiaries, including a credit union and a travel agency, Westworld Travel. The PRCA officers elected in 1985 wish to return to conducting business in the more conservative manner of earlier times.[22] It is possible that the general membership was reluctant to keep pace with the dizzying speed with which changes have often been made.

In recent years, professional rodeo has been almost overly concerned with being compared favorably with other sports and in the process has taken on some of their trappings. While this concern has undoubtedly gained for rodeo and its participants millions of dollars, larger audiences, and greater exposure each year, it has also removed the sport further from its roots, which are deeply entrenched in the cattle industry of a century and a quarter ago. The developments in the next few years will be interesting to follow.

In the past sixty-five years over 125 books about rodeo have been published. The vast majority of these are, predictably, in the nonfiction category. A number of long-established contests had histories written to commemorate anniversaries. Famous people and famous animals have their biographies; well-known photographers have issued collections of their work.

The fiction category is fairly lean with only a few works of note, while the juvenile category has a number of creditable publications. Although no one can learn a sport by reading a book, there have been a number of instruction books aimed at teaching anything from horse training to trick roping to bull riding.

The following is a summary of the works that, in dealing with various facets of the sport, have merit.

It has already been pointed out that Dr. Westermeier's *Man, Beast, Dust: The Story of Rodeo* was a ground-breaking study. This reissue of his book will ensure new readers of an opportunity to learn about the roots and the early years of the sport. *The 101 Ranch* by Ellsworth Collings and Alma Miller England (University of Oklahoma Press, 1937, rep. 1971) is a fascinating tale of the three Miller brothers' 101 Ranch Real Wild West Show, in which many rodeo contestants as well as western-film actors got their start.

The colorful announcer Foghorn (Fred M.) Clancy published his recollections in 1952, entitled *My 50 Years in Rodeo: Living with Horses and Danger* (San Antonio: Naylor Company). Filled with stories and anecdotes of early contests and personalities, the book's main shortcoming is that it is often difficult to pin down exact years.

A light-hearted look at rodeo as it began to emerge into a full-fledged sport is offered in *Rodeo Back of the Chutes* (Denver: Bell Press, 1956). Written by Gene Lamb, first editor of *Rodeo Sports News*, it contains numerous behind-the-scenes stories and interesting tidbits.

Mary S. Robertson's *Rodeo: Standard Guide to the Cowboy Sport* (Berkeley, Calif.: Howell-North, 1961) was indeed a guide, written for the spectator. As such, it has validity to this day. In the same vein, but somewhat more lively, is Sam Savitt's *Rodeo: Cowboys, Bulls and Broncos* (Garden City, N.Y.: Doubleday, 1963). The author surveys the sport to the early 1960s, using interviews with rodeo contestants. It includes explanation of events and stories of famous animals. Robert West Howard and Oren Arnold's *Rodeo: Last Frontier of the Old West* (New York: New American Library) was, when it appeared in 1961, a complete and accurate account of the sport to date. It remains an important and reliable source of information on rodeo through the 1950s.

One of the oldest and best-known rodeos in the United States is the Cheyenne Frontier Days, held continuously since 1897. In time for its seventieth anniversary, Robert D. Hanesworth, who had served on the organizing committee since 1926, wrote a well-illustrated history entitled *Daddy of 'Em All: The History of the Cheyenne Frontier Days* (Cheyenne, Wyo.: Flintlock Publishing Co., 1967). The book, however, lacks an index and is therefore awkward to use for reference.

A companion piece on Canadian rodeo is Fred Kennedy's *The Authentic Story of the Calgary Stampede* (Vancouver, B.C.: West Vancouver Enterprises, Ltd., 1965).

In the biographical and autobiographical category, two books stand out. Thelma Crosby and Eve Ball's *Bob Crosby: World Champion Cowboy* (Clarendon, Tex.: Clarendon Press, 1966) offers a colorful account of the life and career of a man who actually was never a world champion but nevertheless is one of rodeo's all-time greatest stars. In *Rodeo Road: My Life as a Pioneer Cowgirl* (New York: Hastings House, 1974) trick- and bronc rider Vera McGinnis gives a fascinating and realistic picture of the lifestyles of the women in rodeo during a time when they participate in far more events than today.

Coverage of the new breed of cowboy began with Fred Schnell's *Rodeo! The Suicide Circuit* (Chicago: Rand McNally, 1971). It takes a candid look at professional rodeo, and the artistic photographs by the author makes this one of the more outstanding books on the modern contestant as he began to emerge in the 1970s. One of three books by that title, *Let 'Er Buck!* (New York: Saturday Review Press/E. P. Dutton, 1973) by Douglas Kent Hall is another photojournalistic account of modern rodeo. Hall, traveling with the contestants, gained amazing insight into the stuff of which they are made, what makes them do what they do, and why they do it. Long after the term *new breed* has been forgotten, the book will hold up as a study of the man it stood for.

Willard H. Porter, once owner of *Hoofs and Horns* and editor of the *Quarter Horse Journal,* now director of the Rodeo Division of the National Cowboy Hall of Fame, has written two books on the roping events, their contestants, and famous horses. *13 Flat* (1967) contains biographies of thirty all-time great ropers and their mounts, whose names have become as well known as those of their owners. *Roping and Riding-Fast Horses and Short Ropes* (1975) offers a knowledgeable account of the roping events, along with descriptions of the men, horses, and equipment necessary for success. (Both books were published by A. S. Barnes & Company, Cranbury, New Jersey.) Mr. Porter's *Who's Who in Rodeo* (Oklahoma City: Powder River Book Co., 1982) is the sport's only encyclopedia to date, with biographies of

Hall of Fame male and female honorees and PRCA all-around world champions.

Teresa Jordan's *Cowgirls-Women of the West: An Oral History* (Garden City, N.Y.: Anchor Press/Doubleday, 1982) provides excellent profiles of numerous western women, in ranching as well as rodeo. These are further strengthened by the author's thorough examination of accounts of their earlier counterparts in letters, diaries, biographies, and fiction.

The first anthropological study of the sport is Elizabeth Atwell Lawrence's *Rodeo: An Anthropologist Looks at the Wild and the Tame* (Knoxville: University of Tennessee Press, 1982). As such, it disregards the boundaries of professional and amateur that have so far characterized rodeo literature. Instead, Dr. Lawrence looks at rodeo as a rite that expresses a way of life, a symbolic pageant, dealing with man's place in nature in the late twentieth-century cattle culture.

In my own study, *American Rodeo: From Buffalo Bill to Big Business* (College Station: Texas A & M University Press, 1985), I focus on the development of rodeo into an organized, national sport. It deals primarily with the cowboys' early attempts at organizing while also trying to establish for themselves an image that would make them more acceptable to the general public. In 1979–81 I was privileged to be the first person to use Clifford P. Westermeier's collected papers, which have been housed since 1979 in the Western History Collections at the University of Colorado library. The collection includes those documents and photographs used in the compilation of his 1947 book. It contained, and steered me to, additional material without which my own book could not easily have been completed.

NOTES

1. Interview with Earl Lindsey, conducted by telephone by David Stout, August 7, 1982; "RCA-Cowboy Organization Makes Changes," *Hoofs and Horns* 14, no. 11 (May 1945): 16.

2. "RCA-Cowboy Organization Makes Changes," 16; "Statement from Everett Bowman," *Hoofs and Horns* 14, no. 12 (June 1945): 13.

3. "Statement from Everett Bowman," 13.

4. "Champion Cowboys 1929–1944," *Prorodeo 1984 Official Media Guide*, p. 19.

5. Clifford P. Westermeier, *Man, Beast, Dust: The Story of Rodeo* (Denver: World Press, 1947).

6. Jerry Armstrong, "The Collegiate Cowboy's Column," *Western Horseman* 11, no. 2 (March-April 1946): 15; Jerry Armstrong, "Picked Up in the Rodeo Arena," *Western Horseman* 14, no. 3 (March 1949): 10.

7. Armstrong, "The Collegiate Cowboy's Column," *Western Horseman* 12, no. 3 (May-June 1947): 10.

8. Armstrong, "Picked Up in the Rodeo Arena," *Western Horseman* 13, no. 3 (May-June 1948): 37.

9. Armstrong, "Picked Up in the Rodeo Arena," *Western Horseman* 20, no. 7 (July 1955): 20.

10. Interview with Lex Connelly at Studio City, Calif., March 20, 1978; "Event Winners at Larger Rodeos," *Rodeo Sports News*, Championship Edition, 1969, p. 99.

11. Mike Swift, "The Rodeo Information Commission," *Rodeo Sports News*, Championship Edition, 1958, p. 120.

12. "TV, War Threat Making It Tough for Rodeo Hands," *Rocky Mountain News*, January 8, 1951, p. 6; "Two National Telecasts," *Rodeo Sports News*, Championship Edition, 1959, p. 37.

13. "First Finals Rodeo in '59," *Rodeo Sports News*, Championship Edition, 1959, p. 38.

14. Lex Connelly, "Founding and First Years of National Finals Rodeo," *Persimmon Hill* 4, no. 1 (Summer 1973): 15.

15. "National Finals: A Growth Industry," *Rodeo Sports News*, January 25, 1978, p. 4.

16. "First Finals Rodeo in '59."

17. "Interview with Warren Cox, director of animal protection, American Humane Association, at Denver, Colo., September 15, 1978; interview with Bob Eidson, executive vice president, Professional Rodeo Cowboys Association, at Denver, September 14, 1978.

18. "National Finals Rodeo—1967," *Rodeo Sports News*, Championship Edition, 1968, p. 12.

19. "1984 Prorodeo," *Prorodeo Sports News*, Championship Edition, 1985, pp. 6–8.

20. "1985 Prorodeo," *Prorodeo Sports News*, Championship Edition, 1986, pp. 6, 8; "Winston Tour Rodeo," ibid., pp. 54, 56.

21. International Rodeo Fans *Newsletter*, May 1986; "PRCA Compromise Averts 'War,'" *Gazette Telegraph* (Colorado Springs, Colo.), April 2, 1986.

22. International Rodeo Fans *Newsletter*, June-July 1986.

BOOKS: BIBLIOGRAPHY

Adams, Andy, *The Log of a Cowboy*, Houghton Mifflin Company, (Boston and New York, 1936).

———— *Reed Anthony, Cowman, An Autobiography*, Houghton Mifflan Company, (Boston and New York, 1907).

Adams, Ramon F., *Western Words: A Dictionary of the Range, Cow Camp and Trail*, University of Oklahoma Press, (Norman, Oklahoma, 1944).

Altrocchi, Julia C., *The Old Caliornia Trail*, Caxton Printers, Ltd., (Caldwell, Idaho, 1945).

Byers, Charles, *Roping, Trick and Fancy Rope Spinning*, G. P. Putnam's Sons, (New York and London, 1928).

Coolidge, Dane, *Arizona Cowboys*, E. P. Dutton and Company, Inc., (New York, 1938).

———— *Old California Cowboys*, E. P. Dutton and Company, Inc., (New York, 1939).

———— *Texas Cowboys*, E. P. Dutton and Company, Inc., (New York, 1937).

Dale, Edward E., *Cow Country*, University of Oklahoma Press, (Norman, Oklahoma, 1942).

———— *The Range Cattle Industry*, University of Oklahoma, (Norman, Oklahoma, 1930).

Dick, Everett, *Vanguards of the Frontier*, D. Appleton-Century Company, (New York, 1941).

Dobie, J. Frank, *A Vauqero of the Brush Country*, The Southwest Press, (Dallas, 1929).

———— *The Longhorns*, Little, Brown and Company, (Boston, 1941).

Fergusson, Erna, *Our Southwest*, Alfred A. Knopf, (New York and London, 1941).

Fergusson, Harvey, *Rio Grande*, Tudor Publishing Company, (New York, 1945).

Gabriel, Ralph H., ed., *The Pageant of America*, v.15, Yale University Press, (New Haven, Conn., 1929).

Gay, Carl W., ed., *The Breeds of Live-Stock by Live-Stock Breeders*, Macmillan Company (New York, 1916).

Haley, J. Evetts, *Charles Goodnight, Cowman and Plainsman,* Houghton Mifflin Company, (New York, 1936).

Hamner, Laura V., *Short Grass and Longhorns,* University of Oklahoma Press, (Norman, Oklahoma, 1943).

Hastings, Frank S., *A Ranchman's Recollections,* The Breeder's Gazette, publishers, (Chicago, 1921).

Hough, Emerson, *The Story of the Cowboy,* D. Appleton-Century Company, Inc., (New York, 1935).

Hunter, J. Marvin, and Saunders, George W., *The Trail Drivers of Texas,* The Southwest Press, (Dallas, 1925).

James, Will, *All in the Day's Riding,* World Publishing Company, (Cleveland and New York, 1945).

———— *Cowboys North and South,* Charles Scribner's Sons, (New York, 1945).

———— *Lone Cowboy, My Life Story,* Charles Scribner's Sons, (New York, 1946).

———— *The Drifting Cowboy,* Charles Scribner's Sons, (New York, 1946).

Kegley, Max, *Rodeo, The Sport of the Cow Country,* Hastings House, (New York, 1942).

Komroff, Manuel, ed., *The History of Herodotus,* Tudor Publishing Company, (New York, 1936).

Leigh, William R., *The Western Pony,* Harper and Brothers, (New York and London, 1933).

Lomax, John A., and Alan, *Cowboy Songs and Other Frontier Ballads,* Macmillan Company, (New York, 1944).

Mason, Bernard S., *Primitive and Pioneer Sports or Recreation Today,* A. S. Barnes and Company, (New York, 1937).

McCoy, Joseph G., *Historic Sketches of the Cattle Trade of the West and Southwest,* Ramsey, Millett and Hudson, (Kansas City, Missouri, 1874).

Menke, Frank G., *Encyclopedia of Sports,* A. S. Barnes and Company, (New York, 1945).

Osgood, Ernest S., *The Day of the Cattleman,* University of Minnesota Press, (Minneapolis, 1929).

Palmer, Joel, "Journal of Travels Over the Rocky Mountains, 1845-1846," *Early Western Travels,* ed., R. G. Thwaites, v.30, Arthur H. Clark Company, (Cleveland, 1906).

Pelzer, Louis, *The Cattleman's Frontier,* Arthur H. Clark Company, (Glendale, California, 1936).

———— "Trails of the Trans-Mississippi Cattle Frontier, a Decade of Ox-Team Freighting on the Plains," *Trans-Mis-*

sissippi West, ed., C. B. Goodykoontz and J. F. Willard, (Boulder, Colorado, 1930).

Poe, Sophie, *Buckboard Days*, ed., E. Cunningham, Caxton Printers, Ltd., (Caldwell, Idaho, 1936).

Post, C. C., *Ten Years a Cowboy*, (Chicago, 1898).

Ridings, Sam F., *The Chrisholm Trail, A History of the World's Greatest Cattle Trail*, Co-Operative Publishing Company, (Guthrie, Oklahoma, 1936).

Rister, Carl C., *Southern Plainsmen*, University of Oklahoma Press, (Norman, Oklahoma, 1938).

Rollinson, John K., *Pony Trails in Wyoming*, Caxton Printers, Ltd., (Caldwell, Idaho, 1944).

Rush, Oscar, *The Open Range*, Caxton Printers, Ltd., (Caldwell, Idaho, 1936).

Santee, Ross, *Men and Horses*, Century Company, (New York 1926).

Steiner, Jesse F., *Americans at Play, Recent Trends in Recreation and Leisure Time Activities*, McGraw-Hill Book Company, Inc., (New York, 1933).

Strong, Phil, *Horses and Americans*, Garden City Publishing Company, Inc., (Garden City, New York, 1946).

Thorpe, N. Howard, coll., Neil M. Clark, *Pardner of the Wind*, Caxton Printers, Ltd., (Caldwell, Idaho, 1945).

Vestal, Stanley, *Short Grass Country*, Duell, Sloan and Pearce, (New York, 1941).

Webb, Walter P., *The Great Plains*, Houghton Mifflin Company, (Boston and New York, 1936).

Wellman, Paul I., *The Trampling Herd*, J. B. Lippincott Company, (Philadelphia and New York, 1939).

Wyman, Walker D., *The Wild Horse of the West*, Caxton Printers, Ltd., (Caldwell, Idaho, 1945).

Zeublon Pike's Arkansaw Journal: In Search of the Southern Louisiana Purchase Boundary Line, ed., Stephen H. Hart and Archer N. Hulbert, The Stewart Commission of Colorado College and the Denver Public Library, (Denver, 1932).

ARTICLES:

"About Pendleton," *Hoofs and Horns*, 8 (October 1938).

Albert, Paul, "The Romance of the Western Stock Horse," *The Western Horseman*, 4 (May-June 1939); 5 (July-August 1940); 7 (March-April 1942).

"Arizona Men Buy Johnson Rodeo," *Hoofs and Horns*, 7 (August 1937).

Armstrong, "The Collegiate Cowboys' Column," *The Western Horseman*, 10 (March-April 1945); 10 (May-June 1945); 10 (July-August 1945).

"Army Rodeos," *Hoofs and Horns*, 13 (May 1944).

Arnold, O., "Cowboy Looks at the Dudes," *Travel*, 78 (November 1941).

"At the Arena Mike," *Rodeo Fans*, 2 (November 1943).

Barnes, W. C., "On the Trail of the Vanishing Longhorn," *Saturday Evening Post*, 200 (October 15, 1927).

———— "Texas Longhorns and Some Distant Cousins," *Travel*, 61 (October 1933).

———— "Wild Horses," *McClure*, 32 (January 1909).

Bascom, Weldon, "Brahma-Ritus," *Hoofs and Horns*, 6 (May 1937).

Bauman, John, "On a Western Ranch," *The Fortnightly Review*, 47 (April 1887).

Becker, B., "Rodeo," *Popular Mechanic*, 46 (August 1926).

Belden, C. J., "Cowpunchers Still Ride the Ranges," *Travel*, 77 (July 1941).

Bell, William G., "Rose Davis—Cowgirl Bronk Rider," *Hoofs and Horns*, 6 (July 1936).

"Best Bucking Horses Last Ten Years," *The Western Horseman*, 5 (May-June 1940).

Black, C. M., "Suicide Circuit," *Collier's*, 106 (October 26, 1940).

"Black Hills Roundup," *Hoofs and Horns*, 11 (September 1941).

Blake, F., "Wild Horses Run," *Scribners*, 97 (April 1, 1935).

"Boston Garden Rodeo," *Hoofs and Horns*, 7 (September 1937).

Bovee, Sgt. Red, "Rodeo In Italy," *The Western Horseman*, 9 (September-October 1944).

Britt, A., "Ride 'im Cowboy!" *Outlook*, 135 (September 26, 1923).

"Broadway Rodeo," *Time*, 30 (October 18, 1937).

"Broncho-Busting In Gandhi-Land," *The Western Horseman*, 10 (March-April 1945).

"Bucking Horse Deal," *Hoofs and Horns*, 11 (September 1941).

"Bucking Horses Get that Way from Pampering," *Literary Digest*, 116 (July 8, 1933).

"Bulldogging Champions," *Hoofs and Horns*, 7 (May 1938).

Barton, G. L., "Colorado Cow-Punchers on A Round-Up," *Outing*, 36 (May 1900).

"C. A. A. and R. C. A. Working Argeement In Force," *The Buckboard* 1 (March 1946); (April 1946).

Casement J. S., "Why a Steeldust Stud Book?" *The Western Horseman*, 4 (March-April 1939).

"Career Cowboy," *Time*, 34 (October 16, 1939).

Chapman, A., "Bucking Horses Earned $100,000." *Tech World*, 22 (February 1915).

———————— "Rodeo Dollars," *World's Work*, 60 (July 1931).

Clancy, Fog Horn, "Ben the Rodeo Tailor," *Hoofs and Horns*, 9 (October 1939).

———————— "Famous Bucking Horses," *Hoofs and Horns*, 11 (July 1941).

———————— "Memory Trail," *Hoofs and Horns*, 6 (September 1936); 7 (July 1937); 7 (January 1938); 7 (March 1938); 9 (December 1939); 10 (October 1940); 11 (October 1941).

Cline, Eleanor, "Cowboy Bowman," *Hoofs and Horns*, 9 (July 1939).

Clinton, Bruce, "Are Cowboys Athletes?" *Hoofs and Horns*, 8 (March 1939).

———————— "Bronc Rider's Luck," *The Western Horseman*, 6 (July-August 1941).

———————— "Contest Ropers Are Better," *The Western Horseman*, 5 (September-October 1940).

———————— "Cowgirl Cowhands!" *The Western Horseman*, 4 (May-June 1939).

———————— "Famous Bucking Horses!" *The Western Horseman*, 4 (March-April 1939).

———————— "High, Wide, and Handsome," *The Western Horseman*, 5 (November-December 1940).

———————— "It's the Horse!" *The Western Horseman*, 4 (July-August 1940).

———————— "Modern Cowboy Contestants," *The Western Horseman*, 5 (July-August 1940).

———————— "Rodeo Conscious," *Hoofs and Horns*, 10 (February 1941).

———————— "Rodeos, The New Big-Time Business and Sport," *Hoofs and Horns*, 6 (July 1936).

———————— "Smart Rope Horses!" *The Western Horseman*, 4 (September-October 1939).

———————— "The Boys are Speeding Up!" *The Western Horseman*, 7 (January-February 1942).

———————— "Three Out of Four," *The Western Horseman*, 7 (March-April 1942).

———————— "Trained Bucking Horses vs. Wild Horses," *Hoofs and Horns*, 9 (March 1940).

"Clyde Burk Rides On," *Hoofs and Horns*, 14 (March 1945).

Colburn, Walt, "That Five X Beaver Crown," *Hoofs and Horns*, 9 (March 1940).

———————— "They Can't All Win," *Hoofs and Horns*, 10 (March 1941).

Coleman,, Max, "An Endurance Ride," *Hoofs and Horns*, 8 (November 1938).

"Comments of the Ogden Controversy," *Bulletin, Rodeo Association of America*, 3 (August 1939).

Connery, Ed, article on Clay McGonigal, "Old Timers; Men and Women Who Helped to Build the West," *Hoofs and Horns*, 9 (May 1940).

"Convention at Colorado Springs," *Bulletin, Rodeo Association of America*, 6 (February 1942).

Cooper, C. R., "Way Down West In Florida; Cattle Industry," *Saturday Evening Post*, 212 (October 7, 1939).

"Cooperation With Cowboys," *Bulletin, Rodeo Association of America*, 1 (April 12, 1937).

Coryndon, R. T., "Lost Horses," *Living Age*, 291, (December 9, 1916).

Cowan, J. L., "Lingo of the Cow Country," *Outing*, 54 (August 1909).

"Cowboys Attention!" *Hoofs and Horns*, 10 (July 1940).

"Cowboy Organization Makes Change," *Hoofs and Horns*, 7 (May 1945).

"Cowboys' Turtle Association," *Hoofs and Horns*, 6 (December 1936); 7 (January 1938); 7 (June 1938); 7 (July 1938); 9 (October 1939).

"Cowgirls Become Honorary Members of Turtles Ass'n.," *Hoofs and Horns*, 7 (May 1938).

"Cowgirl Bronc Riders Are Now Turtles," *Hoofs and Horns*, 8 (September 1938).

Crates, Mary, "Margie Greenough—Bronc Rider," *Hoofs and Horns*, 8 (May 1939).

———— "Pauline Nesbitt, Trick Rider," *Hoofs and Horns*, 8 (March 1939).

Crichton, Kyle, "Rodeo Ben," *Collier's*, (August 4, 1945).

Curley, Cal, "What's Become of the Cowboy?" *The Western Horseman*, 5 (November-December 1940).

Dean, Frank, "Cooperation Needed," *Hoofs and Horns*, 7 (January 1938).

Denhardt, Robert M., "First Quarter Horse Show," *The Western Horseman*, 5 (July-August 1940).

———— "Quarter Horses Then and Now," *The Western Horseman*, 4 (March-April 1939); 5 (November-December 1940).

———— "Rodeo Time in Old Mexico," *The Western Horseman*, 8 (July-August 1943).

———— "The Quarter Horse," *The Western Horseman*, 5 (November-December 1940).

———— "The Quarter Horse . . . And What He is," *The Western Horseman*, 7 (March-April 1942).

"Denver Rodeo," *Hoofs and Horns*, 10 (March 1941).

Dew, L. E., "Aristocrates of the Texas Range," *Country Life*, 17 (January 1910).

Dillon, Jack M., "Rodeo In Canada," *Hoofs and Horns*, 11 (July 1941).

Dobie, J. Frank, "Outlaws of the Brush," *Saturday Evening Post*, 205 (December 10, 1932).

———— "Pitching Horses and Panthers," *The Western Horseman*, 5 (November-December 1940).

Dodge, Col. C. T., "Horse in America," *North America*, 155 (December 1892).

Don, "Vaquero Lingo," *The Western Horseman*, 5 (July-August 1940); 5 (September-October 1940); 6 (July-August 1941).

Driskill, Leo, "Tipperary, A Great Bucking Horse," *Hoofs and Horns*, 9 (July 1939).

Dye, H., "They Ride 'em at the 4 W," *Sunset*, 59 (November 1927).

Earle, G. W., "Ride 'em Cowboy!" *Popular Mechanic*, 53 (June 1930).

"Eastern Spring Rodeos," *Hoofs and Horns*, 11 (April 1942).

Eisele, Mary L., "Bucking Horses," *Hoofs and Horns*, 11 (July 1941).

——————— "Col. Johnson Today," *Hoofs and Horns*, 10 (May 1941).

Elton, B., "Elimination of Dust," *Bulletin, Rodeo Association of America*, 5 (October 1941).

Fernandez, Virginia E., "Gene Creed—Champion Cowgirl," *Hoofs and Horns*, 7 (August 1937).

"Flying A Ranch," *Hoofs and Horns*, 11 (January 1942).

Foster, Freling, "Keep Up With The World," *Collier's*, (December 8, 1945).

Fox, Capt. Dan, "Tad Lucas," *Hoofs and Horns*, 7 (October 1937).

"Fox Wilson, World's Only Woman Bulldogger," *Hoofs and Horns*, 4 (December 1934).

Fraser, E. J., "Harry Knight of Banff, Alberta," *Hoofs and Horns*, 5 (April 1936).

Gage, E. W., "Ride 'im Cowboy!" *Travel*, 65 (June 1935).

Gardner, Clem, "My Impressions of the Contestants of the 1912 Stampede," *Canadian Cattleman*, Calgary, Alberta, Canada, (June 1945).

Garland, Tex, "Chuck Wagon Chatter," *Rodeo Fans*, 2 (April 1943).

"Gene Autry's Spring Rodeos," *Hoofs and Horns*, 11 (March 1942).

"Girl Bronc Riders Are 'On Their Own' Say the Turtles," *Bulletin, Rodeo Association of America*, 2 (April 1938).

Gleason, A. H., "Art of Bronco-Busting," *Country Life*, 7 (April 1905).

Godshall, Cal, "Rodeos and Their Development," *Hoofs and Horns*, 8 (July 1938).

Grant, Don, "Curtailment of Horse Events," *The Western Horseman*, 7 (May-June 1942).

Haley, J. E., "Longhorn, Lasso and Latigo," *Nature*, 16 (December 1930).

Harger, Charles M., "Cattle Trails of the Prairies," *Scribners*, 2 (June 1892).

"Harry Rowell," *Hoofs and Horns*, 8 (June 1939).

Hegger, G., "Sixteen Hands High," *Sunset*, 38 (June 1917).

"Honolulu Rodeo," *Hoofs and Horns*, 12 (September 1942); 14 (May 1945); 15 (July 1945).

" 'Hoofs and Horns' Place in the Rodeo World," *Bulletin, Rodeo Association of America*, 4 (June 1940).

Hopkins, Ethel A., "This and That," *Hoofs and Horns*, 6 (June 1936); 6 (November 1936); 6 (June 1937); 8 (September 1938); 10 (January 1941); 10 (February 1941); 14 (September 1944).

"Horses Nobody Wants," *Literary Digest*, 84 (January 3, 1925).

Irving, Ralph, "Old-Time Cowhands versus Modern Cowhands," *The Western Horseman*, 9 (July-August 1944).

————— "The Case of the Dale Vuelta versus the Texas Tie," *The Western Horseman*, 8 (January-February 1943).

James, Will, "Bronco Twisters," *Sunset*, 51 (September 1923); (October 1923); (November 1923).

————— "Bucking Horses and Bucking-Horse Riders," *Scribners*, 73 (March 1923).

————— "How Would You Like to Buck this Game," *American*, 113 (June 1932).

————— "Why the High Heels," *Saturday Evening Post*, 199 (February 26, 1927).

————— "Remuda," *Saturday Evening Post*, 200 (November 19, 1927).

"John Jordan—Rodeo Announcer," *Hoofs and Horns*, 9 (April 1940).

Johnson, B., "My Kindom for a Cayuse," *North American*, 223 (September 1926).

Jones, Norman S., "Homer Holcomb," *Hoofs and Horns*, 11 (August 1941).

————— "Misery For Cowboys, Featuring 'Starlight,' 'Sonora Red' and Other Tough Ones of Harry Rowell's Stock," *Hoofs and Horns*, 10 (April 1941).

————— "Tygh Valley," *Hoofs and Horns*, 10 (May 1941).

"Judge Selection is Made Clear; None Protested," *Bulletin, Rodeo Association of America*, 2 (April 1938).

"Junior Rodeo Fans, A Department for Boys and Girls," *Rodeo Fans*, 2 (April 1943).

Kaynor, Cliff, "The Pioneer Background and Traditions of the Old West," *Bulletin, Rodeo Association of America*, 5 (February 1941).

King, Arch, "Hooray Old-Timers," *The Western Horseman*, 5 (July-August 1940).

Kinkead, E. F., "Cowboy Business," *New Yorker*, 16 (October 26, 1940).

Kinney, Jack C., "Rodeo Problems and Experiences of Fifty Years," *Bulletin, Rodeo Association of America*, 5 (September 1941).

Knight, Ethel, "Pete Knight of Crossfield, Alberta," *Hoofs and Horns*, 4 (May 1935).

——————— "The Boys at Calgary," *Hoofs and Horns*, 6 (August 1936).

Koller, J. F., "The Rodeo Map," *Hoofs and Horns*, 9 (April 1940).

La Farge, W. M., "No Turtles Need Apply," *Saturday Evening Post*, 211 (July 9, 1938).

Larom, T. H., "Valley Ranching in Wyoming; Reflections of a Contender in the Madison Square Garden," *Arts and Decoration*, 53 (March 1941).

Lehman, P. E., "Florida Cowpunchers," *Travel*, 73 (August 1939).

"Leo Cremer and His Broncs," *Hoofs and Horns*, 8 (August 1938).

"Legislation," *Bulletin, Rodeo Association of America*, 1 (May 1937).

"Letter of Appreciation," *Hoofs and Horns*, 10 (September 1940).

"Letters to the Bulletin," *Bulletin, Rodeo Association of America*, 3 (September 1939).

"Letter to C.T.A.," *Bulletin, Rodeo Association of America*, 1 (December 13, 1937).

"Letter from Ralph L. Lovelady, Manager of Sidney, Iowa, Rodeo," *Bulletin, Rodeo Association of America*, 6 (September 1936).

"Letter from Herman Linder," *Hoofs and Horns*, 8 (August 1938).

"Letter from Hugh Bennett," *Hoofs and Horns*, 9 (February 1940).

"Letter from Jimmie Minotto," *Hoofs and Horns*, 8 (August 1938).

"Letter to Judge Maxwell McNutt, Pres. R.A.A.," *Hoofs and Horns*, 8 (July 1938).

"Letter from President Maxwell McNutt," *Bulletin, Rodeo Association of America,* 4 (January 1940).

"Letter from Riders," *The Western Horseman,* 10 (September-October 1945).

Lipp, G. A., "Passing of Western Cattle Ranches," *Overland,* n. s. 63 (February 1914).

Long, Hughie, "From a Contestant," *Hoofs and Horns,* 11 (July 1941).

"London All Worked Up Over An American Rodeo," *Literary Digest,* 82 (July 26, 1924).

"Lone Star Barony," *Country Life,* 28 (October 1940).

Love, Clara M., "History of the Cattle Industry in the Southwest," *Southwestern Historical Quarterly,* 19 (April 1916); 20 (July 1916).

Lucas, F. A., "Ancestory of the Horse," *McClure,* 15 (October 1900).

MacFarlane, T. B., "Rodeo Popular in Australia," *Hoofs and Horns,* 10 (July 1940).

Maddy, Herbert S., "Eastern Rodeos," *Hoofs and Horns,* 4 (March 1935); 4 (May 1935); 5 (October 1935); 5 (December 1935); 10 (March 1941).

———— "Eastern Rodeo Chat," *Hoofs and Horns,* 5 (April 1936); 7 (September 1937); 9 (May 1940); 11 (October 1941).

Maloney, Alice B., "The Sport of Kings," *The Western Horseman,* 4 (July-August 1939).

Martin, Chuck, "Prison Bars, Dean of Bucking Horses," *Hoofs and Horns,* 10 (February 1941).

———— "Rodeo in the Deep South," *Hoofs and Horns,* 10 (January 1941).

———— "The Top Hand of Melody Ranch," *Hoofs and Horns,* 11 (April 1942).

———— "The Tucson Doin's," *Hoofs and Horns,* 11 (April 1937).

"Matched Roping Contests," *Hoofs and Horns,* 11 (June 1942); 12 (July 1942); 12 (May 1942); 13 (October 1943); 13 (November 1942); 14 (October 1944); 14 (November 1944); 14 (May 1945); 15 (August 1945); 16 (December 1946); 16 (February 1947).

Mayo, Earl, "A Day's Work on a Cattle Ranch," *World's Work,* 8 (January 1902).

McCann, L. P., "Ride 'em Cowboy!" *Sunset*, 59 (September 1927).

"McNutt Resigns," *Bulletin, Rodeo Association of America*, 4 (July 1940).

Merchant, Richard, "From a Contestant," *Hoofs and Horns*, 11 (July 1941).

Mitchell, John D., "He Would't Lay," *Hoofs and Horns*, 8 (February 1939).

"More About the Ogden Convention," *Bulletin, Rodeo Association of America*, 2 (February 1938).

Morse, Frank I., "Who's to Blame," *Hoofs and Horns*, 7 (October 1937).

Muncaster, Austin, "Let 'er Buck," *Ford News*, 20 (January 1940).

"Newsman Questions Choice of World's Best Bucking Horse," *Bulletin, Rodeo Association of America*, 5 (May 1940).

"Non-Pro Rodeo Has No Future Gardner Says," *Hoofs and Horns*, 9 (August 1939).

"Notice from the President," *Hoofs and Horns*, 9 (July 1939).

Notson, R. C., "Horses, Horses, What's to Become of Wild Horses," *Sunset*, 59 (November 1927).

"No World's Champion Rodeo," *Bulletin, Rodeo Association of America*, 3 (May 1939).

O'Brien, Eddie, "Rodeo Chat," *Hoofs and Horns*, 13 (March 1944).

O'Shaughnessy, Bob, "Van Vleet's Arabian 'Laboratory,'" *The Western Horseman*, 9 (March-April 1944).

"Ogden Promises Still Hold Good Says James Minotto," *Bulletin, Rodeo Association of America*, 2 (May 1938).

"Oklahoma State Prison Rodeo," *Hoofs and Horns*, 8 (January 1939); 3 (January 1934).

"On to Livingston, Montana, January 6-7," *Bulletin, Rodeo Association of America*, 2 (December 1938).

Ortega, Luis B., "Horse Breaking Suggestions," *The Western Horseman*, 7 (September-October 1942).

Osborn, H. F., "Evolution of the Horse in America," *Century*, 69 (November 1904).

"Out of the Wild West They Came," *Literary Digest*, 120 (October 19, 1935).

Parr, V. V. "Brahman (Zebu) Cattle," *Farmer's Bulletin*, 1361 (1923).

"Passing of the Longhorn," *Literary Digest*, 54 (March 17, 1917).

Paxson, F. L., "Cow Country," *American Historical Review*, 22 (October 1916).

———— "The Rise of Sport," *Mississippi Valley Historical Review*, 4 (September 1917).

Pelzer, Louis, "A Cattleman's Commonwealth on the Western Range," *Mississippi Valley Historical Review*, 13 (June 1926)

Perry, Harmon W., "Ogden Pioneer Days Stock Rodeo," *Hoofs and Horns*, 7 (August 1937).

"Pete Knight, Champion," *Hoofs and Horns*, 7 (July 1937).

Phillips, George, "Foothill Filosophy," *Hoofs and Horns*, 8 (February 1939).

Pond, W. P., "Horse in America," *Country Life*, 19 (November 1, 1910).

Porter, Charles A., "Why Blame Them?" *The Western Horseman*, 5 (May-June 1940).

"President McNutt Instructs this Letter be Printed," *Bulletin, Rodeo Association of America*, 2 (August 1938).

"President's Message," *Bulletin, Rodeo Association of America*, 1 (May 1937).

Putnam, G. P., "Pendleton Roundup; A Classic of American Sport," *Outlook*, 132 (October 25, 1922).

"Quarter Horses," *Country Life*, 76 (September 1939); (October 1939); 77 (December 1939); (April 1940).

"R.A.A. Bulletin," *Bulletin, Rodeo Association of America*, 9 (April 1945).

"Rampageous Ways of a Frisky Bronco," *Literary Digest*, 88 (January 2, 1926).

"Reno Pleased With the Convention," *Bulletin, Rodeo Association of America*, 2 (February 1938).

"Report of Fort Worth Controversy Filed," *Bulletin, Rodeo Association of America*, 3 (April 1939).

"Retaliation Controversy Still Important Subject With C.T.A. and R.A.A.," *Bulletin, Rodeo Association of America*, 2 (June 1938).

Rice, Lee M., "The Famous Hamley Saddles," *The Western Horseman*, 8 (November-December 1943).

"Ride 'em Cowboy!" *Popular Mechanic*, 72 (October 1939).

"Riders Bring Wild West Thrills," *Newsweek*, 2 (October 21, 1933).

"Rodeo," *Literary Digest*, 124 (October 30, 1937).

"Rodeo Announcer," *Hoofs and Horns*, 8 (April 1938).

"Rodeo at Kingsley Brothers Ranch," *Hoofs and Horns*, 4 (March 1945).

"Rodeo Briefs," *Bulletin, Rodeo Association of America*, 4 (May 1940).

"Rodeo in China," *Hoofs and Horns*, 15 (October 1945).

"Rodeo in France," *Hoofs and Horns*, 15 (October 1945).

"Rodeo Men Select 'Hell's Angel,'" *Bulletin, Rodeo Association of America*, 4 (March 1940).

"Rodeo Picture Shaping Up Better," *Bulletin, Rodeo Association of America*, 6 (June 1942).

"Rodeo—The American Sport of Today," *Hoofs and Horns*, 5 (June 1935).

"Rodeos Curtailed Along Coast," *The Western Horseman*, 7 (March-April 1942).

Rodriguez, Joe, "Vaqueros; The Originators of Our West," *Hoofs and Horns*, 5 (February 1936).

"Romance of American Cattle," *Review of Reviews*, 69 (May 1924).

Roumell, Mrs. L. E., "Whoopee!" *The Western Horseman*, 5 (September-October 1940).

"San Francisco Rodeo," *Hoofs and Horns*, 11 (December 1941).

Sass, H. R., "Hoofs on the Prairie," *Reader's Digest*, 29 (September 1936).

"Saving the Texas Longhorn," *Literary Digest*, 93 (April 16, 1927).

Schneider, J., "Ace Rodeo Rider Tells How He Tames Vicious Broncs," *Popular Science*, 125 (August 1934).

Schwarz, E., "Story of the Horse," *Nature*, 31, (March 1938.)

Scully, Frank, "In Defense of Amateurs," *Hoofs and Horns*, 6 (September 1936).

"Secretary's Message," *Bulletin, Rodeo Association of America*, 1 (March 11, 1937); (April 12, 1937); (May 5, 1937); (September 3, 1937); (December 13, 1937).

"Shades of the Old West; Juvenile Rodeo, Cheyenne Mountain School Colorado Springs, Colorado," *Literary Digest*, 116 (November 25, 1933).

"Sheriff's Roping Contest," *Hoofs and Horns,* 9 (February 1940).

Sherman, Tex, "Chuck Wagon Chatter," *Hoofs and Horns,* 4 (July 1934); (November 1934); (March 1935); 5 (December 1935); (October 1935).

———— "Rodeo News," *Hoofs and Horns,* 3 (February 1934); (March 1934).

"Shorty Ricker," *Hoofs and Horns,* 7 (March 1938).

Sisty, Alice, "Rodeo Ramblings," *Hoofs and Horns,* 6 (July 1936).

Smith, H. H., "New Wild West," *Outlook,* 159 (October 28, 1931).

Sprott, Darrell B., D.V.M., "We Do Have the Quarter Horse," *The Western Horseman,* 5 (July-August 1940).

"Stars Behind Bars, Texas Prison Rodeo," *Time,* 36 (October 21, 1940).

Steele, R., "Mustangs, Busters and Outlaws of the Nevada Wild Horse Country," *America,* 72 (October 1911).

"Story of a Western Industry," *The Western Horseman,* 4 (July-August 1939).

Taylor, Florence, "Cancelled! So What," *The Western Horseman,* 8 (May-June 1943).

———— "Tipperary . . . The Tri-State Outlaw," *The Western Horseman,* 7 (March-April 1942).

"The Crying Jew," *Hoofs and Horns,* 8 (May 1939).

"The N.R.A. Round-Up," *Hoofs and Horns,* 11 (June 1942).

"The Personal Notes of William Anson," arranged by Robert Denhardt, *The Western Horseman,* 7 (January-February 1942).

"The Rodeo Association of America," *Hoofs and Horns,* 11 (July 1941).

"The Rodeo Friendship Club," *Hoofs and Horns,* 7 (June 1938).

"The Round-Up," *Century,* n.s., (April 1888).

"The Southwest Rodeo Association," *Hoofs and Horns,* 11 (July 1941).

"The Sportive Cowboy," *Atlantic,* 65 (November 1890).

"The $2,000.00 Matched Team Roping," *The Western Horseman,* 7 (September-October 1942).

Thistlethwaite, E. W., "Answer to Cowboys Old and Modern," *Hoofs and Horns,* 11 (April 1937).

"This Week's Cover," *Saturday Evening Post,* 218 (July 21, 1945).

Thompson, Claire, "Dick Griffith," *Hoofs and Horns,* 7 (May 1938).

——————— "Cowgirls' Comments," *Hoofs and Horns,* 8 (July 1938).

——————— "Jimmy Nesbitt, Rodeo Clown," *Hoofs and Horns,* 8 (July 1938).

"Texas Prison Rodeo," *Hoofs and Horns,* 8 (January 1939); 10 (January 1941).

"Tex Austin," *Hoofs and Horns,* 8 (December 1938).

"Too Much Fame For Turk's Gal, Sal," *The American Weekly,* (February 11, 1945).

"Toots vs. Clyde in Texas Roping Contest," *The Western Horseman,* 8 (November-December 1943).

"Touring Bronco Busters Whoop It Up In New York," *Newsweek,* 4 (October 20, 1934).

Trimble, Sanky, "John Lindsey, Rodeo Clown," *Hoofs and Horns,* 11 (December 1941).

Triplett, J. F., "Scouts' Story: from the journal of a cattleman," *Atlantic,* 135 (April 1925).

"Trouble Made For Los Angeles Rodeo," *Bulletin, Rodeo Association of America,* 6 (January 1940).

"Troubles of Members," *Bulletin, Rodeo Association of America,* 2 (September 1938).

"Tucson Rodeo," *Hoofs and Horns,* 9 (February 1940).

"Turtle Association Good," *Hoofs and Horns,* 9 (October 1939).

"Turtles, Attention," *Hoofs and Horns,* 9 (June 1940).

Vachell, H. A., "Rodeo in Southern California," *Living Age,* 240 (January 16, 1904).

Vaden, Clay W., "Trick Riding," *Hoofs and Horns,* 3 (May 1934).

"Vanishing Mustang," reprinted from *Arizona Republican, Current Literature,* 30 (May 1901).

Vernon, A., "Wild Horses," *Scientific Digest,* 9 (January 1941).

"V. H. Famous Roping Horse Dies," *Hoofs and Horns,* 6 (September 1936).

Vincent, Bobby, "Oklahoma Rodeo Roundup—The Princess Passes," *Hoofs and Horns,* 10 (February 1941).

Warrington, J., "Wild Horses of the Old Frontier," *Travel,* 74 (November 1939).

"Wartime Status of Rodeo," *Bulletin, Rodeo Association of America*, 6 (April 1942).

Weadick, Guy, "What Are Rodeos Doing," *Hoofs and Horns*, 7 (January 1938).

"West Moves East and into Madison Square Garden," *Newsweek*, 6 (October 19, 1935).

"Where is the Rodeo Game Going," *Bulletin, Rodeo Association of America*, 3 (July 1939).

"Wild West in New York City," *Literary Digest*, 122 (October 24, 1936).

"Wild West Shows," *Bulletin, Rodeo Association of America*, 4 (January 1940).

Wilkerson, Frank, "Cattle Raising on the Plains," *Harper's*, 72 (April 1886).

Wister, Owen, "The Evolution of the Cowpuncher," *Harper's*, 91 (September 1895).

"World's Championship Rodeo," *Newsweek*, 12 (October 24, 1938).

Wright, Cecil, "Hell Bent," *Hoofs and Horns*, 8 (February 1939).

"Writer Suggests Plan for Training Boys for Rodeo," *Bulletin, Rodeo Association of America*, 3 (May 1939).

Youngs, Daniel, "Death Rides the Rodeo," *Hoofs and Horns*, 7 (July 1937).

Zogbaum, Rufus, "A Day's Drive With Montana Cowboys," *Harper's*, 71 (July 1885).

NEWSPAPERS:

American Weekly
    Febraury 11, 1945.

Boulder Daily Camera, (Boulder, Colorado).
    August 16, 1941.

Buffalo Evening News, (Buffalo, New York).
    September 1, 1942.

Calgary Daily Herald, (Calgary, Alberta,, Canada).
    September 2, 1912.
    September 3, 1912.
    September 4, 1912.
    September 6, 1912.
    September 7, 1912.
    August 2, 1919.

August 20, 1919.
August 27, 1919.
August 30, 1919.
July 15, 1924.
Calgary Weekly Herald, (Calgary, Alberta, Canada).
June 8, 1891.
May 16, 1893.
May 27, 1893.
June 3, 1893.
June 19, 1893.
Cheyenne Daily Leader, (Cheyenne, Wyoming).
July 6, 1872.
September 11, 1873.
May 25, 1882.
August 31, 1882.
October 3, 1882.
November 14, 1882.
June 29, 1883.
October 3, 1883.
August 19, 1902.
August 6, 1903.
August 24, 1903.
August 28, 1903.
Chronicle, (Dallas, Oregon).
August 28, 1913.
Cleveland News, (Cleveland, Ohio).
April 11, 1942.
Courier Express, (Buffalo, New York).
September 1, 1942.
October 4, 1942.
November 1, 1942.
November 8, 1942.
Daily Record, (Ellensburg, Washington).
August 30, 1941.
Daily Sun-Leader, (Cheyenne, Wyoming).
August 30, 1897.
August 31, 1897.
September 3, 1897.
September 6, 1897.
September 7, 1897.

September 9, 1897.
September 23, 1897.
August 24, 1898.
September 6, 1898.
August 17, 1900.

Democratic Leader, (Cheyenne, Wyoming).
February 27, 1887.

Denver Post, (Denver, Colorado).
October 7, 1902.
October 8, 1902.
October 10, 1902.
July 20, 1903.
August 2, 1903.

Denver Republican, (Denver, Colorado).
September 7, 1895.
September 12, 1895.
October 2, 1901.
October 4, 1901.
October 5, 1901.
October 6, 1901.
October 8, 1901.
October 10, 1902.
August 18, 1912.

East Oregonian, (Pendleton, Oregon).
September 11, 1913.
September 22, 1913.
September 1, 1926.
September 8, 1927.

Enterprise, (White Salmon, Washington).
August 29, 1913.

Journal, (Portland, Oregon).
September 23, 1928.

La Hermandad, (Pueblo, Colorado).
August, 1903.
September, 1904.

Live Wire, (Pendleton, Oregon).
September 11, 1913.

Prescott Evening Courier, (Prescott, Arizona).
June 30, 1941.

Rocky Mountain News, (Denver, Colorado).
    August 25, 1895.
    September 6, 1895.
    September 7, 1895.
    September 14, 1895.
    September 30, 1895.
    October 2, 1895.
    October 9, 1895.
    October 14, 1895.
    October 16, 1895.
    October 18, 1895.
    October 1, 1901.
    October 4, 1901.
    October 5, 1901.
    October 7, 1901.
    October 11, 1902.
    August 2, 1903.
    August 30, 1904.
    January 17, 1931.
    January 25, 1931.
    January 18, 1945.
Semi-Weekly Calgary Herald and Alberta Livestock Journal.
    July 13, 1894.
    July 20, 1894.
Sun Star, (Merced, California).
    November 1, 1926.
Times, (Seattle, Washington).
    November 21, 1926.
Waverly Sun, (Waverly, New York).
    November 27, 1941.
Women's Wear Daily, (New York, New York).
    October 6, 1942.
World, (Aberdeen, Washington).
    December 17, 1913.
Wyoming Tribune, (Cheyenne, Wyoming).
    September 18, 1897.
    September 22, 1897.
    September 23, 1897.
    September 24, 1897.
    July 23, 1907.

March 28, 1910.
August 27, 1910.
June 8, 1912.
August 17, 1912.
August 20, 1912.
April 29, 1914.
August 29, 1914.

Documents

A letter—"Santa Fe, 10th June, 1847." Written by Captain Mayne Reid to Samuel Arnold of Drumnakelly, Seaforde, County Down, Ireland. Now in the manuscript collection of Colin Johnston Robb, Drumharriff Lodge, Loughgall, County Armagh, Ireland. (Permission to use granted by Mr. Robb.)

Laws of Texas, 1871, Session 12.

United Staes Congress, 48th Congress, 2nd session, *House Executive Document,* Joseph Nimmo, "Range and Range Cattle Traffic," v. 29, no. 267 (ser. no. 2304).

Yearbook of the United States Department of Agriculture, 1899, "Texas Fever, Splenetic Fever, or Southern Cattle Fever."

PERSONAL LETTERS AND COMMUNICATIONS:

Allison, Oren G., secretary, Pendleton Roundup, Pendleton, Oregon.

Cremer, Leo, stock contractor, Big Timber, Montana.

Elliott, Mrs. Verne, stock contractor, Johnstown, Colorado.

Eskew, Junior, World Champion Trick Roper, Ardmore, Oklahoma.

Griffith, Dick, International Champion Trick Rider, Scottsdale, Arizona.

Hamley, David, vice-president, Hamley and Company, Pendleton, Oregon.

Hanesworth, Robert D., secretary, Frontier Days, Cheyenne, Wyoming.

Hopkins, Ethel A., editor, *Hoofs and Horns,* Tucson, Arizona.

Kaynor, J. Clifford, president, Ellensburg Rodeo, Ellensburg, Washington.

Koller, J. F., secretary-manager, Black Hills Roundup, Belle Fourche, South Dakota.

Maddy, Herbert S., JE Ranch, Waverly, New York.

MacFarlane, Thomas B., Councillor and Assistant Honorary Ringmaster, Royal Agricultural Society of New South Wales, Australia.

Messinger, Marie, (formerly Mrs. Doff Aber) Burbank, California.

McCarger, Fred S., secretary, Rodeo Association of America, Salinas, California.

Perrigoue, Nell, secretary, Days of '76, Deadwood, South Dakota.

Ranney, Harriet, (formerly Mrs. Bill McMackin) Corona, California.

Rowell, Harry, stock contractor, Rowell Ranch, Hayward, California.

Snyder, Smokey, Champion Bull and Bareback Rider, Fullerton, California.

Studer, C. A., district vice-president, International Rodeo Association, Canadian, Texas.

Taylor, Harry A., manager of Southern Division office of Plymouth Cordage Company, Houston, Texas.

Yule, J. Charles, general manager, Calgary Stampede, Calgary, Alberta, Canada.

MISCELLANEOUS:

"Articles of Association, By-Laws and Rules," *The Cowboys' Amateur Association of America,* 1941.

"Articles of Association, By-Laws and Rules," *The Cowboys' Turtle Association,* 1941.

"Constitution and By-Laws and Rules," *The Rodeo Association of America,* 1941.

INDEX OF PROPER NAMES AND PLACES

This index is intended to serve as a reference guide to the subject matter of the book — rodeo. Only the names of those personalities, places and related items which appeared to dominate in the story of the development of rodeo have been indexed. The information in the footnotes is not included.